STUDIES IN ANTIQUITY AND CHRISTIANITY

STUDIES IN ANTIQUITY AND CHRISTIANITY

The Institute for Antiquity and Christianity
Claremont Graduate School
Claremont, California

STUDIES IN ANTIQUITY & CHRISTIANITY

GNOSTICISM, JUDAISM, AND EGYPTIAN CHRISTIANITY

Birger A. Pearson

FORTRESS PRESS   **MINNEAPOLIS**

BT
1390
.P38
1990

GNOSTICISM, JUDAISM, AND EGYPTIAN CHRISTIANITY

Scripture quotations, unless otherwise noted, are from the Revised Standard Version
of the Bible, copyright © 1946, 1952, and 1971 by the Division of Christian Education
of the National Council of Churches.

Library of Congress Cataloging-in-Publication Data

Pearson, Birger Albert.
    Gnosticism, Judaism, and Egyptian Christianity / Birger A.
  Pearson.
      p.   cm. — (Studies in antiquity and Christianity)
    Includes bibliographical references.
    ISBN 0-8006-3104-8
    1. Gnosticism.   2. Egypt—Religion.   3. Judaism—Relations—
  Gnosticism.   4. Gnosticism—Relations—Judaism.   5. Christianity
  and other religions—Gnosticism.   6. Gnosticism—Relations—
  Christianity.   I. Title.   II. Series
  BT1390.P38   1990
  273.1—dc20   89-48945
                                                                      CIP

The paper used in this publication meets the minimum requirements of American
National Standard for Information Sciences—Permanence of Paper for Printed
Library Materials, ANSI Z329.48–1984. ∞™

Manufactured in the U.S.A.   AF 1-3104

94   93   92   91   90   1   2   3   4   5   6   7   8   9   10

In Memoriam

GEORGE WINSOR MACRAE, S.J.
(1928–1985)
Hunc Librum
Auctor
Offert

Contents

Preface

This book is the fifth volume to appear in the series Studies in Antiquity and Christianity. The series, published by Fortress Press for the Institute for Antiquity and Christianity in Claremont, California (James M. Robinson, Director), was founded as a vehicle for the publication of work produced by the various research projects of the Institute. I am grateful to my colleagues on the editorial board for accepting this book into the series. It is the third volume to be published in conjunction with the Institute's project "The Roots of Egyptian Christianity," of which I am privileged to serve as Project Director.

Much of the material included in this book has been published before in various places, and I wish to acknowledge here with thanks the permissions to use previously copyrighted material, as follows: for chapter 2, the Armenian Patriarchate and the St. James Press in Jerusalem; for chapters 3, 4, 9, and 12, E. J. Brill in Leiden; for chapter 5, the Royal Academy of Letters, History and Antiquities in Stockholm; for chapter 8, E. P. Sanders and Fortress Press; for chapter 10, the President and Fellows of Harvard College in Cambridge; for chapter 11, A. H. B. Logan and A. J. M. Wedderburn, and T. & T. Clark in Edinburgh. Earle Hilgert of McCormick Theological Seminary in Chicago, representing the now-defunct Philo Institute, has kindly endorsed my use of material in chapter 1. All of the previously published items have been revised and edited for this book (see my discussion in the Introduction).

I want to express here my special thanks to Ms. Andrea Diem, a graduate student in the Department of Religious Studies at the University of California–Santa Barbara, for help in preparing the manuscript of this book for publication. Without her word-processing skills, this book would have taken much longer to produce. My thanks, as well, to Mr.

Neal Kelsey, a graduate student at the Claremont Graduate School, for help with the indices, to Drs. John A. Hollar† and Marshall Johnson of Fortress Press for their encouragement, and to their very capable staff for excellent work in producing this book.

No scholar ever works in a vacuum. My reliance on the work of others is, of course, documented in footnotes where possible. But beyond that, there is always that intangible inspiration that interaction with teachers, colleagues, and students brings about. I have been richly rewarded by my two decades as a member of the faculty of the Department of Religious Studies at the University of California–Santa Barbara, and have benefited enormously from the stimulation provided by my colleagues and students. My association with the Institute for Antiquity and Christianity in Claremont has also yielded rich, if intangible, rewards. It is not possible for me to name all of the people who have stimulated my research in Gnosticism. But one name I cannot refrain from mentioning here: Father George MacRae, S.J.†, my teacher, colleague, and friend. Readers of this book who are familiar with his work will understand something of the debt of gratitude I owe to him. To his revered memory I dedicate this book.

BIRGER A. PEARSON
Department of Religious Studies
University of California
Santa Barbara, California

Abbreviations

1. GENERAL

ADAIK   Abhandlungen des Deutschen Archäologischen Instituts Kairo

ALGHJ   Arbeiten zur Literatur und Geschichte des hellenistischen Judentums

ANET   *Ancient Near Eastern Texts* (ed. J. B. Pritchard)

ANF   The Ante-Nicene Fathers (ed. A. Roberts and J. Donaldson)

ANRW   *Aufstieg und Niedergang der römischen Welt*

BCNH   Bibliothèque copte de Nag Hammadi

BG   (Codex) Berolinensis Gnosticus

BHT   Beiträge zur historischen Theologie

CBQ   *Catholic Biblical Quarterly*

CBQMS   Catholic Biblical Quarterly Monograph Series

CCL   Corpus Christianorum: Series Latina

CG   (Codex) Cairensis Gnosticus (=NHC)

CIJ   *Corpus Inscriptionum Judaicarum*

CPJ   *Corpus Papyrorum Judaicarum*

CRINT   Compendia Rerum Iudaicarum ad Novum Testamentum

DAWBIO   Deutsche Akademie der Wissenschaften zu Berlin, Institut für Orientforschung

EPRO   Études préliminaires aux religions orientales dans l'Empire Romain

EvTh   *Evangelische Theologie*

FRLANT   Forschungen zur Religion und Literatur des Alten und Neuen Testaments

GBS   *Greek and Byzantine Studies*

GCS   Griechische christliche Schriftsteller

HTR	*Harvard Theological Review*
HUCA	*Hebrew Union College Annual*
JAC	*Jahrbuch für Antike und Christentum*
JBL	*Journal of Biblical Literature*
JE	*The Jewish Encyclopaedia*
JEH	*Journal of Ecclesiastical History*
JJS	*Journal of Jewish Studies*
JSJ	*Journal for the Study of Judaism in the Persian, Hellenistic and Roman Period*
JTS	*Journal of Theological Studies*
LCC	Library of Christian Classics
LCL	Loeb Classical Library
LXX	The Septuagint version of the Bible
NedTTs	*Nederlands theologisch tijdschrift*
NHC	Nag Hammadi Codex (=CG)
NHS	Nag Hammadi Studies
NorTT	*Norsk teologisk Tidsskrift*
NovT	*Novum Testamentum*
NTA	*New Testament Apocrypha* (ed. R. Hennecke and W. Schnee-melcher, trans. R. M. Wilson)
NTS	*New Testament Studies*
OLZ	*Orientalische Literaturzeitung*
OrChr	*Oriens christianus*
OTP	*The Old Testament Pseudepigrapha* (ed. J. H. Charlesworth)
PG	*Patrologia graeca* (ed. J. Migne)
PGL	*A Patristic Greek Lexicon* (ed. G. W. H. Lampe)
PGM	*Papyri Graecae Magicae* (ed. K. Preisendanz et al.)
PTS	Patristische Texte und Studien
RB	*Revue biblique*
RechSR	*Recherches de science religieuse*
REJ	*Revue des études juives*
RevQ	*Revue de Qumran*
RevScRel	*Revue des sciences religieuses*
RGG	*Religion in Geschichte und Gegenwart*
RSPhTh	*Revue des sciences philosophiques et théologiques*
RSRev	*Religious Studies Review*
RSV	The Revised Standard Version of the Bible
RTP	*Revue de théologie et de philosophie*
SAC	Studies in Antiquity and Christianity
SBE	Sacred Books of the East

SBLDS Society of Biblical Literature, Dissertation Series
SBLSCS Society of Biblical Literature Septuagint and Cognate Studies
SBLSP *Society of Biblical Literature, Seminar Papers*
SBT Studies in Biblical Theology
SC Sources chrétiennes
SD Studies and Documents
SGRR Studies in Greek and Roman Religion
SHR Studies in the History of Religions (Supplements to *Numen*)
SNTSMS Society for New Testament Studies Monograph Series
SP *Studia Philonica*
SRivB Supplementi alla Rivista Biblica
ST *Studia Theologica*
STK *Svensk teologisk kvartalskrift*
TDNT *Theological Dictionary of the New Testament* (ed. G. Kittel and
G. Friedrich, trans. G. Bromiley)
ThR *Theologische Rundschau*
TLZ *Theologische Literaturzeitung*
TU Texte und Untersuchungen
UUÅ Uppsala Universitets Årsskrift
VC *Vigiliae Christianae*
VT *Vetus Testamentum*
WMANT Wissenschaftliche Monographien zum Alten und Neuen
Testament
WUNT Wissenschaftliche Untersuchungen zum Neuen Testament
ZÄS *Zeitschrift für ägyptische Sprache und Altertumskunde*
ZAW *Zeitschrift für die alttestamentliche Wissenschaft*
ZPE *Zeitschrift für Papyrologie und Epigraphik*
ZRGG *Zeitschrift für Religions- und Geistesgeschichte*
ZTK *Zeitschrift für Theologie und Kirche*

N.B.: Abbreviations of biblical books and other ancient sources (except the Coptic Gnostic Library) are not given here. The ones used in this book are standard and presumably recognizable.

2. SHORT TITLES OF OFTEN-CITED WORKS

Bauer, *Orthodoxy and Heresy*
Bauer, Walter. *Orthodoxy and Heresy in Earliest Christianity*. Trans. and ed. by R. A. Kraft and G. Krodel. Philadelphia: Fortress Press, 1971.

Berliner Arbeitskreis, "Texte von Nag Hammadi"
   Berliner Arbeitskreis für koptisch-gnostische Schriften. "Die Bedeut-
   ung der Texte von Nag Hammadi für die moderne Gnosisforschung."
   In Tröger, *Gnosis und Neues Testament*, 13–76.
Bianchi, *Origini dello gnosticismo*
   Bianchi, Ugo, ed. *Le origini dello gnosticismo: Colloquio di Messina 13–
   18 Aprile 1966*. SHR 12. Leiden: E. J. Brill, 1970.
Facsimile Edition
   The Facsimile Edition of the Nag Hammadi Codices. Ed. by J. M. Robin-
   son et al. 12 vols. Leiden: E. J. Brill, 1972–84.
Foerster, *Gnosis*
   Foerster, W., ed. *Gnosis: A Selection of Gnostic Texts*. Trans. and ed. by
   R. McL. Wilson. 2 vols. Oxford: Clarendon, 1972, 1974.
Jonas, *Gnostic Religion*
   Jonas, Hans. *The Gnostic Religion: The Message of the Alien God and the
   Beginnings of Christianity*. 2nd ed. Boston: Beacon, 1963.
Layton, *Gnostic Scriptures*
   Layton, Bentley. *The Gnostic Scriptures*. Garden City, N.Y.: Double-
   day, 1987.
Layton, *Rediscovery*
   Layton, B., ed. *The Rediscovery of Gnosticism: Proceedings of the Inter-
   national Conference on Gnosticism at Yale, New Haven, Connecticut
   March 28–31, 1978*. 2 vols. SHR 41. Leiden: E. J. Brill, 1980–81.
MacRae, "Gnostic Sophia Myth"
   MacRae, George W. "The Jewish Background of the Gnostic Sophia
   Myth." *NovT* 12 (1970) 82–101. Repr. in MacRae, *Studies in the New
   Testament and Gnosticism*, ed. by D. J. Harrington and S. B. Marrow.
   Wilmington: Michael Glazier, 1987, 184–202.
Nag Hammadi Library
   The Nag Hammadi Library in English. 3d rev. ed. Ed. by James M.
   Robinson and Richard Smith. San Francisco: Harper & Row, 1988.
Pearson, "Christians and Jews"
   Pearson, B. "Christians and Jews in First-Century Alexandria." In G.
   W. E. Nicklesburg and G. MacRae, eds., *Christians Among Jews and
   Gentiles: Essays in Honor of Krister Stendahl*. Philadelphia: Fortress
   Press, 1986, 206–16. = *HTR* 79 (1984 [1986]) 206–16.
Pearson, *Codices IX and X*
   Pearson, B., ed. *Nag Hammadi Codices IX and X*. NHS 15. Leiden: E. J.
   Brill, 1981.

Pearson, "Earliest Christianity"

Pearson, B. "Earliest Christianity in Egypt: Some Observations." In Pearson-Goehring, *Roots of Egyptian Christianity*, 132–59.

Pearson, "Exegesis of Mikra"

Pearson B. "Use, Authority and Exegesis of Mikra in Gnostic Literature." In M. J. Mulder, ed., *Mikra: Text, Translation, Reading and Interpretation of the Hebrew Bible in Ancient Judaism and Early Christianity*. CRINT II.1. Assen: Van Gorcum/Philadelphia: Fortress Press, 1988, 635–52.

Pearson, "Gnostic Hermeneutics"

Pearson, B. "Some Observations on Gnostic Hermeneutics." In W. O'Flaherty, ed., *The Critical Study of Sacred Texts*. Berkeley Religious Studies Series. Berkeley: The Graduate Theological Union, 1979, 243–56.

Pearson, "Gnostic Interpretation"

Pearson, B. "Gnostic Interpretation of the Old Testament in the *Testimony of Truth* (NHC IX,3)." *HTR* 73 (1980) 311–19.

Pearson, "'Jewish Gnostic' Literature"

Pearson, B. "The Problem of 'Jewish Gnostic' Literature." In C. W. Hedrick and R. Hodgson, eds., *Nag Hammadi, Gnosticism, and Early Christianity*. Peabody, Mass.: Hendrickson, 1986, 15–35.

Pearson, "Jewish Sources"

Pearson, B. "Jewish Sources in Gnostic Literature." In M. Stone, ed., *The Literature of the Jewish People in the Period of the Second Temple*. CRINT II.2. Assen: Van Gorcum/Philadelphia: Fortress, 1984, 443–81.

Pearson, "Philo and Gnosticism"

Pearson, B. "Philo and Gnosticism." In W. Haase, ed., *ANRW* II.21.1: *Religion (Hellenistisches Judentum in römischen Zeit: Philon und Josephus)*. Berlin: Walter de Gruyter, 1984, 295–342.

Pearson, *Pneumatikos-Psychikos Terminology*

Pearson, B. *The Pneumatikos-Psychikos Terminology in 1 Corinthians: A Study in the Theology of the Corinthian Opponents of Paul and Its Relation to Gnosticism*. SBLDS 12. Missoula: Society of Biblical Literature, 1973; repr. Scholars Press, 1976.

Pearson, "Tractate Marsanes"

Pearson, B. "The Tractate Marsanes (NHC X) and the Platonic Tradition." In B. Aland, ed., *GNOSIS: Festschrift für Hans Jonas*. Göttingen: Vandenhoeck & Ruprecht, 1978, 373–84.

Pearson-Goehring, *Roots of Egyptian Christianity*
  Pearson, Birger A., and James E. Goehring, eds. *The Roots of Egyptian Christianity*. SAC 1. Philadelphia: Fortress Press, 1986.
Rudolph, *Gnosis*
  Rudolph, Kurt. *Gnosis: The Nature and History of Gnosticism*. Trans. and ed. by R. McL. Wilson. Edinburgh: T. & T. Clark/San Francisco: Harper & Row, 1983.
Schenke, "Gnostic Sethianism"
  Schenke, H.-M. "The Phenomenon and Significance of Gnostic Sethianism," in Layton, *Rediscovery* 2. 588–616.
Schenke, *Der Gott "Mensch"*
  Schenke, H.-M. *Der Gott "Mensch" in der Gnosis: Ein religionsgeschichtliche Beitrag zur Diskussion über die paulinische Anschauung von der Kirche als Leib Christi*. Berlin: Evangelische Verlagsanstalt, 1962.
Schenke, "Das sethianische System"
  Schenke, H.-M. "Das sethianische System nach Nag-Hammadi-Handschriften." In P. Nagel, ed., *Studia Coptica*. Berlin: Akademie-Verlag, 1974, 165–72.
Scholer, *Nag Hammadi Bibliography*
  Scholer, David M. *Nag Hammadi Bibliography 1948–1969*. NHS 1; Leiden: E.J. Brill, 1971. Annually updated in *NovT*: "Bibliographia Gnostica: Supplementum" (from 1971).
Stroumsa, *Another Seed*
  Stroumsa, G. G. *Another Seed: Studies in Gnostic Mythology*. NHS 24. Leiden: E. J. Brill, 1984.
Tröger, *Altes Testament*
  Tröger, K.-W. *Altes Testament-Frühjudentum-Gnosis: Neue Studien zu "Gnosis und Bibel."* Berlin: Evangelische Verlagsanstalt, 1980.
Tröger, *Gnosis und Neues Testament*
  Tröger, K.-W. *Gnosis und Neues Testament: Studien aus Religionswissenschaft und Theologie*. Berlin: Evangelische Verlagsanstalt, 1973.
van den Broek-Vermaseren, *Studies in Gnosticism*
  van den Broek, R., and M. J. Vermaseren, eds. *Studies in Gnosticism and Hellenistic Religions Presented to Gilles Quispel*. EPRO 91. Leiden: E.J. Brill, 1981.
Völker, *Quellen*
  Völker, W. *Quellen zur Geschichte der christlichen Gnosis*. Tübingen: J. C. B. Mohr (Paul Siebeck), 1932.

The Coptic Gnostic Library:
Table of Tractates

The following table lists for the thirteen Nag Hammadi Codices, the Codex Berolinensis 8502, the Bruce Codex, and the Askew Codex, the tractate titles commonly used and the abbreviations of these titles. A critical edition of the Coptic Gnostic Library is being published as a subseries in the series "Nag Hammadi Studies" (Leiden: E. J. Brill, from 1975). Several of the volumes in that series are cited in this book.

I,1	*The Prayer of the Apostle Paul*	*Pr. Paul*
I,2	*The Apocryphon of James*	*Ap. Jas.*
I,3	*The Gospel of Truth*	*Gos. Truth*
I,4	*The Treatise on the Resurrection*	*Treat. Res.*
I,5	*The Tripartite Tractate*	*Tri. Trac.*
II,1	*The Apocryphon of John*	*Ap. John*
II,2	*The Gospel of Thomas*	*Gos. Thom.*
II,3	*The Gospel of Philip*	*Gos.Phil.*
II,4	*The Hypostasis of the Archons*	*Hyp. Arch.*
II,5	*On the Origin of the World*	*Orig. World*
II,6	*The Exegesis on the Soul*	*Exeg. Soul*
II,7	*The Book of Thomas the Contender*	*Thom. Cont.*
III,1	*The Apocryphon of John*	*Ap. John*
III,2	*The Gospel of the Egyptians*	*Gos. Eg.*
III,3	*Eugnostos the Blessed*	*Eugnostos*
III,4	*The Sophia of Jesus Christ*	*Soph. Jes. Chr.*
III,5	*The Dialogue of the Saviour*	*Dial. Sav.*
IV,1	*The Apocryphon of John*	*Ap. John.*
IV,2	*The Gospel of the Egyptians*	*Gos. Eg.*
V,1	*Eugnostos the Blessed*	*Eugnostos*
V,2	*The Apocalypse of Paul*	*Apoc. Paul*

V,3	*The (First) Apocalypse of James*	1 Apoc. Jas.
V,4	*The (Second) Apocalypse of James*	2 Apoc. Jas.
V,5	*The Apocalypse of Adam*	Apoc. Adam
VI,1	*The Acts of Peter and the Twelve*	
	Apostles	Acts Pet. 12 Apost.
VI,2	*The Thunder: Perfect Mind*	Thund.
VI,3	*Authoritative Teaching*	Auth. Teach.
VI,4	*The Concept of our Great Power*	Great Pow.
VI,5	*Plato, Republic 588b–589b*	Plato Rep.
VI,6	*The Discourse on the Eighth and Ninth*	Disc. 8–9
VI,7	*The Prayer of Thanksgiving*	Pr. Thanks.
VI,8	*Asclepius 21–29*	Asclepius
VII,1	*The Paraphrase of Shem*	Paraph. Shem
VII,2	*The Second Treatise of the Great Seth*	Treat. Seth
VII,3	*The Apocalypse of Peter*	Apoc. Pet.
VII,4	*The Teachings of Silvanus*	Teach. Silv.
VII,5	*The Three Steles of Seth*	Steles Seth
VIII,1	*Zostrianos*	Zost.
VIII,2	*The Letter of Peter to Philip*	Ep. Pet. Phil.
IX,1	*Melchizedek*	Melch.
IX,2	*The Thought of Norea*	Norea
IX,3	*The Testimony of Truth*	Testim. Truth
X,1	*Marsanes*	Marsanes
XI,1	*The Interpretation of Knowledge*	Interp. Know.
XI,2	*A Valentinian Exposition*	Val. Exp.
XI,2a	*On Baptism A*	On Bap. A
XI,2b	*On Baptism B*	On Bap. B
XI,2c	*On Baptism C*	On Bap. C
XI,2d	*On the Eucharist A*	On Euch. A
XI,2e	*On the Eucharist B*	On Euch. B
XI,3	*Allogenes*	Allogenes
XI,4	*Hypsiphrone*	Hypsiph.
XII,1	*The Sentences of Sextus*	Sent. Sextus
XII,2	*The Gospel of Truth*	Gos. Truth
XII,3	*Fragments*	Frm.
XIII,1	*Trimorphic Protennoia*	Trim. Prot.
XIII,2	*On the Origin of the World*	Orig. World
BG 8502,1	*The Gospel of Mary*	Gos. Mary
BG 8502,2	*The Apocryphon of John*	Ap. John

BG 8502,3   *The Sophia of Jesus Christ*   *Soph. Jes. Chr.*
BG 8502,4   *The Act of Peter*   *Act Pet.*

The First Book of Jeu in the Bruce Codex   *1 Jeu*
The Second Book of Jeu in the Bruce Codex   *2 Jeu*
The Untitled Text in the Bruce Codex   Cod. Bruc. *Untitled*
Pistis Sophia, four books in the Askew Codex   *Pist. Soph.*

Introduction

The essays in this book represent aspects of some two decades of research in Gnosticism. Ten of the chapters have been published before as journal articles or as essays contributed to edited volumes such as Festschriften and congress proceedings. These have been selected, edited, and organized for this book. The other three chapters are published here for the first time.

Some of these essays represent research activity that was related to my work in the Coptic Gnostic Project of the Institute for Antiquity and Christianity at the Claremont Graduate School, Claremont, California (James M. Robinson, Director), a collaborative research project of which I have been a member since 1968. My major contribution to that project was the edition of Nag Hammadi Codices IX and X, published in 1981.[1] In that same year I became Director of a new Institute project (based in Claremont and Santa Barbara), "The Roots of Egyptian Christianity." That project is devoted to the study of all aspects of Egyptian Christianity (until the Arab Conquest), not only Gnosticism. This book is intended as a contribution to the work of that project, and is the third volume attached to the "Roots" project to appear in the Institute's series, "Studies in Antiquity and Christianity."[2] Chapter 13 in this book represents particularly well that transition in my work from a focus on Gnosticism to a wider attention to Egyptian Christianity, which includes not only Gnosticism and Gnostic Christianity but also other forms of Christianity as well. Even so, this book as a whole is devoted to Gnosticism, that is, the Gnostic religion, and some of the various forms in which it manifested itself in the period of the early Roman Empire.

1. Pearson, *Codices IX and X.*
2. The other two are Pearson-Goehring, *Roots of Egyptian Christianity,* and Tim Vivian, *St. Peter of Alexandria: Bishop and Martyr* (Philadelphia: Fortress Press, 1988).

1

What I mean by such terms as "Gnosticism" and "the Gnostic religion" will be clarified in what follows, especially in my concluding statement in this introduction. But first, some remarks on each chapter in this book are in order.

Much of my work—some of it is included in this volume—has been devoted to the study of the relationship between Gnosticism and Judaism. In chapter 1 I take up for discussion and analysis the pioneering work in this area published by Moritz Friedländer in 1898, "The Pre-Christian Jewish Gnosticism."[3] Friedländer's thesis is based in large part on his reading of Philo of Alexandria, and my involvement in a collaborative research effort focusing on Philo,[4] coupled with my study of Gnosticism, led me to explore Friedländer's book. This essay was published in 1973 in a journal founded by the aforementioned Philo project, *Studia Philonica*.[5] It has been revised and updated for republication here.

Chapter 2 is devoted to a study of the Gnostic anthropogony constituting part of the basic myth found in one of the Coptic Gnostic tractates, *The Apocryphon of John*. I explore the dependence shown by the Gnostic author on earlier non-Gnostic Jewish traditions of biblical exegesis, with special attention to the exegesis of Gen. 1:26f. and Gen. 2:7. I was invited to contribute this essay[6] by my friend and colleague Michael Stone for inclusion in a book of essays on biblical exegesis. It was published in 1976,[7] and has been edited and updated for republication here.

Chapter 3 is the oldest of the essays in this volume. In it I isolate a passage from *The Testimony of Truth* in Nag Hammadi Codex IX that, in my view, constitutes a kind of Gnostic "midrash," featuring the serpent in the paradise narrative in Genesis 2—3. I explore the various non-Gnostic Jewish exegetical traditions on which the author of that midrash drew, and conclude that it reflects a pre-Christian stage in the development of Gnosticism. This essay was presented orally at the Annual

---

3. *Der vorchristliche jüdische Gnosticismus* (Göttingen: Vandenhoeck & Ruprecht).

4. I refer to the Philo Institute, founded and directed for a time by Robert Hamerton-Kelly. The founding meeting of the Philo Institute took place at McCormick Theological Seminary in Chicago in June 1971. It met annually for some years thereafter, but eventually disbanded after Hamerton-Kelly left McCormick. Six issues of *Studia Philonica* were published (1972–80), and it has recently been revived as *The Studia Philonica Annual: Studies in Hellenistic Judaism* (Brown Judaic Studies; Atlanta: Scholars Press, from 1988).

5. "Friedländer Revisited: Alexandrian Judaism and Gnostic Origins," *Studia Philonica* 2 (1973) 23–39.

6. This essay is largely based on research done for my doctoral dissertation. See Pearson, *Pneumatikos-Psychikos Terminology*, chap. 6.

7. "Biblical Exegesis in Gnostic Literature," in M. Stone, ed., *Armenian and Biblical Studies* (Jerusalem: St. James Press, 1976) 70–80.

Meeting of the Society of Biblical Literature in Atlanta, Georgia, in October 1971, and then published as a contribution to the Festschrift for Geo Widengren in 1972.[8] It was republished in a volume of essays resulting from a colloquium on religious syncretism held at the University of California, Santa Barbara, in April 1972.[9] It has been substantially revised for republication here.

Chapter 4 explores the Gnostic sources and patristic testimonies in order to set forth a typology of the Gnostic savior figure Seth, son of Adam, and shows that Gnostic speculation on Seth is based on scripture interpretation and Jewish traditions of exegesis. It was presented to a special seminar devoted to Sethian Gnosticism as part of the International Conference on Gnosticism held at Yale University, New Haven, Connecticut, in March 1978. It was published in 1981 in the proceedings of that conference.[10] It has been edited and updated for republication here.

Chapter 5 explores the Gnostic sources and patristic testimonies dealing with the figure of Norea, sister of Seth. A history of the traditions pertaining to this figure is presented, showing that the Gnostic Norea is based on non-Gnostic Jewish traditions pertaining to a Canaanite woman, Naamah. As a feminine savior figure, Norea plays an important role in several Gnostic tractates, especially *The Hypostasis of the Archons* (NHC II,4).[11] She has even been "discovered" by a modern novelist.[12] This essay was first presented at the International Colloquium on Gnosticism held in Stockholm in August 1973, and was published in 1977 in the colloquium proceedings.[13] It has been edited and updated for republication here.

In chapter 6 I analyze the sources pertaining to the Gnostic interpreta-

8. "Jewish Haggadic Traditions in *The Testimony of Truth* from Nag Hammadi (CG IX,3)," in J. Bergman et al., eds., *Ex Orbe Religionum: Studia Geo Widengren oblata* (SHR 21–22; Leiden: E.J. Brill, 1972) 1.457–70.
9. In B. Pearson, ed., *Religious Syncretism in Antiquity: Essays in Conversation with Geo Widengren* (Missoula: Scholars Press, 1975) 205–22.
10. "The Figure of Seth in Gnostic Literature," in Layton, *Rediscovery* 2.472–504.
11. See now also Anne McGuire, "Virginity and Subversion: Norea Against the Powers in the *Hypostasis of the Archons*," 239–58, and B. Pearson, "Revisiting Norea," 265–75, in Karen King, ed., *Images of the Feminine in Gnosticism* (SAC 4; Philadelphia: Fortress Press, 1988).
12. On a visit to Sweden in 1987 my cousin showed me a trilogy of novels featuring Eve, Cain, and Norea. In the preface to the third novel, "Noreas Saga," the author refers (as my cousin pointed out) to my introduction to the tractate *The Thought of Norea* (NHC IX,2), published in *The Nag Hammadi Library in English* (1st ed., 1977), 404. See Marianne Fredriksson, *Paradisets Barn* ["Children of Paradise"] (Stockholm: Wahlström & Widstrand, 1985) 443.
13. "The Figure of Norea in Gnostic Literature," in G. Widengren, ed., *Proceedings of the International Colloquium on Gnosticism Stockholm August 20–25, 1973* (Stockholm: Almqvist & Wiksell, 1977) 143–52.

tion of the biblical Cain, son of Adam, showing that in most cases Cain is evaluated negatively by the Gnostics. I also explore the patristic testimonies relating to a Gnostic sect, the "Cainites," and conclude that this alleged group is a figment of the heresiologists' imaginations. An early version of this essay was presented at the Annual Meeting of the Society of Biblical Literature in Dallas, Texas, in December 1983. It is published for the first time here.

Chapter 7 is devoted to an analysis of the (relatively few) Gnostic texts in which the biblical figure of Melchizedek occurs (Genesis 14 and Ps. 110:4). Building on research done in connection with my publication of the tractate *Melchizedek* (NHC IX,1),[14] I trace the history of the interpretation of Melchizedek as found in the sources, concluding that the latest Gnostic speculations on Melchizedek as a heavenly figure actually hark back to pre-Christian Jewish material such as the Melchizedek fragments from Qumran (11QMelch). An earlier version of this essay was presented at the Fourth International Congress of Coptic Studies held at the Catholic University in Louvain-la-Neuve, Belgium, in September 1988. It is published for the first time here.

Chapter 8 explores the Gnostic materials, especially the "Sethian" sources, for evidence concerning the ancient Gnostics' self-understanding, looking particularly at the self-designations used by the Gnostics. A prominent feature of Gnostic self-understanding is a rejection of traditional Judaism, even though scripture and Jewish traditions were freely used—and, of course, reinterpreted—in the process whereby the Gnostics established their own self-definition. This essay was first presented at a special symposium on "Jewish and Christian Self-Definition" at McMaster University, Hamilton, Ontario, in May 1978. It was published in 1980 in a volume containing the symposium papers.[15] It has been edited and revised for republication here.

In chapter 9 I analyze the concluding section of the Hermetic tractate *Poimandres* for evidence of the use of Jewish liturgical traditions in its formulation. Concluding that the author used Jewish prayers and doxologies in his own hymns and prayers composed for use in Hermetic

---

14. See Pearson, *Codices IX and X*, 19–85. Cf. also B. Pearson, "The Figure of Melchizedek in the First Tractate of the Unpublished Coptic-Gnostic Codex IX from Nag Hammadi," in C. Bleeker et al., eds., *Proceedings of the XIIth International Congress of the International Association for the History of Religions* [Stockholm, 1970] (SHR 31; Leiden: E.J. Brill, 1975) 200–208.

15. "Jewish Elements in Gnosticism and the Development of Gnostic Self-Definition," in E. P. Sanders, ed., *The Shaping of Christianity in the Second and Third Centuries* (London: SCM/Philadelphia: Fortress Press, 1980) 151–60.

ritual, I propose a theory as to the historical situation in which this might have occurred. An early version of this essay was presented to the Seventh World Congress of Jewish Studies in Jerusalem in August 1977, in a section chaired by the late Gershom Scholem. It was published in the Festschrift for Gilles Quispel in 1981.[16] It has been substantially revised for republication here.

In chapter 10 I address the issue of the relationship between Gnosticism and Platonist philosophy, with special attention to one of the Nag Hammadi tractates that reflects an advanced stage in the history of this relationship, *Marsanes* (NHC X,1). In that tractate we can infer the kind of give-and-take that would have taken place in discussions between adherents of Gnostic groups and members of philosophical schools, such as that of the famous Plotinus in Rome in the early third century. An early version of this essay was presented to the Symposium on Philosophy and Religion in Late Antiquity, organized by Gedalyahu G. Stroumsa and held in Jerusalem in March 1981, under the auspices of the Israel Academy for Sciences and Humanities. It was also presented at the Annual Meeting of the Society of Biblical Literature in San Francisco in December 1981. The essay was published in 1986,[17] and has been edited for republication here.

Chapter 11 is an essay originally prepared for publication in the Festschrift for R. McL. Wilson and published in 1983.[18] Its title and topic were assigned to me by the editors of that volume. Thus, having been invited to write something on "Philo, Gnosis and the New Testament," I chose to relate my essay to problems addressed by Wilson in various of his publications, and to attempt in my own way to relate the three elements in the essay's title. In it I trace a trajectory of "speculative wisdom" (what Wilson calls "gnosis") from Philo of Alexandria to Paul's Corinth, via Apollos (1 Corinthians 1—4), and back again to Alexandria (NHC VII,4: *Teach. Silv.*). The essay has been updated for republication here.

16. "Jewish Elements in *Corpus Hermeticum* I *(Poimandres),*" in R. van den Broek, ed., *Studies in Gnosticism and Hellenistic Religions presented to Gilles Quispel* (EPRO 91; Leiden: E. J. Brill, 1981) 336–48. In that version of the essay, I acknowledged the important influence that Quispel has had on my work, from the time that he was a Visiting Professor at Harvard University in 1964–65. It was he, too, who introduced me to the writings of this century's greatest scholar of Jewish mysticism, Gershom Scholem, whom I met in Jerusalem in 1977 and again in 1981.

17. "Gnosticism as Platonism: With Special Reference to Marsanes (NHC 10,1)," *HTR* 77 (1984 [appeared 1986]) 55–72.

18. "Philo, Gnosis and the New Testament," in A. H. B. Logan and A. J. M. Wedderburn, eds., *The New Testament and Gnosis: Essays in Honour of Robert McL. Wilson* (Edinburgh: T. &. T. Clark, 1983) 73–89.

In chapter 12 I take up for discussion two quite different examples of
"Gnostic heresiology," both found in tractates contained in Nag Hammadi Codex IX: *Melchizedek* and *The Testimony of Truth*. That "heresiology" should be found among the Gnostic opponents of the great
heresiologists of the orthodox church is an interesting surprise, but the
Nag Hammadi texts contain many surprises, some of them perhaps as
yet undetected. This essay was originally prepared as a contribution to
the Festschrift for Pahor Labib,[19] former Director of the Coptic Museum
in Old Cairo, where the Nag Hammadi manuscripts are now kept. It was
also presented at the annual meeting of the Pacific Coast Region of the
Society of Biblical Literature in San Jose, California, in April 1975. It has
been substantially revised and expanded for republication here.

Chapter 13 is a new essay, hitherto unpublished. A portion of it is
based on a paper presented orally at the Annual Meeting of the Society
of Biblical Literature in Boston in December 1987. In this chapter I take
up for discussion the difficult problem of the origins and early history of
Christianity in Egypt, with special attention to the role played in that
history by Gnostics and Gnosticism. In the course of the discussion I
have occasion to consider the pioneering work of Walter Bauer,[20] whose
views on early Egyptian Christianity are widely endorsed by scholars.
The position that I take here, on the basis of my reading of the evidence,
challenges Bauer's thesis of a heretical origin for Egyptian Christianity.

It will be noted that I regularly use the upper-case *G* in referring to
Gnosticism, Gnostics, and the Gnostic religion. This usage represents a
conscious scholarly decision on my part as to what these terms mean,
and how Gnosticism should be construed historically and phenomeno-
logically. The problem becomes all the more acute when we see how
closely Gnosticism is tied to other religions in antiquity, especially Christianity. Indeed, the argument is still being mounted in some scholarly
circles that Gnosticism began and developed as a Christian heresy.[21]
This position denies what I am seeking to affirm, namely, that Gnosticism first developed independently of Christianity and, even in its continuing development within Christian circles, ought to be seen as a

19. "Anti-Heretical Warnings in Codex IX from Nag Hammadi," in M. Krause, ed.,
Essays on the Nag Hammadi Texts in Honour of Pahor Labib (NHS 6; Leiden: E.J. Brill,
1975) 145–54.
20. Bauer, *Orthodoxy and Heresy*.
21. See esp. Simone Pétrement, *Le Dieu séparé: les origines du gnosticisme* (Paris: Cerf,
1984). Cf. my assessment of her work in "Early Christianity and Gnosticism: A Review
Essay," *RSRev* 13 (1987) 1–8.

discrete religious phenomenon for which the designation "the Gnostic religion"[22] is entirely appropriate.

The use of the term "Gnosticism" has been criticized, notably by Kurt Rudolph, who points out that the term is a seventeenth-century creation.[23] But even he is forced to use it, just because it has become part of the scholarly vocabulary. In my view there are definite advantages in retaining the term because "Gnosticism" (=the Gnostic religion) can then be usefully distinguished from the kinds of "gnosis," that is, esoteric doctrines reserved for a religious elite, that do not share in the radical dualism or other essential features properly reserved for "Gnosticism."[24] I see the term "Gnosticism" as analogous to such other "-isms" as *Ioudaismos* (2 Macc. 2:21, "Judaism"), *Christianismos* (Ignatius *Magn.* 10.1,3; *Phld.* 6.1; *Rom.* 3.3, "Christianity"), and the like. "Mandaeism" is an especially useful example, for it means essentially the same as "Gnosticism" (from Mandaic [East Aramaic] *manda*, "knowledge"). This example reminds us that the ancient Gnostic religion did not die out, but, in the case of the Mandaeans, survives to this day, albeit tenuously, in the marshlands of Iran and Iraq.[25]

What are the essential features of Gnosticism, and why should Gnosticism be treated as a historically discrete religious phenomenon? An extensive answer to this question is hardly possible here, nor is it needed, for it has been supplied by others.[26] Suffice it to say here, by way of summarizing my own views on the matter, first, that adherents of Gnosticism regard *gnosis* (rather than faith, observance of law, etc.) as requisite to salvation. The saving "knowledge" involves a revelation as to the true nature both of the self and of God; indeed, for the Gnostic, self-knowledge *is* knowledge of God. Gnosticism also has, second, a characteristic *theology* according to which there is a transcendent supreme God beyond the god or powers responsible for the world in which we live. Third, a negative, radically dualist stance vis-à-vis the cosmos involves a *cosmology*, according to which the cosmos itself, having been created by an inferior and ignorant power, is a dark prison in which human souls are held captive. Interwoven with its theology and

22. Jonas, *Gnostic Religion.*
23. *Gnosis*, 56.
24. For discussion of these issues see esp. chap. 11 in this book.
25. On the Mandaeans see esp. Rudolph, *Gnosis*, 343–66, and literature cited. Hans Jonas, in his discussion of "Gnostic Imagery and Symbolic Language" (*Gnostic Religion*, chap. 3, pp. 48–99), relies chiefly on the Mandaean evidence.
26. E.g., Rudolph, *Gnosis*; Jonas, *Gnostic Religion.*

its cosmology is, fourth, an *anthropology*, according to which the essential human being is constituted by his/her inner self, a divine spark that originated in the transcendent divine world and, by means of gnosis, can be released from the cosmic prison and can return to its heavenly origin. The human body, on the other hand, is part of the cosmic prison from which the essential "man" must be redeemed. The notion of release from the cosmic prison entails, fifth, an *eschatology*, which applies not only to the salvation of the individual but to the salvation of all the elect, and according to which the material cosmos itself will come to its fated end.

Gnosticism, at first glance, seems to be a highly individualistic religion, and so it is. But, in fact, Gnostics did gather in communities of like-minded persons. Hence, there is, sixth, a *social* dimension to Gnosticism. Closely tied to this is, seventh, a *ritual* dimension as well, for the Gnostics had religious ceremonies of various kinds. There is, also, eighth, an *ethical* dimension, though in this area there was considerable variation from group to group. Most characteristic, reflecting the acosmic nature of Gnosticism, is the propensity toward withdrawal from engagement with the cosmos, which in its most extreme forms involved abstinence from sex and procreation. That all of the aforementioned features of Gnosticism involved, ninth, an *experiential* dimension almost goes without saying. Religious experience, for the Gnostic, involved joy in the salvation won by gnosis, as well as an extreme alienation from, and revolt against, the cosmic order and those beings attached to it. Tenth, what holds everything together for the Gnostic is *myth*. One of the most characteristic features of Gnosticism is its mythopoesis, its impulse to create an elaborate mythical system giving expression to all that gnosis entails. An interesting feature of Gnostic mythopoesis is that there was great variation in the telling of the myth; each Gnostic teacher would create new elements to be added to his or her received myth, and, with such elaborations, Gnostic myths could become more and more complicated as they developed.

I hope I have shown in the foregoing discussion that Gnosticism deserves to be called "a religion."[27] But what makes Gnosticism so hard to define is, finally, its *parasitical* character, a feature that constitutes an eleventh dimension of Gnosticism. This brings up the problem of the relationship between Gnosticism and other religions, chiefly Judaism

27. Cf. my colleague Ninian Smart's discussion of the six dimensions of what constitutes "a religion": doctrinal, mythic, ethical, ritual, experiential, and social; in *Worldviews: Cross Cultural Explorations of Human Beliefs* (New York: Charles Scribner's Sons, 1983) 7–8.

and Christianity. From the foregoing discussion of the essential features of Gnosticism the question would inevitably arise: What has this religion to do with Judaism? Or with Christianity? Precisely such questions are taken up in various ways in this book. In the ensuing chapters we shall see that parasitical dimension of Gnosticism.

I conclude this introduction with two examples, both of which will be further elaborated in the chapters to follow. The first example is the relationship between Gnostic myth and Judaism, more precisely, Jewish scriptures and exegetical traditions. That relationship is parasitical in that the essential building blocks of the basic Gnostic myth constitute a (revolutionary) borrowing and reinterpretation of Jewish scriptures and traditions.[28] But the resulting religious system is anything but Jewish!

The second example is the relationship between the revealer of gnosis in Gnosticism and Christianity, more precisely, the figure of Jesus Christ. In Christian Gnosticism (or Gnostic, i.e., "heretical" Christianity), Jesus Christ is the revealer of gnosis; the entire Gnostic myth is attributed to him (as, e.g., in *Ap. John*). What seems to be reflected here, historically, is an attempt on the part of Gnostics to gain entry into Christian communities, or to gain Christian adherents to their communities, by means of equating their own gnosis with alleged secret teachings of Jesus. This is precisely what causes so much difficulty for modern interpreters, some of whom continue to insist that Gnosticism, in its origins, was sparked by the appearance in history of a suitable savior figure, understood to be Jesus Christ. But this is an illusion. Non-Christian (pre-Christian?) varieties of Gnosticism had other revealer figures to whom to attribute their mythology, the most important of which seems to have been Seth, son of Adam. Of course, later "Christianized" Sethian Gnostics could then equate Seth with Jesus Christ, and regard the latter as the incarnation or avatar of the former.[29]

Such are the issues in modern scholarship on Gnosticism. In this book are examples of my own stance on such matters. It goes without saying that not everyone will agree with my interpretations of the evidence. I shall be content, however, if this book provides a catalyst for further scholarly discussion and debate on the Gnostic phenomenon and its various manifestations in space and time. And if these things are of interest to the general reader as well, all the better.

28. See esp. chaps. 2–9; Pearson, "'Jewish Gnostic' Literature."
29. See esp. chap. 4 in this book.

1

Friedländer Revisited: Alexandrian Judaism and Gnostic Origins

In many fields of human endeavor it sometimes happens that a person sets forth seemingly outlandish theories; the work is dismissed lightly, or perhaps ponderously refuted, and then lies unnoticed by the next generation. At last, however, someone takes notice of what had been proposed many years before, and the earlier work turns out to be exceedingly useful when looked at with new evidence and by a different generation. For example, Alfred Wegener, in a book entitled *The Origin of Continents and Oceans,* published in 1915, put forward the thesis that South America once lay alongside Africa, but that in a process of many aeons the two continents drifted far away from each other, having been split apart by forces generated beneath the earth's crust. He went on to observe that all of the earth's continents have shifted and broken apart over vast spaces of time, and are still in the process of drifting. Wegener was laughed out of court by the geologists of his day, and died in 1930 surrounded by incredulity and derision. Now, as we all know, the theory of continental drift has become almost an orthodoxy.[1]

The field of the history of religions also has its Wegeners, and scholars whose interests lie in the complex history of the religions of the Hellenistic-Roman world are well advised to look into the work of bygone eras of scholarship for "new" light on current areas of interest. Much is currently being written on the question of the origins of Gnosticism[2] and

1. For material on this fascinating subject that is reasonably intelligible to us humanists, see J. T. Wilson, ed., *Continents Adrift* (Readings from *Scientific American;* San Francisco: W. H. Freeman, 1972) and S. W. Matthews, "This Changing Earth," *National Geographic* 143 (1973) 1–37.
2. See esp. Bianchi, *Origini dello gnosticismo.* A complete bibliography of scholarship on Gnosticism since 1948 is now available: Scholer, *Nag Hammadi Bibliography* supplemented annually in *Novum Testamentum.* See also the important work by K.

the relationship of Gnosticism to Judaism.[3] It seems to me useful, for the purpose of further discussion, to exhume from the dust of many decades some interesting and provocative ideas set forth by Moritz Friedländer, whose theses did not meet with the approval of his contemporaries, but which may very well be taken more seriously now. In a book entitled *Der vorchristliche jüdische Gnosticismus,*[4] Friedländer put forth the thesis that Gnosticism is a pre-Christian phenomenon which originated in antinomian circles in the Jewish community of Alexandria. This Gnosticism, against which Philo polemicizes, came early to Palestine; and the rabbinic polemics against the Minim are directed specifically at such Gnostics. Christian Gnosticism is simply a secondary version of the older Gnosticism, which attached itself to the emergent Christian sect and appropriated for itself the figure of Jesus Christ.

FRIEDLÄNDER'S ARGUMENTS

Friedländer's thesis is worth considering in some detail. In this article I first want to set forth his main arguments, concentrating especially on what he derives from his reading of Philo. Then I shall comment briefly on the issues he raised from the vantage point of modern scholarship and on the basis of materials unknown to Friedländer and his generation that we now have at our disposal.

It should be mentioned that Friedländer did not write in a vacuum; others had for many years and even decades written on Gnosticism, and specifically on the relationship of Gnosticism to Judaism. Two of the most important of these are H. Graetz and M. Joël.[5] But Friedländer was

Rudolph, "Gnosis and Gnostizismus, ein Forschungsbericht," *ThR* 34 (1969) 121–75; 181–231; 358–61; and 36 (1971) 1–61; 89–124.
3. See, e.g., several of the chaps. in this book.
4. (Göttingen: Vandenhoeck & Ruprecht, 1898; repr. Farnborough: Gregg International, 1972). Reference will also be made in this article to an earlier work of his, "La secte de Melchisédec et l'epître aux Hébreux," *REJ* 5 (1882) 1–26; 188–98; and 6 (1883) 187–99.
5. Graetz, *Gnosticismus und Judenthum* (Krotoschin: B. L. Monasch & Sohn, 1846; Joël, *Blicke in die Religionsgeschichte zu Anfang des zweiten christlichen Jahrhunderts,* vol. 1 (Breslau: Schottlander, 1880). For Graetz, gnosis is a variety of Hellenistic speculative metaphysics that powerfully influenced Judaism not only in Alexandria (e.g., Philo) but also in Palestine. His book treats the influence of Gnosticism upon Judaism in the Tannaitic period, discusses four important figures in Palestine who were "Gnostics" or influenced by gnosis (the four who "entered Paradise," *Hag.* 14b), and suggests that *Sefer Yetzirah* (the "Book of Creation") is an anti-gnostic work, though influenced by gnosis, and was written by R. Akiba. For Joël, gnosis is rooted especially in Platonic-Pythagorean metaphysics, and comes into Judaism and Christianity under the impetus

the first, to my knowledge, to suggest that Gnosticism *originated* in Judaism.

Friedländer begins his discussion by referring to the cultural and religious situation in the Jewish Diaspora prior to the time of Jesus. It was a situation in which the "new wine" of Hellenistic culture and philosophy was being put into the "old wineskins" of Jewish religion. The allegorical method of scripture interpretation was one of the manifestations of this trend. The Mosaic law was being interpreted allegorically by Jews who had imbibed of Greek philosophy, and the Law was taken to be a "revelation" of "divine philosophy." Indeed, since Moses was more ancient than the Greek philosophers, it was natural to suggest that the latter had learned from the former. Philo is a good example of this trend, but he had forerunners, such as Aristobulus, Pseudo-Aristeas, and Pseudo-Solomon (1–3).[6]

The allegorical interpretation of the Law must have led to divisions in Diaspora Judaism between "conservative" Jews who observed the letter of the Law and "philosophizers" who regarded the letter of the Law as peripheral.[7] Such a division is not merely a hypothetical reconstruction, but is well documented in historical sources. Eusebius (*Praep. Ev.* 7.10) specifically speaks of two parties in Diaspora Judaism whose differences are precisely delineated along the lines here suggested (3–4).

Philo himself provides clear evidence of such divisions. A key text in Friedländer's argument is *On the Migration of Abraham* 86–93,[8] which Friedländer quotes in full. In this text, wherein Philo polemicizes against allegorists who neglect the letter of the Law and derive from it only spiritual truths, we have reflected a full-blown schism in the Diaspora. An "antinomian" party of Jews is referred to here. They differ from the

---

of the desire to read out of (really "into") the Bible the Hellenistic metaphysics so prevalent in the Greco-Roman world. He, too, discusses the extensive influences of gnosis upon Palestinian Judaism, and his work is especially important for its discussion of Jewish-Gnostic elements in the developed systems of Gnosticism known to us from the writings of the church fathers. F. C. Baur, too, should be mentioned in this connection, for he suggested in his still important work, *Die christliche Gnosis oder die christliche Religionsphilosophie in ihrer geschichtlichen Entwicklung* (Tübingen: Osiander, 1835), that the Gnostic religion could only develop in a situation wherein Jewish religion had come into contact with pagan religion and philosophy; see esp. 36–68.

6. Bare page numbers are references to Friedländer's book, *Der vorchristliche jüdische Gnosticismus*.

7. These ideas had been set forth by Friedländer in an earlier book, *Das Judenthum in der vorchristlichen griechischen Welt* (Wien: M. Breitenstein, 1897), but had not met with much enthusiasm on the part of his fellow scholars.

8. References to Philo throughout this article are cited and quoted according to the LCL edition, except where otherwise specified. Friedländer's own references are all to the Mangey edition of 1742.

Therapeutae, the Palestinian Essenes, and Philo himself not so much in their use of allegory, but precisely in their antinomian tendencies (4–9).

A number of Jewish sects are known to us from antiquity whose views were suspect in the eyes of law-abiding Jews, Friedländer continues. Among these are the "Sibyllists" known to Origen (*Contra Celsum* 5.6lf.), probably identical to the "pious ones" referred to in the *Sibylline Oracles*, book 4. Justin Martyr refers to some pre-Christian sects among the Jews (*Dial.* 80), at least one of which, the "Hellenians," is surely a reference to a Diaspora group. Hegesippus derives all Christian heresies from pre-Christian Jewish heresies (Eusebius *Hist. Eccl.* 4.22.7). According to him the Gnostic heresy reared its ugly head in the church soon after the death of the apostles (Eusebius *Hist. Eccl.* 3.32.7f.). The implication of Hegesippus's statement is that "false" gnosis was already extant in apostolic times, but the powerful influence of the apostles kept it from blossoming in the church. The origin of this "false gnosis," if we consider the testimony of Hegesippus, is found in pre-Christian Judaism. The view of some later fathers that heresy is necessarily later than orthodoxy (e.g., Clem. Alex. *Strom.* 7.17; Tertullian *Haer.* 29ff.) is obviously tendentious (9–17).

Friedländer goes on to set forth the daring hypothesis that such "Christian" heresies as those of the Ophites, the Cainites, and the Sethians, as well as the Melchizedekians, are the progeny of the radical antinomians against whom Philo had polemicized. According to the oldest patristic accounts (Irenaeus *Haer.* 1.30; Ps.-Tertullian *Haer.* 2.1; Filastrius 1; Epiphanius *Haer.* 36) the Ophites—who according to some accounts are closely associated with the Sethians (Theodoret *Haer.* 1.14)—were antinomian and venerated the serpent as the revealer of gnosis and as an incarnation of the divine Wisdom. Reflected in these ideas is the Alexandrian-Jewish doctrine of the divine *dynamis*. Philo and other Alexandrian Jews regarded Sophia as a divine *dynamis*. The Ophites simply took up this doctrine and interpreted it in a heretical fashion (17–19).

The Cainites (Irenaeus *Haer.* 1.31; Ps.-Tert. *Haer.* 2.5; Filastrius 2; Epiphanius *Haer.* 37; Theodoret *Haer.* 1.15; Augustine *Haer.* 18) venerated Cain as the divine power, rejected all moral conventions, and rejected the Law along with its God. And what, asks Friedländer, is "Christian" about that? The Alexandrian school provides the most plausible link for the origin of this heresy. Indeed, the Cainite sect was already well known to Philo. Friedländer quotes in this connection *On the Posterity and Exile of Cain* 52–53. In this text "Cain" is a symbol of heresy, and the specifics of the heresy represented by him are such that one can only conclude that Philo is arguing against a philosophizing sect characterized not only by constructing myths contrary to the truth, but by gross antinomianism. Philo speaks against these heretics precisely as Irenaeus speaks against the Gnostics (*Haer.* 2.30.1–2). There can be no doubt that the heretics combated by Philo are the forerunners of the Christian Gnostics later combated by the church fathers (19–23).

The Sethians (Epiphanius *Haer.* 39; Ps.-Tertullian *Haer.* 2.7; Filastrius 3) shared in the errors of the Ophites and Cainites, teaching that the world was created by angels and not by the highest God. The *dynamis* from on high came down into Seth after Abel's death, according to the Sethians, and many held Seth to be the Messiah (24).

Ophites, Cainites, and Sethians all derive from the Jewish Diaspora. Their members were recruited from the Jewish radicals known to us from Philo, and from philosophically oriented proselytes who had attached themselves to the synagogues. Indeed, Filastrius numbers the Ophites, Cainites, and Sethians among the sects that flourished in Judaism "before the advent of Jesus."[9] It is obvious that these sects could not have originated from within Christianity, from the very fact that their chief doctrines are derived from the Old Testament rather than from the New. The divine power was seen by them to reside in the Old Testament figures of the serpent, Cain, and other such biblical personages as were not tied to the Law. These Old Testament figures were adhered to even after the Gnostics came into contact with Christianity. Their origin, in short, is traceable to the situation in Alexandrian Judaism wherein allegorical exposition of the Law flourished, and wherein antinomianism also developed (25–27).

Friedländer turns next to the Melchizedekians. This group held Melchizedek to be a "great Power" (Epiphanius *Haer.* 55; Ps.-Tert. *Haer.* 8.3; Theodoret *Haer.* 2.6; Augustine *Haer.* 34; Filastrius 52), a being higher than the Messiah, a "Son of God" who occupied a place among the heavenly angels. Such a belief cannot have originated in Christianity. The figure of Melchizedek, of course, is derived from the Old Testament, and becomes for antinomian Alexandrian Jews a powerful symbol of Law-free religion. When the Melchizedekians came into contact with

9. P. 26; cf. *REJ* 5 (1882) 2. At neither place does Friedländer provide a reference, and indeed the phrase does not occur in modern editions of Filastrius. The apparatus criticus of that in the Corpus Christianorum (*Eusebii Vercellencis Episcopi quae supersunt* [Series Latina 9; Turnholt: Brepols, 1957]) provides the information that the Sichardi ed. of 1528 had at 1.1, just before the account of the Ophites, Cainites, Sethians, et al., the heading: "catalogus eorum qui ante adventum Christi haereseos arguuntur."

Christianity, Jesus was incorporated into their system, but his position was *below* that of Melchizedek. As Jesus is an advocate for humans, so also is Melchizedek an advocate for the angels (Ps.-Tertullian *Haer.* 8.3) (28–30; cf. REJ 5 [1882] 1–6).

The Alexandrian origin of Melchizedekianism is also demonstrated with reference to Philo himself, for whom Melchizedek is not only a heavenly being but identified with the Logos (*Leg. All.* 3.79–82). Philo nevertheless stresses in his version of the Melchizedek mystery that there is no other God beside God Most High, and he is One (*Leg. All.* 3.82). That in this passage (*Leg. All.* 3.81) a polemic is directed against antinomian heretics is shown also with reference to the "Ammonites" and "Moabites" who are excluded from the divine congregation (30–33).

The Alexandrian author of the Epistle to the Hebrews obviously knew of the Melchizedek mystery, Friedländer continues (referring to Heb. 7:1–3), and indeed presents a modified Melchizedekianism to his erstwhile coreligionists, trying to prove to them that Jesus is indeed superior to Melchizedek. In Heb. 7:3 the Melchizedek mystery is qualified with the phrase ἀφωμοιωμένος δὲ τῷ υἱῷ τοῦ Θεοῦ (33–35; cf. *REJ* 5 [1882] 193–97).

Friedländer distinguishes the Melchizedekians from the Ophites and Cainites, suggesting that the former were not so aggressive in their antinomianism as the latter. He even suggests that Melchizedekianism is the one form of pre-Christian Gnosticism that qualifies best as the point of departure for *Christian* Gnosticism (35–38; cf. *REJ* 5 [1882] 8).

On the origin of pre-Christian Jewish Gnosticism, Friedländer summarizes his position by stating that it began with the "Hellenization of Judaism in the Diaspora."[10] Gnosticism served as the medium by which Judaism should become a world religion. It remained orthodox so long as the Law was observed, as is the case with Philo, and became heretical when the letter of the Law was rejected, as was the case with the "radicals" combated by Philo (44–45).

In the second half of the monograph Friedländer discusses further the content of gnosis and its propagation among the Jews of Palestine. The chief content of the oldest gnosis consists of cosmogonical and theosophical speculation; the means by which an amalgamation of the old religion with newer philosophical ideas was achieved was allegory. This characteristic of Gnosis—evident in the oldest known Gnostic sect, the

---

10. ". . . dass derselbe mit der Hellenisierung des Judenthums in der Diaspora seinen Anfang nahm," 44. Cf. the well-known dictum of A. von Harnack, that Gnosticism is the "acute Hellenization of Christianity."

Ophites—is found also among the most ancient Mishnah teachers under the designations *ma'ăśēh bᵉrēšît* (the "work of Creation") and *ma'ăśeh merkābāh* (the work of the Chariot) (45–46).

That cosmogonic and theosophical speculations had taken a heretical turn very early in Palestine is demonstrated, according to Friedländer, by the following Mishnah, which is referred to as a tradition of the sages by the first-century rabbi, Yohanan ben Zakkai (according to *j.Ḥag.* 77a):

> The laws of incest may not be expounded to three persons, nor the *Story of Creation* (מעשה בראשית) before two persons, nor the subject of the *Chariot* (מרכבה) before one person alone unless he be a Sage and comprehends of his own knowledge. Whoever puts his mind to these four matters it were better for him if he had not come into the world—What is above? What is below? What is beyond? What is in the opposite beyond? And whosoever has no regard for the honour of his Creator it were better for him had he not come into the world.[11]

Clearly reflected in this Mishnah, and severely condemned, is the antinomian Gnostic differentiation between the highest God and an inferior Creator. But one finds a polemic against such obscene esoterica, Friedländer suggests, already in the second half of the second pre-Christian century in Sir. 3:21–24, a passage actually quoted in the Talmud later in an anti-Gnostic polemic (*Ḥag.* 11b). Heretical gnosis reached Palestine at least by the early first century. "Gnostic" mystical doctrines were tolerated and fostered by some in orthodox circles, so long as "the honor of the Father in Heaven" was served and the unity of God maintained. Thus a distinction was made between "true" gnosis and "false" gnosis, the latter characterized by arrogance over against God (48–52).

The Palestinian distinction between true and false gnosis is matched by, and preceded by, a similar distinction in the Alexandrian Diaspora. Philo distinguishes between the true and the false gnosis by stating that the true is characterized by following God, and is typified by righteous Abel (*Sacr.* 2), while the false, typified by Cain, is characterized by ascribing all things to the human mind (*Sacr.* 2), and by self-love, rejection of the truth, and godlessness (*Post.* 53) (52–53).

---

11. *Ḥag.* 2.1 (*Mishnayot*, ed. P. Blackman [New York: Judaica Press, 1963] 2.494). M. Joël (*Blicke in die Religionsgeschichte*, 151ff.) suggests that the first part of this mishnah is earlier than the second, and that the second part was formulated in the early second century when heretical gnosis was rampant. Friedländer takes issue with this, but does agree with Joël that the second part is specifically directed against heretical gnosis (46, n.3). He sees the heretical development as having taken place earlier than is posited by Joël.

Friedländer suggests further that the dependence of Palestinian esoteric speculation upon Alexandrian Judaism can be shown with reference to Philo, both with respect to the practice of reserving the higher
gnosis to the initiated, and with respect to actual content. Several passages in Philo (*Ebr.* 30–32; *Cher.* 42, 48; *Sacr.* 131–133, 59; *Cher.* 27f.) are
cited in this connection. In these Alexandrian speculations we have the
sources of the Palestinian mysteries of the *ma*ʿᵃśēh *b*ᵉrēšît and the
*ma*ʿᵃśēh *merkābāh*. These speculations, if not pursued by such pious
worthies as Philo or R. Yohanan ben Zakkai, could easily lead to heresy.
Philo describes this kind of heresy very appropriately when he refers to
the "self-loving and godless mind which regards itself as equal to God"
(*Leg. All.* 1.49) (53–58).

Friedländer contends that heretical Gnosticism was an important factor in Palestine already in the time of Jesus.[12] The most influential variety
of heretical Gnosticism was Ophitism, transplanted in Palestine from
the Diaspora. The Talmud refers to the Gnostic heretics as *mînîm*, and
the Gnostic heresy itself as *mînût*, terms that cannot be taken—as is
sometimes done—to refer to Christians and Christianity (59–69).

A concrete illustration of the relationship—that is, identity—between
the Ophites described by the Christian fathers, who interpreted her-
etically the Old Testament and cursed the God of the Jews (Origen *Cels.*
6.27–29), and the Minim opposed by the rabbis, is the Midrash (*Gen. Rab.*
1.10) wherein it is stated that the world was created with a *bêt* (referring
to the opening letter of the Torah) instead of an *'alep* because *bêt*
connotes "blessing" (ברכה) and *alep* "cursing" (ארורה), lest the Minim find
justification in their blasphemous suggestion that the world was created
with the language of cursing (69).

Friedländer goes on to give detailed expositions of Talmudic aggadoth
referring to Minim, arguing that these refer specifically to Gnostics. For
example, the story of R. Jonathan's disciple who ran away to the Minim
in Capernaum (recounted in *Eccl. Rab.* 1.8.4) is a clear reference to
antinomian Ophites who practiced free love. Such libertinism as practiced by the Gnostic Minim is decried by R. Jonathan with the exclamation, "Is this the way for Jews to behave!" (ibid.). Free love is attributed by the Christian fathers to the Carpocratian and Cainite branches
of Ophitic Gnosticism (Irenaeus *Haer.* 1.31.2; Epiphanius *Haer.* 26.4;
27.2; 38.1-2; Clem. Alex. *Strom.* 3.2.5); and Philo's polemic against the

12. He refers to the first century as the "Sturm- und Drangperiode der theogonischen
und theosophischen Forschungen" (60).

antinomian allegorists (*Migr*. 90; *Post*. 52–53) reflects the same practice among these Gnostics (70–79).

Further evidence concerning the Ophite Gnostics in Palestine, according to Friedländer, is afforded by the prescription in the Talmud that the *gilyônîm* and the "Books of the Minim" are not to be saved from the fire but are to be burnt in their place, along with the *'azkarôt* (divine names) occurring in them (*Šabb*. 116a; *Yal. Isa*. 57; *Num. Rab*. 9). Contrary to some Talmudists *gilyônîm* cannot refer to Christian "gospels," which of course do not contain *'azkarôt*. The *gilyônîm* are "tablets" and refer specifically to the "Ophite diagram" described by Celsus and Origen (*Cels*. 6.24–38). The great hatred of the Minim displayed in the Talmudic reference by R. Tarfon and R. Ishmael is perfectly understandable when it is seen that the Minim are Ophites and their diagram, containing their heretical use of the divine names and their own heretical speculations on *ma'ªśēh bᵉrēšît* and *ma'ªśēh merkābāh* are referred to under the Hebrew term *gilyôn*. Such heretics are to be hated with "perfect hatred" (Ps. 139:22), for they sow "wrath between Israel and their Father in Heaven" (*Šabb*. 116a). The hatred of the rabbis is matched only by that of the church fathers who polemicized against the same heretics (80–92).

After further discussion of the Gnostics referred to in rabbinic literature—with special attention paid to the arch-heretic Elisha ben Abuya (Aḥer)—and various Gnostic elements in Talmudic doctrines, Friedländer concludes that "jüdische Alexandrinismus" constitutes the root from which Palestinian Gnosticism sprang (93–116).

So far as ethics is concerned, Friedländer continues, the Alexandrian Jewish tendency toward the mortification of the flesh in the interests of higher gnosis could lead either to strict asceticism or to libertinism. This point is given specificity with reference to the Gnostic concept of the "destruction of the womb" (Irenaeus *Haer*. 1.31.2, referring to the Cainites). That this concept is directly dependent upon "Jewish Alexandrianism" is evident from Philo, who in a very striking passage (*Leg. All*. 3.151ff.) discusses how the body, to which we are bound, should be dealt with. In an involved allegory upon Deut. 23:12f. Philo makes the point that the soul, for the sake of knowledge, should disregard the flesh, and allow reason to act as a shovel and cover up all unseemly passions. "The lover of pleasure moves upon the belly, but the perfect man flushes out the entire belly" (ὁ δὲ τέλειος τὴν κοιλίαν ὅλην ἐκπλύνει, ibid., 159). Whereas Philo derives from the Alexandrian Jewish depreciation of the body and its passions a strong ascetic tendency, the Cainites drew the opposite conclusions and taught that the bodily nature could be destroyed only by partaking of the passions of the flesh. Philo polemicizes against such a party in the remarks he makes following the passage just referred to, in an allegory on Gen. 3:14 (*Leg. All.* 3.160). Similar Gnostics were found in Palestine.[13] Those whom Philo encountered in his time were the "fathers and grandfathers" of the Cainites decried by Irenaeus (116–19).

Friedländer refers, finally, to the arrogant predestinarianism of the Gnostics, and derives this, too, from "Jewish Alexandrianism." The Gnostics referred to themselves as "spiritual by nature" (Irenaeus *Haer.* 1.6.2), an idea derived from the Jewish-Alexandrian view exemplified by Philo (*Leg. All.* 3.77) when he says that God produces good natures among men by grace, without giving reasons, and produces also faulty natures among others (120–122).

> Es zeigt sich hier wiederum, dass die Grundlehren des Gnosticismus dem jüdischen Alexandrinismus entnommen sind, wenn sie auch allerdings auf ihren verschiedenen Wanderungen sich mit fremden Anschauungen vermischten und dadurch mancherlei Umgestaltungen erfuhren. (122)

COMMENTS ON FRIEDLÄNDER'S ARGUMENTS

I have presented Friedländer's arguments as fully as space would permit, for I believe that Friedländer deserves to be heard again. I do not suggest that we should accept uncritically everything that he wrote on the subject of the Jewish origins of Gnosticism. For example, we can still agree with the protest raised by E. Schürer in his review of Friedländer's book in 1899[14] against the all-encompassing view adopted by Friedländer on the meaning of the terms *mîn* and *mînût*; for, to be sure, Christians are sometimes referred to in rabbinic literature under these terms, as Schürer rightly points out. On the other hand, subsequent attempts to interpret all occurrences of these terms as references to Jewish Christianity, as is done by R. T. Herford,[15] fall to the ground in face of the facts. There were heretical Jewish Gnostics in Palestine, and they were referred to as Minim.[16] It may also be the case that Fried-

---

13. Friedländer refers here (119) to the "inhabitants of Capernaum" Minim referred to in *Eccl. Rab.* 1.8.4, which he had discussed previously (76ff.), and amongst whom he places Elisha ben Abuya (108f.; cf. *Eccl. Rab.* 7.26.3).

14. *TLZ* 24 (1899) 167–70.

15. *Christianity in Talmud and Midrash* (London: Williams & Norgate, 1903; repr. Clifton, N. J.: Reference Books, 1966), esp. 97ff.

16. This had already been made very clear before Friedländer by Graetz, *Gnosticismus*, esp. 18ff. Recent work has confirmed the correctness of this view. See, e.g., H.-J. Schoeps, "Simon Magus in der Haggada," in *Aus frühchristlicher Zeit* (Tübingen: J. C. B.

länder's interpretation of *gilyônîm* (see above) goes beyond the evidence,[17] though something like the Ophite diagram was apparently known to the Palestinian rabbis, as M. Joël had pointed out even before Friedländer.[18] In short, the specificity of the polemics directed in Talmud and Midrash against heresy makes crystal clear that Jewish Gnostics did exist in Palestine, and that from at least the early second century on, if not earlier, they posed a great threat in many Jewish circles.[19]

The basic questions that arise from Friedländer's work, as I see the matter, are: (1) Can the Philonic passages used by Friedländer to prove the existence of Gnostic sects in Alexandria in Philo's time bear the weight that is made to hang on them? Or, to put it another way, were there actually Gnostic heretics in the Alexandrian Jewish Diaspora? (2) Did Gnosticism derive originally from *Alexandrian* Judaism?

To the first point, it has been argued against Friedländer that Philo's references to allegorizers who regard the observance of the Law as peripheral (esp. *Migr.* 86–93) are not clear indicators of the presence of Gnosticism.[20] This is, of course, true. Although "antinomianism" and esoteric interpretation of Scripture are hallmarks of Gnosticism, there are more specific aspects of Gnosticism that distinguish it from non-Gnostic varieties of "antinomianism" and Scripture allegorization.[21]

Indeed, Friedländer's case could have been strengthened considerably had he referred to yet another class of antinomians in Alexandria, who apparently not only rejected the ritual laws, but did not even bother to resort to allegory in their denunciation of the "objectionable" portions of Scripture. Such a class of "antinomian" Jews is clearly referred to by Philo in *On the Confusion of Tongues* 2f., a passage that was overlooked by Friedländer:

Mohr, 1950) 239–54; H.-F. Weiss, "Einige Randbemerkungen zum Problem des Verhältnisses von 'Judentum' und 'Gnosis,'" *OLZ* 64 (1969) 548ff.

17. So Schürer, *TLZ* 24 (1899) 169. He agrees with Friedländer, however, that *gilyônîm* cannot mean εὐαγγέλια. Herford (*Christianity*, 155) says that the word *gilyôn* means "the unwritten portion of a book, the margin." The Soncino translation of the passage in question in tractate *Šabbat* 116a reads, "the blank spaces and the Books of the Minim. . . ."

18. See *Blicke* 139ff., with special reference to Ḥagiga 11b. Cf. also Friedländer, 84, 112.

19. H.-F. Weiss, "Randbemerkungen." Cf. esp. his book, *Untersuchungen zur Kosmologie des hellenistischen und palästinischen Judentums* (Berlin: Akademie, 1966).

20. Weiss, "Randbemerkungen," 548; M. Simon, "Eléments gnostiques chez Philon," in Bianchi, *Origini dello gnosticismo*, 360; cf. Schürer, *TLZ* 24 (1899) 167–70.

21. E.g., Paul used allegory and rejected the Law—Gal. 4:21–31 is an example of both in one passage—but he can hardly be called a "Gnostic." For our purposes here my use of the term "Gnosticism" will be limited to the heretical variety of gnosis; cf. the definitions proposed in the "Final Document" of the Messina Congress of 1966 in Bianchi, *Origini dello gnosticismo*, xxvi–xxix, and my remarks in the Introduction to this book.

Those who are disgusted with their ancestral institutions and are always taking pains to criticize and find fault with the laws use these and similar passages (Gen. 11:1–9) as excuses for their godlessness. These impious people say, "Do you still regard with solemnity the commandments as though they contained the canons of truth itself? Look, your so-called holy books also contain myths such as those you ridicule whenever you hear them recited by others. Indeed, what is the need to collect the numerous examples scattered throughout the Law, as we might if we had the leisure to press the charges, when we need only remind you of those examples that are ready to hand?" (au. trans.)

The text goes on to set forth the comparisons made by the scoffers between the story of the Tower of Babel and similar myths found in Homer and the mythographers. The point to be made here is that Philo was acquainted not only with "allegorizing" antinomian Jews, but with impious Jews who had rejected their ancestral traditions outright.

Without making a judgment as to whether or not the people referred to in this passage are Gnostics, I would nevertheless like to point out that there are examples of Gnostic literature wherein the literal sense of the biblical text is taken at face value, and no recourse to allegory is necessary for the Gnostic point to be made. The question is: Did Philo know of Jewish apostates who could also be identified as Gnostics?

If one could find in Philo some clear examples of polemics directed against specifically "Gnostic" theologoumena—against Gnostic teachings concerning the inferior Demiurge, for example—then Friedländer's case for the existence of Jewish Gnostics in Alexandria could be made virtually airtight.

In an early "Ophite" Gnostic midrash embedded in the third tractate of Codex IX from Nag Hammadi, which I have treated extensively elsewhere,[22] the following passage occurs (47.14–48.7):

But of what sort is this God? First [he] maliciously refused Adam from eating of the tree of knowledge. And secondly he said, "Adam, where are you?" God does not have foreknowledge; (otherwise), would he not know from the beginning? [And] afterwards he said, "Let us cast him [out] of this place, lest he eat of the tree of life and live forever." Surely he has shown himself to be a malicious grudger (-φθονεῖν). And what kind of a God is this? For great is the blindness of those who read, and they did not know him. And he said, "I am the jealous God; I will bring the sins of the fathers upon the children until three (and) four generations."[23]

22. See chap. 3 in this book.
23. The translation here has been updated to conform to that published in *Nag Hammadi Library*. For the Coptic text see now Pearson, *Codices IX and X*, 162, 164.

In this passage the Gnostic affirmation of the "envy" (φθόνος) of the Demiurge[24] revolves around three texts in Scripture: Gen. 2:17; 3:22; and Exod. 20:5. Does Philo know of the Gnostic interpretation of any or all of these passages in the Torah?

Indeed, he may be countering such an interpretation of Gen. 3:22 in *Questions and Answers on Genesis* 1.55 when he says of this passage, "There is neither doubt nor envy in God."[25] Thereupon he enters into a lengthy explanation of the passage in which he demonstrates to his satisfaction that such an idea must be excluded.[26]

The Gnostic interpretation of Exod. 20:5[27] may be alluded to, and Gnostics are possibly referred to, when Philo says, in the context of his discussion of the First Commandment in *On the Decalogue* 63:

> Some again, seized with a loud-mouthed frenzy, publish abroad samples of their deep-seated impiety and attempt to blaspheme the Godhead, and when they whet the edge of their evil-speaking tongue they do so in the wish to grieve the pious who feel at once the inroad of a sorrow indescribable and inconsolable, which passing through the ears wastes as with fire the whole soul.

With this we may compare the general statement Philo makes about apostates in *On the Special Laws* (1.54), again in the context of a discussion of God and his commandments, and consider the possibility that Gnostic apostates are in his mind:

> But if any members of the nation [he means the nation of Israel, as over against the Gentiles] betray the honour due to the One they should suffer the utmost penalties. They have abandoned their most vital duty, their service in the ranks of piety and religion, have chosen darkness in preference to the brightest light and blindfolded the mind which had the power of keen vision.

This passage immediately calls to mind the anti-Gnostic statement from the Mishnah cited above, "and whosoever has no regard for the

---

24. Plato (*Timaeus* 29E) had said of the Demiurge that he is good, and without any φθόνος whatever. This general statement of the goodness of the Demiurge is also taken up by Philo in *Op*. 21. At that point nothing specifically anti-Gnostic can be seen.

25. I have used the LCL edition with Marcus's translation from the Armenian. Cf. at this point the Greek fragment (J. Rendel Harris, ed., *Fragments of Philo Judaeus* [Cambridge: University Press, 1886], 15: οὔτε ἐνδυασμὸς οὔτε φθόνος περὶ θεόν. . . .

26. Cf. Irenaeus *Haer*. 3.23.6. On rabbinic arguments against the Gnostic contention concerning the envy and jealousy of God, see A. Marmorstein, "The Background of the Haggadah," in *Studies in Jewish Theology* (Arthur Marmorstein Memorial Volume; London: Oxford University Press, 1950) 24ff.

27. Exodus 20:5 is cited regularly in Gnostic texts as a proof for the envy of the Demiurge; see, e.g., *The Apocryphon of John* NHC II 13,8; BG 44,14; Irenaeus *Haer*. 1.29.4.

honour of his Creator, it were better for him had he not come into the world."

It has been argued against Friedländer that he went beyond the evidence in seeing specific Gnostic sects—Ophites, Sethians, Cainites, Melchizedekians—reflected in Philo.[28] In fact, Friedländer's discussion deals mainly with "Melchizedekians" and with "Cainites," whom he identified, along with the "Sethians," as branches of the "Ophite" group. It may be useful to make some observations on these points, to see if his case will stand up under scrutiny.

With respect to the "Cainites," I would suggest that Friedländer assumed too much when judging the reliability of the patristic descriptions. Indeed, the numerous Gnostic texts that have been uncovered since Friedländer's day, especially the Nag Hammadi Library, are calling into question the classification systems used by the heresiologists of the church.[29] It may be doubted, for example, that a sect called the "Cainites" ever existed. I might tentatively suggest that the designation "Cainite" derived originally from the tendency on the part of Jewish interpreters of scripture to see in the figure of Cain a prototype and progenitor of heresy. The designation "Cainite" ultimately came to be thought of by the church fathers as a particular branch of heresy, and the Gnostic sect of the "Cainites" was thereupon invented, becoming a standard part of the heresiological catalogs.[30]

That "Cain" was interpreted as a prototype of heresy among scripture interpreters of Palestine from an early date can be illustrated with reference to the Palestinian Targums, to which Friedländer did not refer. In a striking haggadic expansion of Gen. 4:8, the story of Cain and Abel, the recently published *Targum Neophiti* contains the following passage:

> Cain spoke to Abel his brother, Come, let us both go out to the field. And when they had both gone out to the field Cain answered and said to Abel, I know that the world was not created by love,[31] that it is not governed according to the fruit of good deeds and that there is favor in Judgment. Therefore your offering was accepted from you with delight. Abel answered and said to Cain, I see that the world was created by love and is

28. See esp. E. Schürer, *TLZ* 24 (1899) 167–70; and M. Simon, "Eléments gnostiques," in Bianchi, *Origini dello gnosticismo* 359–76.
29. On this see especially the useful observations made by F. Wisse, "The Nag Hammadi Library and the Heresiologists," *VC* 25 (1971) 205–33.
30. See now chap. 6 in this book.
31. The same aggadah occurs in *Targum Ps.-Jonathan*, but at this point Cain's first statement reads, "I know that the world was created by love." The negative is original and has fallen out of the text, as was seen clearly already by V. Aptowitzer, *Kain und Abel in der Agada* (Wien: R. Löwit, 1922) 10, and now proven by the *Neophiti* parallel.

governed according to the fruit of good deeds. Because my deeds were better than yours my offering was accepted from me with delight but your offering was not accepted from you with delight. Cain answered and said to Abel, There is no Judgment, there is no Judge, there is no other world, there is no gift of good reward for the just and no punishment for the wicked.[32]

Although "Cain" has been interpreted in this passage as a representative of "Sadducean" heresy,[33] the affirmations put into the mouth of Cain could also be seen as representing "Gnostic" heresy. The first statement, especially, is susceptible of this interpretation, that the world was not created in love; but the other statements, too, are found in connection with Gnosticism as, for example, in the account of Simon Magus in the Pseudo-Clementine *Homilies* 2.22. It is also useful to observe in this connection that the affirmations here associated with "Cain" are attributed to the arch-heretic Elisha ben Abuya (*j.Ḥag.* 2.1), and it can hardly be doubted any longer that Elisha ben Abuya (Aḥer) was a Gnostic heretic.[34]

If, now, we raise the question as to whether "Cain" functions in Philo also as a type of Gnostic heresy, at least in some cases, the evidence that emerges from an investigation of the texts is not unimpressive.[35] Unlike Friedländer, however, we do not posit the existence of a specifically "Cainite" sect in Alexandria.

There is, first of all, a parallel in Philo to the haggadic expansion of Gen. 4:8 that we have encountered in the Targums, in that a theological argument between Cain and Abel is associated with the interpretation of Gen. 4:8 presented by Philo.[36] The passage is *The Worse Attacks the Better* 1–2, 32–48. Cain is represented here as attempting to gain the mastery over Abel with recourse to "plausible sophistries" (*Quod. Det.* 1). Whereas Abel represents a "God-loving creed" Cain represents a "self-loving" doctrine (*Quod. Det.* 32), a doctrine that manifests itself in a life devoid of virtue (*Quod. Det.* 34; cf. Friedländer, 20). This theme is reiterated and amplified throughout the rest of the tractate.

---

32. I have used the English translation of S. Isenberg, "An Anti-Sadducee Polemic in the Palestinian Targum Tradition," *HTR* 63 (1970) 437. His article is a brilliant piece of text criticism, and contains some very useful observations, along with considerable bibliography (but curiously omits Aptowitzer's work cited above).

33. Isenberg interprets the text this way.

34. See now esp. G. G. Stroumsa, "Aḥer: A Gnostic," in Layton, *Rediscovery*, 2.808–18.

35. An exposition of these texts here must be selective, for they are too numerous to present *in toto*. See the very useful index in the LCL edition, vol. 10, under the entry "Cain" (295f.).

36. Aptowitzer, *Kain*, 12, suggests that the aggadah in *Targum Ps.-Jonathan* (and now also *Targum Neophiti*) is an outgrowth of the Philonic exposition.

In *On the Posterity and Exile of Cain* 52–53 (quoted in full and commented upon by Friedländer, 21ff.), Cain again represents disputatiousness and the invention of plausible myths contrary to truth (πιθανὰς εὑρέσεις κατὰ τῆς ἀληθείας μυθοπλαστῶν), which results in a life of impiety, self-love, arrogance, false doctrine, ignorance of real wisdom, lawlessness, and so on. Friedländer certainly has a point in seeing here a reference to Gnostic opponents of Philo, for the mode of argument is similar to that of the heresiologists in their struggle with the Gnostics of the second century and later.

In *On the Sacrifices of Abel and Cain* 2f. and 71 Cain represents a "philosophy" in which all things are ascribed to the human mind, whereas Abel represents a philosophy that is subservient to God (cf. Friedländer, 20, 52f.; cf. also *Cher.* 57, 64–66, and Friedländer, 57). Cain's "philosophy" is also labeled "foolish opinion" (δόξα ἄτοπος, *Sacr.* 5), "folly" (ἀφροσύνη, *Quod. Det.* 178), and "madness" (ἀπόνοια, *Post.* 35). In the latter passage "Cain" is regarded as the ancestor of Protagoras's famous dictum that "man is the measure of all things," a notion that could very easily be attributed, in a certain sense, to Gnostics. Finally, Philo's interpretation of Cain's voluntary exile from the presence of God (*Post.* 9–10) could be seen easily enough as paradigmatic of Jewish heresy.

These and other passages relating to Cain in Philo serve to strengthen Friedländer's case for the existence of heretical Gnosticism in Alexandria in the early first century (if not before).

A few remarks are in order with respect to Friedländer's contention that the "Melchizedekian" Gnostic sect was known to Philo, and took its origins in Alexandria. His main sources for this contention are Epiphanius (*Haer.* 55), the Epistle to the Hebrews, and Philo (*Leg. All.* 3.79ff.). From the fourth-century bishop-heresiologist Friedländer derives his basic information on the Melchizedekian sect. From Hebrews, which he takes (possibly correctly) as an Alexandrian product, and from Philo, Friedländer derives his information on the existence of Jewish speculation on the figure of Melchizedek in pre-Christian Alexandrian Judaism. He has been rightly criticized for extrapolating from the earlier texts a full-blown Gnostic sect.[37]

There are now some additional documents, unknown to Friedländer,

---

37. M. Simon, "Eléments gnostiques," in Bianchi, *Origini dello gnosticismo*, 362f.; but see, on the other hand, W. Schmithals, *Gnosticism in Corinth* (Nashville: Abingdon, 1971) 300, where the existence of a pre-Christian Melchizedekian sect is taken for granted.

that shed further light on this problem—one fragmentary text from the Nag Hammadi Coptic Gnostic Library and one fragmentary text from Qumran. The former is a "Melchizedekian" document (CG IX,1) in which the figure of Melchizedek is featured as a heavenly redemption figure and an angelic warrior against the evil archons.[38] Jesus Christ also appears in this text, and in a very interesting anti-docetic passage the reality of Jesus' human nature is stressed. The text from Qumran (11Q Melch)[39] also presents Melchizedek as a heavenly redemption figure,[40] and there are some striking parallels between the Qumran and the Nag Hammadi texts. The evidence of these new documents, when laid alongside our prior information, suggests the following tentative conclusion: (1) Insofar as one can speak of a Gnostic sect of "Melchizedekians," one is dealing with a Christian group in whose speculations the figure of Jesus plays an important role. (2) Their views of Melchizedek develop out of Jewish speculations and traditions surrounding this Old Testament figure. (3) Such speculations existed both in the Alexandrian Diaspora (Philo and, perhaps, Hebrews) and in Palestine, among the Essenes particularly. (4) There is no concrete evidence for the existence of a pre-Christian Jewish Gnostic sect of "Melchizedekians," though the existence of such a sect cannot be ruled out categorically.

Friedländer's main contention, that a pre-Christian Jewish Gnosticism existed in Alexandria, has been seen to be rather plausible. Have we also discovered the origins of Gnosticism?

The evidence continues to mount that Gnosticism is not, in its origins, a Christian heresy, but that it is, in fact, a Jewish heresy.[41] Friedländer's arguments tracing the origins of Gnosticism to a Hellenized Judaism are very strong indeed, and are bolstered with every passing year by newly discovered or newly studied texts, the Nag Hammadi Coptic Gnostic Library providing the bulk of this evidence. It is really only a minor question, then, as to whether the Gnostic heresy originated among

38. See now chap. 7 in this book.
39. See esp. A. van der Woude, "Melchizedek als himmlische Erlösergestalt in den neugefundenen eschatologischen Midraschim aus Qumran Höhle XI," Oudtestamentische Studiën 14 (1965) 354–73; J. Fitzmeyer, "Further Light on Melchizedek from Qumran Cave 11," JBL 86 (1967) 25–41.
40. J. Carmignac ("Le document de Qumran sur Melkisédeq," RevQ 7 [1970] 343–78) objects to this interpretation of the Melchizedek figure in the Qumran fragments, but his arguments are not convincing.
41. See several of the chapters in this book, and the literature cited. It should be stated that G. Quispel was among the first modern scholars to take this position; see his important article, "Der gnostische Anthropos und die jüdische Tradition," Eranos Jahrbuch 22 (1953, i.e., 1954) 195–234. See also, e.g., G. Kretschmar, "Zur religionsgeschichtlichen Einordnung der Gnosis," EvTh 13 (1953) 354–61.

Hellenized Jews of Alexandria,[42] or among Hellenized Jews of Palestine or Syria.[43]

The qualification "Hellenized" is important, for Gnosticism can only be accounted for in a highly syncretistic milieu. Of course, it is no longer possible (if it ever was!) to make a rigid distinction between Hellenistic and Palestinian Judaism, for Hellenization was a very important factor in Palestine as well as in the Diaspora.[44] As an example of the Hellenistic ingredient in Gnosticism one can point to the obviously Platonic (or, as some prefer, Middle-Platonic) elements of its mythology.[45] But this is an element that could flourish as well in Palestine or Syria as in Alexandria. One could argue similarly on the basis of other Hellenistic aspects of Gnosticism, for example, its eclectic character.

It is usually taken for granted that Gnosticism appeared primarily as an intellectual movement. Wisdom circles are frequently referred to as the milieus in which it developed.[46] In this connection, too, one can refer to the philosophical eclecticism of the Jewish wisdom circles of the Hellenistic-Roman period, as well as the growth of a "skeptical" outlook. But the rise of Gnosticism should also be seen as a response not only to a syncretistic conflict-mixture of "traditions" and "ideas" but also to the concrete circumstances of history, to social and political conditions.[47]

42. Cf., e.g., J. Ménard, "Les origines de la gnose," *RevScR* 43 (1968) 24–38, esp. 36ff.; P. Pokorný, "Der Ursprung der Gnosis," *Kairos* 9 (1967) 94–105.

43. Cf., e.g., A. Böhlig, "Der jüdische Hintergrund in gnostischen Texten von Nag Hammadi," in Bianchi, *Origini dello gnosticismo*, 109–40; H.-M. Schenke, "Das Problem der Beziehung zwischen Judentum und Gnosis," *Kairos* 7 (1965) 124–33; K. Rudolph, *ThR* 36 (1971) 89ff.; and esp. Rudolph, "Randerscheinungen des Judentums und das Problem der Entstehung des Gnostizismus," *Kairos* 9 (1967) 105–22, a very important article. I tend to favor the Syro-Palestinian milieu as the place of origin. See, e.g., chap. 3 in this book.

44. See esp. S. Lieberman, *Hellenism in Jewish Palestine* (New York: Jewish Theological Seminary, 1962) and M. Hengel, *Judaism and Hellenism* (2 vols.; Philadelphia: Fortress, 1974).

45. Arthur Darby Nock used the term "Platonism run wild" in connection with Gnosticism in a lecture published after his death in *HTR* 57 (1964) 255–79; reprinted: "Gnosticism" in *Essays on Religion and the Ancient World,* ed. Z. Stewart (Cambridge: Harvard University Press, 1972) 2.940–59. The phrase quoted here occurs on p. 949. Cf. now chap. 10 in this book.

46. See, e.g., A. Adam, "Ist die Gnosis in aramäischen Weisheitsschulen entstanden?" in Bianchi, *Origini dello gnosticismo,* 291–301. On *Jewish* wisdom circles see esp. K. Rudolph, "Randerscheinungen des Judentums," *Kairos* 9 (1967) 119–22; J. Lebram, "Die Theologie der späten Chokma und häretisches Judentum," *ZAW* 77 (1965) 202–11.

47. The "existentialist" interpretation, of course, is best exemplified by Hans Jonas in his epoch-making books. K. Rudolph ("Gnosis und Gnosticismus," *ThR* 36 [1971] 119–24) refers to some attempts at sociological analysis, and remarks that history of religions and sociology should work more closely. For a recent "sociological" analysis of Gnosticism see H. Kippenberg, "Versuch einer soziologischen Verortung des antiken Gnostizismus," *Numen* 17 (1970) 211–31.

This is one aspect of the problem that Friedländer completely overlooked, but which to my mind is absolutely basic to a proper understanding of Gnostic intentionality as well as the question of Gnostic
origins.[48]

Judaism, as a religion that takes history seriously, and that also has a
marked tendency in the direction of messianism, provides ipso facto a
context in which, given the critical circumstances of history, an attitude
of revolt could easily develop.[49] There is a strong case to be made for the
view that ancient Gnosticism developed, in large part, from a disappointed messianism, or rather as a transmuted messianism.[50] Jewish
history is not without parallels to this phenomenon, as G. Scholem's
studies of the Sabbatian movement attest.[51] Such a transmuted messianism, for the ancient period, is better understood as arising in the national
homeland, that is, in Palestine itself, rather than in the Diaspora. But this
is a very tentative judgment.

To conclude: Although much of the detail of Friedländer's argument
is open to question, he has been vindicated in his basic contention, that
Gnosticism is a pre-Christian phenomenon that developed on Jewish
soil.

48. Graetz, on the other hand, was aware of this; see his remarks in *Gnosticismus und
Judenthum*, 9ff.

49. See chap. 3 in this book.

50. Cf. R. M. Grant's thesis that Gnosticism developed out of disappointed apocalyptic hopes after the destruction of Jerusalem, in *Gnosticism and Early Christianity* (New
York: Harper & Row, 1966), esp. 27ff. His view that the fall of Jerusalem was the
decisive historical event out of which Gnosticism arose is surely wrong, and has
subsequently been withdrawn, but otherwise his theory has some merit.

51. See his remarkable essay, "Redemption Through Sin," in *The Messianic Idea in
Judaism* (New York: Schocken, 1971) 78–141. Cf. also his remarks on ancient heretical
Gnosticism in *Jewish Gnosticism, Merkabah Mysticism and Talmudic Tradition* (New York:
Jewish Theological Seminary, 1965) 9. In this context he also expresses, guardedly, an
appreciation for Friedländer's work. In a letter to me (Jan. 28, 1973), Scholem stated his
belief that the Gnostic revolt did indeed arise from within Judaism.

2

Biblical Exegesis in
Gnostic Literature

It is often thought that one of the essential attributes of Gnosticism is a rejection of the Old Testament. In that connection one also finds arguments to the effect that one of the marks of Christian orthodoxy as it developed in the second century was the retention, against Gnostic and Marcionite heretics, of the Old Testament as part of the Christian canon of scripture.[1] There is, of course, no doubt as to the validity of the latter point, but the former assumption requires a great deal of correction and clarification.

A close examination of many Gnostic texts will, in fact, show a considerable indebtedness to the Old Testament (and not only to the Book of Genesis). But beyond that it is interesting to observe the extent to which one finds, *as part of the Gnostic myth itself,* not only quotation from and allusions to the Old Testament texts, but the use of traditions of biblical exegesis, specifically *Jewish* traditions of exegesis. These traditions can be identified as both Hellenistic (presumably Alexandrian) and Palestinian.

In this article I propose to treat, despite the suggestion of inclusiveness in its title, one specific Gnostic text and indeed only part of that, *The Apocryphon of John.* I shall discuss this text with reference to some traditions of exegesis of Gen. 1:26f. and 2:7 reflected in that Gnostic document. Despite the narrowness of focus I think some valid observations of a general nature will be possible regarding the nature of Gnostic myth and the religious-historical context out of which it arose in late antiquity.

The Apocryphon of John is a document now extant in four different

1. See, e.g., "The Old Testament, the Lord, and the Apostles," in Bauer, *Orthodoxy and Heresy,* 195ff. For a general discussion of the issue see now Pearson, "Exegesis of Mikra."

versions: it is found in the Berlin Codex 8502 (= BG) and in three of the Coptic Gnostic codices from Nag Hammadi (CG II, III, IV).[2] Just from the standpoint of genre analysis it is an interesting document, for it consists of a religio-philosophical tract, embodying in turn a running commentary on Genesis 1—8, all set within a framework, probably secondary,[3] of an apocalypse given by the resurrected Jesus to his disciple John.[4]

Since the text of the version in CG III tends to agree with that of BG (the "short recension"), and that of CG IV with that of CG II (the "long recension"), I shall restrict my discussion to the better preserved versions in BG and CG II. The passage of interest to us here deals with the creation of humanity.

The context preceding our focal passage treats the Highest God, eternal and indescribable, whose mystical name is Anthropos, and from whom emanate the various beings that populate the heavenly world. The lowest of the heavenly emanations, Sophia (= "Wisdom"),[5] produces an ugly and abortive offspring called Ialdabaoth,[6] Saklas,[7] and

2. For Coptic text and German translation of BG [Berolinensis Gnosticus] see W. Till, *Die gnostischen Schriften des koptischen Papyrus Berolinensis 8502* (2d ed. rev. H.-M. Schenke; TU 60,2; Berlin: Akademie-Verlag, 1972). For Coptic text and German translation of CG [Cairensis Gnosticus = Nag Hammadi Codex] see M. Krause and P. Labib, *Die drei Versionen des Apokryphon des Johannes im koptischen Museum zu Alt-Kairo* (ADAIK, Kopt. Reihe, 1; Wiesbaden: Harrassowitz, 1962). For Coptic text and English translation of the version in CG II see S. Giversen, *Apocryphon Johannis* (Acta Theologica Danica 5; Copenhagen: Munksgaard, 1963). For an exhaustive bibliography on Gnosticism and the Coptic texts since 1948 see Scholer, *Nag Hammadi Bibliography,* supplemented annually in the journal *Novum Testamentum*.

3. It should be noted that a part of what is now known as *The Apocryphon of John* is represented in Irenaeus's description of the teachings of Gnostics who are also known as "Barbelo Gnostics" (*Haer.* 1.29). It is noteworthy that Irenaeus does not seem to know that this teaching is represented as a revelation of Jesus Christ to John. This would indicate that our document underwent stages of literary development, which also included a "Christianization" process. This is apparent from a formal analysis of the document itself, but is corroborated by the (negative) evidence in Irenaeus. Cf. also J. Doresse, *The Secret Books of the Egyptian Gnostics,* trans. P. Mairet (New York: Viking, 1960) 210f. See now Pearson, "Jewish Sources," 458–64, and "'Jewish Gnostic' Literature," 19–25.

4. The best treatment of the form and composition of *The Apocryphon of John* (hereinafter: *Ap. John*) is that of A. Kragerud, "Apocryphon Johannis. En formanalyse," *NorTT* 66 (1965) 15–38. On the "commentary" aspect of *Ap. John* see also S. Giversen, "The Apocryphon of John and Genesis," *ST* 17 (1963) 60–76.

5. On the Gnostic Sophia and her relationship to the Jewish Wisdom figure see esp. MacRae, "Gnostic Sophia Myth."

6. "Ialdabaoth" is the most frequent name used in *Ap. John* for the Gnostic Demiurge but in CG II 11,16ff. all three names occur together. The name "Ialdabaoth" has often been taken to reflect Aramaic בחות ילדא, "child of chaos." Cf. chap. 3, p. 48 n. 42, where it is noted that contextual references to "chaos" in Gnostic literature tend to support that etymology. But for a contrary view see G. Scholem, *Jewish Gnosticism, Merkabah Mysticism, and Talmudic Tradition* (New York: Jewish Theological Seminary, 1960) 71, n. 23; and Scholem, "Jaldabaoth Reconsidered," *Mélanges d'Histoire des Religions offerts à H.-C. Puech* (Paris: Presses Universitaires de France, 1974), 405–21.

7. "Saklas" is derived from Aramaic סכלא, "fool." Cf. chap. 3, p. 48 and n. 48.

Samael,[8] who in turn produces the lower angels and the lower world. Ialdabaoth declares in his ignorance, "I am a jealous God; beside me there is no other" (BG 44,14f.; CG II 13,8f.; cf. Exod. 20:5; Isa. 45:5,6; 46:9). The Mother, Sophia, realizes her own deficiency and the ignorance of her son and repents. A heavenly voice comes to her, "Man exists and the Son of Man" (BG 47,15f. = CG II 14,14f.). Thereupon Ialdabaoth and his fellow archons see in the waters of chaos the reflection of the image of God. The passage of interest to us now follows, and I quote from the text in BG:[9]

> They (the creator archons)[10] saw in the water the appearance of the image and they said to one another, "Let us create a man according to the image and appearance of God." They created from themselves and from all their powers, and they formed a formation from themselves. And [each one] of the [powers created the aspect and] the power [of] the [soul]. (BG 48,8–49,2)[11]

We see in this passage a conflation of Gen. 1:26f. and 2:7. The latter text is reflected in the use of the Greek words πλάσσειν (and πλάσμα) and ψυχή; cf. the Greek text of Gen. 2:7: καὶ ἔπλασεν τὸν ἄνθρωπον . . . καὶ ἐγένετο ὁ ἄνθρωπος εἰς ψυχὴν ζῶσαν.

The text continues, again with definite allusions to Gen. 1:27:

> They created it (fem. sg., i.e., the soul) according to the image which they had seen, by way of an imitation of the One who exists from the beginning, the Perfect Man. They said, "Let us call him Adam so that the name of that (Being) and his power may become light[12] for us." (BG 49,2–9)

This passage reflects an interpretation of the "image" (εἰκών) of Gen. 1:27,[13] but also has to do with the creation of the human soul, a feature that derives from Gen. 2:7, as has already been observed.

What follows in the text is an elaboration of the work of the creator archons in fashioning man's soul. At this point there are two different versions. In BG each of the creator-angels is referred to as a "soul"

---

8. Samael is the angel of death or the devil in Jewish sources. In Gnostic literature the name "Samael" is explained as "the blind god" (Aramaic ܣܡܐ, "blind" plus אל, "god"). Cf. chap. 3, p. 48, and nn. 42–46.

9. All translations of ancient texts in this article are my own, unless otherwise specifically noted.

10. In CG II 15,1 Ialdabaoth addresses the other powers.

11. The translation is based on the text as established by Schenke with the aid of the other versions where lacunae occur in the text of Codex II.

12. Cf. CG II 15,13, "a power of light."

13. On the εἰκών in Ap. John see esp. Schenke, Der Gott "Mensch," 32–43. On Gnostic exegesis of Gen. 1.26f. see also J. Jervell, Imago Dei (FRLANT 58; Göttingen: Vandenhoek & Ruprecht, 1960) 122–70.

(ψυχή); in CG II each of the angels creates a different feature of man's soul. I present first the text of BG:

> And the powers began from below. The first is Deity, a soul of bone; the second is Lordship,[14] a sinew-soul; the third is Fire, a soul of flesh; the fourth is Pronoia, a soul of marrow and the whole constitution of the body; the fifth is Kingdom, a soul [of blood; the] sixth is Understanding, a soul of skin; the seventh is Sophia, a soul of hair. And they adorned the whole body. And their angels came to them from (among) those who had been prepared at first by the powers, ⟨and they received⟩[15] the hypostases of soul for the ordering of the joint-members. And they created the entire body, joined together from the multitude of angels which I mentioned at first. And it remained inert for a long time, for the seven powers were unable to raise it up, nor could the 360 angels who had put together these joint-members. (BG 49,9–51,1)

The same passage in CG II reads as follows:

> And the powers began. The first, Goodness, created a soul of bone; the second, Pronoia, created a soul of sinew; the third, Deity, created a soul of flesh; the fourth, Lordship, created a soul of marrow; the fifth, Kingdom, created a soul of blood; the sixth, Zeal, created a soul of skin; the seventh, Understanding, created a soul of hair. And the multitude of angels stood up before it. They received from the powers the seven psychic hypostases in order to make the joining of the limbs and the joining of the pieces and the synthesis of the adornment of each of the members.[16] . . . And all the angels and demons worked until they had adorned the psychic body, but their entire work was inert and motionless for a long time. (CG II 15,13–19,15)

Though these texts are slightly different, they both elaborate upon the creation of the soul, or the "psychic body," of man.[17] Insofar as they are working with "soul" (ψυχή) they themselves are referred to as "souls," and their "hypostasis" is a "psychic hypostasis."[18] That we are dealing

14. Accepting Till's emendation of the text, which in the 2d ed. is not followed by Schenke in the text (but reflected in the translation). The text has a reading that can be translated "Messiahship." The emendation is suggested on the basis of the other versions.

15. I derive this meaning of the text from the parallel passage in CG II.

16. At this point in the text there occurs a very long section describing how each of 365 angels (though, fortunately, the full number is not represented) contributed a part to the "psychic body" of man. The angels are given various names, consisting of *nomina barbara*. This section of the text is CG II 15,29–19,10, and is credited to "the Book of Zoroaster" (19,10). The BG text, with its reference to 360 angels, reflects a knowledge of something like this section in CG II, which, however, has been abbreviated out.

17. The reference to body (σῶμα) is a remnant of an earlier tradition concerning the creation by the angels of man's body. Cf. discussion below. See now also R. van den Broek, "The Creation of Adam's Psychic Body in the Apocryphon of John," in van den Broek-Vermaseren, *Studies in Gnosticism*, 38–57.

18. On the meaning of ὑπόστασις see now my article, "Hypostasis," in *The Encyclopedia of Religion* (New York: Macmillan, 1987) 6.542–46.

here with a very involved commentary upon Gen. 2:7 is confirmed by the passage immediately following, wherein we are informed of the origin of the human spirit ($\pi\nu\epsilon\hat{\nu}\mu\alpha$).

The BG text continues:

> And [the Mother (i.e., Sophia) wished to get back] the power which she had given to the archon of Prounikos.[19] She came in innocence, and begged the Father of All rich in mercy, the God of Light. He sent by a holy decree the Autogenes and the four lights[20] in the form of the angels of the first archon. They advised him so that they might bring forth from him the power of the Mother. They said to him, "Breathe into his face from the spirit that is in you, and the thing will rise up." And he breathed upon him from his spirit, which is the power from the Mother, into the body, and it [immediately] moved. (BG 51,1–52,1)

Compare the end of this passage in the CG II version:

> And he blew into him his spirit, which is the power of his Mother; he did not know, because he was in ignorance. And the power of the mother went out from Altabaoth into the psychic body on which they had worked according to the image of him who exists from the beginning. The body moved, and received strength, and shone. (CG II 19,25–33)

The sequel to this passage describes how as a result of this inbreathing the man was stronger and wiser than all of the archons,[21] who thereupon became jealous and cast man down into the lower depths of materiality. In that sphere humans are given "another formation," and chained to the mortal body of corruption, death, and oblivion.

Our attention here, however, is focused upon the passages quoted, in which we have discovered a mythopoetic commentary upon key texts in Genesis dealing with the creation of man, namely, Gen. 2:7, in combination with 1:26f. This commentary is not created ad hoc by the Gnostic author. It is, in fact, a Gnostic synthesis of several *Jewish* (originally non-Gnostic) traditions of Genesis exegesis. These exegetical traditions include (1) the Hellenistic-Jewish (probably Alexandrian) tradition that God relegated the creation of man's mortal nature to the angels, (2) the Hellenistic-Jewish (again probably Alexandrian) distinction, based on the LXX text of Gen. 2:7, between man's lower and higher soul, that is,

19. I.e., Ialdabaoth. "Prounikos" (= whore) is a frequent epithet of Sophia in Gnostic literature. The CG II text reads at this point, "the first Archon." Ialdabaoth, of course, is the first and chief of the seven archons, and functions as the Gnostic creator god.

20. The Autogenes, in the system as described in BG, is "Christus" (cf. 30,14ff.), the Son in the divine triad of Father, Mother, and Son (35,19). The parallel text in CG II reads at this point, "the five illuminators" (19,19).

21. Cf. the rabbinic tradition concerning the "image," interpreted to mean that Adam was larger, more glorious, and wiser than all of the angels. See esp. *Gen. Rab.* 17.4; also on this speculation see J. Jervell, *Imago Dei*, 96.

his ψυχή and his πνεῦμα, and (3) the Palestinian tradition that Adam was created as a "formless mass" (Heb. *gôlem*) into which God breathed his life-giving breath.

1. The earliest witness to the doctrine that God relegated the creation of human mortal nature to the angels is Philo of Alexandria,[22] who states it no less than three times. It is put most succinctly in his treatise *De fuga et inventione* (68–70),[23] immediately following an observation that God takes charge of the more important good things for the soul while leaving the less important to a ministering angel (referring to Gen. 48:15):

> For this reason, I think, when philosophizing on the creation of the world, after having said that all other things come into being by the agency of God, he (Moses) pointed out that man alone was fashioned with the cooperation of fellow-workers. For he says, "God said, 'Let us make man according to our image,'" the words "let us make" indicating many. Thus the Father of all things converses with his powers, to whom he assigned the fashioning of the mortal part of our soul by imitating his own crafts-manship when he formed the rational part in us. He thought it proper that the sovereign part in the soul should be created by the Sovereign, but the subject part by subjects. And he employed the powers that are with him not only for the reason mentioned, but because only the soul of man would receive conceptions of evil things as well as good, and would use one or the other, if it is not possible to use both. Therefore he (God) thought it necessary to assign the origin of evil things to other creators, but to reserve the origin of good things to himself alone.

It is interesting to note that Philo here deals only with the creation of the soul—as does the account in *The Apocryphon of John* presented above—assigning to God the immortal, rational part of man, but to his "powers" (= angels) the irrational part of man, that part of the soul that is susceptible to vices of all sorts. It is probable that in this Hellenistic Jewish tradition is included reference to the creation by the angels of man's body as well as the mortal soul. This is indicated by the testimony of Justin Martyr (Dial. 62), but also, as we shall see, by the source of the doctrine. And we recall the use of the term "psychic body" in the passage from Codex II given above.

The source of this Hellenistic Jewish tradition, which attempts to clarify the use of the plural in Gen. 1:26,[24] is Plato, *Timaeus* 41A–42B.

---

22. This tradition is known to Justin Martyr as a Jewish interpretation of Gen. 1:26f. Justin rejects it (*Dial.* 62).

23. A more lengthy account is given in *Op.* 72–75, and a brief mention of this teaching is made in *Conf.* 168f.

24. That God addressed the angels when he said, "Let us make man," was also the

Plato has his Creator (whom he calls the "Demiurge") fashion with his own hands the immortal part of man, but relegates to the lesser gods human mortal nature, including the body. Plato's "gods" become in Hellenistic Jewish teaching "powers" or "angels."

One of Philo's concerns is to separate from God's own creation the aspects of humanity that incline it toward evil, especially the passions and emotions.[25] In this regard we can compare an interesting passage in *The Testaments of the Twelve Patriarchs* (*T. Reub.* 2f.) wherein it is stated that seven "spirits of error" (πνεύματα τῆς πλάνης) are given to humanity in creation, each spirit identified with a particular vice.

In all of this we have the background of the various details in our passage in *The Apocryphon of John*: the "powers" or "angels" assisting in the creation of the (lower) soul, the identification of the various powers with bodily functions and attributes of the soul, the reference (in CG II) to the "psychic body," and the differentiation of the lower soul from the higher soul, or "spirit" (πνεῦμα).

2. The latter point bears elaboration. The LXX text of Gen. 2:7bc reads, καὶ ἐνεφύσησεν εἰς τὸ πρόσωπον αὐτοῦ πνοὴν ζωῆς καὶ ἐγένετο ὁ ἄνθρωπος εἰς ψυχὴν ζῶσαν. Hellenistic Jewish interpreters saw in this passage, with its use of the terms "breath" (πνοή) and "soul" (ψυχή), scriptural proof for the doctrine, common in Hellenistic philosophy,[26] that the human soul consists of a lower, mortal part (the ψυχή) and a higher, immortal part, usually referred to as the "mind" (νοῦς).[27] In Jewish circles the higher, immortal element in man is frequently referred to as the "spirit" (πνεῦμα) on the basis of the use of the term "breath" in Gen. 2:7.

Again, our best source is Philo. Of many examples that could be cited,[28] Philo's comment on the incorporeal mind within man at *De Somniis* 1.34 (the context is an allegorical interpretation of Lev. 19:24) is brief enough to be quoted here:

> For that which is holy among things that have come into being in the universe is the heaven, and in man the mind (νοῦς), since it is a divine fragment,[29] as Moses, especially, says: "He breathed into his face a breath of life (πνοὴν ζωῆς) and man became a living soul."

---

view of certain of the rabbis: see, e.g., *Tg. Ps-J.*, Gen. 1:26. For other interpretations see also *Gen. Rab.* 8.3.

25. Cf. also Plato, *Tim.* 42B.

26. Cf., e.g., Plato, *Tim.* 69C.

27. Man's bodily nature is related to the "dust from the ground" in Gen. 2:7a.

28. I have treated these passages in chap. 3 of my dissertation (Harvard, 1968); see Pearson, *Pneumatikos-Psychikos Terminology*.

29. ἀπόσπασμα θεῖον is a Stoic term. See, e.g., Epictetus *Diss.* 1.14.6; 2.8.11; and cf. M. Pohlenz, *Die Stoa* (Göttingen: Vandenhoeck & Ruprecht, 1955) 1.229ff.

Sometimes Philo quotes Gen. 2:7 using the term πνεῦμα instead of πνοή (Leg. All. 3.161), thus making the point that the higher soul of man (as explicitly stated at Spec. Leg. 4.123) is "divine spirit" (πνεῦμα θεῖον), and as such the higher self has its roots in heaven (Det. 84).[30]

It is also important to observe that Philo sometimes interprets Gen. 2:7 with reference to what is said of the "image" in 1:27. Thus we are told (Her. 56) that the human's higher soul is that which was fashioned "according to the image of the Creator."[31]

We are now in a better position to understand the background of what is said in The Apocryphon of John of the "soul" created by the archons, as differentiated from the "spirit" breathed into it by Ialdabaoth, the Gnostic creator god. But insofar as Ialdabaoth himself (according to the Gnostic view) is a lower creature of the spiritual Mother, it is necessary for the Gnostic author to affirm that the "spirit" breathed into the human by Ialdabaoth derives from heaven, from a source higher than himself, that is, ultimately from the highest God.

3. There is also reflected in The Apocryphon of John the Palestinian interpretation of Gen. 2:7, which describes the creation of Adam as an inert gôlem.[32] I refer to this tradition as "Palestinian" because it is based on the Hebrew text of the Bible, and is attested in rabbinic (Hebrew) midrashim. It is also reflected in 4 Ezra 3:4f.

Genesis Rabbah 14.8 contains the following comment on part of Gen. 2:7 ("And He breathed into his nostrils"):

This teaches that He set him up as a lifeless mass (גולם) reaching from earth to heaven[33] and then infused a soul (נשמה) into him.[34]

And again (Gen. Rab. 8.1, commenting on Gen. 1:26):

R. Tanhuma in the name of R. Banayah and R. Berekiah in the name of R. Leazar said: He created him as a lifeless mass (גולם) extending from one end

30. He uses the term φυτὸν οὐράνιον in Det. 85, evidently quoting Plato, Tim. 90A. Cf. also Plant. 17.
31. Cf. also Plant. 18.
32. See the valuable article by G. Scholem, "The Idea of the Golem," in his collection of essays entitled On the Kabbalah and Its Symbolism, trans. R. Manheim (London: Routledge & Kegan Paul, 1965) 158–204.
33. Lit. "the firmament," הרקיע. The phrase "reaching from earth to heaven," indicating Adam's cosmic proportions, is probably a secondary feature. This is suggested by Scholem, "Idea of the Golem," 161. This feature of the tradition was read out of Deut. 4:32, as can be seen in Gen. Rab. 8.1, where Deut. 4:32 is expressly quoted in that connection.
34. I have used H. Freedman's translation in the Soncino ed. here and in the other quotation from Midrash Rabbah. For the text I have used J. Theodor and Ch. Albeck, Midrash Bereshit Rabba (repr. Jerusalem: Wahrmann, 1965).

of the world to the other; thus it is written, "Thine eyes did see mine unformed substance (גלמי)."

The latter version provides us with a key to the origin of the description of Adam as a *gôlem:* it was read out of Ps. 139:16, the only passage in the Bible where the term *gôlem* occurs. This psalm was put into the mouth of Adam in Jewish tradition.[35]

One additional text, of many that could be adduced,[36] contains the following teaching of R. Acha b. Chanina:

> The day consisted of twelve hours. In the first hour, his [Adam's] dust was gathered; in the second, it was kneaded into a shapeless mass; in the third, his limbs were shaped; in the fourth, a soul was infused into him; in the fifth, he arose and stood on his feet; in the sixth, he gave [the animals] their names; in the seventh, Eve became his mate; in the eighth, they ascended to bed as two and descended as four;[37] in the ninth, he was commanded not to eat of the tree; in the tenth, he sinned; in the eleventh, he was tried; and in the twelfth, he was expelled [from Eden] and departed, for it is written "Man abideth not in honour."[38]

Our interest centers upon the second and fourth hours in R. Acha's schema: Adam is first a lifeless mass (גולם), and then is animated by the inbreathing of his soul (נשמה). This colorful tradition concerning the creation of Adam is clearly to be seen in the background of our passage in *The Apocryphon of John,* as in fact is the case in a number of other Gnostic texts.[39]

Thus we have discovered in the anthropogonic myth in *The Apocryphon of John*[40] a highly sophisticated use of the biblical text and Jewish traditions of interpretation thereon. What is of special interest, however, is the hermeneutical principle at work in the Gnostic synthesis.

This hermeneutical principle can be described as one of revolt.[41] In the

35. So Scholem, "Idea of the Golem," 161.
36. Cf. J. Jervell's discussion, *Imago Dei,* 105f.
37. I.e., with Cain and his twin sister.
38. *Sanh.* 38b, J. Shachter's translation in the Soncino ed. of the Babylonian Talmud. The scripture quotation is Ps. 49:13 (12).
39. Probably the earliest Gnostic system in which it occurs, at least so far as our extant evidence allows us to determine, is that of Saturninus (Satornilus) of Antioch, described by Irenaeus (*Haer.* 1.24). It may possibly derive from Menander before him, according to a hint given by Tertullian (*De carn. resur.* 5). It may even go back to Simon Magus; cf. K. Rudolph, "Ein Grundtyp gnostischer Urmensch-Adam-Spekulation," *ZRGG* 9 (1957) 7; and G. Quispel, "Der gnostische Anthropos und die jüdische Tradition," *Eranos Jahrbuch* 22 (1953) 202.
40. I have discussed the interpretation of Gen. 2:7 in various other Gnostic documents in my dissertation, *Pneumatikos-Psychikos Terminology,* chap. 6.
41. Cf. H. Jonas, "Delimitation of the Gnostic Phenomenon: Typological and Historical," in Bianchi, *Origini dello gnosticismo,* 28–60.

Gnostic reinterpretation the God of Israel, the God of history and creation, is demonized; the Creator and his creation are considered to be the
product of a tragic fall within the divine realm; and humanity is seen to
be a part of the transcendent God imprisoned by hostile powers in an
alien environment. Inasmuch as the Gnostic synthesis reflects the use
and reinterpretation of Jewish scripture and tradition, it is apparent that
the Gnostic phenomenon itself originates in a Jewish environment as an
expression of alienation from ("orthodox") Judaism.[42] As a result a new
religion, which can no longer be called "Jewish," is born.

Precisely when and where the new religion emerged in the syncretistic context of the history of late antiquity is a matter that may be
settled when all of the available evidence has been thoroughly studied.[43]
One thing is clear, however: Gnosticism early in its development came
to be attached in many areas to yet another religion that had been born
out of Judaism, namely, Christianity. In "Christian" Gnostic circles the
figure of Jesus Christ became the focal point for Gnostic revelation, and
important apostolic figures from early Christianity became, in a developing Gnostic literature, interlocutors with Jesus for the dissemination
of the Gnostic revelation. That is precisely the situation presented to us
in *The Apocryphon of John*. The Gnostic myth is now attributed to Jesus,
and a context is provided that consists of a discussion between Jesus and
his apostle, John. As has already been pointed out,[44] this is a secondary
feature, attributable to the final stage in the literary history of the document.

A final comment is in order. Much as the rabbis of the synagogue and
the fathers of the Church differed in their theology, they could definitely
agree on one point: "Whosoever takes no thought for the honour of his
Maker, it were better for him if he had not come into the world."[45]

42. Although the Jewish origin of Gnosticism was argued long ago by M. Friedländer
(*Der vorchristliche jüdische Gnosticismus* [Göttingen: Vandenhoeck & Ruprecht, 1898]),
Friedländer was considered to be a maverick by his own generation. It is therefore only
in comparatively recent times, as a result of new evidence such as the Nag Hammadi
texts, that the Jewish factor in Gnostic origins is coming to be recognized. On
Friedländer see chap. 1 in this book.
43. I have made a tentative guess (in chap. 3 of this book): Palestine-Syria in the first
century B.C.E. or C.E.
44. See n. 3 above.
45. *Mishnah Ḥagigah* 2.1, trans. H. Danby (London: Oxford University Press, 1933).

3

Jewish Haggadic Traditions in *The Testimony of Truth* From Nag Hammadi (CG IX,3)

The Jewish factor in the origins and development of Gnosticism[1] has gained considerable attention in recent scholarly discussions,[2] especially as more and more of the Coptic documents discovered near Nag Hammadi, Egypt, have appeared in print.[3] This chapter was originally an article intended to provide some information on a then-unpublished text,[4] and at the same time to serve as a modest contribution to the ongoing discussion concerning the origins and essence of Gnosticism.

---

1. See the pioneer work of M. Friedländer, *Der vorchristliche jüdische Gnosticismus*, and chap. 1 in this book. On the history of scholarship dealing with the problem of Gnostic origins see, e.g., B. Frid, "Diskussionen om gnosticismens uppkomst," *STK* 43 (1967) 169–85; G. Widengren, "Les origines du gnosticisme et l'histoire des religions," in Bianchi, *Origini dello Gnosticismo*, 28–60; H. Drijvers, "The Origins of Gnosticism as a Religious and Historical Problem," *NedTTs* 22 (1968) 321–51.

2. For some important treatments of the problem see esp. O. Betz, "Was am Anfang geschah," in *Abraham Unser Vater* (Festschrift O. Michel; Leiden: E. J. Brill, 1963) 24–43; A. Böhlig, "Der jüdische und judenchristliche Hintergrund in gnostischen Texten von Nag Hammadi," in Bianchi, *Origini dello Gnosticismo*, 109–40; H. Jonas, "Delimination of the Gnostic Phenomenon—Typological and Historical," in *Origini dello Gnosticismo*, 90–104; MacRae, "Gnostic Sophia Myth"; K. Rudolph, "Randerscheinungen des Judentums und das Problem der Entstehung des Gnostizismus," *Kairos* 9 (1967) 105–22; H.-M. Schenke, "Das Problem der Beziehung zwischen Judentum und Gnosis," *Kairos* 7 (1965) 124–33.

3. For early progress reports on the publication of these texts see M. Krause, "Der Stand der Veröffentlichung der Nag Hammadi Texte," in Bianchi, *Origini dello Gnosticismo*, 61–88; J. M. Robinson, "The Coptic Gnostic Library Today," *NTS* 14 (1968) 356–401; K. Rudolph, "Gnosis und Gnostizismus, ein Forschungsbericht," *ThR* 34 (1969) 121–75, 181–231, 358–61; J. M. Robinson, "The Institute for Antiquity and Christianity," *NTS* 16 (1970) 185–90; and idem "The Coptic Gnostic Library," *NovT* 12 (1970) 81–85. In the last-named publication a new monograph series was announced, "Nag Hammadi Studies" (E.J. Brill, Leiden), the first volume of which was Scholer, *Nag Hammadi Bibliography*. "The Coptic Gnostic Library," the English-language critical edition of the Nag Hammadi Codices, is a subseries within that series. See the Table of Tractates in this book, p. xvii.

4. See now Pearson, *Codices IX and X*, 101–203.

The Jewish factor in Gnostic origins, underscored here, is still an important topic in discussions about Gnosticism.

The third tractate in Nag Hammadi Codex IX (CG IX,3: 29,6-74+, end of codex)[5] has been assigned the title, *The Testimony of Truth*.[6] It is an extremely interesting, but unfortunately fragmentary, document. Some entire pages are missing, and other pages are represented only by fragments. But judging from what has been preserved this tractate is clearly a most important document of Christian Gnosticism.

Formally, and as a whole, our document is a Gnostic tract that holds up the ideal of ascetic continence and renunciation of the world. In it are woven together, as in a multicolored garment, arguments of a soteriological, hortatory, and anti-heretical character. Its opening passage indicates that it is addressed to "those who know to hear not with the ears of the body but with the ears of the mind" (29,6-9). A polemical passage argues against those who have been gripped by error and by the authority of the Law. The ensuing material consists of alternate passages dealing with the redemptive work of "the Son of Man" (the usual title of the Redeemer in this tractate, explicitly identified with Jesus Christ in a number of passages) and warning against the error of opponents who are easily identifiable as catholic Christians. In the second half of the document the soteriological teaching is interspersed with extensive polemic against "heretics" who are clearly not catholic Christians but rather other Gnostics! This section is fragmentary, but the names "Valentinus" (56,5, restored at 56,1,) and "Isidore" (57,6) are preserved, and the names "Basilides" and "the Simonians" are very probable readings at 57,8 and 58,2. Other proper names occurred in the document, but are lost in lacunae.

Most pertinent for the purposes of this chapter are passages that contain haggadic discussions of texts and personae from the Old Testament. Indeed, these passages appear clearly to be *Fremdkörper*, already existing material editorially inserted into our tractate for purposes that are not altogether clear. The first and most important of these passages (45,23—49,10) consists of a midrash on the serpent of Genesis 3. The

5. The thirteen codices from Nag Hammadi carry either the designation "CG" (= Cairensis Gnosticus) or "NHC" (Nag Hammadi Codex); cf. "BG" (= Berolinensis Gnosticus 8502, ed. W. Till, TU 60, Berlin: Akademie-Verlag, 1956; 2nd ed., H.-M. Schenke, 1972).

6. Since the last two pages of the manuscript are lost it is not known what title, if any, the tractate originally carried. The assigned title has been supplied by the editor on the basis of key expressions occurring in the text of the tractate ("truth," "the word of truth," "the true testimony," "witness," etc.).

second of these passages (70,4–30) is an excursus—in a very fragmentary section of the document—discussing King David's propensity to idol worship and King Solomon's use of the demons in building the Jerusalem temple. Both of these passages exhibit considerable contact with Jewish haggadic traditions. Both sections are editorially treated as containing "mysteries" (45,20; 70,30), which, presumably, can be probed only through Gnostic hermeneutical insight. Limitations of space permit discussion of only the first of these passages here.[7]

THE SERPENT MIDRASH

The section preceding the passage in question deals with the virgin birth of Christ, in contrast to the natural birth of John the Baptist (45,6–18). This is followed by an exhortation: "Why then, do you (pl.) [err] and not seek after these mysteries which were prefigured for our sake?" (45,19–22). A horizontal line (a *paragraphus*) occurs in the left margin of the manuscript between lines 22 and 23, apparently indicating that the scribe saw at this point a clear dividing point in the text. A source critic would see at this point—even without the scribe's mark—a clearly defined "seam." We are encountering a literary source, previously existing and well defined. Why the author-editor of the tractate put this source precisely here is a question for which I have no adequate answer.

The passage (45,23—49,7) reads as follows:[8]

> It is written in the Law concerning this,[9] when God gave a command to Adam, "From every [tree] you may eat, [but] from the tree which is in the midst of Paradise do not eat, for on the day that you eat from it you will surely die." But the serpent was wiser (46,1) than all the animals that were in Paradise, and he persuaded Eve, saying, "On the day when you eat from the tree which is in the midst of Paradise the eyes of your heart will be opened." And Eve obeyed, and she stretched forth her hand; she took from the tree and she ate; she also gave to her husband with her. And immediately they knew that they were naked, and they took some fig leaves (and) put them on as girdles.
>
> But [God] came at the time of [evening] walking in the midst [of] Paradise. When Adam saw him he hid himself. And he said, "Adam, where are you?" He answered (and) said, "[I] have come under the fig tree." And at that very moment God [knew] that he had eaten from the tree of which he

7. On the other passage see now Pearson, "Gnostic Interpretation."
8. The translation here has been updated to conform to that published in *Nag Hammadi Library*.
9. It is not clear what "this" refers to; its antecedent is presumably lost in a portion of the source not utilized by the author-editor of the tractate.

had commanded him, "Do not eat of it." And he said to him, "Who is it (47,1) who has instructed you?" And Adam answered, "The woman whom you have given me." And the woman said, "It is the serpent who instructed me." And he cursed the serpent, and called him "devil." And he said, "Behold, Adam has become like one of us, knowing evil and good." Then he said, "Let us cast him out of Paradise lest he take from the tree of life and eat and live for ever." But of what sort is this God? First [he] maliciously refused Adam from eating of the tree of knowledge. And secondly he said, "Adam, where are you?" God does not have foreknowledge; (otherwise), would he not know from the beginning? [And] afterwards he said, "Let us cast him [out] of this place, lest he eat of the tree of life and live for ever." Surely he has shown himself to be a malicious grudger. And (48.1) what kind of a God is this? For great is the blindness of those who read, and they did not know him. And he said, "I am the jealous God; I will bring the sins of the fathers upon the children until three (and) four generations." And he said, "I will make their heart thick, and I will cause their mind to become blind, that they might not know nor comprehend the things that are said." But these things he has said to those who believe in him [and] serve him!

And [in one] place Moses writes, "[He] made the devil a serpent ⟨for⟩ [those] whom he has in his generation." Also, in the book which is called "Exodus" it is written thus: "He contended against the [magicians], when the place was full [of serpents] according to their [wickedness; and the rod] which was in the hand of Moses became a serpent, (and) it swallowed the serpents of the magicians." Again it is written, "He made a serpent of bronze (and) hung it upon a pole[10] (49,1) [. . .] which [. . .] for the [one who will gaze] upon [this] bronze [serpent], none [will destroy] him, and the one who will [believe in] this bronze serpent [will be saved]."

This passage can be called a "Gnostic midrash." In the style of Jewish expository midrash it takes its chief point of departure from scripture, in this case from the Torah, and comments interpretively upon it. Much of it is also targumic, that is, paraphrasing the text of scripture. The focal point of this midrash is the serpent of Gen. 3:1, but, in interpreting the significance of the serpent, recourse is had to other passages of the Torah, on the basis of the *Stichwort* principle, which also deal with the "serpent" figure.[11] It is, of course, a *Gnostic* midrash; the theological

10. Unfortunately p. 49 is represented by only small fragments, so much of the text is lost. In the 1972 version of this chapter I erroneously thought that pp. 49–50 were completely lost, and took fragments of p. 49 as belonging to p. 51. Cf. the *Facsimile Edition* of Codex IX, published in 1977.

11. The use of the *Stichwort* device in Jewish, especially rabbinic, exegesis of scripture is too well known to require further documentation. Examples can be found on virtually every page of the Talmud and the Midrashim. For examples using the term "serpent" (נחש) see *Pirqe R. El.* 53, comparing the serpent of Num. 21:9 with that of Genesis 3; cf. also *Num. Rab.* 19.22 and Philo *Leg. All.* 2.79–81. See also *Exod. Rab.* 3.12, comparing the serpent of Exod. 4:2 with that of Genesis 3; cf. also Philo *Leg. All.* 2.88 where the serpent of Exod. 4:2 is interpreted as "pleasure" (ἡδονή) and is thus equated with the serpent of Genesis 3 (ibid., 2.71ff.).

stance of the piece is at numerous points diametrically opposed to the traditional assumptions of Jewish (and Christian) theology. It is thus a piece of "Protestexegese."[12] As to the specific branch of Gnosticism with which this piece is to be identified, a likely assumption is that it derives from the "Ophite" branch, and probably from a very early (probably even pre-Christian) stage of its development.[13]

An array of Jewish haggadic traditions is reflected in this piece, either taken over unchanged or twisted to yield new meanings. These traditions will be discussed under three headings: (A) The Serpent, (B) The Tree, (C) The Creator God.

A. The Serpent

Although the thrust of our midrash is to interpret the serpent figure positively, consonant with Ophite gnosis,[14] there is nevertheless reflected in it the common Jewish (and Christian) identification, serpent= devil ($\delta\iota\acute{a}\beta o\lambda os$, 47,6 and 48,16ff).[15] It should be noticed, however, that the designation "devil" is given to the serpent by a hostile and envious God as an aspect of the curse inflicted upon him.[16] It might also be inferred that the expression "Moses writes" (48,16) is a signal that the truth is to be sought elsewhere than in the bare words of Moses.[17]

The serpent is introduced in our midrash as "wiser (ογϲⲁⲃⲉ) than all the animals that were in Paradise." The adjective "wise" is stronger than the word used in the biblical text of Gen. 3:1 (LXX $\phi\rho o\nu\iota\mu\acute{\omega}\tau a\tau os$, Aquila $\pi\acute{a}\nu o\nu\rho\gamma os$, Heb. ערום *Tg. Onq.* ערים),[18] and is suggestive of the serpent's role—in the Gnostic view—as revealer of wisdom and knowledge. The *Targum Ps.-Jonathan* also uses the word "wise" (חכים), but adds the

---

12. The term is used by K. Rudolph, "Randerscheinungen des Judentums" (cit. n. 2), 117.

13. See below for further discussion. There is, of course, a problem in simply taking over such patristic designations as "Ophite," "Sethian," "Cainite," etc. See chap. 6 in this book.

14. It is, of course, true that some Gnostic groups placed a negative valuation upon the serpent of Genesis 3. See, e.g., the Gnostics described by Irenaeus (*Haer.* 1.30.5-7; cf. 1.30.15, Sophia = the serpent); the Severians described by Epiphanius (*Haer.* 45.1); the system of the book *Baruch*, described by Hippolytus (*Ref.* 5.26ff. ['Naas']); *The Gospel of Philip* (CG II,3) 61,5-12.

15. See, e.g., Wis. 2:24; *Apoc. Sedrach* 4; *2 Enoch* 31; *Vita Adae* 12ff.; *3 Apoc. Bar.* 4.8; Rev. 12:9; etc. Of the many proper names attached to him, "Samael" is probably the most common in Jewish tradition. See, e.g., *Targum Ps.-Jonathan* Gen. 3:6; *3 Apoc. Bar.* 4.8; *Zohar* 35b; *Pirqe R. El.* 13, 21 (where, however, the serpent is the *instrument* of Samael).

16. 48,18 is exceedingly difficult; I have emended the text to read: ⟨ⲛ̄⟩[ⲛⲉ]ⲧⲉ ογⲛ̄ⲧⲁϥϲⲉ ϩⲙ̄ ⲡⲉϥϫⲡⲟ. See now Pearson, *Codices IX and X*, 166.

17. Cf. the continuing refrain in *The Apocryphon of John*, "not as Moses said" (BG 45,9; 58,17; 59,17; 73,4; CG II (Krause ed.) 13,19; 22,22; 23,3; 29,6; etc.

18. The Bohairic version (ed. Lagarde) also uses the word ογϲⲁⲃⲉ.

phrase "for evil" (לביש).[19] The "wisdom" of the serpent is the subject of a saying attributed to R. Meir: "Because the wisdom of the serpent was so great, therefore the penalty inflicted upon it proportionate to its wisdom."[20]

The serpent's role as "teacher" is underscored in the interchange between God, Eve, and Adam (47,1–4), where it is stated that the woman "instructed" Adam, and the serpent had "instructed" the woman.[21] Indeed, the teaching role of both the serpent and Eve is the subject of considerable speculation in Gnostic literature. The two most important of the Gnostic documents that should be considered in this connection are The Hypostasis of the Archons (CG II,4) and On the Origin of the World (CG II,5).[22]

In The Hypostasis of the Archons, in a passage paraphrasing and interpreting the Paradise narrative of Genesis 2—3, the "Spiritual Woman" (= heavenly Eve, Sophia)[23] comes into the serpent, the "Instructor" (ⲡⲣⲉϥⲧⲁⲙⲟ), and gives instruction to the fleshly Adam and Eve.[24] Similar speculations occur in On the Origin of the World, also in passages dealing with the Paradise story of Genesis 2—3. At 113 [Böhlig 161], 21ff., there is an involved discussion of the origin of the "Instructor" whose mother

19. M. Ginsburger, ed., Thargum Jonathan ben Usiël zum Pentateuch (Berlin: S. Calvary, 1903).

20. Eccl. Rab. 1.18, comparing Gen. 3:1 and 3:14. The translation is that of A. Cohen in the Soncino edition of the Midrash Rabbah. It is, of course, true that the serpent is credited with "wisdom" or special intelligence not only in ancient Judaism and Gnosticism, but in many and diverse cultures. See on this T. Gaster, Myth, Legend, and Custom in the Old Testament (New York: Harper & Row, 1969) 35f.

21. The Coptic word used is ⲧⲥⲁⲃⲟ-, literally "to make wise"; cf. the adjective ⲥⲁⲃⲉ.

22. The edition used here of Hyp. Arch. is R. Bullard, The Hypostasis of the Archons (PTS 10; Berlin: Walter de Gruyter, 1970); that of Orig. World is A. Böhlig (with P. Labib), Die Koptisch-gnostische Schrift ohne Titel aus Codex II von Nag Hammadi (DAWBIO 58; Berlin: Akademie-Verlag, 1962). It should be noted that the titles and abbreviations of the Nag Hammadi tractates referred to in this article are those employed in the Coptic Gnostic Library edition of the Nag Hammadi Codices and other publications, such as the Journal of Biblical Literature. It will also be observed that my citation of pages from CG II differs (by forty-eight pages) from the pagination employed by Bullard and Böhlig. The reason is that Bullard and Böhlig in their publications used the pagination of the volume of plates published by P. Labib, Coptic Gnostic Papyri in the Coptic Museum at Old Cairo (Cairo: Government Press, 1961), rather than that of the Codex itself.

23. Cf. Irenaeus Haer. 1.30.15 (Harvey ed. 1.28.8): "Quidam enim ipsam Sophiam serpentem factam dicunt"; Hipp. Ref. 5.16 (of the Peratic Gnostics): ὁ καθολικὸς ὄφις, φησίν, οὗτός ἐστιν ὁ σοφὸς τῆς Εὔας λόγος; cf. also The Apocalypse of Adam (CG V,5) 64,12ff. On the Gnostic Sophia as a heavenly projection of Eve see the important article by MacRae, "Gnostic Sophia Myth."

24. CG II, 89 [Bullard 137], 30ff. The term "instructor" is used of the serpent at 89,32 and again at 90,6. The same Coptic word (ⲡⲉϥⲧⲁⲙⲟ) is used with a feminine article at 90,11 to refer to the "Spiritual Woman."

"the Hebrews" call "Eve-Zoe" (ⲉ ⲩ ⲍ ⲁ ⲛ ⲍ ⲱ ⲏ), "which is 'the Instructor of Life'" (113,33f.). As for the "Instructor" himself, he has another name given to him by the "Authorities": the "beast" (θήριον), which is interpreted to mean the "instructor," "for they found him to be wiser than them all" (114,3f.; cf. Gen. 3:1). Curiously, the term "serpent" does not appear in this text, but he is there under the names "instructor" and "beast." Subsequently in the text Eve comes as an "instructor" to Adam (115,33) to rouse him from his sleep (cf. Gen. 2:21ff.). And later, when the archons command Adam and Eve not to eat of the tree of knowledge, "the one who is wiser than them all, who was called 'the beast' (θήριον)" (118,25f.) comes and instructs Eve about the tree and about the envious nature of the Creator. Eve, confident of the good counsel of the "Instructor," eats of the tree and gives the fruit to her husband.

Now all of these speculations involving the serpent and Eve and their teaching functions are based on wordplays that clearly derive from Aramaic sources.[25] The Aramaic word for "serpent," חיויא,[26] is brought into wordplay with the name "Eve," חוה, which already in the text of Gen. 3:20 is etymologically related to the word "live" (Heb. חיה, Aram. חיא). Both the serpent and Eve, in turn, are related via wordplay to the Aramaic verb חוא, "to show, tell," hence "instruct." Only in Aramaic is this conjunction of words, ḥewyā' –ḥawāh –ḥawā', possible.[27]

Furthermore, it is probable that this wordplay arises on Jewish soil, our midrash (and the other texts cited) representing a Gnostic interpretation of Jewish aggadah. Such aggadah occurs in *Genesis Rabbah* 20.11 in a comment on Gen. 3:20, "The man called his wife's name *Hawwah*": "She was given to him for an adviser [or "instructor," text: חיויתה], but she played the eavesdropper like the serpent [חיויה]." Another comment immediately follows, clarifying the role of the serpent: "He showed [חיווה] her how many generations she had destroyed."[28] A third comment, credited to R. Aha, reads (as though addressed to Eve) "The serpent was thy serpent, and thou art Adam's serpent" (חויה חוויך ואת חוויה דאדם).[29]

25. Cf. Böhlig's notes in his edition, 73f.
26. See Jastrow, *Dictionary*, 452. In *Targum Onqelos* (ed. Sperber) the word occurs in its full form, חייא at Gen. 3:1 et passim; in *Targum Ps.-Jonathan* (ed. Ginsburger) it occurs as חויא.
27. The figure of the beast (θήριον) in *Orig. World* carries this wordplay even further. The term in Aramaic is חיוא (Jastrow, *Dict.* 452); thus, the possibility for wordplay involving the verb חוא. Cf. Böhlig's edition, 73f.
28. Trans. H. Freedman in the Soncino ed.; text ed. Albeck (repr. Jerusalem: Wahrmann, 1965).
29. Ibid.; cf. also *Gen. Rab.* 22.2.

All of these comments are based on the same linguistic puns as those noted in the Gnostic sources. It can hardly be doubted that the Gnostic interpretations are derived from Jewish sources (whether precisely these or others of a similar nature); it is most improbable that the rabbis would base their interpretations upon Gnostic sources.

Not much can be said about the short and fragmentary passages in our midrash commenting upon the rod of Moses that became a serpent (Exod. 4:2–4; 7:8–12) and the bronze serpent in the wilderness (Num. 21:9). There are parallels in other Gnostic sources,[30] but nothing from Jewish aggada can be adduced to shed further light on our text.[31]

B. The Tree

Our midrash is the only Gnostic text I know of identifying the tree of knowledge in Genesis as a fig tree.[32] That identification is clearly made at 46,18ff.: Adam hides, and in reply to God's query, "Where are you?" Adam says, "I have come under the fig tree."[33] Then God knows that he has eaten from the forbidden tree.

In fact, the identification of the tree of knowledge as a fig is a widespread tradition in early Jewish sources, apocryphal,[34] rabbinic,[35] and (derivatively) early patristic.[36] The identification made in our midrash between the tree under which Adam hid (cf. Gen. 3:8) and the fig tree =

---

30. On Moses' rod, see Hippolytus on the Peratae (*Ref.* 5.16). On the bronze serpent see Hippolytus (ibid.); Epiphanius (on the Ophites, *Haer.* 37.7.1); etc. See below, on the identification with Christ.

31. For an interesting, though late, account of the history of Moses' rod, see *The Book of the Bee*, ed. and trans. E. Budge (Oxford: Clarendon, 1886), chap. 30: It originated as a branch from the forbidden (fig-)tree in Paradise, and was handed down from Adam to Moses. It became a serpent in Egypt, and served as the standard for the bronze serpent, and finally became a part of the Lord's cross. On this passage see G. Widengren, *The King and the Tree of Life in Ancient Near Eastern Religion* (UUÅ 1951:4, Uppsala, 1951) 38ff. Cf. *Numbers Rabbah* 18.23 (on Aaron's rod in Num. 17:21): this was originally the rod of Judah; it later belonged to Moses, then Aaron; it served as the scepter of every king until the temple was destroyed, and in the end time will be held in the hand of King Messiah.

32. Cf. the description of the two trees of Paradise in *Orig. World*, CG II, 110 [158],2ff.: The tree of life has leaves like those of the Cypress and fruit like clusters of grapes (reminiscent of "the tree of wisdom" in *1 Enoch* 32); the tree of knowledge has leaves like those of the fig, and its fruit resembles dates. It gives power to those who eat of it to condemn the Authorities and their angels.

33. Cf. the following passage from the Ethiopic *Book of Adam and Eve* (trans. Malan; London, 1882), Bk. 1, chap. 36 ". . . and the word of God came to Adam and Eve and said unto them, 'Adam, Adam, where art thou?' And Adam answered, 'O God, here am I. I hid myself among fig trees. . . .'"

34. E.g., *Apoc. Mos.* 20.4f.

35. R. Jose, according to *Gen. Rab.* 15.7; *Eccl. Rab.* 5.10; *Pesiq. Rab. Kah.* 20; *Pesiq. R.* 42.1; and R. Nehemiah, according to *b. Ber.* 40a and *b. Sanh.* 70b.

36. E.g., Tertullian *Adv. Marc.* 2.2.

tree of knowledge (deduced from Gen. 3:7) reflects a possible use of an aggada that appears (in variant forms) in the *Apocalypse of Moses* and in a saying of R. Jose: Adam after his sin looked for a tree under which to hide, and none of the trees of Paradise would receive him except the tree whose fruit he had eaten in his sin against God.[37] Of course the Gnostic version does not regard the eating of the forbidden fig tree[38] as a sin; in our midrash Adam is sinned against by a God who envies him both knowledge and life.[39]

C. The Creator-God

We have in our midrash clear, though quite undeveloped, lineaments of the monstrous figure of the Gnostic Demiurge, Ialdabaoth-Saklas-Samael. Although these names do not occur in our text,[40] his attributes are clearly present: blindness (typified especially in the name "Samael"), ignorance (expressed in the name "Saklas"), and malicious envy (prominent in texts describing the monstrous "child of chaos," Ialdabaoth).[41] It

37. *Apoc. Mos.* 20.4f., and *Gen. Rab.* 15.7. This tradition may be reflected in Philo, *Quaest. in Gen.* 1.44 (on Gen. 3:8): ". . . whereas they ought to have fled far away from the tree whence came their transgression, in the very midst of this place he was caught . . ." (trans. R. Marcus in the LCL ed.).

38. In Jewish sources other identifications of the tree of knowledge are proposed (grapevine, ethrog, wheat, date), the most common being the grapevine. See, e.g., *Gen. Rab.* 15.7; *Pesiq. Rab. Kah.* 20; *Pesiq. R.* 42.1; *b. Ber.* 40a; *b. Sanh.* 70ab; *Lev. Rab.* 12.1; *Num. Rab.* 10.2; *Esth. Rab.* 5.1; *Apoc. Abr.* 23; *3 Apoc. Bar.* 4.8 (where the vine is planted by the angel Samael!). Cf. the Gnostic Severians described by Epiphanius (*Haer.* 45.1.5ff.): the vine is the product of the wicked serpent-devil, and its fruit are like globules of poison.

39. There are many other more fully developed examples of Gnostic interpretation of the tree(s) in Genesis 2—3. See especially *Ap. John* BG 56,3ff.; CG II, 21[69],21ff.; *Orig. World* 118[166],16ff.; etc. See also the amulet published by E. Goodenough, "A Jewish-Gnostic Amulet of the Roman Period," GBS 1 (1958) 71–80. On one side of the amulet there is a figure of Adam and Eve on either side of a tree around which is coiled a serpent. Their stance, uncharacteristic of early Christian representations, expresses Gnostic shamelessness (Goodenough, 73). Goodenough was unable to interpret the two Hebrew (square Aramaic) letters in the engraving, a *heth* beside Adam and "a *resh* or *daleth* beside Eve" (ibid). I offer the following solution: the two letters are *heth* and *daleth*, standing for חיים, "life," and דעת, "knowledge," the two trees of Gen. 2:9 understood gnostically as a single tree portrayed on the amulet.

40. In *Testim. Truth*, outside of our midrash, the name Sabaoth is used of the God of the Law and of error at 73,30. The figure of Sabaoth, a transparent reference to the God of the Old Testament, is sometimes differentiated from Ialdabaoth in Gnostic texts, as, e.g., in *Orig. World* 103[151],32ff.; there Sabaoth is the repentant son of Ialdabaoth. Cf., e.g., the Severians (Epiphanius *Haer.* 45.1.4), where Ialdabaoth and Sabaoth are explicitly equated. Cf. also *Haer.* 26.10.6, where Sabaoth is said by the Gnostics there described to have the form of an ass or a pig!

41. It is unusual for all three of these names of the Demiurge to occur in a single context, but that is the case in the *Ap. John* CG II,11[59], 15ff., and in *Trim. Prot.* CG XIII, 1 at 39,21ff.,: "the great demon who rules over the nether region of hell and chaos . . .," called "Saklas," i.e., "Samael," "Ialdabaoth" (au. trans.).

is, moreover, evident that the figure of the Gnostic Demiurge derives in large measure from the Jewish devil and angel of death, usually called "Samael."[42]

The name "Samael" in Gnostic sources is defined as "the blind god" or "the god of the blind"[43] (Aramaic סמא, "blind" plus אל, "god").[44] This etymology probably arises in pre-Gnostic Jewish tradition dealing with the figure of the devil.[45] However, the most common understanding of the name "Samael" in Jewish sources involves a different etymology (סם or סמא "poison" plus אל "god").[46] In addition to his function as "devil" and "angel of death" Samael is also, in Jewish sources, the chief "accusing angel."[47]

In our midrash "blindness" is only indirectly attributed to God; he is, however, described as bringing blindness to his people so as to prevent them from seeing the truth. The exclamation, "Great is the blindness of those who read" (48,2f.), coupled with a paraphrase of Isa. 6:10 (48,8ff.), accuses God of veiling the truth from his people, perhaps out of his own blindness or ignorance but especially out of malice. God is, in other words, playing the part of Samael, the accusing angel; indeed he has become Samael.

Another attribute of the Creator God frequently occurring in Gnostic literature is that of foolishness or ignorance. The name "Saklas" (Aramaic סכלא, "fool" plus Greek ending) is used in this connection in a number of sources.[48] In our text the foolishness or ignorance of the

42. "Samael" is the only one of the three names that occurs in Jewish (non-Gnostic) sources, although all three are Semitic constructions. On Samael and Saklas see below. The etymology of "Ialdabaoth" (ילדא בהות, "child of chaos") proposed already by A. Hilgenfeld (*Die Ketzergeschichte des Urchristentums* [Leipzig, 1884; repr. Darmstadt: Wissenschaftliche Buchgesellschaft, 1963] 238) is cogent. For Coptic texts that strengthen this etymology see *Orig. World* 103[151],24; *Soph. Jes. Chr.* BG 119,9f.; and the quotation from *Trim. Prot.*, above, n. 41.

43. See, e.g., *Orig. World* 103[Böhlig 151],18; *Hyp. Arch.* 94[142],25f.; 87[135],3f. ("the god of the blind").

44. Cf Böhlig's note in his edition, 49.

45. It may be reflected in the New Testament in 2 Cor. 4:4; if so, the designation would involve not the "blindness" of the "god of this world" himself, but his activity in bringing blindness upon the "unbelievers." Cf. on the other hand *Acta Andreae et Matthiae* 24: the devil cannot see Andrew, and Andrew says to him, ἐπικέκλησαι Ἀμαήλ [read Σαμαήλ]; οὐχ ὅτι τυφλὸς εἶ μὴ βλέπων πάντας τοὺς ἁγίους; (Tischendorf ed.)

46. Cf. *JE*, "Samael," and *b.ʿAbodah Zarah* 20b; *Test. Abraham* (ed. M. R. James) chaps. 16–17 (rec. A).

47. See, e.g., *Exod. Rab.* 18.5; *Deut. Rab.* 11.10. Samael's chief antagonist is Michael.

48. See, e.g., *Apoc. Adam* 74,3; *Hyp. Arch.* 95[143],7; also the texts cited above, n. 41. Cf. the Valentinian description of the Demiurge as ἄνους καὶ μωρός, Hippolytus *Ref.* 6.33. On the Manichaean equivalent of Saklas, *Ašaqlūn*, see A. Adam, "Ist die Gnosis in

Creator is tied to the question in Gen. 3:9, "Adam, where are you?" (47,19ff.), a passage that precipitated considerable exegetical genius in orthodox circles.[49]

But the attribute of God most emphasized in our text is malicious envy. That God envies (φθονεῖν) Adam both knowledge and life is derived from the prohibition in Gen. 2:17 (47,15ff.) and the determination on God's part in Gen. 3:22 to banish Adam from the tree of life (47,23ff.).[50]

The envy (φθόνος) of the Creator here and elsewhere in Gnostic literature is derived from that of the devil in Jewish aggada. One of the earliest sources documenting the latter is the Wisdom of Solomon 2:24: φθόνῳ δὲ διαβόλου θάνατος εἰσῆλθεν εἰς τὸν κόσμον ("through the envy of the devil death came into the world").[51] The envy of the devil is mentioned in early pseudepigraphical works as well.[52]

The use of the word βάσκανος, translated "malicious" in the rendition supplied above, is reminiscent of an aggada in *Pirqe Rabbi Eliezer* 13. The serpent says to Eve concerning the prohibition against eating of the tree of knowledge, "This precept is nought else except the evil eye (עין רעה), for in the hour when ye eat thereof, ye will be like Him, a God."[53] The word βάσκανος is used to translate רע עין in the Greek Old Testament, and it is possible that our Gnostic midrash, with its use of the rather rare word βάσκανος, is aware of the aggada. What is seen in the latter as a piece of the serpent's slander is seen in the Gnostic text as a true statement.[54]

Aramäischen Weisheitsschulen entstanden?" in Bianchi, *Origini dello Gnosticismo*, 291–301.

49. The rabbis read, אַיֶּכָּה, "where are you?" as אֵיכָה, "how . . . !," expressing a lament over man's fallen state. See, e.g., *Gen. Rab.* 19.9; *Lam. Rab.* Proem 4; 1.1.1; *Pesiq. Rab. Kah.* 15; Philo also reads the question as a reproach, though obviously without knowledge of the ambiguities of the Hebrew text, *Quaest. in Gen.* 1.45; cf. *Leg. All.* 3.52. Cf. also Justin *Dial.* 99, and Tertullian *Adv. Marc.* 2.25, both explicitly denying any ignorance on God's part and explaining it in terms of a lament or reproach.

50. Theophilus of Antioch (*Ad. Autol.* 2.25) specifically denies that there was any φθόνος in God's prohibition in Gen. 2:17. Philo (*Quaest. in Gen.* 1.55) and Irenaeus (*Haer.* 3.23.6) specifically deny any φθόνος in God's resolve in Gen. 3:22, perhaps arguing against the Gnostic interpretation. Cf. Plato's Demiurge: ἀγαθὸς ἦν, ἀγαθῷ δὲ οὐδεὶς περὶ οὐδενὸς οὐδέποτε ἐγγίγνεται φθόνος (*Tim.* 29E).

51. Cf. Josephus *Ant.* 1.41: the serpent became envious (φθονερῶς μὲν εἶχεν) of Adam. On the serpent's envy of Adam cf. also *b. Sanhedrin* 59b and *'Abot R. Nat.* 1.

52. *Vita Adae* 12–17; 3 *Apoc. Bar.* 4.8; 2 *Enoch* 31.3.

53. Trans. G. Friedländer (London, 1916, repr. New York: Herman Press, 1965); Heb. text ed. D. Luria (Warsaw: Bomberg, 1852). The last part of the sentence would be better translated, "you shall be like gods."

54. Cf. the good counsel of the "Instructor" in *Orig. World* 118[166],32ff.

The envy of the Creator is underscored in our midrash with the quotation from Exod. 20:5, a text that appears regularly in Gnostic literature in connection with the Demiurge's arrogance and malice.[55]

SIGNIFICANCE OF THE MIDRASH

The last part of our midrash is badly damaged, but it probably ends at 49,7. An editorial comment immediately follows: "For this is Christ." The identification of Christ with the various manifestations of the serpent is a well-known aspect of (Christianized) Ophite gnosis.[56] Yet our midrash had shown no signs (up to that point) of any Christian influence at all. It is most probable, therefore, that the reference to Christ is part of the editorial framework belonging to the larger tractate. The larger tractate is, of course, a Christian Gnostic document.

The midrash, which we have identified as a literary source, reflects only Jewish, not Christian, influence: Jewish scripture, Jewish forms of interpretation, specifically Jewish haggadic traditions, some of which, of course, are deliberately perverted in a Gnostic direction. Moreover, as a Gnostic piece it is remarkably undeveloped and bears all the marks of a very early (pre-Christian?) form of Ophite gnosis. This text may therefore be very significant indeed for what it can tell us about Gnostic origins.

Much scholarly effort has been expended in the effort to probe the background and origin of Gnosticism. Geo Widengren, for example, has elucidated the Iranian components in the background of Gnosticism.[57] Yet the precise historical matrix out of which Gnosticism qua Gnosticism arises is still a matter of debate, and the factor of Judaism is attracting more and more scholarly attention.[58] The answer to the problem of

55. See *Ap. John* CG II 13[61],8; BG 44,14; Iren. *Adv. Haer.* 1.29.4; *Treat. Seth* CG VII,2:64,22ff.

56. Hippolytus *Ref.* 5.16.9–10; 5.17.8; Ps.-Tertullian *Haer.* 2; Epiphanius *Haer.* 37.2.6; 37.8.1. Cf. my article, "Did the Gnostics Curse Jesus?" *JBL* 86 (1967) 301–5. This is doubtless a secondary Christianization of an originally non-Christian Ophite gnosis.

57. See esp. "Der iranische Hintergrund der Gnosis," *ZRGG* 4 (1952) 97–114; "Les origines du gnosticisme" (cit. n. 1); *Mani and Manichaeism* (New York: Holt, Rinehart & Winston, 1965); *The Great Vohu Mana and the Apostle of God* (UUÅ 1945:5, Uppsala, 1945); and *The Gnostic Attitude* (trans. B. Pearson; Santa Barbara: Institute of Religious Studies, 1973). On the powerful influence of Iranian religion upon Judaism in the pre-Christian centuries see his articles, "Iran and Israel in Parthian Times with Special Regard to the Ethiopic Book of Enoch," in *Temenos* (1966) 138–77; "Quelques rapports entre Juifs et Iraniens à l'époque des Parthes," *Volume du Congrès Strasbourg 1956* (*VT* Suppl. 4; Leiden: E.J. Brill, 1957) 197–241.

58. See above, n. 2; and several of the chaps. in this book.

Gnostic origins requires a precise definition of what Gnosticism is in its essence, as well as the isolation of the historical and existential factors that brought it into being.

H. Jonas is doubtless right in stressing the element of revolt in Gnosticism, though he is reluctant to see this as arising within Judaism.[59] In my opinion the sources we now have tend to show that this revolt did indeed arise from *within* Judaism, though it is axiomatic that once Gnosticism is present Judaism has been abandoned.[60] The text discussed in this chapter can be taken as a paradigm. It is a Gnostic midrash utilizing Jewish traditions; at the same time it is very simple and undeveloped, evidently a piece of primitive Gnosticism. One can hear in this text echoes of existential despair arising in circles of the people of the Covenant faced with a crisis of history, with the apparent failure of the God of history: "What kind of a God is this?" (48,1); "These things he has said (and done, failed to do) to those who believe in him and serve him!" (48,13ff.). Such expressions of existential anguish are not without parallels in our own generation of history "after Auschwitz."[61]

Historical existence in an age of historical crisis, for a people whose God after all had been the Lord of history and of the created order, can, and apparently did, bring about a new and revolutionary look at the old traditions and assumptions, a "new hermeneutic."[62] This new hermeneutic arising in an age of historical crisis and religiocultural syncretism is the primary element in the origin of Gnosticism.

Where and when? This is a vexing but important question, one that I am not competent to answer definitively. My guess is: Palestine and Syria[63] in the first century B.C.E., or the first century C.E.[64]

59. See "Delimitation of the Gnostic Phenomenon" (cit. n. 2).
60. See also Böhlig, "Der jüdische und judenchristliche Hintergrund," 110; MacRae, "Gnostic Sophia Myth," 97; Schenke, "Problem der Beziehung," 132f. (articles cit. above, n. 2).
61. See, e.g., R. Rubenstein, *After Auschwitz: Radical Theology and Contemporary Judaism* (Indianapolis: Bobbs-Merrill, 1966).
62. For an interesting treatment of Jewish apocalyptic as a reflection of the changes necessitated by new understandings of history see P. Hanson, "Jewish Apocalyptic Against Its Near Eastern Environment," *RB* 78 (1971) 31–58. See also K. Rudolph's important observations on the skeptical stance in Jewish wisdom circles as a factor in the development of Gnosticism, "Randerscheinungen des Judentums" (cit. n. 2), 119f.
63. So also Rudolph, "Randerscheinungen des Judentums," 109.
64. So A. Adam, "Aramäischen Weisheitsschulen" (cit. n. 48), 294, though Adam does not take seriously the probability of intra-Jewish origins (300).

4

The Figure of Seth in Gnostic Literature

Gnostic speculation on the figure of Seth, son of Adam, is gaining greater attention among scholars interested in the origins and history of Gnosticism. Studies on this subject have recently multiplied,[1] and the publication of an important monograph on Seth by A. F. J. Klijn, *Seth in Jewish, Christian and Gnostic Literature*, is especially noteworthy.[2] Indeed, the ground covered in Klijn's book can be said to pose the question whether it is profitable to presume to carry the investigation any further. It is thus with some hesitation, and perhaps some presumptuousness, that I offer herewith some observations of my own on this subject, though I should perhaps add that I began to work on this topic before I had had a chance to read Klijn's book.

In this chapter I shall try to build upon evidence presented by Klijn and others, as well as upon research done in connection with my own previous study,[3] in order to show, hopefully with greater precision than

1. See esp. the papers presented to a special joint seminar of the Pseudepigrapha Group and the Nag Hammadi Section of the Society of Biblical Literature at the Society's One Hundred Thirteenth Annual Meeting in San Francisco, December 1977. The following papers prepared for this seminar are published in the volume of proceedings, *SBLSP 1977* (Missoula, Mont.: Scholars Press, 1977): Anitra Bingham Kolenkow, "Trips to the Other World in Antiquity and the Story of Seth in the Life of Adam and Eve," 1–11; William Adler, "Materials Relating to Seth in an Anonymous Chronographer ('Pseudo-Malalas') and in the Chronography of George Syncellus," 13–15 (an introduction to texts and translations); George W. MacRae, "Seth in Gnostic Texts and Traditions," 17–24; and Birger A. Pearson, "Egyptian Seth and Gnostic Seth," 25–43. The following items were presented to the seminar but are as yet unpublished: William Adler et al., "Materials Relating to Seth in an Anonymous Chronographer ('Pseudo Malalas') and in the Chronography of George Syncellus" (texts and translations); William Adler, "Notes to Text of George Syncellus and Pseudo-Malalas"; John T. Townsend, "Seth in Rabbinic Literature: Translations of the Sources"; and Dennis Berman, "Seth in Rabbinic Literature: Translations and Notes." Other studies will be cited below.
2. Leiden: E. J. Brill, 1977.
3. "Egyptian Seth and Gnostic Seth." Part of the research done for both of these

heretofore achieved, the extent to which Gnostic speculation on Seth is based upon scripture interpretation and Jewish traditions of exegesis. Out of considerations of space, I shall confine my discussion to the chief patristic sources on Gnosticism and to the Coptic Gnostic texts, omitting extended treatment of the Manichaean and Mandaean sources.[4]

SURVEY OF THE EVIDENCE

A. Patristic Sources

Irenaeus, in his description of the doctrines of a group of Gnostics sometimes called "Sethian-Ophites" (*Haer.* 1.30),[5] presents a version of the primeval history based on the opening chapters of Genesis. The birth of Seth "by the providence of Prunicus (= Sophia)," and that of his sister Norea,[6] are recounted; Seth and Norea are said to be the progenitors of the rest of humankind (*Haer.* 1.30.9). Nothing further is said of Seth in this account.

The earliest known patristic description of the "Sethian" Gnostic sect (*Sethoitae*) is that of Ps.-Tertullian, *Against All Heresies*,[7] a Latin work possibly based on Hippolytus's lost *Syntagma*. It is said there (chap. 8) that two men, Cain and Abel, were created by the angels. After the death of Abel, the "Mother" (= Sophia) intervened and Seth was born. The chapter concludes with the report that the Sethians identify Christ with Seth.

Epiphanius's account of the Sethian Gnostics (Σηθιανοί, see *Haer.* 39) is dependent upon Pseudo-Tertullian,[8] though Epiphanius tells us that he had personal knowledge of the group, presumably in his travels in

---

studies was supported by an NEH Senior Stipend for the summer of 1977. I am grateful to the Endowment for its support.

4. For brief surveys of the Mandaean and Manichaean evidence see my paper "Egyptian Seth and Gnostic Seth," 34–35, and Klijn, *Seth*, 107–111. It might be noted that the genetic and phenomenological relationships between Mandaean/Manichaean and other Gnostic speculations on Seth could very profitably be investigated, but this would require a more extensive study than could be attempted in this chapter. On the Manichaean material see now my article, "The Figure of Seth in Manichaean Literature," in P. Bryder, ed., *Manichaean Studies: Proceedings of the First International Conference on Manichaeism* (Aug. 5–9, 1987, Lund, Sweden: Lund; Plus Ultra, 1988) 147–55.

5. The characterization "Sethian-Ophite" is based on Theodoret of Cyrus's restatement of Irenaeus's description, *Haer.* 1.14: οἱ δὲ Σηθιανοὶ οὓς ᾿Οφιανοὺς ἤ ᾿Οφίτας τινὲς ὀνομάζουσιν. Irenaeus's text has only, "alii . . ." (1.30.1).

6. On Norea see chap. 5 in this book.

7. Cf. Klijn, *Seth*, 82–83.

8. Ibid., 83–86.

Egypt, and had gotten access to some of their books (*Haer.* 39.1.2). He reports that the Sethians trace their race (γένος) from Seth, son of Adam, and identify him with Christ (39.1.3). Seth was born at the instigation of the Mother (= Sophia) after Abel's death, and received the spark of divine power (39.2.4,7). The Mother destroyed Cain's wicked race in the Flood and preserved the righteous race of Seth (39.3.1), though the wicked angels installed Ham into the ark in order that wickedness might be preserved (39.3.2–3). Jesus Christ, appearing in the world miraculously, is none other than Seth (39.3.5). The Sethians have seven books in the name of Seth, as well as other books (39.5.1). They honor a certain Horaia (= Norea)[9] as the wife of Seth and regard her as a spiritual power in her own right (39.5.2–3).

Two other groups described by Epiphanius, the "Archontics" ('Αρχοντικοί, *Haer.* 40)[10] and the libertine "Gnostics" (Γνωστικοί, *Haer.* 26)[11] of various stripes, seem clearly to be related to the Sethians (*Haer.* 39). Indeed, Michel Tardieu has recently argued that the three sects described by Epiphanius in chapters 26, 39, and 40 of his opus against heresies are ultimately manifestations of one and the same Gnostic ideology.[12]

Epiphanius locates the Archontics in Palestine. In their system Cain and Abel are the product of a liaison between Eve and the devil (40.5.3), but Seth is the real son of Adam (40.7.1). This Seth, also called "Allogenes," was endowed from on high with spiritual power, and therefore recognized the highest God in distinction from the creator of the world and his archons (40.7.2–3). The Archontics have books in Seth's name and in the name of his seven sons, who are also called "Allogeneis" (40.7.4–5). Of the "Gnostics" Epiphanius reports that they, too, have books in the name of Seth (26.8.1). "Noria" (= Norea)[13] also plays a role in their system (26.1.3–9).

Hippolytus's description of a group he identifies as Sethians (Σηθιανοί)[14] is remarkably different from the accounts of Ps.-Tertullian and

9. Cf. Irenaeus, *Haer.* 1.30.9, and n. 6 above.
10. Cf. Klijn, *Seth*, 89.
11. Ibid., 87 n. 21.
12. Michel Tardieu, "Les livres mis sous le nom de Seth et les Séthiens de l'hérésiologie," in *Gnosis and Gnosticism: Papers read at the Seventh International Conference on Patristic Studies, Oxford, September 8th–13th, 1975* (ed. Martin Krause; NHS 8; Leiden: E. J. Brill, 1977) 206. He cites Epiphanius, *Haer.* 40.7.5., as an indication that Epiphanius himself was aware of the relationship among the three groups. See now also Layton, *Gnostic Scriptures*, 185–214.
13. Cf. nn. 6 and 9 above, and chap. 5 in this book.
14. Cf. n. 5. Klijn mentions this group in a footnote; see *Seth*, 89 n. 32.

Epiphanius on the Sethians; it also differs from Irenaeus's account of the "others," later identified as Sethians (*Haer.* 1.30). Hippolytus's group has an elaborate system based on three principles: Light, Darkness, and intermediate Spirit. Seth is mentioned only once, where the three principles (λόγοι) are related allegorically to various biblical triads: Adam, Eve, the serpent; Cain, Abel, Seth; Shem, Ham, Japheth; Abraham, Isaac, Jacob (*Haer.* 5.20). Hippolytus also reports that their system is propounded in a book entitled *Paraphrase of Seth* (5.22).

The Valentinian Gnostics are credited by Irenaeus and other heresiologists with an allegorical interpretation of Cain, Abel, and Seth somewhat comparable to that of Hippolytus's Sethians: the three classes of men, "material" (ὑλικοί), "psychic" (ψυχικοί), and "spiritual" (πνευματικοί), correspond to Cain, Abel, and Seth.[15] Seth is therefore the symbolic progenitor and representative of "spiritual" (i.e., Gnostic) humankind, according to the Valentinians.

The aforementioned patristic accounts constitute all that we know of the Gnostic interpretation of Seth from the point of view of the orthodox heresiologists. There are, of course, other patristic accounts and references—for example, Filaster, Isidore of Seville, Paulus, Honorius, the *Anacephalaiosis* attached to Epiphanius's *Panarion* (*Haer.*), John Damascene, Joseppus, Augustine, Praedestinatus, Ps.-Jerome, Didymus the Blind, Serapion of Thmuis, and Origen—but these are all dependent upon the earlier patristic writers.[16]

B. Coptic Gnostic Sources

The first extensive study of the Nag Hammadi codices was carried out by Jean Doresse, who also propounded the theory that these codices constituted *in toto* a Sethian-Gnostic "library."[17] Further study has dramatically reduced the number of tractates in the Nag Hammadi collection that can properly be labeled as "Sethian." Hans-Martin Schenke, in a very important article, defines the following documents as Sethian: *The Apocryphon of John* (Nag Hammadi Codex II,1; III,1; IV,1; and Berlin Gnostic Codex, 2, plus parallel in Irenaeus *Haer.* 1.29), *The Hypostasis of the Archons* (NHC II,4), *The Gospel of the Egyptians* (NHC III,2; IV,2), *The Apocalypse of Adam* (NHC V,5), *The Three Steles of Seth* (NHC VII,5),

---

15. Irenaeus, *Haer.* 1.7.5; *Exc. Theodot.* 54.1; Tertullian, *Adv. Val.* 29.
16. Cf. Klijn, *Seth*, 88.
17. Jean Doresse, *The Secret Books of the Egyptian Gnostics* (trans. Philip Mairet; London: Hollis & Carter, 1960); see esp. 249–51. For a critique of Doresse's views see Frederick Wisse, "The Sethians and the Nag Hammadi Library," *SBLSP* 1972, 601–7.

Zostrianos (NHC VIII,1), *Melchizedek* (NHC IX,1), *The Thought of Norea* (NHC IX,2), and *Trimorphic Protennoia* (NHC XIII,1).[18] In two of these the name "Seth" does not occur *(Norea, Trim. Prot.).* In *Melchizedek* the name occurs only in the isolated phrase, "the children of Seth" (5,20); other tractates similarly designate the spiritual race (i.e., Gnostics) as the "children," "seed," or "race" of Seth *(Ap. John, Zost., Steles Seth,* and *Gos. Eg.).* The birth of Seth is mentioned briefly in *The Hypostasis of the Archons.*

One of the most important of the tractates usually labeled as "Sethian" is *The Apocalypse of Adam.* In this work Adam is represented as giving his son Seth a testamentary revelation. He reveals the future course of the world's history and the fact that Seth will be the progenitor of the Gnostic race.

Two of the Nag Hammadi tractates bear titles with Seth's name, *The Second Treatise of the Great Seth* (NHC VII,2) and the *Three Steles of Seth.* No mention is made of Seth in the text of the *Treatise,* though Seth may (perhaps secondarily) be regarded as the putative revealer = "author" of the document. In *The Three Steles of Seth* one Dositheos is represented as interpreting the "steles."

In *The Apocryphon of John* Seth is the (heavenly) son of the perfect Man, Adam, and is placed over the second pleromatic light, Oroiael. The preexistent souls constituting the seed of Seth dwell in the third light, Daveithe. The heavenly Adam and Seth have their earthly counterparts as well, and the birth of Seth is narrated in the text.

The Gospel of the Egyptians contains a highly developed doctrine of Seth. This tractate is represented as a book written by the "Great Seth"

---

18. Schenke, "Das sethianische System," 165–66. In his other major article on the same issue, "Gnostic Sethianism," he adds *Allogenes* (NHC XI,3) and *Marsanes* (NHC X,1), as well as the untitled tractate from the Bruce Codex. For another list of Gnostic documents implicitly identified as Sethian see Alexander Böhlig and Pahor Labib, *Koptisch-Gnostische Apokalypsen aus Codex V von Nag Hammadi* (Sonderband, Wissenschaftliche Zeitschrift der Martin-Luther Universität Halle-Wittenberg; Halle/Saale, 1963) 87. Böhlig omits *The Hypostasis of the Archons, Melchizedek, Thought of Norea,* and *Trimorphic Protennoia* (probably because he was not familiar with them), and adds *Allogenes, The Second Treatise of the Great Seth,* and the untitled tractate from the Bruce Codex. Cf. Klijn's discussion of the Nag Hammadi texts, *Seth,* 90–107.

Citations of the Nag Hammadi texts in this chapter are according to page and line of the codex. Translations quoted here are taken from *Nag Hammadi Library.* The Coptic text of all of the Nag Hammadi Codices is available in *Facsimile Edition.* Critical editions of various tractates will be cited below. For bibliography citing publications of, and studies on, the Nag Hammadi tractates and other Gnostic materials see Scholer, *Nag Hammadi Bibliography,* annually supplemented in *NovT.*

Translations of ancient texts other than the Nag Hammadi materials appearing in this chapter are my own, except where otherwise specified.

and placed on a high mountain to be reserved for the elect of the last times. The "Great Seth" is the heavenly son of the incorruptible Man, Adamas. He also plays a savior role, for he is sent into the lower world to rescue the elect, "putting on" Jesus for that purpose.

As we shall see, there is reason to include in our purview documents that have not hitherto been labeled as Sethian, or in which Seth is not named. In two versions of *The Apocryphon of John* Seth is referred to as the "image" of the Son of Man; the latter could, at first glance, be taken as a designation for the heavenly Seth. The "Son of Man" terminology occurs in *Eugnostos the Blessed* (NHC III,3; V,1) and *The Sophia of Jesus Christ* (NHC III,4; BG 3). We shall therefore have to consider whether Seth, though unnamed, lies in the background.

Two additional tractates present special problems: *The Paraphrase of Shem* (NHC VII,1) and *Allogenes* (NHC XI,3). *The Paraphrase of Shem* contains material related to the "Sethian" system described by Hippolytus and supposedly derived by him from a document called "the *Paraphrase of Seth*." We shall have to consider, therefore, whether *The Paraphrase of Shem* in the Nag Hammadi collection should really be called "the Paraphrase of Seth," even though Seth is never mentioned in the text.[19] *Allogenes* could be regarded as a "Sethian" document on the testimony of Epiphanius that the Sethians possessed books called "*Allogenes*" (*Haer.* 39.5.1) and that Seth himself was called "Allogenes" (*Haer.* 40.7.7).[20]

As has already been noted in the citations, two of the Nag Hammadi tractates already discussed (*The Apocryphon of John* and *The Sophia of Jesus Christ*) occur also in the Berlin Gnostic Codex (BG).[21] Of the other extant Coptic Gnostic codices, the Askew Codex[22] contains no reference to Seth; but Seth does occur as a divine being, under the name "Setheus," in the untitled tractate of the Bruce Codex.[23]

In what follows, the sources surveyed above will be utilized to build a typology of the Gnostic figure of Seth,[24] and comparable non-Gnostic

19. For discussion of this problem see esp. Frederick Wisse, "The Redeemer Figure in the Paraphrase of Shem," *NovT* 12 (1970) 138; and Tardieu, "Les livres mis sous le nom de Seth," 205.

20. Böhlig includes *Allogenes* in his list of Sethian books, and Schenke adds it to his list in his more recent treatment. Cf. n. 18.

21. See Walter C. Till and Hans-Martin Schenke, eds., *Die Gnostische Schriften des koptischen Papyrus Berolinensis 8502* (TU 60.2; Berlin: Akademie-Verlag, 1972).

22. See Carl Schmidt and Violet MacDermot, *Pistis Sophia* (NHS 9; Leiden: E. J. Brill, 1978).

23. See Carl Schmidt and Violet MacDermot, *The Books of Jeu and the Untitled Text in the Bruce Codex* (NHS 13; Leiden: E. J. Brill, 1978). Cf. Klijn, *Seth*, 111–12.

24. A similar procedure is followed by George MacRae, "Seth" (cf. n. 1, above);

materials will be considered in order to achieve some clarity regarding the sources of Gnostic speculation on the figure of Seth, son of Adam.

TYPOLOGY OF THE GNOSTIC SETH

Our typology will be arranged according to what the texts tell us of the identity of Seth (A–C) and the function of Seth (D–E). Under each heading, we consider the primary sources first, and then bring in the patristic testimonies.

A. The Birth of Seth[25]

There are several Gnostic accounts of the birth of Seth, and all of them consist of midrashic restatements of the key passages in Genesis 4 (esp. 4:25) and 5 (esp. 5:3). These accounts of the birth of Seth are also designed to counterbalance similar midrashic restatements of the story of Cain and Abel (Gen. 4:1–16).

The Hypostasis of the Archons (91,11–92,2)[26] contains a midrash on Gen. 4:1–15, which is especially important for our purposes. The births of Cain and Abel are narrated as follows:

> Now afterwards (i.e., after the expulsion of Adam and Eve from Paradise) she (Eve) bore Cain, their son; and Cain cultivated the land. Thereupon he (Adam) knew his wife; again becoming pregnant, she bore Abel. (91,11–14; parentheses added)

In this passage, interpreting Gen. 4:1–2, Cain is identified as the son of the archons ("their son"). The rape of Eve by the archons had been reported earlier in the text (89,18–30). This idea of the parentage of Cain is based on a widespread Jewish haggadic tradition according to which Cain was the product of a liaison between Eve and the angel of death or the devil, Sammael.[27] *Targum Ps.-Jonathan* follows this tradition in its rendering of Gen. 4:1–2:

> And Adam was aware that his wife had conceived from Sammael the angel, and she became pregnant and bore Cain, and he was like those on high, not like those below; and she said, "I have acquired a man, the angel of the Lord." And she went on to bear from Adam, her husband, her twin

---

MacRae's paper has been of particular help to me in my own treatment of the figure of Seth.

25. Cf. MacRae, "Seth," 19–20.
26. The definitive edition is that of Bentley Layton, "The Hypostasis of the Archons," *HTR* 67 (1974) 351–425; 69 (1976) 31–101.
27. See chap. 6 in this book.

sister and Abel. And Abel was a keeper of sheep, but Cain was a man working in the earth.[28]

The birth of Seth is recounted in *The Hypostasis of the Archons* as follows:

> And Adam [knew] his female counterpart Eve, and she became pregnant, and bore [Seth] to Adam. And she said, "I have borne [another] man through God, in place [of Abel]." (91,30–33)

This passage is an interpretive restatement of Gen. 4:25; and the restorations of the names "Seth" and "Abel" in the lacunae are therefore certain. However, it is to be noted that Gen. 4:1 is reflected here, too, in the saying attributed to Eve: "I have borne [another] man through God." Cf. Gen. 4:1 (LXX): $\dot{\epsilon}\kappa\tau\eta\sigma\acute{a}\mu\eta\nu$ $\ddot{a}\nu\theta\rho\omega\pi\sigma\nu$ $\delta\iota\grave{a}$ $\tau\sigma\hat{v}$ $\theta\epsilon\sigma\hat{v}$. "Another man" interprets $\sigma\pi\acute{\epsilon}\rho\mu a$ $\ddot{\epsilon}\tau\epsilon\rho\sigma\nu$ in Gen. 4:25. *The Hypostasis of the Archons* does not, therefore, extrapolate from $\sigma\pi\acute{\epsilon}\rho\mu a$ $\ddot{\epsilon}\tau\epsilon\rho\sigma\nu$ a doctrine of a special race or seed of Seth, as a number of other Gnostic texts do. Instead, special significance for Gnostic humankind is derived from the birth of the heroine Norea, sister of Seth:

> Again Eve became pregnant, and she bore [Norea]. And she said, "He has begotten on [me a] virgin as an assistance [for] many generations of mankind." She is the virgin whom the Forces did not defile. (91,34–92,3)

Norea, sister of Seth, thus renders for mankind the "assistance" ($\beta\sigma\acute{\eta}$-$\theta\epsilon\iota a$; cf. Gen. 2:18) requisite for salvation. Her begetting is from God; "he" in Eve's exclamation is clearly a reference to God, the Father of the All.[29] As a virgin she is "undefiled," in contrast to the earthly Eve, whose rape by the archons is narrated earlier in the text.

In view of the notable parallels between *The Hypostasis of the Archons* and *On the Origin of the World* (NHC II,5),[30] one would expect to find in the latter some reference to the birth of Seth. But that is evidently not the

---

28. Trans. by John Bowker, *The Targums and Rabbinic Literature* (Cambridge: University Press, 1969) 132. Cf. Klijn, *Seth*, 3–4. For the text see now David Rieder, *Pseudo-Jonathan: Targum Jonathan Ben Uziel on the Pentateuch* (Jerusalem: Salomon, 1974), an improved collation of the London manuscript used by Ginsburger in his edition. For other testimonies to this tradition of the origin of Cain cf. *Pirqe R. El.* 21; *2 Enoch* 31:6; *b. Yebam.* 103b; *b. 'Abod. Zar.* 22b; *b. Šabb.* 146a; *Zohar* 3.76b; and in the NT John 8:44 and 1 John 3:12. Cf. chap. 6 in this book.

29. So Layton, "Hypostasis," 62. This narrative of the birth of Norea has a parallel in the reference to the birth of Cain's unnamed twin sister in *Tg. Ps.-J.*, quoted above.

30. See Alexander Böhlig and Pahor Labib, *Die Koptisch-Gnostische Schrift ohne Titel aus Codex II von Nag Hammadi im Koptischen Museum zu Alt-Kairo* (DAWBIO 58; Berlin: Akademie-Verlag, 1962). My references are to the codex pagination, and not to the pagination assigned by Böhlig, following Pahor Labib's publication of plates, *Coptic Gnostic Papyri in the Coptic Museum at Old Cairo* (Cairo: Government Press, 1956).

case. Eve is described as "the first virgin, not having a husband" (114,4). After giving birth she sings a hymn, the last line of which is, "I have borne a lordly man" (114,15). This appears to refer to Cain, for Gen. 4:1 (esp. the Hebrew: קניתי איש את יהוה) is in the background.[31] In a later passage the rape of the earthly Eve by the seven archangels is narrated (117,2–15), followed immediately by the birth of Abel and others: "First she was pregnant with Abel, by the first ruler. And it was by the seven authorities and their angels that she bore the other offspring" (117,15–18).

Whether Seth was meant to be included in this reference is impossible to say; in any case he is not mentioned in the text. Nothing is said, either, of the birth of Norea. Her name is mentioned only in the title of a book referred to earlier, "The First Book of Noraia" (102,10–11) or "The First Treatise of Oraia" (102,24–25).[32]

We turn to *The Apocryphon of John*. The longer recension (NHC II,1) has the fuller account of the birth of Seth, and I follow that version here.[33] This account is preceded by the story of the birth of Cain and Abel. The seduction of Eve by the chief archon results in the birth of two sons, Eloim called "Cain," and Yawe called "Abel" (24,15–26). The result is the planting of "sexual intercourse" in the world (24:27–31).

That both Cain and Abel are the product of Eve's illicit union with the "chief archon" probably reflects a Jewish interpretation of Gen. 4:1–2, according to which both Cain and Abel were sons of the devil rather than of Adam.[34]

The birth of Seth is narrated as follows:

> And when Adam recognized the likeness of his own foreknowledge, he begot the likeness of the son of man. He called him Seth according to the way of the race in the aeons. Likewise the mother also sent down her spirit, which is in her likeness and a copy of those who are in the pleroma, for she will prepare a dwelling place for the aeons which will come down . . . Thus the seed ($\sigma\pi\acute{\epsilon}\rho\mu\alpha$) remained for a while assisting (him) in order that, when the Spirit comes forth from the holy aeons, he may raise up and heal him from the deficiency, that the whole pleroma may (again) become holy and faultless. (24,34–25,16)

31. MacRae suggests that this passage is a "probable allusion to the birth of Seth" ("Seth," 19). See now chap. 6 in this book.

32. Cf. chap. 5 in this book.

33. See Martin Krause and Pahor Labib, *Die Drei Versionen des Apokryphon des Johannes im Koptischen Museum zu Alt-Kairo* (ADAIK, Koptische Reihe 1; Wiesbaden: Harrassowitz, 1962).

34. Cf. Klijn's discussion of *Gen. Rab.* 24.6; *Pirqe R. El.* 22; *Zohar* 1.55a; *Adam and Eve* 22:3; *1 Enoch* 85:6-8; and the Samaritan *Malef* in *Seth*, 7–10, 16, 21, 28–30.

In this passage the focal text in Genesis is not 4:25 but 5:3. The key word is "likeness" (ειмε), rendering both ἰδέα and εἰκών in Gen. 5:3 (LXX). The product of Adam's begetting is "the likeness of the son of man," and he is called Seth, "according to the way of the race in the aeons." The text is here referring back to the "race" or "seed" of the heavenly Seth (cf. 9,11–16). The "Son of Man" in whose "image" Seth is begotten would seem, at first glance, to be a heavenly Seth, but this will have to be tested in another context to be discussed later. In any case, we have here an interpretation of Gen. 5:1–3:[35] earthly Seth is an "image" of his heavenly prototype, the Son of Man.[36]

It is to be noticed that the "Mother" plays a special providential role in *The Apocryphon of John*, and in that connection we read of the descent of her "spirit" (πνεῦμα) and the "seed" (σπέρμα). The use of the latter term here may reflect interpretation of the key term ἕτερον σπέρμα in Gen. 4:25. The heavenly counterpart of the "seed" below is the aforementioned "seed of Seth," dwelling in the third light. The "Mother," of course, is Sophia, who is obliged to intervene in the world below "in order to rectify her deficiency" (cf. 23,20–26).[37]

The patristic reports of Gnostic interpretations of the birth of Seth present ideas similar to those encountered in our primary sources, although there are some differences in detail. The "others" discussed by Irenaeus (*Haer.* 1.30), in contrast to *The Hypostasis of the Archons* and *The Apocryphon of John*, attribute the birth of both Cain and Abel to the sexual intercourse of Adam and Eve (1.30.9). The birth of Seth is treated as follows:

> After these they say that Seth was generated by the providence of Prunicus (secundum providentiam Prunici), then Norea. From these were generated the remaining multitude of men. (1.30.9)

These Gnostics had a version of the birth of Seth showing points of similarity to both *The Hypostasis of the Archons* and *The Apocryphon of John*. In common with the former Norea is mentioned; and in common with the latter the providential role of Sophia ("Prunicus") is stressed. However, nothing is said of a special "seed" of Seth; all mankind is derived from Seth and Norea.

The Sethians described by Ps.-Tertullian attribute the generation of both Cain and Abel to the angels. Klijn reads Ps.-Tertullian's obviously

---

35. Cf. MacRae, "Seth," 19.
36. For discussion of the "birth" of the heavenly Seth see below.
37. On Gnostic Sophia see above all MacRae, "Gnostic Sophia Myth."

garbled account to mean that Cain and Abel were "really the first crea-
tures,"[38] but probably these Gnostics had a story of the parentage of
Cain and Abel similar to that of *The Apocryphon of John*. It is then said
that the "Mother" (= Sophia) "wanted Seth to be conceived and born in
Abel's place." Here, too, an account similar to *The Apocryphon of John* lies
in the background, but the phrase "in Abel's place" shows that their
version held closer to the text of Gen. 4:25 ($\dot{a}\nu\tau\dot{\iota}$ "Aβελ). The "seed" is
mentioned in the following context (cf. $\ddot{\epsilon}\tau\epsilon\rho\sigma\nu$ $\sigma\pi\dot{\epsilon}\rho\mu\alpha$, Gen. 4:25). The
Mother's purpose is to make the wicked angels ineffective by means of
the "seed."

The Sethians described by Epiphanius evidently attributed the birth
of Cain and Abel to Adam and Eve ($\delta\dot{\nu}o$ $\dot{a}\nu\theta\rho\dot{\omega}\pi\sigma\nu s$, *Haer.* 39.2.1). The
death of Abel was caused by the quarreling of the angels (39.2.2). After-
ward the "Mother" caused Seth to be born, "and in him she placed her
power, depositing in him the seed ($\sigma\pi\dot{\epsilon}\rho\mu\alpha$) of the power from on high
and the spark ($\sigma\pi\iota\nu\theta\dot{\eta}\rho$) which is from above, sent for the first deposit of
the seed and the formation" (*Haer.* 39.2.4). This account of the birth of
Seth resembles that of *The Apocryphon of John*, though it differs from the
latter on the origin of Cain and Abel. Epiphanius later reports that these
Sethians also taught that Seth had a wife named Horaia (39.5.2), a detail
that puts us in some contact with *The Hypostasis of the Archons*, according to which Norea is the sister of Seth. "Horaia" and "Norea," of course,
are one and the same.[39]

Epiphanius reports of the Archontics that they had a myth according
to which Cain and Abel were children of Eve and the devil (*Haer.* 40.5.3).
Seth, on the other hand, was the real son of Adam ($\phi\dot{\nu}\sigma\epsilon\iota$ $\ddot{\iota}\delta\iota\sigma s$ $a\dot{\nu}\tau\sigma\hat{\nu}$
$\upsilon\dot{\iota}\dot{\sigma}s$). Afterward the "Power" ($\delta\dot{\nu}\nu\alpha\mu\iota s$) from above snatched up Seth and
taught him heavenly revelations. The "Power" referred to here may be a
reference to Sophia; if so we are again in contact with the account in *The
Apocryphon of John*.

As we have seen, all of the various Gnostic accounts of the birth of
Seth (and of Cain and Abel) consist of reinterpretations of key passages
in scripture; and we have also seen that Jewish exegetical traditions are
sometimes to be seen in the background.

B. Names and Titles of Seth

A number of special names or titles are attached to Seth in Gnostic
literature. In this section, which necessarily overlaps other portions of

38. Klijn, *Seth*, 82.
39. See chap. 5 in this book.

this chapter, I shall treat together the various names by which Seth is known.

1. "The Great Seth"[40]

In *The Gospel of the Egyptians*,[41] the characteristic designation for Seth is "the great Seth" (passim). This title refers not to the earthly Seth, whose birth we have discussed above, but to a Platonic heavenly prototype of the earthly Seth, undoubtedly originating in Gnostic speculation as a projection of the latter onto the transmundane, precosmic plane. The heavenly Seth is then regarded as the "Son" of a heavenly Adam, similarly projected by the Gnostics into the precosmic realm.[42] This can be seen in the following account of the emanation, or "birth," of the great Seth:

> The incorruptible man Adamas asked for them a son out of himself, in order that he (the son) may become father of the immovable, incorruptible race, so that, through it (the race), the silence and the voice may appear, and, through it, the dead aeon may raise itself, so that it may dissolve. And thus there came forth, from above, the power (δύναμις) of the great light, the Manifestation (προφάνεια). She gave birth to the four great lights: Harmozel, Oroiael, Davithe, Eleleth, and the great incorruptible Seth, the son of the incorruptible man Adamas. (III 51,5–22)

Later on in the text the great Seth is presented as residing in the second light, Oroiael (III 65,16–17) or (anomalously) in the third light, Daveithe (III 56,20; IV 68,3–5). The great Seth initiates the salvation of the elect. The great Seth is also presented as the "author" of *The Gospel of the Egyptians* (III 68,1–2.11). The great Seth is similarly credited with the authorship of another Nag Hammadi tractate, *The Second Treatise of the Great Seth*.

2. "Emmacha Seth"

The heavenly Seth is also designated under names probably meant to heighten his transcendent, mysterious character. These names are probably to be understood as *nomina barbara*. In *The Three Steles of Seth*, the heavenly Seth, in blessing his father Geradamas (or "Pigeradamas"), calls himself "Emmacha Seth." The heavenly "son of Adamas" is called "Seth Emmacha Seth" in *Zostrianos* (6,25; 51,14–15). And in *The Gospel of*

---

40. Cf. MacRae, "Seth," 20–21.
41. See Alexander Böhlig and Frederick Wisse, *Nag Hammadi Codices III,2 and IV,2: The Gospel of the Egyptians* (NHS 4; Leiden: E. J. Brill, 1975).
42. Cf. MacRae, "Seth," 20. It should be noted here that the Gnostic Sophia is a similar kind of projection of Eve, the "Mother of the Living." Cf. MacRae, "Gnostic Sophia Myth," esp. 99–101.

the Egyptians the heavenly Seth gives praise to yet another, even more exalted, heavenly Seth figure, "the thrice-male child, Telmael Telmael Heli Heli Machar Machar Seth" (III 62,2–4), also called "the incorruptible child Telmael Telmachael Eli Eli Machar Machar Seth" (IV 59,18–21), "the great power Heli Heli Machar Machar Seth" (III 65,8–9), and "the great power Telmachael Telmachael Eli Eli Machar Machar Seth" (IV 77,2–4)!

Klijn has suggested an etymology for "Emmacha," אמה, namely, "servant,"[43] but this does not seem likely. An Egyptian etymology has also been suggested.[44] But in dealing with *nomina barbara* etymological analysis is hazardous at best.

3. "Son of Man"(?)

The problem of the Gnostic "Son of Man" is very complex, and certainly cannot be treated here in the detail it deserves.[45] We shall have to be satisfied with a consideration of those texts in which Seth appears to be called "Son of Man," or something similar.

As an example of the complexity of this problem we refer first to the passage from *The Apocryphon of John* quoted earlier in connection with the birth of Seth (II 24,34–25,16). We saw evidence there of an interpretation of Gen. 5:1–3, and indicated that at first glance one might tend to identify the "Son of Man" in whose image the earthly Seth is begotten as the heavenly Seth. However, a closer look at Gen. 5:3 itself, wherein Seth is born as "a son in his own (i.e., Adam's) likeness," will clarify the identity of the "Son of Man" in *The Apocryphon of John*. The title "Son of Man," in fact, applies to a heavenly *Adam* ("Man"), not a heavenly Seth. Earlier in the text of *The Apocryphon of John* a voice comes from heaven as a rebuke to the creator-archon Ialdabaoth: "Man exists and the Son of Man" (II 14,14–15). "Man" in this *bath qôl* is none other than the Highest God; the "Son of Man" is another Anthropos figure called "Adamas," "Pigeradamas," and so on.[46] His son, in turn, is the heavenly Seth (cf. *Ap. John* II 8,28–9,14). The heavenly Seth would then, more consistently, be called "the Son of the Son of Man."

In fact, the designation "the Son of the Son of Man" does occur in another Nag Hammadi tractate, *Eugnostos the Blessed:*

---

43. *Seth*, 105 n. 137.

44. See below for discussion.

45. For a useful discussion of the evidence see Frederick H. Borsch, *The Christian and Gnostic Son of Man* (SBT, 2d series 14; London: SCM, 1970) esp. 58–121.

46. See esp. Schenke, *Der Gott "Mensch,"* 34–43. As Schenke has convincingly demonstrated, the Gnostic "Man" speculation consists essentially of interpretation of Gen. 1:26b. Cf. also "Das sethianische System."

The first aeon, then, is that of Immortal Man. The second aeon is that of Son of Man, the one who is called "First Begetter." ⟨The third is that of son of Son of Man,⟩ who is called "Savior." (III 85,9–14)[47]

Though the name "Seth" is not found in *Eugnostos the Blessed*, there can be hardly any doubt that "the Son of Son of Man" in this passage is Seth.[48] More specifically, he is the heavenly Seth. Curiously, the "third aeon" referred to as "the Son of the Son of Man" is missing from the Christianized parallel text, *The Sophia of Jesus Christ*. The figure of Seth has therefore disappeared altogether from the latter.

Something like a "Son of Man" title is given to the heavenly Seth in some Nag Hammadi tractates. In *The Gospel of the Egyptians* "the great Seth" is also called "the son of the incorruptible man, Adamas" (III 51,20–22; 55,16–18), but in this tractate, as in *The Apocryphon of John*, the "Son of Man" referred to in the voice from heaven ("Man exists and the Son of Man," III 59,1–3) is probably not Seth, but a heavenly Adam/Anthropos, "Son" of the highest Deity ("Man").

The heavenly Seth is called "the son of Adamas" in *Zostrianos* (6,25–26; 30,9–10; 51,14). And in the first stele of *The Three Steles of Seth* he addresses his father Geradamas (or "Pigeradamas," 118,25–27). But, in fine, it does not appear that Seth is ever given the simple title "Son of Man," either in his heavenly or his earthly manifestation.[49]

4. "Allogenes"

The names and titles for Seth already discussed are ultimately tied to speculative interpretation of Gen. 5:1–3 (in relation to Gen. 1:26–27), but in the case of the name "Allogenes" we have an interpretation of the other key text, Gen. 4:25, with its reference to Seth as a ἕτερον σπέρμα ("other seed").

In Epiphanius's account of the Archontics we learn of the name "Allogenes" as applied to Seth (*Haer.* 40.7.1). The same name is given to Seth's seven sons by the Archontics (*Haer.* 40.7.1). In addition, we are told in the same report that the Archontics make use of books called "Allogenes" (καὶ τοῖς Ἀλλογένεσι καλουμένοις, 40.2.2). Epiphanius later adds that the Archontics have written books in Seth's own name, as well as others in his and his seven sons' name (40.7.4).

---

47. The material in angular brackets is restored on the basis of the parallel in Codex V (13,12–13).

48. See Douglas Parrott, "Evidence of Religious Syncretism in Gnostic Texts from Nag Hammadi," in B. Pearson, ed., *Religious Syncretism in Antiquity: Essays in Conversation with Geo Widengren* (Missoula, Mont.: Scholars Press, 1975) 173–89, esp. 179–80.

49. Unless the term "son of man" in *Trim. Prot.* 49,19 is to be understood as referring to a manifestation of Seth. Seth is not named at all in the tractate, however.

This coheres well with what we are told of the Sethians. While Epiphanius does not tell us directly that the Sethians call Seth "Allogenes," one can make that assumption nevertheless, for he speaks of seven books in the name of Seth, and "others" called "Allogeneis" (*Haer.* 39.5.1). The seven books of Seth and the "others" are probably the same; Epiphanius has garbled his sources. Perhaps, too, the "many books in the name of Seth" mentioned by Epiphanius in use among the libertine "Gnostics" (*Haer.* 26.8.1) are the same books. Thus we can presume that the epithet "Allogenes" is a Sethian-Gnostic designation for Seth.[50]

Accordingly, it is reasonable to regard the Nag Hammadi tractate *Allogenes* as a "Sethian" book, and to assume that the revealer "Allogenes" is to be understood as a manifestation of Seth himself.[51]

A name similar to Allogenes is used once in *Zostrianos*, "Allogenios" (128,7). Allogenios, together with Eleleth, Kodere, and Epiphanios, constitute "the fourth aeon of the fourth Light." This name is doubtless modeled on "Allogenes," but is not a designation for Seth.

5. "Setheus"

This variation on the name Seth—essentially a Graecization of the Hebrew name—is found in the untitled tractate of the Bruce Codex (passim).[52] In that tractate Setheus is an aspect of the highest God, and has a demiurgic function.[53] As Klijn says, "He has clearly lost all contact with the historical setting in which he was originally placed in the beginning of Genesis."[54] What we see in the Bruce Codex, in fact, is an advanced point along the trajectory of Gnostic speculation on Seth as a heavenly being.

The name "Setheus" occurs also in *Zostrianos* of a figure in the "third light" of the "third aeon" (*Zostrianos* 126,12–16). Here the name seems to

50. It might be added here that the Sethians, contrary to Klijn (*Seth*, 35), did not call Seth ἀνταλλαγή (cf. *Haer.* 39.5.7). This designation is Epiphanius's own interpretation of the name Seth (ὅπερ ἑρμηνεύεται ἀνταλλαγή), based on the phrase ἀντὶ ''Aβελ in Gen. 4:25.

51. Cf. the reference to "apocalypses" in the name of Allogenes and others in Porphyry, *Vit. Plot.* 16, and the "Apocalypse of the Stranger" (= Allogenes) reported by Theodore bar Konai in use among the Audians. On the latter see esp. Henri-Charles Puech, "Fragments retrouvés de l'"Apocalypse d'Allogène'," *Mélanges Franz Cumont* (Annuaire de l'Institut de Philologie et d'Histoire Orientales et Slaves de l'Université libre de Bruxelles 4; Brussels, 1936) 955–62.

52. Cf. n. 23.

53. This is a very peculiar development in Gnostic speculations on Seth, but the Mandaean Seth, Šitil, plays a similar role in the Mandaean *Book of John*. See, e.g., M. Lidzbarski, *Das Johannesbuch der Mandäer* (Giessen: Töpelmann, 1915) 93, 7; pp. 213,24–216,3; cf. Pearson, "Egyptian Seth and Gnostic Seth" (cf. n. 1), 34.

54. Klijn, *Seth*, 112.

be applied to a figure other than Seth, but along the lines of "Allogenios" discussed above.

All of the names and epithets we have discussed refer to the heavenly aspect of Seth, and are to be seen as the product of Gnostic reflection on the transcendent meaning of those key references to Seth in Gen. 5:1–3 and 4:25. Thus far, however, we have not discussed the question of Gnostic attempts at wordplay or etymology of the name "Seth," such as occurs in the text of Genesis itself: "She bore a son and called his name 'Seth' (שֵׁת), for she said, 'God has "set" (שָׁת) for me another offspring instead of Abel.'"[55] A variety of such wordplays on the name "Seth" is displayed in Jewish and Christian literature, and we might therefore expect to find examples of the same kind of thing in Gnostic literature.

Klijn discusses one possible wordplay of this kind, based on Coptic, in *The Apocalypse of Adam* (65,6–9), where Adam says to his son Seth, "I myself have called you by the name of that man who is the seed of the great generation or from whom (it comes)." Klijn,[56] following a suggestion made by Rodolphe Kasser,[57] finds a wordplay based on the similarity of the name Seth (cHΘ) to the Coptic word for "seed" (cιτε). But this suggestion has to be rejected, not only because the original language of *The Apocalypse of Adam* was Greek rather than Coptic, but also because the word for "seed" in this passage is the Greek word σπορά, not cιτε. Adam is telling his son Seth here that he is named for the heavenly progenitor (i.e., the heavenly Seth) of the Gnostic race; the word "seed" reflects a Gnostic interpretation of Genesis 4:25 (ἕτερον σπέρμα).

Another wordplay suggested by Klijn[58] is more likely. In *The Gospel of the Egyptians* it is said that the number of the aeons brought forth by the great Seth is "the amount of Sodom" (III 60,9–12). The text goes on to say:

> Some say that Sodom is the place of pasture of the great Seth, which is Gomorrah. But others (say) that the great Seth took his plant out of Gomorrah and planted it in the second place to which he gave the name Sodom. (60,12–18)

The word "plant" (τωбε, both verb and noun) is to be understood as a play on the meaning of the name "Seth" according to a traditional Jewish

55. Ibid., 33.
56. Ibid., 92.
57. "Bibliothèque Gnostique V, Apocalypse d'Adam," in *RTP* 17 (1967) 318 n. 2; "Textes Gnostiques, Remarques à propos des éditions récentes du Livre Secret de Jean et des Apocalypses de Paul, Jacques et Adam," in *Muséon* 68 (1965) 93 n. 56.
58. *Seth*, 102 n. 122.

explanation, wherein the words שת־לי in Gen. 4:25 ("he has established for me") are related to the word for "plant," שתיל.[59]

Finally, in another passage not noticed by Klijn, we find an indication that some Gnostics were aware of the Hebrew wordplay found in the text of Genesis itself, שׁת/שׁת. Epiphanius reports that, according to the Sethians, the Mother "placed" (ἔθετο, cf. Gen. 4:25 Aquila)[60] her own power in Seth, "setting down (καταβαλοῦσα) in him the seed (σπέρμα) of the power from above . . ." (*Haer.* 39.2.4). The use of the words τίθημι and καταβάλλω would possibly indicate a knowledge of the original Hebrew wordplay on the name "Seth" in Gen. 4:25, שׁת/שׁת, for the Hebrew word שׁית can be rendered with either of these Greek verbs. The LXX rendering of Gen. 4:25, on the other hand, uses the word ἐξανίστημι.[61]

C. Seth as Progenitor of the Gnostic Race

Probably the most important feature of Gnostic speculation on Seth is the idea that Gnostics constitute a special race of Seth. Indeed this should be seen as "the fixed point of what may be called Sethian Gnosticism."[62]

This idea is fully elaborated in *The Apocalypse of Adam*, wherein Adam reveals the future to his son Seth. In a passage already treated in another context (65,6–9), Adam tells Seth, "I myself have called you by the name of that man who is the seed of the great generation or from whom (it comes)." As we observed, "that man" is the heavenly Seth; he is the "seed" referred to in Gen. 4:25 (ἕτερον σπέρμα), and from him there comes the "generation" (γενεά) of Seth, that is, the Gnostics. Later in the text it is said that the men who came from this seed, who have received the "life of the knowledge," are "strangers" (ϣⲙ̄ⲙⲟ) to the Creator (69,12–18), and in this we detect another allusion to the phrase ἕτερον σπέρμα in Gen. 4:25.

The revelation to Seth in *The Apocalypse of Adam* consists largely of a

59. Cf. Klijn, *Seth*, 34. The source for this tradition is late—Klijn cites the Syriac *Book of the Bee*—but the wordplay in *The Gospel of the Egyptians* would seem to indicate that the tradition is at least as old as the latter. For additional discussion of this passage, see below.

60. Cf. Frederick Field, *Origenis Hexaplorum quae supersunt sive veterum interpretum Graecorum in totum Vetus Testamentum Fragmenta* (Oxford, 1875; reprinted, Hildesheim: Olms, 1964) 1.20.

61. (Non-Gnostic) Christian interpretation of Gen. 4:25 capitalized on the apparent reference in Gen. 4:25 LXX to the resurrection of Christ; see Klijn, *Seth*, 34–35.

62. MacRae, "Seth," 21.

"salvation history" of the race of Seth, its origin, its survival of flood and fire, and its final salvation through the coming of a savior, the "Illuminator." This kind of "salvation history" is a regular feature in presumably "Sethian" Gnostic materials. In *The Apocalypse of Adam* we have what seems to be an early stage of this tradition, modeled on Jewish apocalyptic texts and especially on the Jewish apocryphal Adam literature.[63]

The Gospel of the Egyptians presents similar features, though more highly developed. In a passage already treated in another context (III 51,5–22) the heavenly Adamas requests a son, "in order that he (the son) may become father of the immovable, incorruptible race" (III 51,7–9). Thereafter we learn of the birth of "the great incorruptible Seth" (III 51,20) and, in turn, the placing of his seed in the third great light, Davithe (III 56,19–22). After the sowing of the seed of Seth into the created aeons (III 60,9–11) the "great incorruptible race" (cf. III 60,25–26) suffers through perils of flood and fire, and is ultimately saved by Seth himself. The great Seth passes through "three parousias" (flood, conflagration, and judgment) in order to save his race (III 63,48), "putting on" Jesus for that purpose (III 64,1–3).

In *The Apocryphon of John*, as in *The Gospel of the Egyptians*, we are told of the precosmic origin of the "seed ($\sigma\pi\acute{\epsilon}\rho\mu\alpha$) of Seth" which consists of the preexistent "souls of the saints"; and, as in *The Gospel of the Egyptians*, Seth's seed is located in the third light, Daveithai (II 9,14–17; cf. BG 36,1–7). However, in the "salvation history" that is subsequently revealed, the "seed of Seth" is not explicitly mentioned. We do read of "the immovable race" (ⲧⲅⲉⲛⲉⲁ ⲛ̄ⲁⲧⲕⲓⲙ, II 25,23 et passim) in this connection, and we should probably take this as an implicit reference to the "seed" or the "race" of Seth.[64]

In *The Three Steles of Seth* the heavenly Seth is designated as "the Father of the living and unshakeable race" (118,12–13). In praise of his father, Geradamas, Seth says, "Thy place is over a race, for thou hast caused all these to increase, and for the sake of my seed" (120,8–10). Similarly in *Zostrianos* we read of "the sons of Seth" (7,8–9), the "living seed" that came from Seth (30,10–14), and "the holy seed of Seth" (130,16–17). On the other hand, at the beginning of the tractate the

---

63. See, e.g., Pheme Perkins, "Apocalyptic Schematization in the Apocalypse of Adam and the Gospel of the Egyptians," *SBLSP* 1972, 591–95. See now also Pearson, "'Jewish Gnostic' Literature," 26–33.

64. On "the immovable race" and other such Gnostic self-designations see chap. 8 in this book.

heavenly messenger addresses Zostrianos as the one who should save those who are worthy (4,7–18). Is Zostrianos to be understood as an incarnation of Seth? A similar question is posed in *Melchizedek*, where we find the elect referred to as both "the children of Seth" (5,20) and "the race of the High-priest," that is, Melchizedek (6,17). We shall have to return to this problem.

In patristic sources we find further evidence of Gnostic speculation on Seth as the father of a special race. Epiphanius begins his description of the Sethian Gnostics with the observation that they trace their "race (γένος) back to Seth, son of Adam" (*Haer.* 39.1.3), and to the action of the "Mother" (Sophia) in depositing in Seth the "seed of the power from above" (39.2.4–6). A "salvation history" of the race of Seth is also presented in Epiphanius's account, resembling those we have encountered in the Coptic sources.

As has already been observed, Hippolytus's account of Sethian Gnosticism differs remarkably from that of Epiphanius. There we find no reference to the "seed" or "race" of Seth. Seth merely functions as an allegorical symbol for the principle of Light, in contrast to Cain (Darkness) and Abel (Intermediate Spirit; see *Ref.* 5.20). Similarly, the Valentinians look upon Seth as an allegorical symbol of the "spiritual" (πνευματικός) class of mankind, that is, the Gnostics.[65] Finally, in contrast, we should recall that one Gnostic system evidently looked upon Seth as the father of all mankind, not just of the Gnostic "race" (Irenaeus, *Haer.* 1.30.9, discussed above).

The theory of a Gnostic race of Sethian ancestry has important parallels in Jewish speculation on Seth. As an example from Jewish apocalyptic literature, the dream visions of Enoch in *1 Enoch* (chaps. 85–90) could be cited. In that passage a kind of "salvation history" is narrated, telling of the history of the world from creation to the coming of the Messiah. Seth is presented symbolically as a white bull, the people of Israel as a nation of white bulls, and the Messiah as a white bull. The rest of humankind, in contrast, is presented as black oxen. This suggests that Seth is looked upon as the progenitor of the elect race, and finally of the Messiah.[66]

65. Cf. discussion above, and the references in n. 15.
66. Cf. Klijn, *Seth*, 20–23. A number of other texts trace the generations of the righteous back to Seth with a focus on Gen. 5:1–3, according to which Seth is the bearer of the "image of God." See, e.g., *Pirqe R. El.* 22 and the Samaritan *Molad Mosheh;* cf. Klijn, *Seth*, 8–10, 29–30.

Especially important for our purposes, however, is Philo's treatise *On the Posterity and Exile of Cain*. Commenting on Gen. 4:17–25, Philo remarks that all lovers of virtue are descendants of Seth (*Post.* 42), in contrast to the race of Cain. Again, commenting on the term ἕτερον σπέρμα in Gen. 4:25, Philo says that Seth is the "seed of human virtue" (*Post.* 173), sown from God (*Post.* 171). For Philo, therefore, all virtuous people are the race of Seth, which means that actual human generation is irrelevant. The Gnostics look upon spiritual or Gnostic mankind in the same way, as symbolic "descendants" of Seth. In both cases this doctrine is read out of Gen. 4:25. Indeed it would appear that the Gnostic interpretation of Gen. 4:25 is influenced by a Jewish exegetical tradition similar to that encountered in Philo. In any case, no such interpretation of Gen. 4:25 is ever found in (non-Gnostic) Christian sources.

D. Seth as Recipient/Revealer of Gnosis[67]

A very prominent aspect of Gnostic speculation on Seth is the role that he is thought to play in the transmission of redemptive knowledge, and in that connection Seth is credited with the "authorship" of a number of books. In discussing Seth's role in the transmission of revelation, *The Apocalypse of Adam* is the obvious starting point, for this document represents the earliest stage in the development of this idea in Gnostic literature.

The *incipit* of *The Apocalypse of Adam* reads, "The revelation which Adam taught his son Seth in the seven hundredth year, saying . . ." (64,2–4). The revelation is to be seen as a "testamentary" revelation, for the "seven hundredth year" is to be understood as the last year of Adam's life.[68] Adam tells his son Seth of his and Eve's experience in paradise, and transmits revelation that he had received from three angelic informants regarding the future adventures of the elect race, the coming destructions by flood and fire, and the coming of a savior. It is specified that special revelation will be written by angels "on a high

---

67. Cf. MacRae, "Seth," 17–19.
68. The "seven hundredth year" indicates the time since the birth of Seth, which (according to the LXX text of Gen. 5:3) took place 230 years after Adam's creation. Cf. the parallel in *Adam and Eve*, where however, the eight hundred years reflects the use of the Hebrew text of Gen. 5:3 (130 years). The parallel in *Apoc. Mos.* 5:1–2 specifically states that Adam has lived 930 years (cf. Gen. 5:5), and he calls his sons to him to hear his dying words. On *The Apocalypse of Adam* as a "testament," and its relationship to the Jewish Adam literature, see esp. Perkins, "Apocalyptic Schematization," 591–94.

mountain, upon a rock of truth" (85,10–11). The conclusion to the book informs us that Adam's son, Seth, "taught his seed" about the revelations he had received from Adam (85,19–24).

The Apocalypse of Adam is, in a sense, part and parcel of the Jewish apocryphal Adam literature known to have circulated from at least the first century C.E., and shows special affinities with the *Life of Adam and Eve*. In *Adam and Eve* one finds important parallels to *The Apocalypse of Adam*, both in form and content, beginning especially at 25:1. Compare the opening passages of the revelation to Seth in *The Apocalypse of Adam* and *Adam and Eve*:

The Apocalypse of Adam	*Adam and Eve*
Adam taught his son Seth . . . saying, "Listen to my words, my son Seth. When God had created me out of the earth along with Eve your mother . . ." (64,2–8).	Adam said to Seth, "Listen, Seth, my son, and I will pass on to you what I heard and saw. After your mother and I had been driven out of Paradise . . ." (25:1). Cf. 32:1: And Adam answered and said, "Listen to me, my sons. When God made us, me and your mother. . . ."[69]

In *Adam and Eve*, as in *The Apocalypse of Adam*, Adam not only tells Seth of his experiences in paradise, but also prophesies the future salvation of the elect (cf. esp. 29:1–10). At the end of *Adam and Eve*, Eve instructs her children to write what they had heard from Adam and Eve on tables of stone and clay, stone to survive a judgment of flood, and clay to survive a judgment of fire (50:1–2). Seth thereupon makes the tables (51:3).

In this connection we recall the tradition found in Josephus (*Ant.* 1.69–71): the progeny of Seth inscribed their (astronomical) discoveries on two steles, one of brick and one of stone, that their lore might survive the destruction by fire and deluge predicted by Adam. The stone stele, Josephus reports, still survives "in the land of Seiris" ($\kappa\alpha\tau\grave{\alpha}$ $\gamma\hat{\eta}\nu$ $\tau\grave{\eta}\nu$ $\Sigma\epsilon\iota\rho\acute{\iota}\delta\alpha$).

The reference in *The Apocalypse of Adam* to angelic revelations written on stone on a high mountain reflects this tradition found in Josephus

---

69. The translation used here is that of M. D. Johnson in *OTP*, vol. 2.

and *Adam and Eve.* "The land of Seiris" in Josephus may be understood as the land of Egypt,[70] but other testimonies to the tradition refer to "Mount Sir."[71] "Mount Sir" is to be identified as the mountain of the Flood story (cf. the "mountains of Ararat," Gen. 8:4). This identification is made explicitly in *The Hypostasis of the Archons* 92,14; and the name may have been assimilated to the Babylonian name for the mountain of the Flood story, "Nisir."[72]

Seth's role in the transmission of gnosis in *The Apocalypse of Adam* consists essentially of handing on to his "seed" the revelations he had heard from Adam. In this respect *The Apocalypse of Adam* adheres to the pattern established in the Jewish Adam books, such as *Adam and Eve.* The intentionality in *The Apocalypse of Adam*, of course, is radically different; the Gnostic author is obviously critical of the Jewish apocryphal Adam tradition,[73] and breathes the Gnostic spirit of defiance vis-à-vis the Creator.

Seth's role as revealer of gnosis is escalated in other Gnostic documents. *The Gospel of the Egyptians* represents such an escalation in its treatment, although at numerous points it shares common traditions with *The Apocalypse of Adam*, including a similar handling of "salvation history." No mention is made of Adam's role in the transmission of knowledge in the gospel. At the end of it we are informed that "the great Seth" (i.e., the heavenly Seth) wrote the book and placed it "in high mountains" (III 68,1–3), "in the mountain that is called Charaxio" (III 68,12–13), that it might be used as revelation for the elect of the end time.

---

70. Josephus's κατὰ γῆν τὴν Σείριδα can be taken as equivalent to ἐν τῇ Σηριαδικῇ γῇ in a Hermetic text ascribed to Manetho and preserved by Syncellus; see W. G. Waddell, trans., *Manetho* (LCL; Cambridge: Harvard University Press, 1940) 208–9. The σειριὰς γῆ is the home of Isis, who is herself called σειριάς in Greco-Egyptian texts. For discussion see esp. Richard Reitzenstein, *Poimandres: Studien zur griechisch-ägyptischen und frühchristlichen Literatur* (Leipzig: Teubner, 1904; repr. Darmstadt: Wissenschaftliche Buchgesellschaft, 1966) 183.

71. E.g., the *Chronology* of Ps.-Malalas 6.5: εἰς τὸ Σίριδος ὄρος. See William Adler, "Materials Relating to Seth" (cf. n. 1). Cf. also Adler's "Notes to Text of George Syncellus and Pseudo-Malalas"; but Adler overlooks the possibility that "the land of Seiris" is Egypt. Cf. n. 70, and the excursus below.

72. Cf. "The Epic of Gilgamesh," *ANET*, 94 (tablet XI, line 140). Unfortunately the Hellenistic author Berossos does not specify the name of the mountain; he merely reports that the flood hero Xisouthros's boat came to rest ἐν τοῖς Κορδυαίων ὄρεσι τῆς Ἀρμενίας. See fr. 34 in Paul Schnabel, *Berossos und die Babylonisch-Hellenistische Literatur* (Berlin: Teubner, 1923) 266. Alternatively, the name "Mount Sir" may reflect assimilation to the biblical mountain of the Edomites, Mount Seir (Σηιρ), which was also a mountain of divine revelation (cf., e.g., Isa. 21:11). I owe this suggestion to John Strugnell of Harvard. See now also Stroumsa, *Another Seed*, 115–19.

73. Cf. Perkins, "Apocalyptic Schematization," 591.

The Gospel of the Egyptians is meant to reveal gnosis about the highest God, and as such is also given the title "The Holy Book of the Great Invisible Spirit" (III 69,16–19; cf. 40,12–14).

In *The Three Steles of Seth* the heavenly Seth is credited with three steles inscribed with praises offered up by Seth to the heavenly triad of Father, Mother, and Son. The reference to "steles" reflects the Jewish legend of revelatory steles of stone and brick (discussed above). A certain Dositheos is credited with reading and transmitting the contents of Seth's steles for the benefit of the elect. The occurrence of the name "Dositheos" may reflect Samaritan influence.[74]

In this context we should compare *Zostrianos*. At the end of that document Zostrianos reports, "I wrote three tablets (and) left them as knowledge for those who come after me, the living elect" (130,1–4). This seems to reflect the tradition concerning the Sethian "steles" discussed above, though the word translated "tablets" ($\pi \acute{v} \xi o s$) indicates a wooden tablet rather than one of stone. The colophon at the end poses another question: "Zostrianos. Words of truth of Zostrianos. God of Truth. Words of Zoroaster" (132,6–9). Recalling that Zoroaster may have been identified with Seth in certain circles,[75] and noting the redemptive role assigned to Zostrianos in the tractate, we are entitled to wonder whether Zostrianos might not have been regarded as an incarnation of Seth in the minds of the author and his circle.

The Second Treatise of the Great Seth presents an analogous problem, for it is attributed (in a probably secondary title at the end: 70,11–12) to the "great Seth." In the body of the text Jesus Christ is the revealer, but it is probable that the *Treatise* was used (if not composed) in circles in which Jesus Christ was venerated as an incarnation of Seth.[76]

This brings us to the testimony of Epiphanius regarding the Sethian Gnostics. As we have already noted, the Sethians known to Epiphanius not only had seven books in the name of Seth (*Haer.* 39.5.1) but also regarded Jesus Christ as a manifestation of Seth himself (39.1.3; 39.3.5). In addition, they had books called "Allogenes" (39.5.1). The Archontics, too, had books called "Allogeneis" (40.2.2), as well as books in Seth's own name (40.7.4). Seth himself, in their system, bore the name "Allo-

74. So Schenke, "Das Sethianische System," 171–72.
75. See esp. Wilhelm Bousset, *Hauptprobleme der Gnosis* (Göttingen: Vandenhoeck & Ruprecht, 1907) 378–82.
76. See now Louis Painchaud, *Le Deuxième Traité du Grand Seth (NH VII,2)* (BCNH, "Textes" 6; Québec: Université Laval, 1982), esp. 21.

genes" (40.7.1). Books in the name of Seth circulated also among the libertine "Gnostics" (*Haer.* 26.8.1).[77]

The information we have from Epiphanius regarding the use of books called "Allogenes," and the identity of "Allogenes" and Seth, allows us to inquire whether the "Allogenes" who addresses his son "Messos" in the Nag Hammadi tractate *Allogenes* is to be understood as a manifestation of, or incarnation of, Seth. In *Allogenes* the feminine revealer-angel Youel guides Allogenes on a visionary ascent to the heavenly realm; the same kind of revelatory ascent is attributed to Seth-Allogenes by the Archontics, according to Epiphanius (*Haer.* 40.7.1–2).[78] At the end of the tractate Allogenes is commanded to write down the revelations, and to leave the book upon a mountain for the sake of those who are "worthy" (68,16–21). These details recall the end of *The Gospel of the Egyptians* (discussed above).[79] At the very end of *Allogenes*, there is a possible reference to other books of Allogenes: "all [the books of] Allo[ge]nes" (69,17–19), corroborating Epiphanius's statements regarding a plurality of Allogenes books (*Haer.* 39.5.1; 40.2.2).

Hippolytus's information regarding a *Paraphrase of Seth* in use among the Sethians (*Ref.* 5.22), plus the similarity in content between *The Paraphrase of Shem* and the "Sethian" system described by the church father, poses the question whether the title given to the Nag Hammadi tractate is a mistake for the title given by Hippolytus, or vice versa. Alternatively, we might consider the possibility that the names "Shem" and "Seth" were interchangeable among some Gnostics.[80] In *The Paraphrase of Shem*, Shem, in a state of ecstasy, receives a revelation from a redeemer figure called "Derdekeas." At one point in the text, Derdekeas says to Shem, "I shall reveal to you completely that you may reveal them to those who will be upon the earth the second time" (26,21–25). This refers

---

77. In the same passage we read also of "apocalypses of Adam"; it is possible, therefore, that the Nag Hammadi *Apocalypse of Adam* was known to them.

78. The Cologne Mani Codex (pp. 50–52) quotes from an apocalypse of Seth(el) describing a similar revelatory journey to heaven. See Albert Henrichs and Ludwig Koenen, eds., "Der Kölner Mani-Kodex (P. Colon. inv. nr. 4780) ΠΕΡΙ ΤΗΣ ΓΕΝΝΗΣ ΤΟΥ ΣΩΜΑΤΟΣ ΑΥΤΟΥ, Edition der Seiten 1–72," *ZPE* 10 (1975) 50–52. The parallels between this quotation and the tradition preserved by Epiphanius suggest that the Manichaeans and the "Archontics" shared a common source.

79. Perhaps this passage in *Allogenes* might be of help in determining the meaning of the name given to the mountain of revelation in *The Gospel of the Egyptians*, "Charaxio," i.e., "Mountain of the worthy," reflecting a combination of the Hebrew word for "mountain" (הר) and the Greek word for "worthy" (ἄξιος). For criticism of this suggestion see now Stroumsa, *Another Seed*, 116.

80. Cf. Frederick Wisse, "The Redeemer Figure" (cit. n. 19), 138; cf. also Klijn, *Seth*, 88.

to the postdiluvian world, of which Shem (son of Noah) is regarded as a representative. It is therefore possible that Hippolytus's *Paraphrase of Seth* was really a secondary, Sethianizing version of a document originally having nothing to do with Seth.[81] Be that as it may, "Shem" plays a largely passive role in the text; "Derdekeas" is the revealer-savior.[82]

As we have seen, the earliest stage in the Gnostic treatment of Seth as a transmitter of gnosis is represented by *The Apocalypse of Adam*, which, in turn, is based upon Jewish apocryphal Adam traditions. However, it should be added that there are also Jewish testimonies to the tradition that Seth (and other antediluvian patriarchs) wrote revelations in his own name.[83] On the other hand, there are no (non-Gnostic) Christian sources that ascribe any special knowledge to Seth, apart from Christian adaptations of the traditions found in *Adam and Eve* and Josephus. Thus Klijn's conclusion regarding the role of Seth as a transmitter of knowledge in Gnosticism is correct: "The Gnostics derived their ideas from Jewish sources."[84]

E. Seth as Savior[85]

Seth's role as a revealer of knowledge, described above, is also to be seen as a saving role, for in Gnosticism the purpose of the Savior's descent is to reveal the salutary knowledge to the elect here below. Indeed, from the Gnostic point of view, any proclaimer of saving knowledge is performing the function of a "savior."[86] Thus we have already discussed an aspect of Seth's role as "Savior" in the previous section.

Nevertheless there is more to be said. In *The Apocalypse of Adam*, part of the revelation given to Seth has to do with the coming of a savior figure called the "Illuminator of Knowledge." The identity of this savior is not given, but MacRae's suggestion that this figure "is meant to be a (docetic) incarnation of Seth" is very plausible.[87] The role of Seth as Savior is clearer in *The Gospel of the Egyptians*, but there one finds explicit identification of Seth with Jesus Christ: the great Seth is sent

81. Cf. Wisse, "The Redeemer Figure."
82. "Derdekeas" means "child" (Aram. דרדקא); see Stroumsa, *Another Seed*, 79, who suggests a connection with Seth.
83. See, e.g., 2 *Enoch* 33:10; cf. Klijn, *Seth*, 20.
84. Klijn, *Seth*, 112.
85. Cf. MacRae, "Seth," 21; Klijn, *Seth*, 114–15.
86. Cf. Walter Schmithals's discussion of the "apostle" in Gnosticism, in *The Office of Apostle in the Early Church* (trans. John E. Steely; Nashville: Abingdon, 1969) 114–97.
87. Other scholars see in the passage dealing with the Illuminator evidence of Christian influence. For discussion see, e.g., George MacRae, "The Apocalypse of Adam Reconsidered," *SBLSP* 1972, 575. See now Pearson, "'Jewish Gnostic' Literature," 26–33.

from above, passes through "three parousias" (flood, fire, and the judgment of the archons), and "puts on" Jesus in order to save the straying race of Seth (III 63,24–64,9).[88]

In our previous discussion of the use of the epithet "Son of the Son of Man" in *Eugnostos the Blessed* III 85,9–14, we saw that this is a reference to Seth despite the fact that the name "Seth" does not occur in the document. We also recall that this reference to the heavenly Seth has an additional specification, "the one who is called 'Savior'" (85,13–14). In *Eugnostos the Blessed*, however, there is no explicit reference to an earthly manifestation of the Savior, though "Eugnostos the blessed," writing "to those who are his," may plausibly be assumed to be playing this role (III 70,1–2).

In the previous section we also noted the possibility that Zostrianos, in the tractate that bears his name, might be regarded as an incarnation of Seth, for he plays the role of a revealer of gnosis. At the beginning of the tractate Zostrianos is commanded by the heavenly messenger to "preach to a living [race . . .] and to save those who are worthy, and to strengthen the elect" (4,15–17). At the end, after Zostrianos's ascent and descent, he addresses the "erring multitude" with these words:

> Release yourselves, and that which has bound you will be dissolved. Save yourselves so that your soul may be saved. The kind Father has sent you the Savior and given you strength. (131,10–16)

We have already noted the numerous references in *Zostrianos* to the heavenly Seth and to the "race of Seth." Given the saving role played by Zostrianos in this tractate, we should probably regard him as an incarnation of the heavenly Seth. Thus in *Zostrianos*—using the terminology of *The Gospel of the Egyptians*—Seth has "put on" Zostrianos in order to awaken his seed to gnosis.

This leads us to take another look at the tractate *Melchizedek*, in which we have noted the use of the phrase "the children of Seth." In *Melchizedek* the Savior is the "high priest" Melchizedek himself, who is also envisaged as performing the final work of salvation in the form of the

88. Language similar to that employed in *The Gospel of the Egyptians* is found in *Trimorphic Protennoia*, where the heavenly Protennoia, a Sophia-figure, says, "As for me, I put on Jesus . . . and my Seed, which is mine, I shall [place] into the Holy Light within an incomprehensible Silence" (50,12–20). Cf. *Ap. John* II 30,11–31,25. In the *Trimorphic Protennoia* the role of Seth has been bypassed; the heavenly Mother ("Protennoia") puts on Jesus herself, without first having become manifest as Seth. Contrast *The Apocryphon of John*, where the heavenly Mother sows (as a father!) her seed in Seth; see *Ap. John* II 24,34–25,16, quoted above.

crucified and risen Jesus Christ.[89] But given the reference to the "children of Seth" (5,20), and the parallel reference to the "race of the high priest" (i.e., Melchizedek, 6,17), we should entertain the possibility that in Melchizedek the priest-savior Melchizedek is regarded as an earthly incarnation of the heavenly Seth.

As a result of these observations, it might be posited that a constitutive feature of "Sethian" Gnosticism is the notion of Seth as a heavenly redeemer who can manifest himself in a variety of earthly incarnations, such as Zostrianos, Zoroaster, Melchizedek, Jesus Christ, and so on.[90]

The patristic testimonies add little to this picture. It is simply reported of the Sethians that they equate Christ with Seth (Ps.-Tertullian, *Haer.* 8; Epiphanius, *Haer.* 39.1.3; 39.3.5), which means that some (Christian) Sethians regarded Christ as an earthly manifestation of the heavenly Seth. One passage in Epiphanius may be of special interest, however:

> But from Seth, according to the seed ($\kappa\alpha\tau\grave{\alpha}$ $\sigma\pi\acute{\epsilon}\rho\mu\alpha$) and by succession of race, came the Christ, Jesus himself, not by human birth but appearing in the world miraculously. He is the one who was Seth then and is manifest now to the race of men as Christ, having been sent from the Mother above. (*Haer.* 39.3.5)

In this passage the identification of "the Christ" (Jesus) with Seth is tied to an interpretation of the phrase $\H{\epsilon}\tau\epsilon\rho\text{o}\nu$ $\sigma\pi\acute{\epsilon}\rho\mu\alpha$ in Gen. 4:25. In the previous context in Epiphanius's account, the usual Sethian "salvation history" is reported. The manifestation of Seth as "the Christ" is therefore to be understood as an eschatological event. This, of course, puts us in contact with *The Apocalypse of Adam* and *The Gospel of the Egyptians*, discussed above, but also raises an additional issue of considerable interest.

As we have seen, much of the Gnostic speculation on Seth is derived from Jewish traditions. We are therefore led to inquire into the possibility that the Gnostic notions of Seth as Savior might also be based on Jewish traditions. The aforementioned passage from Epiphanius is of special interest because it may reflect some use of Jewish messianic speculation on Gen. 4:25. As an example of this, the following passage from *Midrash Genesis Rabbah* is relevant:

---

89. See chap. 7 in this book, and Pearson, *Codices IX and X*, 19–85.
90. As is well known, the same idea is found in Manichaeism. On "Sethel our Savior" in Manichaean literature, see Pearson, "Egyptian Seth and Gnostic Seth," 35, and references cited there; also Pearson, "Seth in Manichaean Literature" (cit. n. 4), 153–54.

And she called his name Seth, "For God has set me an alien seed," etc. Rabbi Tanḥuma in the name of Samuel Kozit said: (She set her eyes on) that same seed who will arise from an alien place. And who is this? This is the Messianic King.[91]

Although this passage, as indicated especially by its context, refers to the birth of the Messiah from an alien nation (the Moabitess Ruth), it is nevertheless notable that the expected Messiah is referred to in the context of speculation on the story of the birth of Seth. The association of the Messiah with Seth and his "seed" is made elsewhere in Jewish literature as well. As we have already noted, the Messiah and the elect are tied together with Seth by means of apocalyptic animal symbolism in 1 Enoch 85–90. And there are Samaritan parallels for the same basic idea.[92]

It should also be noted that there are numerous Jewish parallels for the idea that a biblical patriarch such as Seth can appear in another incarnation. Indeed, Melchizedek, according to 2 Enoch, undergoes several incarnations[93] and in the Dead Sea Scrolls (11QMelch) he emerges as an end-time redeemer.[94] A comparable idea seems to be reflected in those passages in the New Testament where Jesus is identified with one or another of the prophets.[95] The identification of John the Baptist with Elijah reflects the same idea.[96] One can add to this the idea of a pre-existent heavenly redeemer who assumes human form—this is what we find in the case of the "Son of Man" in 1 Enoch 37, 71, implicit in his identification with the patriarch Enoch (chap. 71). There, too, the "Son of Man" (Enoch) is clearly identified as the Messiah of the end time (esp. chap. 46).

Thus, though no certainty can be achieved on this point, it is reasonable to suppose that the Gnostic view of Seth as eschatological Savior is ultimately based on sectarian Jewish messianic traditions. In any case, the identification of Seth with Jesus Christ seems clearly to be a secondary development of an originally non-Christian, perhaps even pre-Christian, tradition.

91. Gen. Rab. 23.5; trans. by Dennis Berman, "Seth in Rabbinic Literature," 5. Cf. Ruth Rab. 8.1, where the same tradition is credited to R. Ḥuna. Cf. also Klijn, Seth, 7.
92. See Klijn, Seth, 31. The late date of the Samaritan sources used by Klijn poses a problem, however.
93. Cf. 2 Enoch 21–23 (ed. Vaillant), on which see esp. M. Delcor, "Melchizedek from Genesis to the Qumran Texts and the Epistle to the Hebrews," JSJ 2 (1971) 127–30.
94. See esp. Ithamar Gruenwald, "The Messianic Image of Melchizedek" (Hebrew), Mahanayim 124 (1970) 88–98; and chap. 7 in this book.
95. "Elijah . . . Jeremiah or one of the prophets," Matt. 16:14.
96. Matt. 11:10–14.

EXCURSUS:
EGYPTIAN INFLUENCES?

It is often averred that the figure of Seth in Gnosticism is identifiable with, assimilated to, or otherwise related to, the Egyptian god of the same name.[97] Usually no evidence is given for this assertion, for the very good reason that there is none.[98] To be sure, the Egyptian god Seth is ubiquitous in Greco-Roman magic, in such materials as the magical papyruses and curse tablets; and he occurs also in the so-called Gnostic gems and amulets.[99] But he is virtually absent from materials that can properly be labeled "Gnostic,"[100] and in any case is never identified with Seth, son of Adam.

However, it might be useful to examine here two recent suggestions of possible influences from the Egyptian cult of Seth in the Nag Hammadi library.

In the case of *The Gospel of the Egyptians* A. Böhlig and F. Wisse have suggested that the reason for the use of the title ("The Gospel of the Egyptians") is the prominence of Seth in this document, and the association in the minds of Egyptian readers with the Egyptian god of the same name.[101] Such an association is suggested in the document itself, they argue, in a passage where it is said that the number of the seed of Seth is "the amount of Sodom" (πϣι ⲛ̄ⲥⲟⲇⲟⲙⲱⲛ, III 60,11–12).[102] In the same passage, it is also said that Sodom is the "dwelling place" or "place of pasture" (πⲙⲁ ⲙ̄ⲙⲟⲛⲉ) of the great Seth, which is Gomorrah (III 60,13–14). Since the Egyptian Seth had been accused of sodomy (i.e., homosexual intercourse with Horus), and Gnostics can be expected to interpret as good what traditionally is considered evil, we have here an indication of an Egyptian Gnostic attempt to "rehabilitate" the Egyptian god by interpreting him in terms of Seth, son of Adam. Of course, nothing in the text of *The Gospel of the Egyptians* suggests any "sodomite" tendencies on the part of the "great Seth," nor, indeed, does the use of the names "Sodom" and "Gomorrah" indicate any connection with homosexuality, much less a justification of, or denial of, the Egyptian god's rape of his brother! The symbolic use of "Sodom" and "Gomorrah" has biblical precedents (Isa. 1:10 and Rev. 11:8, meaning Jerusalem!), though, to be sure, "Sodom" and "Gomorrah" are given reverse evaluations in *The Gospel of the*

---

97. See, e.g., Georg Kretschmar, "Sethianer," *RGG*[3] 5, 1715; S. G. F. Brandon, "(Egyptian) Set (Seth)" in *Dictionary of Comparative Religion* (London: Weidenfeld & Nicolson, 1970) 570; H. Bonnet, *Reallexikon der ägyptischen Religionsgeschichte* 715; Doresse, *Secret Books*, 104–5; et al.

98. I have come to this conclusion in my previous study where I examined this question; see "Egyptian Seth and Gnostic Seth."

99. Cf. Pearson, "Egyptian Seth and Gnostic Seth," 26–30.

100. Egyptian Seth occurs in a fragmentary writing in the Bruce Codex and in *Pistis Sophia* under his Greek name "Typhon," and also influences the Gnostic descriptions of Iao. For discussion see Pearson, "Egyptian Seth and Gnostic Seth," 34, 32. Cf. also Wolfgang Fauth, "Seth-Typhon, Onoel und der eselsköpfige Sabaoth: Zur Theriomorphie der ophitisch-barbelognostischen Archonten," *OrChr* 57 (1973) 79–120; this important article was not available to me when I wrote "Egyptian Seth and Gnostic Seth."

101. In their edition of *The Gospel of the Egyptians* (cit. n. 41), 35.

102. This passage is quoted above, p. 67.

Egyptians, as cities destroyed by the evil Demiurge; this is a typical feature of Gnosticism.[103]

Another suggestion associating the Gnostic Seth with the Egyptian god Seth has been advanced by Konrad Wekel and the Berliner Arbeitskreis für koptisch-gnostische Schriften, in an attempt to arrive at an Egyptian etymology for the name "Emmacha" (cf. "Emmacha Seth," *Steles Seth* 118,28).[104] It is proposed that "Emmacha" is derived from an epithet of the Egyptian god Seth attested from the Ptolemaic period, ḥm-m ꜣꜣ.[105] But this is linguistically improbable, for a word beginning with Eg. ḥ would normally come into Greek either with an initial σ or an initial χ (Coptic ϣ).[106] As has already been noted in the case of this epithet,[107] it seems fruitless to attempt any etymology at all for such a *nomen barbarum.*

If we are to look for Egyptian influence in the development of the Gnostic figure of Seth, we might do better to relate the Gnostic Seth to a god in the Egyptian pantheon other than the wicked Seth-Typhon, namely, Thoth, the Egyptian Hermes.[108] Manetho is credited by Syncellus with composing his history of Egypt on the basis of hieroglyphic inscriptions written by the god Thoth "in the Seriadic land" (ἐν τῇ Σηριαδικῇ γῇ), that is, Egypt,[109] and it is probable that the temples of Egypt had in their archives, from ancient times, hieroglyphic tablets ascribed to Thoth, the divine scribe.[110] In *The Discourse on the Eighth and Ninth* (NHC VI,6) Hermes Trismegistus commands his "son" to write his revelation in hieroglyphic characters on turquoise steles for the temple at Diospolis (61,18–30), presumably commanding the son to follow a venerable precedent established by himself. We might therefore look to the lore associated with the god Thoth in Egypt for the origins of the tradition, discussed above, that Seth wrote revelations on stone steles.

However, it is clear that the Gnostic traditions pertaining to Seth's steles cannot be derived directly from Egyptian sources, for the Gnostic traditions reflect details that have no parallel in Egyptian sources. They are derived, instead, from Jewish sources, such as the apocryphal Adam literature and the tradition preserved by Josephus to the effect that the Sethites had antediluvian

103. For Sodom cf. also *Paraph. Shem* 29,1. For additional discussion see Pearson, "Egyptian Seth and Gnostic Seth," 33–34. For the suggestion that Sodom and Gomorrah are meant as purely geographical references (i.e., the Dead Sea region), see Doresse, *Secret Books,* 299.

104. "Die drei Stelen des Seth," *TLZ* 100 (1975) 572–73.

105. Citing the Erman-Grapow *Wörterbuch,* 3, 280: ḥm-m ꜣꜣ "als Bez. des Seth."

106. Cf., e.g., Plutarch *Isid.* 79 (383D), where Eg. ḥry (Coptic ϣⲁⲗ, "myrrh") is transliterated into Greek as σαλ; and *Isid.* 37 (365E), where Eg. ḫt (Coptic ϣⲉ, "wood") is reflected in Plutarch's designation for a special ivy sacred to Osiris, χενόσιρις ("plant of Osiris"). Cf. the notes in J. Gwyn Griffiths, *Plutarch's "De Iside et Osiride"* (Cambridge: University of Wales, 1970) 568, 108.

107. Cf. discussion above, p. 64.

108. Klijn brings up this possibility in his discussion regarding Seth as the discoverer of letters, but then quickly dismisses it (*Seth,* 50). Cf. on this point Adler, "Notes to Text of George Syncellus and Pseudo-Malalas" (cit. n. 1) 5/6,1–5.

109. Cf. n. 70.

110. Cf. A.-J. Festugière, *La Révélation d'Hermès Trismégiste* I (Paris: Gabalda, 1950) 74–76.

revelations on steles of brick and stone.[111] Josephus, possibly our earliest witness to this tradition, may have gotten his information from a source in which a function of the Egyptian god Thoth-Hermes had been transferred to the pre-Flood patriarch Seth, son of Adam. The Gnostic tradition is based on Jewish sources, and only indirectly—via the Jewish sources, if at all—on Egyptian lore pertaining to the god Thoth.

CONCLUSIONS

As we have seen, the Gnostic figure of Seth is largely defined on the basis of scripture interpretation, especially of the key passages, Gen. 4:25 and 5:1–3. We have also noted that the Hebrew text of Genesis is sometimes utilized as well as the Greek. The Gnostic narratives of the birth of Seth—as well as those of Cain and Abel—are presented in the form of midrashim on the key texts in Genesis, showing parallels in form and content with Jewish haggadic traditions. The notion of a heavenly Seth represents a specifically Gnostic interpretation of the Genesis accounts whereby the earthly figures of Adam and Seth are projected onto the precosmic transmundane plane. The Gnostic traditions pertaining to a special race of Seth show clear influence from Jewish traditions regarding the righteous lineage of Seth. The development of the idea of Seth as a transmitter of gnosis is based on such Jewish sources as the apocryphal Adam literature. The "salvation history" of the Gnostic (Sethian) race is derived from Jewish apocryphal sources, and the notion of Seth as an eschatological savior seems also to reflect Jewish Messianic speculation on the future Messiah as a scion of Seth. In short, virtually every aspect of the typology of Seth discussed above reflects the influence of Jewish scripture and tradition. The sole Christian component of our typology, the identification of Seth with Jesus Christ, is obviously secondary, reflecting a Christianizing stage in the development of the Gnostic interpretation of Seth.

I have not attempted here to define the constitutive elements of the "Sethian" Gnostic system,[112] but it does seem clear that the items we have discussed would constitute important elements in the evolution and development of "Sethian" Gnosticism.[113] Inasmuch as the Gnostic

---

111.   Cf. discussion above, p. 72.

112.   Cf. esp. Schenke, "Das Sethianische System" and "Gnostic Sethianism."

113.   Although Frederik Wisse has raised some important caveats in his provocative essay, "Stalking Those Elusive Sethians" (in Layton, *Rediscovery*, 2.563–76), I believe it is still useful to speak of a "Sethian" Gnostic system, such as has been isolated by Schenke in his seminal articles. In holding to this terminology we do not need to commit ourselves to any rigid theory of a single Sethian sect. Nor do we have to conclude that

traditions pertaining to Seth derive from Jewish sources, we are led to posit that the very phenomenon of Sethian Gnosticism per se is of Jewish, perhaps pre-Christian, origin.[114]

the term "Sethian" is a self-designation of one or more Gnostic groups, for, in fact, that particular adjective does not occur in any of our primary texts, and may be an invention of the heresiologists. The heresiologists, nevertheless, would presumably have had some reasons for coming up with this epithet. The material in this paper has hopefully shed some light on their bases for coining the designation "Sethian," if that is what they did.

114. For all the material he has presented in his book, Klijn seems to me to arrive at very weak conclusions. He notices the Gnostic use of Jewish material but does not want to jump to conclusions about historical relationships; see esp. *Seth*, 119. But what conclusions can we draw, on the basis of the evidence, other than those posited here?

5

The Figure of Norea
in Gnostic Literature

One of the most interesting figures in Gnostic myth and lore is a
feminine personage most frequently called "Norea," but known also
under other names, such as "Noria," "Noraia," "Horea," "Orea," "Horaia,"
and "Nuraita." Her appearance in some of the Coptic Gnostic texts from
Nag Hammadi provides a good occasion for a discussion of the relevant
texts in which she appears, with the purpose of defining with greater
precision than heretofore her original name, the history of the traditions
in which she plays a role, and her function in Gnostic myth.

A brief rundown of the Gnostic evidence will be useful at the outset:

In the fourth tractate of Codex II from Nag Hammadi,[1] entitled *The
Hypostasis of the Archons*,[2] Norea or Orea (both names occur interchangeably) is the virgin daughter of Eve, but also plays a role in the
story of Noah and the flood. When Noah builds the ark she attempts to
board it, and when she is refused she blows against the ark and destroys
it with fire. When the wicked creator-archons attempt to seduce her, as
they had attempted to seduce her mother Eve, she cries out for help.
Eleleth, one of the heavenly Illuminators, comes to rescue her. He reveals to her the truth concerning the archons and the heavenly world.

1. For a complete bibliography on the Coptic texts and on Gnosticism in general, see
Scholer, *Nag Hammadi Bibliography*, with annual supplements in *NovT*.
2. For this essay I have used R. A. Bullard, *The Hypostasis of the Archons: The Coptic
Text with Translation and Commentary* (PTS 10; Berlin: Walter de Gruyter, 1970), and P.
Nagel, *Das Wesen der Archonten* (Wissenschaftliche Beiträge der Martin-Luther Universität Halle-Wittenberg, 1970/6; Halle, 1970). Bullard's and Nagel's pagination of the text
follows the plate numbers in P. Labib, *Coptic Gnostic Papyri in the Coptic Museum at Old
Cairo* (Cairo: Goverment Press, 1956). Page references in this article will be to the
pagination of the codex itself. There is a difference of forty-eight pages; i.e., in the
aforementioned editions the text of this document runs from 134, line 20, to 145, line 23,
whereas the text in the codex is 86,20–97,23. Cf. *Facsimile Edition* (1974).

In CG IX,2: *The Thought of Norea*,[3] Norea is represented as crying out to the heavenly world and receiving aid from the "four holy helpers," the Gnostic Illuminators, and is brought into the heavenly Pleroma.

In CG II,5: *On the Origin of the World*,[4] we are informed that the feminine names of the seven powers of chaos can be found "in the first book of Noraia."[5] We are also informed that the history of the various (lower) heavens and their glories is recorded "in the first treatise of Oraia."[6]

The earliest patristic evidence for the figure of Norea in Gnostic traditions is Irenaeus. In his account of the system of the "Sethian Ophites,"[7] we learn that after the birth of Cain and Abel, Adam and Eve brought forth, by the providence of Prounikos, Seth and then Norea.[8] Seth and Norea thus represent the ancestry of spiritual humankind. This evidence is supplemented by Epiphanius's account of the Sethians, where we are informed that the Sethians assert that "a certain Horaia is the wife of Seth."[9] Epiphanius goes on to say that other heretical sects as well honor "a certain power" ($\delta \acute{v} \nu a \mu \acute{\iota} \nu$ $\tau \iota \nu a$) under the name Horaia ('$\Omega \rho a \acute{\iota} a$), but the Sethians identify her specifically as the wife of Seth. Thus from Irenaeus we learn of a "Norea" who is sister of Seth, and from Epiphanius we learn that she is called "Horaia," and is Seth's wife and, as a member of the second generation of humankind, necessarily Seth's sister.[10]

---

3. See now Pearson, *Codices IX and X*, 87–99.

4. See A. Böhlig and P. Labib, *Die Koptisch-Gnostische Schrift ohne Titel aus Codex II von Nag Hammadi im Koptischen Museum zu Alt-Kairo* (DAWBIO 58; Berlin: Akademie-Verlag, 1962). Böhlig's edition follows the pagination in Labib's volume of plates. Page references in this article will be to the pagination of the Codex itself. The text runs from 97,24 (Böhlig, 145,24) to 127,17 (Böhlig 175,17).

5. 102,10-11: ϨΝ ΤϢΟΡΠ ΝΒΙΒΛΟϹ ΝΝϢΡΑΙΑϹ. Böhlig translates, "im ersten Buch der Norea." Note the Greek genitive ending preserved (anomalously) in the Coptic.

6. 102,24–25. Böhlig's text: ϨΜ ΠϢΟΡΠ ΝΛΟΓΟϹ Ν⟨Ν⟩ϢΡΑΙΑϹ. His translation: "im ersten Logos der Norea." Again the Greek genitive ending is preserved. Cf. the interchangeable ΝϢΡΕΑ and ϢΡΕΑ in *Hyp. Arch.* There is no doubt that the two references are to one and the same document, circulating presumably under the name of Norea or Noraia. Cf. the testimony of Epiphanius, cited below.

7. In *Haer.* 1.30.1 (Harvey ed. 1.28.1) the Latin text identifies these Gnostics as "alii" (he has previously dealt with the "Barbelognostics" in 1.29); the Greek text as preserved (and modified) by Theodoret identifies them as "the Sethians whom some refer to as Ophians or Ophites."

8. "Post quos secundum providentiam Prunici (=Sophia) dicunt generatum Seth, post Noream," *Haer.* 1.30.9 (=Harvey 1.28.5).

9. $\gamma \upsilon \nu a \hat{\iota} \kappa \acute{a}$ $\tau \iota \nu a$ '$\Omega \rho a \acute{\iota} a \nu$ $\lambda \acute{e} \gamma o \upsilon \sigma \iota \nu$ $\epsilon \hat{\iota} \nu a \iota$ $\tau o \hat{\upsilon}$ $\Sigma \acute{\eta} \theta$, *Haer.* 39.5.2 (GCS ed. Holl). Holl suggests in a note that '$\Omega \rho a \acute{\iota} a$ is possibly a scribal error for $N \omega \rho \acute{e} a$, and refers us to Iren. *Haer.* 1.30.9. That '$\Omega \rho a \acute{\iota} a$ is not a "scribal error" will become clear in the course of our argument.

10. Epiphanius "refutes" the Sethians by referring to the *Book of Jubilees*, according to which the wife-sister of Seth was Azura ('$A \zeta o \upsilon \rho \acute{a}$); cf. *Jub.* 4;11.

According to the cryptic remarks of Filastrius, the Nicolaitan Gnostics venerated Barbelo and a certain woman (called) Nora.[11] This Nora is doubtless meant to be a reference to Norea. Epiphanius tells us that a group of Gnostics who followed the heresy of Nicolaus and the Nicolaitans fabricated books, among which is a book called "Noria."[12] These heretics, Epiphanius goes on to say, refer to this Noria as Noah's wife, intending to translate the name of the Pyrrha of Greek mythology into a pseudo-Semitic name, Nora.[13]

What is of special interest is the Gnostic myth that Epiphanius relates in this connection. Noria, Noah's wife, was refused permission to enter the ark; so she burned it, not once but three times. Noria was acting on behalf of the higher power, Barbelo, whereas Noah was obedient to the lower Archon. Thus Epiphanius provides us with a version of the same myth concerning Norea and the ark that we find in *The Hypostasis of the Archons*, although we are not told in the Nag Hammadi document that Norea is Noah's wife. Epiphanius also tells us that Noria reveals to Gnostic humankind the duty of gathering the seed of men and women which represents the seed stolen by the Archon from the heavenly Mother. Thus the motif of the sexual seduction of the archon(s) occurs also, though in a form different from that in the Nag Hammadi text.

Our heroine occurs also in Mandaean and (probably) Manichaean literature. In the second book of the *Ginza (R)* Noah and the flood are mentioned, and the wife of Noah is given the name "Nuraita."[14] However, in another passage a "Nhuraita" appears as the wife of Noah's son, Šum (=Shem).[15] And in yet another text[16] "Nuraita" is the wife of the heavenly scribe Dīnānūkht.[17]

---

11. "Isti Barbelo venerantur et Noram quandam mulierem," *Her.* 33.3 (CCL ed. Heylen). In a note Heylen informs us that Fabricius's edition (1721) reads "Noriam," but we are invited to compare νοῦρα in Epiphanius *Haer.* 24.1 (a mistaken reference; it should be 26.1.5).

12. καὶ βίβλους πλάττουσι Νωρίαν τινὰ βίβλον καλοῦντες, *Haer.* 26.1.3.

13. On Epiphanius's remarks on the etymology of "Nora" see below. Epiphanius goes on to say that Noah's wife's name was neither "Nora" nor "Pyrrha" but "Barthenos" (Βαρθενώς, 26.1.6). Perhaps Βαρθενώς is a corruption of παρθένος, and we recall that in some of our texts dealing with Norea/Horaia she is called a "virgin." Cf. also Holl's note referring us to the name of Noah's mother in *Jubilees* 4:28, "Bētēnōs." This name is probably a corruption of *bath 'enōš*, "daughter of Enos." Cf. L. Ginzberg, *The Legends of the Jews* (Philadelphia: Jewish Publication Society, 1925) 5.146.

14. *Ginza R* 2.1.121, Lidzbarski trans., 46, line 4.

15. *GR* 18, Lidzbarski 410,7. Cf. Lidzbarski's remarks in *Das Johannesbuch der Mandäer* (Giessen: Töpelmann, 1915) 58. Cf. also prayer no. 170 in *The Canonical Prayerbook of the Mandaeans* (ed. E. S. Drower; Leiden: E. J. Brill, 1959) 152.

16. *GR* 6, Lidzbarski 211,36; 39. On these texts see K. Rudolph, *Die Mandäer* (FRLANT 74; Göttingen: Vandenhoeck & Ruprecht, 1960) 1.83 n. 1; 1.169 n. 2.

17. Dīnānūkht=Iranian *Denanuχt*, "the one who speaks in accordance with religion,"

In the Manichaean system as described in the *Acta Archelai* a very interesting passage occurs in the context of a description of Manichaean soteriology. This passage represents the Manichaean understanding of the phenomenon of physical death:

A certain virgin comely and well-adorned (παρθένος τις ὡραία κεκοσμημένη)[18] attempts to despoil the archons that had been borne up and crucified in the firmament by the Living Spirit, and she appears to the male archons as a beautiful woman, but to the female archons as a handsome and lusty young man. The archons, whenever they look at her in her beautiful appearance, are overcome with the passion of love, and unable to grasp her they burn terribly, out of their minds with the pangs of love. Whenever they run after her the virgin disappears.[19]

The resultant wrath of the archons brings about pestilence and death.

We are here very close to the myth of the seduction of the archons[20] that we have encountered in other Gnostic texts dealing with Norea/Horaia. We have now only to raise the logical question as to the identity of the beautiful and seductive virgin in this Manichaean passage, and it appears that we have the answer in the text itself. For there is no reason necessarily to take the Greek word ὡραία as a simple adjective. Why not interpret the phrase in question as meaning "a certain well-adorned virgin, Horaia"?[21]

Thus we have been presented with a number of Gnostic texts dealing with a figure called "Norea," "Horaia," and so on, who is associated with the patriarchs of the diluvian and antediluvian era (Seth, Noah, Shem) and who attracts sexually the "archons" of the world.

according to Andreas. Cf. Lidzbarski, *Ginza*, 205. Lidzbarski points out certain features of Dīnānūkht which are reminiscent of the Babylonian Noah, Ut-Napištim. It is therefore understandable that his wife should be called Nūraitā (=Norea). Note also that in the passage in which Nuraita appears in this sixth book, she is opposing her husband. This motif is very much in character with some of the traditions concerning Noah's wife, not only the Gnostic tradition already mentioned, but others yet to be brought out.

18. Lat: "Virgo quaedam decora et exornata."

19. Hegemonius, *Acta Archelai* 9 (GCS ed. Beeson). The translation is my own.

20. The myth of the seduction of the archons is a very prominent aspect of the Manichaean soteriology. The Third Messenger sails in his vessel of light (the moon) across the vault of heaven and shows himself to the demonic powers, as a "virgin of light" to the males and as a naked resplendent youth to the females. On this myth and the possible Iranian background of some of the details see G. Widengren, *Mani and Manichaeism* (trans. C. Kessler; New York: Holt, Rinehart & Winston, 1965) 56–58. W. Bousset emphasizes the parallels in other Gnostic sources; see *Hauptprobleme der Gnosis* (Göttingen: Vandenhoeck & Ruprecht, 1907) 76–77. Bousset sees a difference between the "virgin of light" in the other texts (and in *Acta Archelai* 13) and the virgin in the passage quoted above, but the myth is ultimately the same. On the mythological complex involving the seduction of the archons see now Stroumsa, *Another Seed*, 35–70.

21. Cf. also R. Bullard, *The Hypostasis of the Archons*, 98.

Who is this figure? What is her original name, and what is the origin of the myths and legends revolving around her?

A number of etymologies for the name "Norea" have been proposed. Epiphanius, in the context of his discussion of the Nicolaitans and related sects (*Haer.* 26.1.5), saw in the name "Noria" an attempt to translate the name of the Greek flood-heroine Pyrrha (Πύρρα = "fiery") into Aramaic: νοῦρα = נורא, "fire." Epiphanius thus contrives a wordplay on the activity of Noria in burning Noah's ark. His etymology can hardly be considered the correct one, at least with respect to the origin of the name, although it is possible that the "Nicolaitans" (or whoever they were) arrived at this (secondary) etymology themselves in explaining a figure they had gotten from earlier tradition.[22] Nor are any of the other etymologies thus far suggested any better than that of Epiphanius. Bousset, for example,[23] sees in "Noria" a Hebrew equivalent of the name Epiphanius himself gives to Noah's wife, Βαρθενώς. Bousset takes this name to be a corruption of παρθένος, and thus proposes a derivation from Hebrew נערה = "young maiden." Bullard[24] understands the original form of Norea to be "Orea," to which the Coptic particle ṉ has been attached to yield the name "Norea." "Orea" is thus an Egyptian name, in Bullard's view, and he connects it with the fire-breathing snake, the uraeus. This interpretation is far-fetched. But we ought not simply dismiss the name "Norea" and its various equivalents as an ad hoc invention similar to names found in such pseudepigraphic books as *Jubilees.*[25]

I think we can find the original name of Norea and the origin of the

22. It is also possible that the story of the burning of the ark is based upon an understanding of the name "Norea" as meaning "fire." The word *nūra*ʾ can also mean "light"; cf. the "virgin of light" in the Manichaean system referred to above. On the cult of *Panagia Al Nouria* in Beirut see the interesting comment of E. Segelberg, "Old and New Testament Figures in Mandaean Version," in S. Hartman, ed., *Syncretism* (Stockholm: Almquist & Wiksell, 1969) 235. I am grateful to Segelberg for calling my attention to this article.

23. *Hauptprobleme*, 14, commenting on the same passage in Epiphanius.

24. *Hypostasis of the Archons*, 95–98. P. Nagel, assuming the original form of the name to be Norea (Gr. Νωραία), supplies an interesting note in his edition to account for the dropping of the N in the Coptic text of *The Hypostasis of the Archons*: "Der Ausfall von N in 140,11 [=Codex, 92,11] ⲁⲥⲉⲓ ⲇⲉ ⲛⲟ̄ⲓ ⲱⲣⲉⲁ ist m.E. nicht als innerkoptischer Kopierfehler, sondern durch falsche Wortabgrenzung der griechischen Vorlage erklärbar: ΚΑΙ/ΗΛΘΕΝ/ΩΡΑΙΑ." Thus in his Greek retroversion he reads at this point in the text: καὶ ἦλθε Νωραία. See *Das Wesen der Archonten*, 76. Bentley Layton of Yale University has kindly called my attention to this note. Of course, the absence of the N in so many other occurrences of the name Norea makes Nagel's ingenious suggestion quite impossible.

25. As Preuschen does. See "Die apokryphen gnostischen Adamschriften aus dem Armenischen übersetzt und untersucht," in *Festgruss für Bernhard Stade* (ed. W. Diehl et al.; Giessen: Töpelmann, 1900) 242 n. 2. Preuschen mentions the name "Azura" as an example. Cf. *Jub.* 4:11 and Epiphanius *Haer.* 39.6; and cf. n. 10 above.

myths about her by referring to non-Gnostic Jewish material of a haggadic nature, rabbinic and pseudepigraphical. It is true that the name "Norea" does not occur in these materials,[26] but we are undaunted by this. For if we press the search we soon encounter the figure of Naʿamah, and she, in turn, leads us back to: Hōraia. Indeed, they are one and the same!

"Naʿamah" is a biblical name. It is the name of the daughter of the Cainite Lamech, the sister of Tubal-cain, in Gen. 4:22. And in 1 Kings 14:21 "Naʿamah" is the name given to the mother of Rehoboam. It is the first occurrence of the name that is of relevance to us.

In the *Midrash Rabbah* on Genesis there occurs an interesting debate on Gen. 4:22. R. Abba b. Kahana comments, "Naamah was Noah's wife; and why was she called Naamah? Because her deeds were pleasing."

R. Abba is contradicted by the majority, however ("the Rabbis"), who says, "Naamah was a woman of a different stamp, for the name denotes that she sang to the timbrel in honour of idolatry."[27]

The name "Naʿamah" (נעמה) means "pleasing, lovely," from the verb נעם, "be pleasing, lovely." R. Abba's comment reflects a prior tradition in which Noah's wife is given the name Naʿamah, and is equating this Naʿamah with the sister of Tubal-cain in Gen. 4:22. He is also making a pun on her name in his remark that "her deeds were pleasing" (Heb.: מעשיה נעימים). The majority position is also a pun on the name "Naʿamah," for a secondary meaning of the verb naʿem is "to sweeten the voice, to sing."[28] Naʿamah was not a pious woman, as R. Abba alleges, because "she sang to the timbrel in honour of idolatry" (מנעמת בתוף לעבודה זרה). The majority position is capable of (at least) three different interpretations: (a) Noah's wife Naʿamah, the sister of Tubal-cain, was an evil woman, and not a pious one; (b) Noah's pious wife, Naʿamah, is a different Naʿamah from the Cainite woman of the same name; (c) Noah's wife is not to be confused at all with Naʿamah, for her name and lineage are completely different. And, in fact, all three possibilities occur in Jewish aggadah.[29]

26. My good friend Michael Stone of Hebrew University in Jerusalem suggests that "Noaba" in Ps.-Philo *Ant. Bibl.* 1.1 may be a corruption of "Norea." That is possible, but I think it is more probable that the original name here was "Naʿamah." See below.
27. *Gen. Rab.* 23.3 (trans. H. Freedman; London: Soncino, 1939). Text: J. Theodor and Ch. Albeck, eds. (Jerusalem: Wahrmann, 1965).
28. Cf. Jastrow's *Dictionary*, ad loc.
29. (b): On Noah's pious wife, Naʿamah, the daughter of Enosh (*bat ʾenōš*, cf. Bētēnōs in *Jub.* 4:28 and n. 13 above) see *Yashar Noah* 14b; cf. Ginzberg, *Legends* 1.159; 5.179. In Tob. 4:12 Noah is listed as one of the patriarchs who "took wives from among their brethren." Thus Noah's wife would be a Sethian woman and not a Cainite. But her

We are especially interested in the traditions concerning the wicked-ness of Na'amah. In late medieval legends, preserved in English and Slavonic texts but reflecting much earlier traditions, Noah's wife is represented as in league with the devil in order to thwart the building of the ark.[30] Even in the Koran the wife of Noah is regarded as a wicked woman. In *Sura* 66.10 the (unnamed) wife of Noah and the wife of Lot are paradigms of unbelief. "They were under two of our righteous ser-vants, but they betrayed them."[31]

One of the most interesting features of the legend concerning the Cainite Na'amah is her sexual liaison with the "sons of God" (angels) referred to in Gen. 6:2.[32] As a Cainite woman she was amongst those who went about stark naked,[33] and because of her striking beauty Na'a-mah was able to seduce the angels Aza and Azael.[34] In some Cabbalistic legends Na'amah, the sister of Tubal-cain, produced the arch-demon Ashmedai (=Asmodeus)[35] as the result of a liaison with the angel Sham-dan.

Now as a beautiful Cainite woman, Na'amah is simply living up to her lineage. For, after all, Cain himself, according to a well-known Jewish tradition found in the Palestinian Targum, the Talmud, and Midrash, was said to be the product of a liaison between Eve and the devil, Samael.[36]

---

name is not given in Tobit. *(c)*: According to *Jubilees* 4:33 Noah married 'Emzārā, the daughter of Rākēēl, the daughter of his father's brother. 'Emzārā is a corruption of אם זרע, "mother of the seed (of man)." Cf. Ginzberg, *Legends*, 5.146. According to the *Book of the Cave of Treasures* Noah's wife's name was Haikal, the daughter of Namos, the daughter of Enoch. See Bezold, ed., *Die Schatzhöhle*, 17.

30. On these legends see M. R. James, *The Lost Apocrypha of the Old Testament* (London: SPCK, 1920) 13–15. James sees in these legends later forms of a folktale concerning Noah's wife used and reinterpreted by the Gnostics described by Epi-phanius. I concur with this view.

31. See Arberry's translation, vol. 2 (London: George Allen & Unwin, 1955).

32. The identification, בני אלהים = angels, is already current in some Jewish circles before Christ. See, e.g., *1 Enoch* 6–9. Cf. P. Alexander. "The Targumim and Early Exegesis of 'Sons of God' in Genesis 6," *JJS* 23 (1972) 60–71.

33. See *Pirqe de Rabbi Eliezer* 22, a tradition attributed to R. Meir. Cf. also *Targum Ps.-Jonathan*, Gen. 6:2.

34. *Zohar* I, 55a. "Azael" and "Shamhazai" are singled out among the angels in *Targum Ps.-Jonathan*, Gen. 6:4. Cf. also *1 Enoch* 6–9 and the role of Semjāzā and Azāzēl. But Na'amah does not occur here in the Targum, or in *1 Enoch*. According to *Zohar* III, 76b Na'amah seduced the "sons of God" (Gen. 6:2) and produced various kinds of demons. Na'amah herself, according to the same passage, appears to men in their dreams in order to excite their lust.

35. Cf. Ginzberg, *Legends* 5.147f. On the demon Ashmedai/Asmodeus, who first appears in Jewish literature in the Book of Tobit (3:8), see L. Ginzberg, "Asmodeus or Ashmedai" in the *Jewish Encyclopedia*. The Iranian derivation, disputed by Ginzberg, seems to me to be most plausible: *aešma-daeva*. On the activity of Aešma see, e.g., *Bundahišn* 28.15–17 (in SBE 5).

36. See now chap. 6 in this book.

One other (possible) occurrence of the name "Naʿamah" is relevant here. The opening passage of pseudo-Philo's *Biblical Antiquities* reads as follows (1.1):

> Initium mundi. Adam genuit tres filios et unam filiam, Cain, Noaba, Abel et Seth. ("Beginning of the world. Adam begat three sons and one daughter, Cain, Noaba, Abel, and Seth.")[37]

"Noaba," the daughter of Adam, strikes us as vaguely familiar. Compare the *Chronicles of Jerahmeel* 26.1:

> Adam begat three sons and three daughters, Cain and his twin wife Qalmana, Abel and his twin wife Deborah, and Seth and his twin wife Noba.[38]

Seth's twin wife "Noba" in the latter passage is manifestly the same as "Noaba" in the former. This is not surprising, for it is well known that the *Chronicles of Jerahmeel* is dependent upon the Latin text of pseudo-Philo.[39] Bearing in mind that pseudo-Philo's Latin reflects a translation process in two stages, from Hebrew into Greek into Latin,[40] we should not be surprised at the corrupt state of personal names in the Latin text. I suggest that "Noaba" is a textual corruption of Greek Νόεμα (= Hebrew נעמה, Naʿamah.)[41]

Thus, from pseudo-Philo and *Jerahmeel*, we can ascertain that in certain Jewish circles of a comparatively early period the twin sister of *Seth* (not Cain) was given the name "Naʿamah."

Now we perceive, too, that the Gnostic myths and legends surrounding Norea/Horaia are, in fact, the same as, or similar to, stories circulating in Jewish aggadah concerning Naʿamah: She is the (wife-) sister of Seth, or the wife of Noah. She attempts to thwart the construction of the ark. She attracts the amorous attentions of angelic beings. We have only to remark that, in fact, Naʿamah and Norea are one and the same!

37. G. Kisch, ed., *Pseudo-Philo's Liber Antiquitatum Biblicarum* (Notre Dame: University of Notre Dame Press, 1949).
38. M. Gaster, trans., *The Chronicles of Jerahmeel* (London 1899; repr. with a Prolegomenon by H. Schwarzbaum, New York: Ktav, 1971). Cf. Josephus *Ant.* 1.52: Adam and Eve had two male children and also daughters; cf. 1.68 for Seth and many others.
39. Cf. Schwarzbaum's remarks on pp. xxxivff. of his Prolegomenon.
40. For an ingenious attempt to reconstruct the Hebrew original of a portion of Ps.-Philo by a process of retroversion, Latin-Greek-Hebrew, see J. Strugnell, "More Psalms of David," *CBQ* 27 (1965) 207–16.
41. Νόεμα is the LXX form of Naʿamah in Gen. 4:22. Cf. also Josephus *Ant.* 1.65: πατὴρ δὲ θυγατρὸς γενόμενος ὁ Λάμεχος Νοεμᾶς ὄνομα (LCL ed.). Robert Kraft of the University of Pennsylvania has indicated to me in private conversation that the *M* and the *B* appear very similar in many Greek manuscripts of wide-ranging date, thus confirming the probability of a corruption from Νοεμα (or, hypothetically, Νοαμα) to Νοαβα.

The original form of the name Norea is, in fact, Hōraia (ʿΩραία, "pleas-
ant, lovely"), the equivalent in Greek of the Hebrew name Naʿamah
(נעמה).

The change of name, from Naʿamah to Noraia, can be accounted for
by suggesting that aggadoth dealing with Naʿamah were appropriated
in Greek-speaking Jewish communities, and in the process the name
was translated into Greek, a phenomenon found even in the LXX (e.g.,
Eve-Ζωή, Gen. 3:20).[42] And, in fact, ʿΩραία is attested as a personal
name amongst the Jews of the Diaspora.[43]

The form "Norea" is easily explained. The ai-e interchange, of course,
is standard as a result of the similarity in pronunciation (from at least the
early Roman period) of ε and the diphthong αι. "Noraia/Norea" is a
mixed form: the initial letter of Naʿamah (נ) has become attached to the
name (H)ōraia. An exact analogy is found in the Armenian Gospel of Seth
edited by Preuschen. Noah's wife's name is given as Noʿemzara, a
transparent combination of Naʿamah and ʾEmzara (Jub. 4:33).[44] The
Mandaean form "Nuraita" (נוראיתא) is simply the stem Norai with the
feminine emphatic ending -ta. The other variations require no comment.

Thus we have discovered in Jewish aggadah[45] the origins of the figure
of Norea, an important personage in Gnostic mythology. Of course, it is
evident that the Gnostics did not simply take over without change the
various aggadoth relating to Naʿamah/Horaia. Gnostic hermeneutics
effect a rather dramatic change in the character of the figure, a change in
valence and, even more important, an escalation of her symbolic significance.

A final look at two of the Nag Hammadi texts with which we began
will illustrate this point. First, The Hypostasis of the Archons:

The villains of this piece are Samael and his fellow archons. "Samael"
is the Creator-God of the Old Testament, who thinks he is the only
God.[46] The Gnostic author of this document has thus equated YHWH,

---

42. It is also possible that legends arising in the Diaspora concerning Horaia were
appropriated in Semitic-speaking areas and amalgamated with those of Naʿamah.
Horaia, or the mixed form Norea, also has come to be used in Semitic-speaking circles.
Cf. Mandaean Nuraita.

43. See CIJ ed. Frey. No. 1509, an epitaph of a girl named ʿΩραία. Cf. "Prosopo-
graphy of the Jews in Egypt," Appendix II in Tcherikover-Fuks, ed., CPJ III.

44. See Preuschen, "Gnostischen Adamschriften," 199. The o in Noʿemzara reflects
the influence of the Hebrew ayin in Naʾamah; cf. Νοεμα in LXX. A less likely explanation for the initial N- in Norea and the No- in Noʾemzara is to suggest influence from
the name "Noah," the husband of Norea-Noʾemzara.

45. Other examples of the appropriation of Jewish aggadah by the Gnostics are
found in other essays in this book.

46. CG II: 86,27–87,4.

who declares his sole Deity in Isa. 43:11–13; 44:6; 45:6, with the devil of Jewish aggadah, Samael.[47] The wicked creator-archons are bent upon holding under their demonic power Adam and Eve and their progeny, whereas a higher power intervenes in order to bring gnosis and freedom to humans. The narrative of the first four chapters of Genesis is presented according to this perspective.

When after the birth of Seth Eve brings forth a daughter, Norea, it is said that she is to be a "help for future generations of men" (91,34–92,2). The text moves quickly to focus upon Genesis 6, and the resolve of the wicked archons to destroy humanity with a flood. In the destruction of Noah's ark Norea functions as a representative of the heavenly world, whereas Noah is ignorantly obedient to the lower powers of creation. Thus a personage who is regarded as wicked in Jewish aggadah for her machinations against Noah is regarded oppositely in the Gnostic version of the myth. And when the archons attempt to seduce Norea, as they had also attempted to seduce her mother Eve,[48] they are unsuccessful. And we perceive that the story of wicked Naʿamah and the angels of Genesis 6 is similarly reversed.[49] In her cry for help to the heavenly world, answered by the appearance of the Illuminator Eleleth (92,33–93,32), Norea becomes a poignant symbol of Gnostic humankind, fettered to the material world, but presented with the possibility of salvation. To Norea this salvation comes in the form of the revelation that Eleleth gives her (94,2–end), a revelation that ends with a glorious Trishagion!

Norea thus functions in this text as both a feminine heavenly power, a redeemer figure working in behalf of Gnostic humanity against the machinations of the world rulers, and a symbol of spiritual humanity in need of redemption. She is, in other words, a Gnostic "Sophia" figure.[50]

The "Sophia" symbolism attached to Norea is even clearer in another text from Nag Hammadi, *The Thought of Norea* (CG IX,2).[51] In this text Norea cries out[52] to the exalted beings of the heavenly Pleroma.

47. On Samael see chap. 3, above, p. 48.
. 48. See 89.21ff. and 92.19ff. In the story of the adventures of the archons with Eve the archons spend the night with a substitute, her "shadow." We have here a "docetic" interpretation of the seduction of Eve by the archons. Cf. the Jewish tradition of the seduction of Eve by Samael, referred to above.
49. But cf. Noria and the archons according to Epiphanius, *Haer.* 26.1.9, a myth acted out in the Gnostic ritual, if we can believe Epiphanius's testimony, *Haer.* 26.4.1–5.6. Cf. what Augustine reports of the Manichaeans, *Haer.* 46.2.
50. On the Gnostic Sophia see esp. MacRae, "Gnostic Sophia Myth."
51. See now Pearson, *Codices IX and X*, 87–99.
52. Cf. *Hyp. Arch.* (CG II,4) 92,32–93,2.

They [heard], (and) they received her into her place forever. They gave it to her in the Father of Nous, Adamas, as well as the voice of the Holy Ones, in order that she might rest in the ineffable Epinoia, in order that ⟨she⟩ might inherit the first mind which ⟨she⟩ had received, and that ⟨she⟩ might rest in the divine Autogenes . . . There will be days when she will [behold] the Pleroma, and she will not be in deficiency, for she has the four holy helpers[53] who intercede on her behalf with the Father of All, Adamas.[54]

This passage reminds us very much of the Valentinian Gnostic myth of the redemption of Sophia and her restoration to the Pleroma.[55]

Thus Norea, a naughty girl in Jewish legend, has become for the Gnostics a moving symbol of acosmic redemption.

53. A reference to the four "Illuminators" ($\phi\omega\sigma\tau\hat{\eta}\rho\epsilon\varsigma$) who appear frequently in Gnostic texts (e.g., *The Apocryphon of John*, CG II,1: 7,30–8,21), one of whom is Eleleth, who appears to Norea as "helper" and revealer in *Hyp. Arch.* (cf. 93,8, et passim).
54. The translation here has been brought into conformity with that published in *Nag Hammadi Library*.
55. See, e.g., Irenaeus *Haer.* 1.2.5–6 on the restoration of the "Upper Sophia," and 1.7.1 on the eventual restoration of the "Lower Sophia," Achamoth.

6

Cain and the Cainites

Ever since Jean Doresse, in his famous book, *The Secret Books of the Egyptian Gnostics*,[1] propounded the view that the Nag Hammadi codices constituted a "library" of a Sethian Gnostic sect, much attention has been given to the problem of delineating "Sethianism" as a Gnostic system,[2] and establishing the historical contours of the "Sethian" Gnostic sect. The Yale congress on Gnosticism held in 1978 was devoted chiefly to Valentinian Gnosticism on the one hand,[3] and Sethian Gnosticism on the other.[4] Now a reaction has set in. Gilles Quispel, for one, has complained that "the danger is very real that everything not Valentinian in the field of Gnosticism will be called 'Sethian.'" Quispel implies that I have fallen into this trap, too, with some of my recent publications.[5]

Thus chastised, I turn my attention to another of the Gnostic sects cataloged by the church fathers, namely, that named for Seth's infamous brother, the "Cainites." Anticipating our conclusion, I can state at the outset that the Cainites will turn out to be more elusive than the Sethians.[6] At stake will be the credibility of the heresiologists, at least as to what they say about this particular group of heretics. We consider this evidence first.

1. *Secret Books* (New York: Viking, 1960) esp. 249–309.
2. See esp. H.-M. Schenke, "Das sethianische System"; and idem, "Gnostic Sethianism."
3. Layton, *Rediscovery*, vol. 1.
4. Ibid., vol. 2.
5. G. Quispel, "Judaism, Judaic Christianity and Gnosis," in A. H. B. Logan and A. J. M. Wedderburn, eds., *The New Testament and Gnosis: Essays in Honour of Robert McL. Wilson* (Edinburgh: T. & T. Clark, 1983) 46–68, esp. 60.
6. Cf. F. Wisse, "Stalking Those Elusive Sethians," in Layton, *Rediscovery* 2.563–76. Wisse is among those who are especially skeptical about the heresiological reports on the Sethians.

THE CAINITES

The earliest extant references to a heretical sect of "Cainites," named as such, are found in Clement of Alexandria, Tertullian, Hippolytus, and Origen. Clement speaks of the various heresies, some of which are named after founders (Valentinus, Marcion, Basilides), some for places or nations (Peratics, Phrygians), some for life-style (Encratites), some from particular dogmas (Docetae, Haematites), some from suppositions or from individuals they have honored—here he names "Cainists" and "Ophians"—and some from nefarious practices and enormities, as those of the Simonians called "Entychites" (Clement *Strom.* 8.17).[7]

Tertullian, in his *Prescriptio* against heretics (chap. 33), discusses certain heresies present already in apostolic times, including that of the Nicolaitans (Rev. 2:6, 15; cf. Acts 6:5). He goes on to say, "There are even now another sort of Nicolaitans: theirs is called the Caian heresy." The designation "Caian" can probably be read as "Cainite," for in *De Baptismo* (chap. 1), Tertullian refers to "a viper of the Cainite heresy, lately conversant in these quarters, who has carried away a great number with her most venomous doctrines, making it her aim to destroy baptism."[8]

Hippolytus, at the end of Book 8 of his *Refutatio*, says:

> Even though there have been denominated certain other heresies—I mean those of the Cainites, Ophites, or Noachites;[9] and of others of this description—I have not deemed it requisite to explain the things said or done by these, lest on this account they may consider themselves somebody, or deserving of consideration.[10]

I shall treat Hippolytus's lost *Syntagma* presently.

Origen, in his *Contra Celsum* (3.13), allows that Celsus has gained some knowledge of "the so-called Ophians and Cainites and whatever other similar doctrine has sprung up which has completely abandoned Jesus."[11]

Note that Clement, Hippolytus, and Origen associate the "Cainites" clearly with the "Ophite" (or "Ophian") group. Tertullian associates them

---

7. See A. Hilgenfeld's discussion of that passage in *Die Ketzergeschichte des Urchristentums* (repr. of 1884 ed.; Darmstadt: Wissenschaftliche Buchgesellschaft, 1963) 43.

8. Translations in ANF 3.

9. "Noachites" is probably based on Hebrew *nāḥāš*, "serpent," and would thus be equivalent to the Naassenes treated by him in Book 5, although Hippolytus is probably unaware of this.

10. Translation in ANF 5.

11. Translation in Foerster, *Gnosis* 1.99.

with the Nicolaitans. No description of their doctrines, however, is given in these references.

Irenaeus, in his *Adversus haereses*, is the first to describe a system (if one can call it that) that only later came to be identified as "Cainite." Right after his lengthy treatment in 1.30 of a group of "other" Gnostics (i.e., other than those described in 1.29)[12] he says,

> Others again say that Cain was from the superior power, and confess Esau and (the tribe of) Korah and the Sodomites and all such as their kinsmen. They were attacked by the creator, but none of them suffered any ill. For Sophia snatched away from them to herself what belonged to her. This Judas the traitor knew very well, and he alone of all the apostles recognized the truth and accomplished the mystery of the betrayal, by which everything earthly and heavenly is dissolved, as they say. And they produce a fabrication, which they call the Gospel of Judas.
>
> I have also collected writings of theirs, in which they urge the destruction of the works of Hystera (the womb); Hystera is the name they give to the fabricator of heaven and earth. And they say they cannot be saved in any other way, except they pass through all things, just as Carpocrates also said. And at every sinful and base action an angel is present and instils in him who ventures the deed audacity and impurity; what it is in act they say in the angel's name: "O thou angel, I make use of thy work; O thou power, I accomplish thy deed." And this is the perfect "knowledge," to enter without fear into such operations, which it is not lawful even to name.[13]

Note that Irenaeus does not pin a label on these "others." The system that he describes is labeled for the first time as "Cainite" by the author of Pseudo-Tertullian, *Against All Heresies*, a work presumably based on Hippolytus's lost *Syntagma*,[14] and also clearly dependent upon Irenaeus:[15]

> There also broke out another heresy, called that of the Cainites. For they glorify Cain, as if conceived by some potent power which operated in him. Abel was conceived and brought forth by an inferior power, and was

12. The system described in 1.30 is not identified by Irenaeus, but was later labeled as that of the "Sethians, whom some call Ophians or Ophites" (Theodoret, *Haer.* 1.14). In Foerster's translation it is presented as "Ophite" (*Gnosis* 1.84–93). The so-called Barbelognostic system described by Irenaeus in *Adversus haereses* 1.29 is essentially parallel to a part of *The Apocryphon of John*. See the translation and discussion in Foerster, *Gnosis* 1.100–105.

13. Irenaeus *Haer.* 1.31.1–2; translation in Foerster, *Gnosis* 1.41–2.

14. See R. M. Grant, *Second Century Christianity* (London: SPCK, 1957) 123–24.

15. It is impossible to determine what Irenaeus's sources were. A. Hilgenfeld and others claimed a role for the lost *Syntagma* of Justin Martyr (*Ketzergeschichte*, 21–30). For criticisms of this view see F. Wisse, "The Nag Hammadi Library and the Heresiologists," *VC* 25 (1971) 205–23.

therefore found to be inferior. Those who assert this also defend Judas the traitor, saying that he was admirable and great because of the benefits which he is claimed to have brought to the human race. For some of them think that thanksgiving should be rendered to Judas for this reason. "For Judas," they say, "observing that Christ wanted to subvert the truth, betrayed him that the truth might not be overthrown." Others dispute this, saying: "Since the powers of this world did not wish Christ to suffer, that salvation might not be provided for the human race through his death, he betrayed Christ out of concern for the salvation of mankind, in order that the salvation which was being hindered by the powers opposed to the suffering of Christ might not be prevented altogether, and therefore through the passion of Christ the salvation of the human race might not be delayed."[16]

Epiphanius has a rather lengthy description of the Cainites (*Haer.* 38), based essentially on Irenaeus and Pseudo-Tertullian,[17] to which he has added a few extra vituperations. A few details are added to the discussion. Epiphanius quotes from a book of theirs that he claims to have obtained (he does not say how):

"This," he says, "is the angel who blinded Moses, and these are the angels, who hid those about Korah and Dathan and Abiram (Num. 16) and brought them to another place."[18]

Epiphanius goes on to claim that these people use a book that is also in use among the "Gnostics" (the "Borborites" of *Haer.* 26) entitled "The Ascent of Paul." This book is allegedly based upon Paul's experience described in 2 Cor. 12:4.[19]

It used to be assumed, and sometimes still is, that the church fathers' description of the various Gnostic and other heretical sects could be taken at face value. With regard to the Cainites, for example, most handbooks and encyclopedia articles simply present the patristic testimonies without much discussion.[20] Moritz Friedländer went even further, arguing that the Christian Cainites described by the church fathers originated out of a pre-Christian Jewish sect of Cainites in Alexandria,

16. Ps.-Tertullian, *Haer.* 2; translation in Foerster, *Gnosis* 1.42. Cf. also Grant, *Second Century Christianity*, 129–30.

17. Note that Epiphanius's description of the Cainites is immediately preceded by a discussion of the "Ophites" (*Haer.* 37), just as in Ps.-Tertullian and Irenaeus (in the latter without that label).

18. *Haer.* 38.2.4; translation in Foerster, Gnosis 1.43.

19. *Haer.* 38.2.5; Foerster, *Gnosis* 1.43. Later patristic discussions of the Cainites (Filastrius, Theodoret, Ps.-Augustine) add nothing to the picture already obtained.

20. See the listings in the standard bibliography by Scholer, *Nag Hammadi Bibliography*. The recent work by Kurt Rudolph is a case in point; see Rudolph, *Gnosis*, 17, 256f., 309.

who, he says, were well known to Philo of Alexandria.[21] More recently, especially since the discovery and gradual publication of the Nag Hammadi texts, some scholars have tended to be much more critical of the patristic accounts.[22] Before going any further, then, it will be useful to look at what is said about Cain in the primary texts now available to us.

CAIN IN GNOSTIC SOURCES

We turn first to *The Apocryphon of John* (NHC II,1; III,1; IV,1; BG,2). Ialdabaoth, the "First Archon" brought forth by Sophia, begets in turn twelve "authorities" or "powers," by which we should understand the Zodiacal constellations.[23] These are enumerated, and "Cain" is the name given to the sixth one ("Abel" to the seventh) in the version in NHC II (10,34); in the BG version Cain is the seventh, and Abel the sixth (40,13). Other names occurring in these lists include variations on names associated with the biblical Creator, such as "Adonaios" and "Sabaoth." A parallel to this passage occurs in *The Gospel of the Egyptians* (NHC III,2: 58,15; Cain is in sixth place).

These passages should be compared to another one later in *The Apocryphon of John*, where we read of the banishment of Adam and Eve from paradise, and its aftermath:

> And the chief archon saw the virgin who stood by Adam, and that the luminous Epinoia of life had appeared in her . . . And the chief archon seduced her and he begot in her two sons; the first and the second (are) Eloim and Yave. Eloim has a bear-face, and Yave has a cat-face. The one is righteous but the other is unrighteous. Yave he set over the fire and the wind, and Eloim he set over the water and the earth. And these he called with the names Cain and Abel with a view to deceive. (NHC II 24,8–25)[24]

These passages reflect a very interesting speculative exegesis of Gen. 4:1–2. This is a problematic biblical passage, especially in the Hebrew version, for one can read Eve's statement, "I have gotten a man with the

---

21. *Der vorchristliche jüdische Gnosticismus* (Göttingen: Vandenhoeck & Ruprecht, 1898) esp. 19–23. Cf. chap. 1 in this book.

22. E.g., Wisse, "The Nag Hammadi Library" (cit. n. 15). Cf. also H.-M. Schenke, "Die Relevanz der Kirchenväter für die Erschliessung der Nag-Hammadi-Texte," in *Das Korpus der griechischen christlichen Schriftsteller* (TU 120; Berlin: Akademie-Verlag, 1977) 209–18.

23. See A. J. Welburn, "The Identity of the Archons in the 'Apocryphon Johannis,'" *VC* 32 (1978) 241–54.

24. Translations of Nag Hammadi texts here and elsewhere in this article are taken from *Nag Hammadi Library*. Cf. the parallel text in BG 62,3–63,2 (translation in Foerster, *Gnosis* 1.117).

help of the Lord" (RSV) in a different way: "I have gotten a man, namely Yahweh" *(qānîtî 'iš 'et YHWH)*. The identification of Cain with "Yahweh" is therefore easily deduced from the text; Abel then becomes "Elohim" by analogy. The notion of "righteousness" and "unrighteousness" associated with these divine names recalls Jewish speculation on the meaning of these names, such as is found in Philo of Alexandria.[25]

In addition, a rabbinic aggadah to the effect that Cain was born of a liaison between Eve and the devil (or "angel of death"), frequently called "Sammael," is also to be seen in the background of our Gnostic texts. The Gnostics demonize the Creator God, and even call him by the name of the devil, "Sammael."[26] The Jewish aggadah in question is exemplified by *Targum Ps-Jonathan*, Gen. 4:1–2:

> And Adam was aware that his wife had conceived from Sammael the angel, and she became pregnant and bore Cain, and he was like those on high, not like those below; and she said, "I have acquired a man, the angel of the Lord." And she went on to bear from Adam, her husband, his (Cain's) twin sister and Abel.[27]

The Jewish tradition regarding the birth of Cain from Sammael is also reflected in *The Hypostasis of the Archons* (NHC II,4), in the context of a midrash on Genesis 4. The births of Cain and Abel are recounted as follows:

> Now afterwards (i.e., after the expulsion of Adam and Eve from paradise) she (Eve) bore Cain, their son; and Cain cultivated the land. Thereupon he (Adam) knew his wife; again becoming pregnant, she bore Abel.[28]

Cain is called "their son," meaning the son of the "Authorities," that is, the Creator and his wicked henchmen. The text goes on to narrate the

---

25. E.g., *Spec. Leg.* 1.307: κύριος = the "punitive power" of God; θεός = the "beneficent power." On this kind of speculation and its bearing on the Gnostic material see (with reference to *Quaest. in Exod.* 2.68 and *Eugnostos* [NHC III 77,9–13 and V 6,14–22]) R. van den Broek, "Jewish and Platonic Speculations in Early Alexandrian Theology: Eugnostos, Philo, Valentinus, and Origen," in Pearson-Goehring, *Roots of Egyptian Christianity*, 190–203, esp. 193–95.

26. So, e.g., *Ap. John* NHC II 11,15–18, where three names are given to him: Samael, Ialdabaoth, and Saklas. On these names see chap. 3, above, pp. 47–48. On the confusion between Yahweh and Satan suggested in biblical and extrabiblical materials see R. M. Grant, "Yahweh as Satan," in *Gnosticism and Early Christianity* (New York: Harper & Row, 1966), 56–61.

27. Translation by J. Bowker, *The Targums and Rabbinic Literature* (Cambridge: Cambridge University Press, 1967) 132. Note the addition of "the angel of" to Eve's statement. The targumist wishes to derail any possible identification of Cain with Yahweh. On this and related texts see now Stroumsa, *Another Seed*, 47–49.

28. II 91,11–14, parentheses added. Cf. Irenaeus *Haer.* 1.30.7: the archontic angels beget other angels from Eve.

murder of Abel by his brother, Cain, and the subsequent birth of Seth, whose sister Norea is the real hero of the story.[29]

The treatise *On the Origin of the World* (NHC II,5), which at places shows a number of parallels to *The Hypostasis of the Archons*, does not contain a reference to Cain by name. He is there, nevertheless. In a very interesting passage the text narrates the birth of "the Instructor," who later enlightens the fleshly Adam and Eve in paradise. The following section is particularly pertinent:

> The Hebrews call (his mother) Eve of Life, namely, the female instructor of life. Her offspring is the creature that is lord. Afterwards, the authorities called it "Beast," so that it might lead stray their modelled creatures. The interpretation of "the beast" is "the instructor." For it was found to be the wisest of all beings. Now, Eve is the first virgin, the one who without a husband bore her first offspring. It is she who served as her own midwife. For this reason she is said to have said . . . (113,32–114,7)

There follows a hymnic passage in which Eve expresses herself in several "I am" sayings, ending with the strophe,

> I am the process of becoming.
> Yet I have borne a man as lord. (114,14–15)

The first part of this passage reflects a sophisticated interpretation of Genesis 2—3 involving an Aramaic wordplay: "serpent" (*ḥewyā'*)—"Eve" (*ḥawwāh*)—"life" (verbal form *ḥᵃyā'*, Heb. *ḥāyāh*)—"instruct" (*ḥᵃwā'*). This wordplay is continued in the text of *On the Origin of the World* (II 118,25ff.) in the paradise story, and is found in a parallel passage in *The Hypostasis of the Archons* (II 89ff.). It is also reflected in the midrash on the serpent of Genesis 2—3 embedded in *The Testimony of Truth* (NHC IX 45,23–49,7). These wordplays derive from Jewish aggadah.[30]

What is of special interest here, though, is that the child of the "instructor of life" is called both "lord" ($\mathbf{x}\mathbf{o}\epsilon\mathbf{i}c = \kappa\acute{\upsilon}\rho\iota o\varsigma$ = "Yahweh" of Gen. 4:2, commented on above) and the "beast" ($\theta\acute{\eta}\rho\iota o\nu$) who is "wiser than all of them" (Gen. 3:1). Thus the implication is clear: Cain and the serpent are identified. That the reference here is to Cain (left unnamed as such) is confirmed in the last sentence of Eve's hymn: "I have borne a man as lord," almost word-for-word what Eve says in Gen. 4:2 at the birth of Cain.

While the texts we have treated previously all imply a negative evalu-

---

29. On Norea, see chap. 5 in this book.
30. See, e.g., *Gen. Rab.* 20.11. See chap. 3, above, pp. 43–46, and Pearson, *Codices IX and X*, 158–69.

ation of Cain (whether as murderer of his brother, child of Ialdabaoth-
Samael, starry constellation, "Yahweh," or whatever), here for the first
time we encounter a piece of Gnostic exegesis that evaluates Cain positively. He is the lordly revealer of gnosis, sharing this honor with the
biblical serpent. It should also be noted that all of this is based on the
text of Genesis and Jewish aggadah related thereto.

The connections among Eve, as a kind of Sophia figure, the serpent,
and Cain, so far as I have been able to determine, are to be found
elsewhere only in Hippolytus's description of the "Peratae," a group
Hippolytus describes right after his discussion of the Naassenes, an
"Ophitic" group. Here is the relevant passage:

> The universal serpent is the wise word of Eve. This is the mystery of Eden,
> this is the river (that flowed) out of Eden, this is the sign that was marked
> on Cain so that anyone who found him should not kill him. This is (that)
> Cain whose sacrifice was not accepted by the god of this world.[31]

On the other hand, Irenaeus's description of a type of Gnosis often
referred to as "Ophite" (*Haer.* 1.30) presents a mixed account, positing a
good serpent (from the Gnostic point of view) = Sophia, who taught
men *gnosis* (1.30.15; cf. 30.7), and an "objectionable serpent," son of
Ialdabaoth, who corrupted Cain so that he killed his brother Abel and
thus introduced envy and death into the world (1.30.9). Cain is thus
evaluated negatively here, as is usually the case in Gnostic sources.

To round off our treatment, let me touch briefly on those texts from
Nag Hammadi in which Cain appears, uniformly in a negative light:

The Apocalypse of Adam (NHC V,5): Adam, in his revelation to his son
Seth, says: "Then the god, who created us, created a son from himself
[and] Eve [your mother]" (V 66,25–28). Here Cain, unnamed, is the issue
of the lower Creator God (Ialdabaoth-Samael in *Ap. John*) and Eve,
according to the exegesis of Gen. 4:1 we have already discussed.

This same thing is reflected in the Valentinian *Gospel of Philip* (NHC
II,3), where Cain also remains unnamed:

> First adultery came into being, afterward murder. And he (i.e., Cain) was
> begotten in adultery, for he was the child of the serpent (= Samael = the
> devil). So he became a murderer, just like his father, and he killed his
> brother (Abel). (II 61,5–10)

This passage also reflects the common Jewish and Christian belief that
the Genesis serpent is really the devil.[32]

---

31. *Ref.* 5.16.8–9; translation in Foerster, *Gnosis* 1.288–89.
32. See chap. 3, above, p. 43 for the relevant texts.

Finally, a brief mention is made of Cain in *A Valentinian Exposition* (NHC XI,2): "Cain [killed] Abel his brother, for [the Demiurge] breathed into [them] his spirit" (XI 38,24–27).

While texts from patristic sources pertaining to Cain could be brought in to supplement the Nag Hammadi evidence,[33] they add nothing of significance to the picture already obtained. With the exception of the passage in the treatise *On the Origin of the World* (together with the parallel in Hippolytus), all of our extant Gnostic sources look at Cain in a negative light. And in the exception cited, the association between Cain and the serpent is underscored. Their positive valuation is based on a Gnostic reading of the text of Genesis, together with an appropriation and reinterpretation of certain Jewish exegetical traditions. None of this material, however, can be related to any specific "Cainite" sect, nor to the system described by Irenaeus and subsequently labeled as "Cainite" (discussed above). Whence, then, comes Irenaeus's detailed description? And how did the notion of a Cainite sect come about?

The key to answering the latter question is to recall that "Cainite" is a general designation for "heretic" in both early Judaism and early Christianity.

"THE WAY OF CAIN"

"Woe to them! For they walk in the way of Cain . . ." (Jude 11, RSV). Thus does the author of the New Testament epistle of Jude denounce his theological opponents (who may very well have been Gnostics of some sort).[34] Jude is clearly utilizing a topos in early Judaism, adopted readily by anti-heretical Christian writers, according to which Cain is the prototype and progenitor of theological heresy.[35] A good Palestinian example of this topos is found in the Palestinian targumim, wherein Gen. 4:8 is expanded by presenting Cain and Abel in a theological dispute. Cain's argument goes like this:

> I know that the world was not created by love, that it is not governed according to the fruit of good deeds and that there is favor in judgment. There is no Judgment, there is no Judge, there is no other world, there is no gift of reward for the just and no punishment for the wicked.[36]

33. Valentinians: Iren. *Haer.* 1.7.5 = *Exc. Theod.* 54. "Sethians": Hipp. *Ref.* 5.20.2. Cf. also Epiphanius on the "Archontics" and the "Sethians" (*Haer.* 39 and 40).
34. Cf. F. Wisse, "The Epistle of Jude in the History of Heresiology," in M. Krause, ed., *Essays on the Nag Hammadi Texts in Honour of Alexander Böhlig* (NHS 3; Leiden: E. J. Brill, 1972) 133–43.
35. On what follows cf. chap. 1, above, pp. 23–25.
36. Translation in S. E. Isenberg, "An Anti-Sadduccee Polemic in the Palestinian

Such a statement could be pressed into duty to cover a multitude of heresies, including Gnostic ones, even if it originally seems to have been directed against the Sadduccees.[37]

Cain also functions as a prototype of heresy in Alexandrian Judaism, at least as represented by Philo. Philo, too, expands Gen. 4:8 into a theological dispute between Cain and Abel (*Quod Det.* 1–2, 32–48). Cain is represented as attempting to gain the mastery over Abel with recourse to "plausible sophistries," and represents a "self-loving" doctrine, devoid of virtue. Such a picture of Cain is reinforced in other Philonic texts. An especially noteworthy example is Philo's statement that "impious and atheistic opinion" is to be assigned to the "race" ($\gamma \acute{\epsilon} \nu o s$) of Cain (*Post.* 42). In contrast, Seth (not Abel) is the "seed of human virtue"; Philo is commenting here on Gen. 4:25 ($\acute{\epsilon} \tau \epsilon \rho o \nu \ \sigma \pi \acute{\epsilon} \rho \mu a$, *Post.* 171–73). All virtuous people are, by implication, the "race of Seth."[38]

Thus, by the first century at the latest, there is an established Jewish tradition that assigns to Cain the role of the first heretic. All subsequent heretics are of his (spiritual) lineage, his *genos*. They are, in other words, "Cainites."

To this same complex of tradition belongs the designation "First-born of Satan," discussed in an important article by Nils Dahl.[39] The term is used as a designation for "heretic" both in Palestinian Jewish texts ($b^e k\hat{u}r$ $\dot{s}\bar{a}t\bar{a}n$) and in patristic Greek texts: $\pi \rho \omega \tau \acute{o} \tau o \kappa o s \ \tau o \hat{v} \ \sigma a \tau a \nu \hat{a}$. The latter first appears in Polycarp (*Phil.* 7.1):

> Whosoever perverts the oracles of the Lord for his own lusts, and says that there is neither resurrection nor judgment,—this man is the first-born of Satan.[40]

The allusion to Cain is transparent, particularly when we recall the Palestinian Targum to Gen. 4:8. Of course, the notion that Cain is a child of the devil is based on the Palestinian Jewish interpretation of Gen. 4:1 (discussed above).

Polycarp is later reported by Irenaeus (*Haer.* 3.3.4) to have said to

Targum Traditions," *HTR* 63 (1970) 433–44, 437. Cf. also M. McNamara, *The New Testament and the Palestinian Targum to the Pentateuch* (Analecta Biblica 27; Rome: Pontifical Biblical Institute, 1966) 156–60.

37. So Isenberg, "Anti-Sadduccee Polemic in the Palestinian Targum Traditions."

38. This passage is relevant to the origins of the various ("Sethian") Gnostic ideas regarding the role of Seth and his "seed" or "race" in Gnostic *Heilsgeschichte*. Cf. chap. 4, above, pp. 68–71; also Stroumsa, *Another Seed*, esp. 71–134.

39. "Der Erstgeborene Satans und der Vater des Teufels (Polyk. 7:1 und Joh 8:44)," in *Apophoreta: Festschrift für Ernst Haenchen* (Berlin: Töpelmann, 1964) 70–84.

40. Translation in C. C. Richardson, *Early Christian Fathers* (LCC 1; New York: Macmillan, 1970) 134.

Marcion, "I recognize you, the first-born of Satan." One could deduce from this that Polycarp, and other ecclesiastics like him, could easily refer to Marcionites or Gnostics as "Cainites."

CONCLUSIONS

We can conclude from all of this that there never was any such thing as a particular Cainite sect of Gnostics. There were, instead, varieties of Gnostic heretics who could, from time to time, be labeled generically as Cainites, according to a well-established topos in early Judaism and Christianity. The Cainite system of *gnosis*, delineated as such by the heresiologists, is nothing but a figment of their imagination, an artificial construct.

We still have to answer the other question: How did the heresiologists construct the "Cainite" system? Let us take another look at the passage from Irenaeus quoted earlier (*Haer.* 1.31). It seems evident to me, first of all, that this passage is a continuation of the discussion of the "other" Gnostics beginning at 1.30.1. This material appears to be based on a catalog of heretical opinions to which Irenaeus has gained access (probably not that of Justin's lost *Syntagma*).[41] The passage, 1.30.1–14, presents a reasonably coherent set of beliefs, and shows some contact with mythologoumena found in *The Apocryphon of John, The Hypostasis of the Archons, The Gospel of the Egyptians*, and other Nag Hammadi texts of this group. But then Irenaeus muddies the waters with an appendix of miscellanea, mixed with vituperative comment. I quote 1.30.15:

> Such are their teachings; from which like the Lernaean Hydra a many-headed monster has been bred from the school of Valentinus. For some say that Sophia herself became the Snake, that she therefore was hostile to the creator of Adam, and put knowledge in men, and for this reason the serpent was said to be wisest of all (Gen. 3:1). But also because of the position of our intestines through which nutriment flows, and because they have such a shape, they point to the hidden parent with the shape of a snake which is within us.[42]

To this passage belongs the so-called "Cainite" material already cited, beginning with: "Others again say that Cain was from the superior power."

An analysis of this so-called "Cainite" material from 1.31.1–2 shows the following main points:

41. Cf. Wisse, "The Nag Hammadi Library and the Heresiologists," 214–15.
42. Translation in Foerster, *Gnosis* 1.93.

1. Cain is from a superior power.

2. These heretics "confess" other Old Testament villains, such as Esau, Korah, and the Sodomites.

3. Sophia snatched away her own, protecting them from the Creator.

4. Judas the traitor is one of their heroes, and they have a "Gospel of Judas."

5. They have writings urging the destruction of the "Womb" (Hystera).

6. Salvation, "perfect gnosis," comes by experiencing all manner of sin.

7. This libertine behavior is acted out in ritual, which includes the invocation of certain angels.

This hodgepodge of beliefs and practice—each item has parallels in other Gnostic and/or patristic sources[43]—can hardly have constituted any coherent sectarian system. It is a heresiological construct, growing "like Topsy" with fanciful elaborations added by Pseudo-Tertullian and Epiphanius.

In sum, while the figure of Cain attracted considerable speculative attention (for the most part, negative) among various Gnostics, who based their speculations on scripture exegesis and already existing Jew-

43. (1) Cain as a superior power: *On the Origin of the World* and the "Peratae" (discussed above). (2) Old Testament villains as heroes: Marcionites, according to Iren. *Haer.* 1.27.3. (3) Sophia's protection of the (Gnostic) victims of the Creator: Iren. *Haer.* 1.30.9 ("Ophites," see discussion above). The rescue of Gnostics from various catastrophes is a prominent motif in some of the Nag Hammadi texts, especially *The Apocalypse of Adam*. (4) Judas as hero: The glorification of Judas might be expected of those who heroize the Old Testament villains (point 2); but this is a piece of polemic, and probably has no real basis in any Gnostic belief. On the other hand, the expansion in Ps.-Tertullian has Judas acting out of concern for an almost Pauline doctrine of the *theologia crucis* (cf. 1 Cor. 2:8), hardly a Gnostic theologoumenon! As for the "Gospel of Judas," H.-C. Puech (in *NTA* 1.313–14) does his best to make sense out of Irenaeus's report, even speculating on the supposed gospel's contents. More probably, this is a faulty reference to *The Gospel of* (Judas) *Thomas* (NHC II,2), used by various Gnostic (and other) groups. Similarly, the "Ascent of Paul" referred to by Epiphanius may be *The Apocalypse of Paul* (NHC V,2). (5) The "Womb": This notion is probably spun out of an exegesis of the Hebrew text of Exodus 34:6 (reading *raḥôm*, "compassion," as *raḥam*, "womb"), as suggested by R. M. Grant (*Gnosticism and Early Christianity*, 60). Gnostic parallels to this "womb" speculation include the Nicolaitans of Epiphanius (*Haer.* 25.5.1–3) and *The Paraphrase of Shem* (NHC VII,1, passim). (6) Salvation by libertine behavior: the Carpocratians, according to Iren. *Haer* 1.25.1–6 (cf. Clem. Alex. *Strom.* 3.2). This is a topos in heresiology; Irenaeus even claims to know of Valentinian libertines (*Haer.* 1.6.3f. (7) Ritual invocations of angels: This could be spun out of what was said of the Carpocratians and their angelology. Ritual invocations of angels are attributed to other "libertine" Gnostic groups, such as those described by Epiphanius (*Haer.* 25–26; cf. *Pistis Sophia* 3, chap. 147). Cf. also the "ascent" invocations of the "Ophites" described by Origen (*Contra Celsum* 6.24–38).

ish aggadah, there never was a "Cainite" Gnostic sect. "Cainite" was originally a convenient designation for "heretic," and only gradually came to be used as a designation for a particular group of Gnostics, a group that existed only in the minds of the heresiologists. The case of the Cainites here explored shows how necessary it is to take the patristic accounts of heretical groups, beliefs, and practices with a liberal dash of the proverbial salt.

7

The Figure of Melchizedek in Gnostic Literature

The writer of the epistle to the Hebrews refers to Jesus Christ as having been "designated by God a high priest after the order of Melchizedek" (Heb. 5:11), quoting (and reinterpreting) Ps. 110:4, "You are a priest for ever, after the order of Melchizedek." The author goes on to say that this is something "hard to explain" ($\delta\upsilon\sigma\epsilon\rho\mu\eta\nu\epsilon\upsilon\tau\sigma$, Heb. 5:6), belonging to the category of "solid food" fit for "mature" people (5:14). When he finally gets around to elaborating his teaching on Jesus as "a high priest for ever after the order of Melchizedek" (6:20), he begins with a series of comments on "this Melchizedek" (7:1ff.) depicted in the story of Abraham's encounter with Melchizedek in Gen. 14:17–20.

It is evident from the way in which the author of Hebrews argues that, already by his time, the mysterious figure of the ancient priest-king Melchizedek, mentioned in the Bible only in Psalm 110 and Genesis 14, had become a subject of considerable speculation among scripture interpreters in Jewish circles. Speculation on Melchizedek developed also in Christian circles, and since Hebrews is the only New Testament book in which the figure of Melchizedek is treated, it was inevitable that this epistle would play an important role in the further elaboration of the Melchizedek gestalt in Christian literature. The figure of Melchizedek did not escape the notice of Gnostic writers, either, although it is somewhat surprising that the mysterious Melchizedek does not play a larger role in Gnostic literature than he actually does.[1]

---

1. See the important monographs on the Melchizedek traditions by Fred L. Horton, Jr., *The Melchizedek Tradition: A Critical Examination of the Sources to the Fifth Century A.D. and in the Epistle to the Hebrews* (SNTSMS 30; Cambridge: Cambridge University Press, 1976); and Claudio Gianotto, *Melchisedek e la sua tipologia: Tradizioni giudiche, cristiane e gnostiche (sec II a.C.–sec. III d.C.)* (SRivB 12; Paideia, 1984). The Gnostic evidence is surveyed by both Horton (131–51) and Gianotto (187–235).

In what follows, I take up for discussion the available Gnostic texts that treat Melchizedek, and see if we can discern any lines of development in the interpretation of that figure. We shall take special note of the role played or not played by the epistle to the Hebrews in Gnostic interpretations of Melchizedek. The texts are as follows, arranged in the chronological and typological order that appears to me most plausible:[2] the Gnostic fragment from Bala'izah, the tractate *Melchizedek* from Nag Hammadi Codex IX, the so-called *Second Book of Jeu* in the Bruce Codex, *Pistis Sophia*, Book 4, in the Askew Codex, and *Pistis Sophia*, Books 1–3.

THE BALA'IZAH FRAGMENT[3]

Among the numerous Coptic manuscripts found in Flinders Petrie's excavations at the ruins of the Monastery of Apa Apollo at Deir al-Bala'izah (ca. twenty km. south of Asyut, ancient Lycopolis)[4] are a parchment leaf and fragments of two others containing an apocryphal text of obvious Gnostic character. The text in question consists of a dialogue between Jesus and his disciple John[5] wherein Jesus gives allegorical interpretations of key figures and events from the opening chapters of Genesis.

The first fragment, which is very damaged, seems to deal with the Paradise-Fall narrative, with the words "body," "naked," and "sinless" partially preserved. Also inscribed on this fragment at the right margin are the letters]ελεκ, which Kahle takes as the final letters of the name Melchizedek.[6] Of course, "Melchizedek" is not the only proper name that ends in -ελεκ (part of Hebrew ṣedeq, which is used in a number of biblical names),[7] and it is not immediately evident what role Melchizedek might play in this particular context.

In any case, Melchizedek does occur later in the text, right after

2. This is also the chronological order posited by Gianotto in his treatment. Horton omits NHC IX,1 (it had not yet been published when Horton wrote his book); otherwise his order is the same.

3. The fragment was first published by Walter E. Crum: "Coptic Anecdota. I. A Gnostic Fragment," *JTS* 44 (1943) 176–79. It was reedited and published by Paul E. Kahle as text no. 52 in his edition of the Coptic texts from Deir El-Bala'izah: *Bala'izah: Coptic Texts from Deir El-Bala'izah in Upper Egypt* (London: Oxford University Press, 1954) 1.473–77. Cf. Horton, *Melchizedek Tradition*, 131–35; and Gianotto, *Melchisedek*, 187–93.

4. For a discussion of the excavations, the manuscript finds, and the Monastery of Apa Apollo, see Kahle, *Bala'izah* 1.1–21.

5. Cf. *The Apocryphon of John*.

6. *Bala'izah*, 1.477.

7. E.g., Adonizedek (Josh. 10:1, 3); Jehozadak (Hag. 1:1; Zech. 6:11). Cf. 'Ιωσεδεκ (Jer. 23:8 LXX).

discussion of "Paradise and the five trees,"[8] Cain and Abel, and Noah and his ark. The immediate context is a question put by John to the Savior:

Moreover, [I wish] to [ask that you] explain
[to me] about Mel[chizedek]. Is it not
said [about him], "he is [without]
[father, without] mother,
his generation not being [mentioned],
not having a beginning of days, nor
end of life, resembling the Son [of]
God, being a priest forever?" Moreover
it is said about him, that . . .[9]

Unfortunately, the text breaks off at this point. What is said of Melchizedek in John's question is a word-for-word quotation of Heb. 7:3. It is probable that the lost material included another scripture reference about Melchizedek, perhaps again from Hebrews. What we have here is a (scriptural) statement about Melchizedek that the Savior is asked to interpret (ἑρμηνεύειν). What the Savior might have said in response is anyone's guess; presumably it would have been an "intellectual symbol" (σύμβολον νοερόν) consisting of Gnostic lore, such as is found previously in the text concerning Adam and the five trees in Paradise.[10]

Although the Melchizedek material occurs in the context of a "Gnostic midrash"[11] on principal figures of Genesis, the Genesis passage in which Melchizedek occurs (14:17–20) is evidently not cited. The occurrence of Melchizedek right after the interpretation of Noah and the ark may reflect knowledge of Jewish lore identifying Melchizedek with Shem.[12] However that may be, Heb. 7:3 is the key text,[13] the starting point for the allegorical interpretation that we now lack.

NHC IX:1: *MELCHIZEDEK*[14]

This very fragmentary text can properly be called an "Apocalypse of Melchizedek," in which "the priest of God Most High" (12,10–11; cf.

8. For one role played by Melchizedek in Paradise see 2 *Enoch* 72:1, 9: The archangel Michael places the child Melchizedek, son of Nir, in the paradise of Eden, where he is preserved during the Flood. See also below, p. 121.

9. Lines 78–90, au. trans.

10. Line 32 and context.

11. This is a designation aptly applied to this text by Horton (*Melchizedek Tradition*, 134).

12. So Horton (ibid.). Cf. H.-M. Schenke, "Die jüdische Melchisedek-Gestalt als Thema der Gnosis," in Tröger, *Altes Testament*, 111–36, esp. 132, 135.

13. Heb. 7:3 appears in another Bala'izah fragment, with a variant Coptic text. See Kahle, *Bala'izah* 1.360 (Text 17, frg. f).

14. For the critical edition, with introduction, translation, and notes, see Pearson,

Gen. 14:18b) receives and transmits revelations mediated by heavenly emissaries. The core of the revealed material has to do with the future career of the Savior, Jesus Christ, and the ultimate identification of Jesus Christ with the recipient of the revelation, Melchizedek himself.[15] There can hardly be any doubt that the identification posited in this text of Jesus Christ with Melchizedek is based on an interpretation of Heb. 7:3, especially the phrase ἀφωμοιωμένος δὲ τῷ υἱῷ τοῦ θεοῦ. In the Hebrews passage itself, as Horton has shown,[16] the eternal Son of God is regarded as the priestly type, and Melchizedek is the antitype. The tractate *Melchizedek* takes this doctrine one step further in positing Jesus Christ as the heavenly counterpart to, or alter ego of, the earthly priest, Melchizedek. This is expressed in various ways in the text. At 15,12 the term "image" is used (as restored in a lacuna): Melchizedek is "[the image of], the true High-priest of God Most High." At 26,2ff. the victorious risen Savior is referred to directly as "Melchizedek, great [High-Priest] of God [Most High]." A very close analogy to this doctrine is found in Jewish speculation on the figure of Enoch, especially in the "Similitudes" of *1 Enoch* (chaps. 37–71). In that text Enoch is ultimately identified with the preexistent heavenly "Son of Man" (71:14).[17]

But there is more to be said. While the epistle to the Hebrews constitutes a formative influence in *Melchizedek*,[18] there are clearly other influences bearing upon this text's interpretation of the figure of Melchizedek. These influences derive directly from Jewish apocalyptic speculation, unmediated by Christianity. They can be seen in the depiction of Melchizedek in an eschatological role as a heavenly "holy warrior," a heavenly "high-priest" who does battle with demonic forces. The key passage is found on p. 26 of the manuscript, which, however, is severely damaged. In this passage, part of the visionary revelation making up the third major section of the text (18,11–27,10), a victorious Melchizedek is greeted by heavenly figures, presumably angels:

Codices IX and X, 19–85. For a German translation, see Schenke, "Jüdische Melchisedek Gestalt," 115–23. For an Italian translation, see Gianotto, *Melchisedek*, 194–207; see also Gianotto's discussion, 207–16.

15. See my discussion in *Codices IX and X*, 28–31.
16. Horton, *Melchizedek Tradition*, 160–64.
17. Cf. my discussion in *Codices IX and X*, 29.
18. See the table of allusions to Hebrews in *Melch.* in *Codices IX and X*, 35. It should be noted that my views on the influence of Hebrews in *Melch.* have changed, as a result of further study of the text, from the position taken in an earlier study. See "The Figure of Melchizedek in the First Tractate of the Unpublished Coptic Gnostic Codex IX from Nag Hammadi," in C. Bleeker, G. Widengren, and E. Sharpe, eds., *Proceedings of the XIIth International Congress of the International Association for the History of Religions* (SHR 31; Leiden: E. J. Brill, 1975) 200–208, esp. 207 n. 29.

greeted [me]
they said to me, "Be [strong, O Melchizedek,]
great [High-priest]
of God, [Most High, for the archons],
who [are] your [enemies],
made war; you have [prevailed over them, and]
they did not prevail over you, [and you]
endured, and [you]
destroyed your enemies [. . .[19]

In this passage, fragmentary though it is, we have Melchizedek portrayed as a heavenly figure, a "High-priest" (ἀρχιερεύς) who emerges
victorious from an eschatological battle with supernatural forces, here
called "archons."

Precisely this combination of roles and attributes ascribed to Melchizedek in our text is found in an apocalyptic Jewish text from Qumran,
usually dated to the first century B.C.E.: 11QMelch.[20] In that text, unfortunately preserved only in fragments, Melchizedek is a heavenly warrior-
priest identical to the archangel Michael. He appears in the tenth and
final jubilee of world history (ii,7) to rescue his "children" (ii,5), the "men
of the lot of Melchizedek" (ii,8), from Belial and his fellow spirits (ii,13,
etc.). This triumph is described as a high-priestly act of "expiation" (ii,8).
Melchizedek is thus implicitly regarded as a "high priest," although he is
not explicitly referred to as such in the extant fragments. The high-
priestly role of both Melchizedek and Michael is, in any case, amply
attested in other Jewish literature.[21]

It should also be noted that the identification of Melchizedek with
Michael in 11QMelch accounts for Melchizedek's role in that text as a
heavenly "holy warrior," for the archangel Michael is the angelic pro-
tector par excellence of God's people in Jewish tradition. As such, he is
the "Commander-in-Chief" (ἀρχιστρατηγός) of the heavenly hosts of
God (Dan. 8:11 LXX).[22] As a matter of fact, the term ἀρχιστρατηγός
occurs in Melchizedek as a title for Jesus Christ (18,5), and we recall that
Melchizedek is ultimately identified with Jesus Christ in that text.

19. 26,1–9; Pearson, Codices IX and X, 83.
20. This fragmentary text was first published by A. S. van der Woude, "Melchisedek
als himmlische Erlösergestalt in den neugefundenen eschatologischen Midraschim aus
Qumran Höhle XI," Oudtestamentische Studiën 15 (1965) 354–73. For this essay I have
used the more recent edition, with commentary and translation, by Paul J. Kobelski:
Melchizedek and Melchireša' (CBQMS 10; Washington, D.C.: Catholic Biblical Association, 1981). On the date of this text (first century B.C.E.) see Kobelski, Melchizedek, 3;
and G. Vermes, The Dead Sea Scrolls in English (3d rev. ed.; London: Penguin, 1987) 300.
21. E.g., Tg. Neof. Gen 14:8, b. Ḥag. 12b, etc.; cf. Kobelski, Melchizedek, 64–66.
22. Cf. my discussion in Codices IX and X, 33.

So far, in our discussion of the figure of Melchizedek in the Nag Hammadi tractate, we have dealt only with Christian and Jewish traditions. But for all of its Jewish and Christian features, *Melchizedek* is a Gnostic text. It is usually associated, together with other Gnostic tractates, with "Sethian" Gnosticism.[23] Just how the Gnostic features in *Melchizedek* are to be accounted for, in terms of the compositional history of the text, is debatable. I tend to look upon the Gnostic features as secondary,[24] but *Melchizedek* has also been taken as an example of "eine vollständig christianisierte sethianische Gnosis."[25] It is clear that the specifically Gnostic features of the text tend to be concentrated in certain sections of it. Moreover, these sections are stamped with a liturgical character and provide evidence for actual Sethian Gnostic cultic practice.[26]

The first of these passages (5,24–6,14) is a prayer, involving invocations of such divine beings in the Gnostic version of the heavenly world as Barbelo, the four "Luminaries" (Harmozel, Oroiael, Daveithe, Eleleth), and others.[27] The prayer is introduced with a self-revelation of an angelic informant, presumably Gamaliel:[28]

> . . . I am]
> [Gamaliel] who was [sent]
> to [   ] the congregation of [the]
> [children] of Seth, who are above
> [thousands of] thousands and [myriads]
> of myriads [of the] aeons.[29]

The reference here to "the children of Seth" is especially interesting in view of the occurrence of the phrase, "race of the High-priest," later in the text (6,17), and the reference in a prayer attributed to Melchizedek to "those that are mine" (16,8). Implied here, evidently, is an identification of Melchizedek with Seth.[30]

The main liturgical section features a prayer offered up by Melchize-

---

23. See esp. Schenke, "Das sethianische System"; and idem, "Gnostic Sethianism."
24. Pearson, *Codices IX and X*, 38.
25. Berliner Arbeitskreis, "Texte von Nag Hammadi," 67; Schenke, "Jüdische Melchisedek-Gestalt" (cit. n. 12), 123–25
26. See the important contribution by J.-M. Sevrin, *Le dossier baptismal séthien: Études sur la sacramentaire gnostique* (BCNH, "Études" 2; Québec: Université Laval, 1986) 222–46.
27. See Sevrin's discussion of this prayer, *Dossier baptismal*, 243–45.
28. "Gamaliel" is a conjectural restoration here. The text has only [. . . . .] ιηλ. See Pearson, *Codices IX and X*, 50, where other occurrences of Gamaliel in Sethian Gnostic literature are noted. Cf. also n. 57, below.
29. 5,17–22; translation in Pearson, *Codices IX and X*, 51.
30. Cf. chap. 4, above, p. 78; Sevrin, *Dossier baptismal*, 226f., 245.

dek (14,15–16,6), an oblation in which Melchizedek offers himself and his own to God (16,7–11), and a baptism that also includes the pronunciation of his name (16,11–16).[31] This is followed by an invocational hymn (16,16–18,7), in which most of the names found in the earlier invocations (5,24–6,14) are repeated.[32]

In these cultic sections Melchizedek (=Seth=Jesus Christ), as Highpriest, also functions as the paradigm for the Gnostic initiate in his reception of the sacrament of baptism. We have here a convergence of (originally non-Christian) Sethian Gnostic ritual with Christian sacramental theology and practice.[33] The tractate as a whole is generically an apocalypse infused with Christian traditions and a strong influence from the epistle to the Hebrews, together with pre-Christian Jewish speculations on the figure of Melchizedek.[34]

THE SECOND BOOK OF JEU[35]

Melchizedek appears in two passages in *2 Jeu*. As in the Nag Hammadi tractate, Melchizedek is a heavenly being who is involved in baptismal ritual. He has a double name: "Zorokothora Melchizedek," a name that reflects Egyptian magical traditions.[36] In the larger context, Jesus is revealing to his disciples the mysteries of the Treasury of Light. He describes how the soul is borne out of the body by the "receivers" of the Treasury of Light, released from its sins, and brought into the world of light (chaps. 42–44). Jesus then invites them to receive three baptisms, of fire, of water, and of the Spirit. The disciples are sent to Galilee for the necessary ritual paraphernalia: two pitchers of wine, vine-branches,

31. See Sevrin's discussion, *Dossier baptismal*, 229–38.
32. Ibid., 238–42.
33. See Sevrin's conclusions, ibid., 245f.
34. *Melch.* also shows some features in common with the teachings of the "Melchizedekian" sect described by Epiphanius (*Haer.* 55). See Pearson, *Codices IX and X*, 38–40, for discussion. I omit any discussion of the Melchizedekians in this essay on the grounds that they were not a Gnostic group. On the Melchizedekians and their treatment of the figure of Melchizedek see esp. H. Stork, *Die sogennanten Melchisedekianer, mit Untersuchungen ihrer Quellen auf Gedankengehalt und dogmengeschichtliche Entwicklung* (Leipzig: A. Deichert, 1928); Horton, *Melchizedek Tradition*, 90–101; and Gianotto, *Melchisedek*, 237–54.
35. For text and translation see Carl Schmidt, ed., and Violet MacDermot, trans., *The Books of Jeu and the Untitled Text in the Bruce Codex* (NHS 13; Leiden: E. J. Brill, 1978) 98–141. For discussion see Horton, *Melchizedek Tradition*, 145–47; Gianotto, *Melchisedek*, 220–23.
36. The name occurs as one in a string of *nomina barbara* in PGM XIII.958, in a "holy name" attributed to the scribe of "King Ochos." Cf. H.-D. Betz, ed., *The Greek Magical Papyri in Translation* (Chicago: University of Chicago, 1986), 193.

herbs, and oils. The disciples are clothed in linen. Holding various ritual objects in their hands, they are placed before an altar of "offering," on which are placed linens, a cup of wine, bread, and olive branches. Sealing his disciples with a secret seal, Jesus offers up a prayer, consisting of *verba barbara* (glossolalia) with "amens," and calls upon the Father to send the fifteen "helpers" (παραστάται) and Zorokothora to come and administer the baptism:

> May they come and baptize my disciples in the water of life of the seven virgins of the Light[37] and forgive their sins, and purify their iniquities and number them among the inheritance of the Kingdom of the Light. If now you have heard me and have had mercy on my disciples, and if they are reckoned in the inheritance of the Kingdom of the Light, and if you have forgiven their sins and erased their iniquities, may a sign happen. And may Zorokothora[38] come and bring forth the water of the baptism of life in one of these pitchers of wine.[39]

The wine in one of the pitchers at the altar then changes into water. The disciples are baptized by Jesus, given some of the "offering" (προσ-φορά), that is, bread and wine, and sealed with a special seal.

Jesus then has the disciples prepare for reception of the baptism of fire by bringing vine branches. Offering up incense, and preparing the altar and the disciples, Jesus offers up a prayer somewhat similar to the previous one, in which the Father is asked that Melchizedek again bring the baptismal water:

> . . . And purify them all and cause Zorokothora Melchizedek[40] to come in secret and bring the water of the baptism of fire of the Virgin of the Light, the judge.[41] . . . Hear me, my Father, father of all fatherhoods, infinite Light, as I call upon imperishable names which are in the Treasury[42] of the

37. The word "Light," here and elsewhere in the text, is rendered with the sign ⊙, an Egyptian hieroglyph used as a determinative in words for light. Cf. Horton, *Melchizedek Tradition*, 146.
38. The full name, "Zorokothora Melchizedek," occurs in the next prayer, and in *Pistis Sophia* (see below).
39. 2 *Jeu*, chap. 45, Schmidt-MacDermot, 107–8. Translations of 2 *Jeu* in this chapter are essentially those of MacDermot, but modified.
40. The name Melchizedek is abbreviated in the text: ⲘⲈⲀⲬ, i.e. ⲘⲈⲀⲬ(ⲓⲤⲈⲀⲈⲔ).
41. Wilhelm Bousset relates this figure (who also occurs in *Pistis Sophia*) to the "Virgin of Light" in Manichaean mythology, and suggests that the common features in the two systems can be accounted for by positing a source used in common by both. See *Hauptprobleme der Gnosis* (Göttingen: Vandenhoeck & Ruprecht, 1907) 349. Cf. also the figure of Norea, and my discussion in chap. 5, 87–88. For a possible Iranian background see C. Colpe, "Daēnā, Lichtjungfrau, Zweite Gestalt: Verbindungen und Unterschiede zwischen zarathustrischer und manichäischer Selbst-Anschauung," in van den Broek-Vermaseren, *Studies in Gnosticism*, 58–77.
42. The word "Treasury," here and elsewhere in this text, is rendered with the sign ▣,

Light. Cause Zorokothora to come and bring the water of the baptism of
fire of the Virgin of the Light, that I may baptize my disciples in it. . . .[43]

As Jesus prays, the requested sign occurs, and Jesus baptizes his
disciples. A third baptismal ceremony then ensues, that of the Holy
Spirit (chap. 47), but Melchizedek plays no role in that baptism.

These are the only passages in the *Books of Jeu* featuring Melchizedek.
It is clear that in *1-2 Jeu* as a whole Melchizedek is not the main
character. Even so, he is portrayed as a heavenly being whose "bringing
forth" of the water of baptism is crucial to its performance. Melchizedek's role is, in effect, that of a heavenly priest. It should be noted that
despite the Christian coloring of the text and the influence of the New
Testament (especially the gospels) at some places in it, the epistle to the
Hebrews plays absolutely no role in *1-2 Jeu*, either in the Melchizedek
sections or in the rest of the text.[44] There is probably an allusion to
Genesis 14 in the Melchizedek material (but not to Ps. 110:4), specifically
in the prayers where Melchizedek is to "bring forth" the baptismal water.
This seems to be an allusion to Gen. 14:18, where Melchizedek "brings
out" bread and wine.[45] The presence of bread and wine on the altar in *2
Jeu* could be taken as another allusion to Gen. 14:18, although the use of
the term προσφορά in this context indicates influence from Christian
liturgical traditions.[46]

How do we account for Melchizedek's heavenly status in *2 Jeu*, and
his connection with baptism? This is obviously part of the tradition
about Melchizedek known to the author of *2 Jeu*. I would suggest the
possibility that the author of that work was aware of the Nag Hammadi
tractate, *Melchizedek*.

PISTIS SOPHIA, BOOK 4[47]

Pistis Sophia is the name given to all of the disparate Gnostic materials
found in the Askew Codex, now organized into four books. Book 4 is

---

a modified form of the Egyptian hieroglyph ⵣⵣ, "treasury." Cf. Horton, *Melchizedek
Tradition*, 146; and the sign list in Alan Gardiner, *Egyptian Grammar* (3d ed.; London:
Oxford University Press, 1957) 493.

43. *2 Jeu*, chap. 46, Schmidt-MacDermot, 110–11.

44. See index in Schmidt-MacDermot, 339ff.

45. So also Horton, *Melchizedek Tradition;* and Gianotto, *Melchisedek*, 222.

46. Cf. Irenaeus *Haer.* 4.18.1; and other references in *PGL* 1184b.

47. For text and translation of *Pistis Sophia* see Carl Schmidt, ed., and Violet
MacDermot, trans., *Pistis Sophia* (NHS 9; Leiden: E. J. Brill, 1978). This work is referred
to by page numbers in nn. 48–68. For discussion of book 4 see Horton, *Melchizedek
Tradition*, 142–45; Gianotto, *Melchisedek*, 223–26.

usually regarded as the oldest, in terms of its content. What is said of Melchizedek in Book 4, as compared to the other books, bears out that judgment.

Melchizedek is featured in a revelation discourse given by Jesus, who is also called "Aberamentho,"[48] in response to a question posed by Mary as to how souls are taken "by theft." Jesus reveals that his father, Jeu, is "the provider ($\pi\rho\text{o}\nu\text{o}\eta\tau\text{ó}s$) of all the archons and the gods and the powers which have come into existence in the matter of the light of the Treasury." The other light figure is Melchizedek:

> And Zorokothora[49] Melchizedek is the envoy ($\pi\rho\epsilon\sigma\beta\epsilon\acute{\upsilon}\tau\eta s$) of all the lights which are purified in the archons, as he takes them into the Treasury of the Light. These two alone are the great lights. Their rank is this, that they come down to the archons and they (the lights) are purified in them. And Zorokothora Melchizedek takes what is purified of the lights which have been purified in the archons and takes them to the Treasury of the Light. When the cipher ($\psi\hat{\eta}\phi$os) and the time of their rank comes and causes them to come down to the archons, they oppress and afflict them, taking away what is purified from the archons. But at the time that they cease from oppression and affliction, they withdraw to the places of the Treasury of the Light. It happens when they reach the places of the Midst, Zorokothora Melchizedek bears the lights and takes them into the gate of those of the Midst, and takes them to the Treasury of the Light; and Jeu also withdraws himself to the places of those of the right, until the time of the cipher that they should go forth again.[50]

Jesus goes on to tell how the angry archons then snatch up by theft such souls as they can, and consume them in smoke and fire.

Later on in the text, in a discussion of Hekate's role in the punishment of souls, Melchizedek appears again:

> And after these things, when the sphere turns, the Little Sabaoth, the Good, he of the Midst, who is called Zeus in the world, comes; and he comes to the eighth aeon of the sphere which is called Scorpion (Scorpio). And Bubastis, who is called Aphrodite, comes, and she comes to the second aeon of the sphere which is called the Bull (Taurus). Then the veils which are between those of the left and those of the right are drawn aside. And Zorokothora Melchizedek looks forth from the height, and the world with

48. Cf. also *Pistis Sophia* 4, chaps. 136, 141 (pp. 354, 367). "Aberamentho" is a magical name (part of a palindrome) that occurs rather frequently in the Greek magical papyri from Egypt. For discussion and references see M. Tardieu, "Aberamentho," in van den Broek-Vermaseren, *Studies in Gnosticism*, 412–18.

49. Cf. n. 36, above. At the beginning of book 4 (chap. 136), "Zorokothora" is one of the *nomina barbara* in a prayer offered by Jesus (p. 353).

50. *Pistis Sophia* 4, chap. 139 (pp. 360–61). Translations of passages from *Pistis Sophia* in this chapter are essentially those of MacDermot, but modified.

the mountains moves, and the archons are in agitation. And he looks upon all the places of Hekate, and her places are dissolved and destroyed. And all the souls which are in her punishments are carried off and returned once more to the sphere, because they were perishing in the fire of her punishments.[51]

Leaving aside any discussion of the involved syncretism in these passages, featuring Greek and Egyptian mythology and astrological lore, we can see that the role of Melchizedek in *Pistis Sophia* 4 is a very important one. As a light being, Melchizedek divests the cosmic archons of the light (human souls) and brings them into the "Treasury of Light" (what in other Gnostic systems would be called the "Pleroma"). In the case of those souls captured by Hekate and other forces of darkness, he causes them to be reborn in the world and thus given another chance at reaching the Treasury of Light. Melchizedek is, therefore, a heavenly savior par excellence, whose rank in the divine hierarchy is clearly superior to that of Jesus Christ himself, though perhaps inferior to that of Jeu.

It is probable that the author of *Pistis Sophia* 4 was familiar with 2 *Jeu*—note the use of the double name Zorokothora Melchizedek—but the ritual baptismal role played by Melchizedek in 2 *Jeu* is replaced by much loftier duties in the process of purifying human souls for entry into the light; indeed, he himself transports them to the light. There is no trace left in this material of the biblical texts from which the figure of Melchizedek derives.

PISTIS SOPHIA, BOOKS 1–3[52]

The role played by Melchizedek in book 4 is further elaborated in books 1–3, though we note the absence now of his other name, Zorokothora. His first appearance is in a revelation discourse given by Jesus in response to a question posed by Mary regarding the destiny of souls:

Before I preached to all the archons of the aeons, and all the archons of the Heimarmene and the sphere, they were all bound with their bonds, in their spheres and their seals, according to the manner in which Jeu, the Overseer ($\epsilon\pi\iota\sigma\kappa\sigma\sigma\sigma$) of the Light, had bound them from the beginning. And each one of them was continuing in his rank and each one was proceeding according to his course, according to the manner in which Jeu, the Overseer of the Light, had settled it. And when the time should come of the number

---

51. *Pistis Sophia* 4, chap. 140 (pp. 363–64).
52. Cf. Horton, *Melchizedek Tradition*, 135–42, Gianotto, *Melchisedek*, 226–33.

($\dot{\alpha}\rho\iota\theta\mu\dot{o}s$) of Melchizedek,[53] the great Receiver of Light, he would come to the midst of the aeons, and to all the archons which were bound in the sphere and in the Heimarmene, and he would take away what was purified of the light from all the archons of the aeons, and from all the archons of the Heimarmene, and from those of the sphere, for he would take away that which was agitating them. And he would move the hastener that is over them and make their cycles turn quickly; and he (Melchizedek) would take away their power which is in them, and the breath of their mouths, and the tears of their eyes, and the sweat of their bodies. And Melchizedek, the Receiver of the Light, would purify those powers, he would carry their light to the Treasury of the Light . . .[54]

Whereas in *Pistis Sophia* 4 Melchizedek was referred to as an "envoy" ($\pi\rho\epsilon\sigma\beta\epsilon\acute{\upsilon}\tau\eta s$), in this passage he is called the "Receiver" ($\pi\alpha\rho\alpha\lambda\acute{\eta}\mu\pi\tau\omega\rho$) of the Light. The role played by Melchizedek is basically the same: he is assigned to transfer particles of light to the Treasury of Light. He is called "the great Receiver of Light" here and elsewhere in *Pistis Sophia* 1–3,[55] that is, the Receiver par excellence; for, in fact, he has subordinates to do the actual work for him, "the receivers of Melchizedek,"[56] who transfer the light from other "receivers," such as those of the moon and the sun. For example, in the material following the passage just quoted (from chap. 25), it is said that "the receivers of the sun would prepare to lay it (the 'light-power') down until they should give it to the receivers of Melchizedek, the purifier (ⲡⲣⲉϥⲥⲱⲧⲃ̄) of the light." Melchizedek, therefore, does not need to descend into the cosmos himself for the purpose of transferring the light into the Treasury of Light.

The epithet "receiver" used here of Melchizedek and his helpers has an interesting history in Gnostic tradition. In *The Apocryphon of John* (BG 66,1–7) reference is made to unnamed "receivers" ($\pi\alpha\rho\alpha\lambda\acute{\eta}\mu\pi\tau\omega\rho$) who remove saved souls from the world into eternal life. In *The Gospel of the Egyptians* there are four such receivers: "the receivers ($\pi\alpha\rho\alpha\lambda\acute{\eta}\mu\pi\tau\omega\rho$) of the great race, the incorruptible mighty men of the great Seth, the ministers of the four lights, the great Gamaliel, the great Gabriel, the great Samblo, and the great Abrasax."[57] Indeed, *2 Jeu* (chap. 42) refers to

53. Cf. the expression "the cipher ($\psi\hat{\eta}\phi os$) and the time of their rank" in *Pistis Sophia* 4, chap. 139 (quoted above).
54. *Pistis Sophia* 1, chap. 25 (pp. 34–35).
55. See *Pistis Sophia* 1, chap. 26 (p. 36); chap. 86 (p. 194); 3, chaps. 112, 131 (pp. 291, 334). The Greek words $\pi\alpha\rho\alpha\lambda\acute{\eta}\mu\pi\tau\omega\rho$ and $\pi\alpha\rho\alpha\lambda\acute{\eta}\mu\pi\tau\eta s$ are used interchangeably in these passages.
56. See *Pistis Sophia* 1, chap. 25 (p. 35); 3, chaps. 112, 128, 129 (pp. 291, 324, 326).
57. NHC III 64,22–65,1 (*Nag Hammadi Library* translation). These four beings are "ministers of the four lights," i.e., of the "illuminators" of the "Sethian" Gnostic system. Cf. *Gos. Eg.* III 52,19–53,1, where Gamaliel is connected with Harmozel, Gabriel with

(unnamed) "receivers (παραλήμπτης) of the Treasury of the Light" who perform the task of bringing souls to the light. As we have seen, Melchizedek's role in that text is another one altogether. Now, in *Pistis Sophia*, he has taken over the role of "Receiver."

The activity of Melchizedek and his fellow "receivers" is referred to several times in *Pistis Sophia* 1–3.[58] One passage, in book 3, deserves special mention, for reference is made in the context to "baptisms" and "sealing." Jesus is revealing to Mary the fate of a good soul who has not listened to the "counterfeit spirit."[59] The receivers take it to the Virgin of the Light,[60] who, together with seven other virgins of the light, examines the soul. After the Virgin of the Light seals the soul,

> the receivers of the light baptize that soul and give it the spiritual chrism. And each one of the virgins of the light seals it with their seals. And also the receivers of the light give it into the hands of the Great Sabaoth, the Good, who is above the gate of life in the place of the right, who is called Father.[61] And that soul gives him the glory of his songs of praise and his seals and his defences. And Sabaoth the Great and Good seals it with his seals. And the soul gives its knowledge and the glory of the songs of praise and the seals to the whole place of those of the right. They all seal it with their seals, and Melchizedek, the great Receiver of the Light, who is in the place of those of the right, seals that soul. And the receivers of Melchizedek seal that soul and they take it to the Treasury of the Light; and it gives glory and honor and the eulogy of songs of praise, and all the seals of all the places of the light. And all those of the place of the Treasury of the Light seal it with their seals, and it goes to the place of the inheritance.[62]

In this passage, Melchizedek functions again as the main Receiver of the Light, who gives the soul its final "seal." It is to be noted, however, that he plays no role in the baptism of the soul; in this text "sealing" and "baptism" refer to different cultic acts.

One additional passage in *Pistis Sophia* calls for comment here, the association of Melchizedek with "the five trees" in the Treasury of Light.

Oroiael, Samlo (sic) with Davithe, and Abrasax with Eleleth. Gamaliel is featured in *Melch.*, as noted above (p. 113; n. 28).

58. Cf. nn. 55, 56, above.

59. Chap. 112 (p. 286). On the "counterfeit spirit" (ἀντίμιμον πνεῦμα) see esp. *Ap. John* BG 71,4–75,10. Cf. Pearson, "Jewish Gnostic' Literature," 25, and A. Böhlig, "Zum Antimimon Pneuma in den koptisch-gnostischen Texten," in Böhlig, *Mysterion und Wahrheit: Gesammelte Beiträge zur spätantiken Religionsgeschichte* (Leiden: E. J. Brill, 1968) 162–74.

60. On the "Virgin of the Light" see above, and n. 41.

61. Cf. the figure of Sabaoth in *Hyp. Arch* (NHC II,4) 95,13–96,3 and *Orig. World* (NHC II,5) 103,32–106,19, on which see Francis T. Fallon, *The Enthronement of Sabaoth: Jewish Elements in Gnostic Creation Myths* (NHS 10; Leiden: E. J. Brill, 1978).

62. Chap. 112 (p. 291).

The context (in book 2) is a discussion of several light entities, "seven amens," "seven voices," "twelve saviors of the Treasury," and so on, including "five trees." A different divine being is associated with each of the five trees:

> For Jeu and the guardian (φύλαξ) of the place of those of the right, and Melchizedek the great Receiver of the Light, and the two great leaders (ἡγούμενος) have come forth from the purified and very pure light of the first tree, as far as the fifth tree.[63]

Each of these divine beings is said to have "come forth" from one of the trees, Melchizedek from the fifth. Here we recall the five trees in Paradise referred to in the Bala'izah fragment,[64] and the saying of Jesus in the *Gospel of Thomas:*

> For you have five trees in Paradise which do not move in summer or in winter, and their leaves do not fall. The one who knows them will not taste death.[65]

To conclude our discussion of *Pistis Sophia*, we may observe that the role of Melchizedek is a highly developed one, building upon several layers of Gnostic tradition rather unsystematically thrown together. We can also say of all four books of *Pistis Sophia* that there is no trace left of the biblical texts from which the figure of Melchizedek derives. While a number of New Testament passages are alluded to in the work as a whole, the epistle to the Hebrews is nowhere utilized. *Pistis Sophia* thus stands far outside the mainstream of Christian tradition in its interpretation of Melchizedek.

SUMMARY AND CONCLUSIONS

In our survey of the Gnostic treatments of Melchizedek, we have noted a trajectory of interpretation in which the epistle to the Hebrews provides a major starting point: Heb. 7:3 is the focal text for the Bala'izah fragment, and is a major factor in the treatment of Melchizedek in the Nag Hammadi tractate. In this respect, these two texts conform to the treatment of Melchizedek in non-Gnostic patristic literature. However, with the *Books of Jeu* and the two parts of *Pistis Sophia* treated above, there is no trace of influence from Hebrews, something that puts

63. Chap. 86 (pp. 194–95).
64. See discussion above (p. 110; n. 8).
65. Logion 19, au. trans. On the "five trees" in *Gos. Thom.* see Margaretha Lelyfeld, *Les logia de la vie dans l'Évangile selon Thomas* (NHS 34; Leiden: E. J. Brill, 1987) 47–48.

these Gnostic works outside of the mainstream of Christian interpretive traditions pertaining to Melchizedek.

Melchizedek is a heavenly figure in the Nag Hammadi tractate. We do not have the interpretation that was given to Heb. 7:3 in the Bala'izah text, but it is likely that Melchizedek was treated as a heavenly figure by its author as well. As for Hebrews itself, Melchizedek is not treated by its author as a heavenly being, although it is likely that the author knew of such an interpretation of Melchizedek.[66] We have seen, in any case, that Melchizedek's role as a heavenly warrior-priest is not derived from Hebrews but from Jewish apocalyptic speculation, such as is reflected in the Qumran fragments, 11QMelch.

Melchizedek's role as a heavenly priest in *2 Jeu* depends on a tradition something like that found in NHC IX,1; and it is not out of the question that the author of *2 Jeu* knew the Nag Hammadi tractate, despite the differences in interpretation displayed between them.

With *Pistis Sophia* new lines are drawn. The author of *Pistis Sophia* 4 probably knew *2 Jeu*—the double name Zorokothora Melchizedek is one indication of that—but he drops the priestly aspect of Melchizedek altogether, concentrating now on Melchizedek's role as a heavenly being who transfers particles of light from the domain of the archons to the Treasury of Light. That role is further elaborated in the material found in *Pistis Sophia* 1–3.

With *Pistis Sophia* there is no trace left of any scriptural influence, whether from Hebrews or from the two Old Testament texts. (Genesis 14 is dimly reflected in *2 Jeu*, as we have seen.) There may, however, be a reflection of noncanonical Jewish traditions concerning Melchizedek in *Pistis Sophia*'s presentation of the crucial role played by Melchizedek in the transfer of particles of light (saved souls) to the Treasury of Light. Here 11QMelch again comes into the picture. In that text, Melchizedek is a heavenly savior who restores the "sons of light," the "men of the lot of Melchizedek," to the company of the "sons of heaven," from which they had been cut off during the "dominion of Belial."[67] *Pistis Sophia*'s treatment of Melchizedek can easily be seen as a Gnostic reinterpretation of

---

66. In Horton's discussion of Hebrews (*Melchizedek Tradition,* 160–64) he is so intent on denying any heavenly status for Melchizedek in Hebrews that he does not take into account the possibility that the author of Hebrews was aware of such a doctrine and could have been implicitly arguing against it in his own presentation of Melchizedek. Cf. Friedländer's interpretation of Hebrews, discussed in chapter 1 of this book (pp. 14–15; see now also H. W. Attridge, *The Epistle to the Hebrews* (Hermeneia; Philadelphia: Fortress, 1989) 191–95.

67. See esp. 11QMelch ii,4–8.

that found in 11QMelch. Indeed, when one thinks about such a possibility, one can see that Jewish lore concerning Melchizedek could just as easily have reached the Egyptian Gnostic author(s) of *Pistis Sophia* as Jewish lore concerning the antediluvian patriarch Enoch, such as is found in books 2 and 3 of that Gnostic work.[68]

If that is true, we must also conclude that the Christian interpretive tradition concerning Melchizedek, begun by the author of Hebrews, is simply a caesura in the case of the Gnostic evidence. The constant trajectory of interpretation runs from pre-Christian Judaism (11QMelch) to the "decadent" Gnosticism of third- or fourth-century Egypt represented by the books of *Pistis Sophia*, a Gnosticism whose Christian character is but a thin veneer, and, in the case of the Melchizedek lore, totally lacking.

68. In *Pistis Sophia* (chaps. 99, 134; pp. 274, 349) Enoch is said to have written the two "Books of Jeu" in Paradise and deposited them on the rock of (Mount) Ararat. This is a reflex of Jewish lore concerning Enoch as a heavenly scribe. On Enoch traditions in Egypt, see my article, "The Pierpont Morgan Fragments of a Coptic Enoch Apocryphon," in G. W. E. Nickelsburg, ed., *Studies on the Testament of Abraham* (SBLSCS 6; Missoula: Scholars Press, 1976) 227–83, esp. 236–39. See also Pearson, "Jewish Sources," 449–50.

8

Jewish Elements in Gnosticism and the Development of Gnostic Self-Definition

Scholars in the field of patristics and early Christian history have customarily looked upon Gnosticism simply as an aberrant form of Christianity. The concomitant tendency among church historians has been to dismiss Gnosticism as unworthy of serious study. Historians of religion, on the other hand, have devoted a good deal of attention to Gnosticism, with the result that numerous theories have developed regarding the origins of Gnosticism. The assumption of an inner-Christian origin for the Gnostic movement has long been challenged among historians of religion. Recourse has been taken to Greek philosophy and Hellenistic mystery religions, to the various oriental religions of Iran, Babylon, and Egypt, or to Judaism for alternative historical theories pertaining to the genesis of Gnosticism.[1] While the arguments for the Jewish origins of Gnosticism propounded by Moritz Friedländer in 1898 did not gain much currency,[2] the Jewish factor in the origins of Gnosticism is now gaining ever greater attention in scholarly discussion, especially as a result of the new evidence from the Nag Hammadi Coptic Codices.[3] For example, in his important book on Gnosticism (a standard reference work on the subject), Kurt Rudolph sets forth a convincing case for the origins of the Gnostic religion in Syro-Palestinian Jewish circles.[4]

---

1. For the history of scholarship see esp. Kurt Rudolph, "Gnosis und Gnostizismus, ein Forschungsbericht," *ThR* 34 (1969) 121–75; 181–231; 358–61; and 36 (1971) 1–61; 89–124. See also the important volume of essays presented to the Messina Colloquium on the origins of Gnosticism: Bianchi, *Origini dello gnosticismo*. For a recent restatement of the "Christian heresy" model see S. Pétrement, *Le Dieu séparé: les origines du gnosticisme* (Paris: Cerf, 1984); cf. my review in *RSRev* 13 (1987) 1–6.
2. See chap. 1 in this book.
3. For bibliography see Scholer, *Nag Hammadi Bibliography*, supplemented annually in *Novum Testamentum*.
4. Rudolph, *Gnosis*, esp. 276–94. Cf. also Rudolph, "Randerscheinungen des Juden-

In my own publications I have been particularly interested in how the Gnostics interpreted the Bible (i.e., the Old Testament). I have attempted to show that the building blocks of the central Gnostic myth consist of interpretations of key Old Testament texts and reflect the utilization of specifically Jewish aggadoth and traditions of scripture exegesis, reinterpreted in a radical new direction.[5] As a result of my research thus far I am prepared to posit that Gnosticism, as a religious movement of late antiquity, originated in sectarian Jewish circles independent of, and perhaps even prior to, Christianity.

Given the massive Jewish influence discoverable in Gnostic texts, how does one interpret the Gnostics' attitude vis-à-vis their roots? It is obviously not enough to speak of "Jewish Gnosticism,"[6] for once the Gnostic hermeneutical shift has occurred one can no longer recognize the resultant point of view as Jewish. One finds, instead, an essentially non-Jewish, indeed anti-Jewish, attitude, and one must interpret this attitude on its own terms as a radically new hermeneutical program, giving birth to a radically new religious movement. Concomitantly, one finds reflected in the Gnostic texts a radically new self-understanding, expressed, to be sure, in many different ways.

In what follows I shall attempt to interpret the significance of the Jewish elements in Gnosticism and the attitude toward Judaism expressed in the Gnostics' use of the Jewish traditions. I shall also attempt to interpret the essential characteristics of the Gnostic self-understanding manifest in the various expressions utilized by Gnostics to refer to themselves and their fellow Gnostics. From such an investigation some interesting historical conclusions may be drawn.

JEWISH ELEMENTS IN GNOSTICISM:
AN INTERPRETATION

For the purposes of this study I shall restrict our discussion to primary Gnostic sources, and thus omit from consideration here the patristic

tums und das problem der Entstehung des Gnostizismus," *Kairos* 9 (1967) 105–22; and his "Forschungsbericht" (cited in n. 1).

5. See esp. chaps. 2–7 in this book; and Pearson, "Gnostic Hermeneutics," "Gnostic Interpretation," "Jewish Sources," "'Jewish Gnostic' Literature," and "Exegesis of Mikra."

6. The "Jewish Gnosticism" referred to in the title of one of Gershom Scholem's important books, *Jewish Gnosticism, Merkabah Mysticism, and Talmudic Tradition* (New York: Jewish Theological Seminary, 1965), is not the "Gnosticism" referred to here, and would be better designated by some other name, such as "Jewish Mysticism." It should be added, however, that Scholem has (orally) expressed his essential agreement with my (and others') arguments for the Jewish origins of Gnosticism (in the technical sense of the word used here).

testimonies. Since we now have a wealth of primary materials as a result of the publication of the Nag Hammadi Codices,[7] it will also be useful to restrict our attention to a representative body of material from which generalizations can safely be made. The best possible group of texts for our purposes consists of those tractates in the Nag Hammadi Library that have been labeled as Sethian Gnostic:[8] *The Apocryphon of John* (Nag Hammadi Codex II,1; III,1; IV,1; Codex Berolinensis Gnosticus, 2; + parallel text in Irenaeus *Haer.* 1.29 [Harvey ed., pp. 221–26]); *The Hypostasis of the Archons* (NHC II,4); *The Gospel of the Egyptians* (NHC III,2; IV,2); *The Apocalypse of Adam* (NHC V,5); *The Three Steles of Seth* (NHC VII,5); *Zostrianos* (NHC VIII,1); *Melchizedek* (NHC IX,1); *The Thought of Norea* (NHC IX,2); *Marsanes* (NHC X,1); *Allogenes* (NHC XI,3); and *The Trimorphic Protennoia* (NHC XIII,1). These documents do, of course, display important differences one from another. For example, some of them show no Christian influence (*Steles Seth, Allogenes, Marsanes, Norea,* and probably *Apoc. Adam*);[9] others reflect only the slightest knowledge of Christianity (*Zost.,* possibly *Apoc. Adam*); some belong to what might properly be called Christian Gnosticism (*Ap. John, Hyp. Arch., Melch.*) or show a considerable Christian veneer (*Trim. Prot., Gos. Eg.*). In the case of some of them—notably, *The Apocryphon of John*—one can clearly discern in the text as it now stands multiple stages of literary development, and a concomitant process of "Christianization."[10] Others (*Zost., Marsanes, Allogenes, Steles Seth*) show an increasing degree of interplay between Gnostic and philosophical—especially Middle-Platonic speculation—and thus provide interesting points of contact with the accounts of Plotinus (*Enn.* 2.9) and Porphyry (*Vit. Plot.* 16) regarding the Gnostics in Rome known to the members of Plotinus's school.[11] What holds these documents together is a (Sethian) Gnostic "system" of ideas and traditions that underlies, or is reflected in, the various trac-

---

7. See *Nag Hammadi Library,* and Scholer, *Nag Hammadi Bibliography.*

8. I cite here the list of tractates included by Hans-Martin Schenke in his important articles, "Das sethianische System" and "Gnostic Sethianism."

9. Considerable controversy exists regarding *Apoc. Adam,* as to whether or not some key passages do or do not reflect Christian influence; see, e.g., George W. MacRae, "The Apocalypse of Adam Reconsidered," in *Society of Biblical Literature, 1972 Proceedings* (Missoula: Scholars Press, 1972) 573–77. See now also Pearson, "'Jewish Gnostic' Literature," 26–33.

10. Cf. my remarks on this aspect of *Ap. John* in chap. 2, above, p. 30, and n. 3; and Pearson, "'Jewish Gnostic' Literature," 19–25. For a good analysis of the form and composition of *Ap. John* see Alf Kragerud, "Apocryphon Johannis: en formanalyse," *NorTT* 66 (1965) 15–38.

11. See chap. 10 in this book.

tates.[12] Moreover, the underlying system represents a very early form of Gnosticism.

The essentials of the Sethian-Gnostic system include the following elements: the figure of Seth,[13] son of Adam, who functions both as a heavenly being and as a redeemer, and whose spiritual descendants constitute the Gnostic elect; a primordial divine Triad of Father (sometimes called "Anthropos" or "Man"), Mother ("Barbelo"), and Son ("Autogenes," "Adamas," etc.); four "luminaries" (Harmozel, Oroiael, Daveithe, and Eleleth) of the divine Son Autogenes; and an apocalyptic schematization of history, focusing on the judgments of the Creator and his archons in the Flood, in fire (Sodom and Gomorrah), and in the end time.[14] The Sethian system also includes a Sophia ("Wisdom") figure, as well as the evil demiurge, Ialdabaoth. But these features are not specifically Sethian, for they occur in other early Gnostic systems and mythic structures as well.

The Sethian Gnostic system is essentially non-Christian, and probably even pre-Christian in its origins. Such Christian elements as occur in some of the Sethian texts are clearly secondary features, reflecting a process of Christianization.[15] For example, in *The Gospel of the Egyptians* Seth "puts on" Jesus in order to redeem the elect imprisoned in the world (III 63,4–64,9), but in principle Seth can "put on" any important prophetic figure, such as Zoroaster, Melchizedek, and so on.[16] On the other hand, the Jewish features observable in the texts are absolutely basic to the Sethian system.[17] The importance of the biblical Seth as a redemptive and revelatory figure is obviously derived from Jewish sources.[18] The Gnostic doctrine of the unknown highest God (see esp. *Ap. John* II

12. This has been cogently argued by H.-M. Schenke in the articles cited above. For a skeptical view of this and other attempts to define a Sethian Gnosticism see Frederik Wisse's article, "Stalking Those Elusive Sethians," in Layton, *Rediscovery*, 2.563–76.

13. See chap. 4 in this book.

14. See esp. Schenke, "Das sethianische System," 166-67.

15. The clearest example of such a Christianization process in the Nag Hammadi Library is the relationship between *Eugnostos* (NHC III,3; V,1) and *Soph. Jes. Chr.* (NHC III,4; BG,3); the former contains no trace of Christian influence, while the latter presents the content of *Eugnostos* as the revealed teaching of Jesus Christ!

16. See my remarks on this in chap. 4 in this book.

17. Schenke has suggested a Samaritan origin for Sethian Gnosticism, taking his cue from the attribution of *Steles Seth* to one Dositheos, presumably intended to be identified as the Samaritan teacher by that name ("Das sethianische System," 171-72), and it is clear that Samaritan sources should be taken into account in any discussion of the Jewish origins of Gnosticism. On the other hand, non-Samaritan Jewish materials frequently turn out to be more fruitful for comparative purposes than the Samaritan sources.

18. See chap. 4 in this book.

2,25–4,26) carries to radical conclusions the tendencies everywhere in early Jewish theology to stress the transcendence of God over the world.[19] Specific features of the Gnostic doctrine of the highest God—such as his mystical designation "Anthropos" and his "image" in humanity—derive from exegesis of key texts in scripture, especially Gen. 1:26–27.[20] The four "luminaries" are probably developed from Jewish speculations on the angels surrounding the throne of God.[21] The feminine divine hypostases, such as Barbelo and Sophia, are developed from Jewish wisdom speculations.[22] And the apocalyptic schematization of history is developed out of Jewish apocalyptic traditions.[23]

It is especially instructive, however, to consider the attitude toward Judaism expressed in the Gnostic literature as part of the Gnostic reinterpretation of the Jewish materials utilized. This attitude is best exemplified in the Gnostic treatment of the biblical creator and the Jewish Law.

Gnostic theology actually splits the biblical God into a transcendent, "unknown" God and a lower creator deity. In his aspect as Creator of the world the biblical God is portrayed as a demonic being of illegitimate origin (*Ap. John* II 9,25–10,19 and parallels; cf. *Hyp. Arch.* II 94,5–9). The names assigned to him by the Gnostics are meant to indicate his true character: "Ialdabaoth" ("Child of Chaos," *Ap. John* II 24,12, etc.; *Hyp. Arch.* II 95,11, etc.; *Trim. Prot.* XIII 39,27); "Samael" ("Blind God," *Ap. John* II 11,18; *Hyp. Arch.* II 87,3, etc.; *Trim. Prot.* XIII 39,27); "Saklas" ("Fool," *Ap. John* II 11,17; *Hyp. Arch.* II 95,7; *Gos. Eg.* III 57,16, etc.; *Apoc. Adam* V 74,3, etc.; *Trim. Prot.* XIII 39,27).[24] The Gnostics portray the "ignorance,"

19. Even the notion that God is essentially *(kat' ousian)* "unknowable" or "unknown" *(agnōstos)* is a topos of Hellenistic Jewish theology; see, e.g., Josephus *Ap.* 2.167.
20. See esp. H.-M. Schenke, *Der Gott "Mensch,"* and chap. 2 in this book.
21. Alexander Böhlig, "Der jüdische Hintergrund in gnostischen Texten von Nag Hammadi," in Böhlig, *Mysterion und Wahrheit: Gesammelte Beiträge zur spätantiken Religionsgeschichte* (Leiden: E. J. Brill, 1968) 84.
22. See esp. MacRae, "Gnostic Sophia Myth."
23. The relationship between *Apoc. Adam* and Jewish pseudepigraphical literature, particularly the Adam literature and the Enoch materials, is especially instructive. See, e.g., George W. E. Nickelsburg, "Some Related Traditions in the Apocalypse of Adam, the Books of Adam and Eve, and 1 Enoch," in Layton, *Rediscovery*, 2.515–39; Pheme Perkins, "Apocalyptic Schematization in the Apocalypse of Adam and the Gospel of the Egyptians," in *Society of Biblical Literature 1972 Proceedings*, 591–95; and Rudolph, *Gnosis*, 135–39.
24. See chap. 3, above, pp. 47–49. It should be pointed out that Gershom Scholem does not accept the usual etymology of Ialdabaoth as (Aramaic) "Child of Chaos," and interprets the name as "begetter of [S]abaoth" instead; see "Jaldabaoth Reconsidered," in *Mélanges d' histoire des religions offerts à Henri-Charles Puech* (Paris: Presses Universitaires de France, 1974) 405–21. It should also be observed that these names of the Gnostic Demiurge are not confined to Sethian sources. For Ialdabaoth see, e.g., *Orig. World* II 100,14, etc.; *Soph. Jes. Chr.* BG 119,5; *Treat. Seth* VII 53,13, etc.); for Samael *Orig.*

"jealousy," and "sin" of the Creator in graphic terms, by means of a midrash on key texts from the Law and the Prophets (Exod. 20:5; Isa. 45:5, 6; 46:9), according to which the Creator boasts that he is the only God beside whom there is no other (*Ap. John* II 11,19–21; 13,8–13; *Hyp. Arch.* II 86,27–87,4; *Gos. Eg.* III 58,23–59,1; *Trim. Prot.* XIII 43,31–44,10).[25] For this idle boast he is appropriately rebuked by a *bath qol* from heaven ("Man exists and the Son of Man").[26] The man he and his archontic henchmen create (Adam) turns out to be superior to him, by virtue of the "inbreathing" of the heavenly spirit (*Ap. John* II 15,1–19,33; *Hyp. Arch.* II 87,23–88,15; cf. *Apoc. Adam* V 64,1–29).[27] As a result the Creator strives with all his power to keep humanity imprisoned in this world, and seizes every opportunity to persecute the Gnostic seed (esp. *Ap. John; Hyp. Arch.; Gos. Eg.; Apoc. Adam,* passim).

The Gnostics' view of the real nature of the Creator is matched by their view of his Law and his promises. Paradoxically, the Gnostics proclaim their sovereignty over the Old Testament scriptures, especially the Torah, but at the same time utilize them as sources upon which to construct their own worldview. Just as they split the Deity into a transcendent, highest God and a lower Creator, upon whom the source of cosmic evil can be foisted, so also they split the scriptures in the same fashion. Thus, while utilizing the scriptures as a canonical authority for their own doctrines, they can baldly "correct" the text of the Torah ("not as Moses said," *Ap. John* II 13,19–20; 22,22–23; 23,3; 29,6). They can regard the Old Testament prophets as "false prophets" (*Gos. Eg.* III 61,15), though they can also learn from the prophets the real purposes of the Creator, namely, to "make their hearts heavy that they may not pay attention and may not see" (*Ap. John* II 22,25–28; cf. Isa. 6:10). The commandments of the Creator are seen to reflect his ill will and "envy" (*Hyp. Arch.* II 90,6–10). Those who obey his commandments are in bondage, serving him "in fear and slavery" (*Apoc. Adam* V 65,20–21; 72,21–22), and those who rely on his promises are duped, for the essence

---

World II 103,18. The last name is a Jewish designation for the Devil and/or Angel of Death; cf. chap. 3, above, p. 48.

25. I am citing here only the "Sethian" sources, though this and other features of the Gnostic attitude to the biblical God are found in many other Gnostic texts. See now N. Dahl's important study, "The Arrogant Archon and the Lewd Sophia: Jewish Traditions in Gnostic Revolt," in Layton, *Rediscovery* 2.689–712.

26. "Man" is the highest God, and the "Son of Man" is the "Son" in the divine Triad of Father, Mother, and Son. Cf. Schenke, "Das sethianische System," 166–67; *Der Gott* "Mensch," 64–68; 94–107.

27. On the Gnostic use of Gen. 2:7 see chap. 2, above, and Pearson, *Pneumatikos-Psychikos Terminology,* chap. 6.

of his promises is death (*Ap. John* II 21,23–24). The Gnostics, on the other hand, are free, for they are by nature foreign to the Creator, and do not belong to him (*Apoc. Adam* V 64,16–19; 69,17–19).

The Gnostic attitude to Judaism, in short, is one of alienation and revolt,[28] and though the Gnostic hermeneutic can be characterized in general as a revolutionary attitude vis-à-vis established traditions, the attitude exemplified in the Gnostic texts, taken together with the massive utilization of Jewish traditions, can in my view only be interpreted historically as expressing a movement of Jews away from their own traditions as part of a process of religious self-redefinition.[29] The Gnostics, at least in the earliest stages of the history of the Gnostic movement, were people who can aptly be designated as "no longer Jews."[30]

GNOSTIC SELF-UNDERSTANDING

If the Gnostics are "no longer Jews," who, then, are they? Curiously enough, even their own self-definition turns out to be based to some extent on Jewish tradition! This can be seen in some of the designations by which they identify themselves and their fellow Gnostics, as a survey of the evidence from our Sethian tractates will readily show.

Basic to the biblical doctrine of the chosenness of Israel is the use of the term "elect" (*eklektos, bāḥir*) to designate the people of the Covenant, both in the Old Testament itself (1 Chr. 16:13; Ps. 105:6, 43; 106:5, 23; Isa. 43:20; 45:4; 65:9, 15, 22) and in extrabiblical Jewish literature (e.g., *Jub.* 1.29; *1 Enoch* passim; 1 QS ix,14; etc.). Surprisingly, this is one of the self-designations of the Gnostics as well (*Zost.* VIII 4,17; *Melch* IX 10,17). The Gnostics can also utilize as self-designations such apocalyptic Jewish terms as "saints" (*Gos. Eg.* III 63,14; 67,26; cf. Dan. 7:18, 21, 22; 1 QM x,10; etc.) and "children (sons) of Light" (*Hyp. Arch.* II 97,13–14; *Trim. Prot.* XIII 41,1.16; 42,16; 49,25; 45,33; cf. 1 QS i,9; ii,16; iii,13,24; lQM i,1, et passim). It may also be the case that we should understand the use of the self-designation "perfect" (*teleios*) (*Steles Seth* VII 124,8.25; Zost. VIII 48,1–2; 59,17–18; 60,23; 129,17; *Allogenes* XI 45,7) at least partially against the

28. Hans Jonas has stressed this element of "revolt" in Gnosticism; see esp. his seminal article, "Delimitation of the Gnostic Phenomenon—Typological and Historical," in Bianchi, *Origini dello gnosticismo*, 28–60.

29. In this respect I must differ with Jonas, who does not see the Gnostic phenomenon as arising from within Judaism; see his "Delimitation of the Gnostic Phenomenon," 102. Cf. my remarks in chap. 3, above, pp. 50–51.

30. Irenaeus applies this phrase to the Basilidian Gnostics (*Haer.* 1.24.6 [Harvey ed., pp. 202f.]).

background of biblical (Gen. 6:9; 2 Sam. 22:26) and apocalyptic Jewish usage (cf., e.g., 1 QS iii,3; I QM vii,5). Of course the Gnostics would relate their status as "perfect" and "elect" "children of Light" to their attainment of *gnosis,* by which they would also be able to discern that other claims to such an exalted status should be adjudged as inherently false. On the other hand, the very exclusivism of the Gnostic claim is itself derived from sectarian Jewish tradition.

One of the most characteristic notions of the Sethian Gnostics—indeed, "the fixed point of what may be called Sethian Gnosticism"[31]—is their self-designation as the "seed" (*Ap. John* II 9,15; *Gos. Eg.* III 54,9–11; 59,25–60,2; 60,8.10; *Apoc. Adam* V 66,4; 83,4; 85,22.27–29; *Zost.* VIII 30,10–14; 130,16–17), "race" (*Gos. Eg.* III 59,13–15; *Steles Seth* VII 118,12–13), or "children" (*Melch.* IX 5,20; *Zost.* VIII 7,8–9) of Seth. This terminology is used both of the pre-Christian souls of the elect in heaven prior to their descent to the world (see esp. *Ap. John* II 9,14–17; cf. *Gos. Eg.* III 56,19–22) and of the Gnostic elect on the earth. The figure of Seth is similarly understood as a precosmic, heavenly being, as well as an incarnate savior-revealer.[32] These ideas concerning Seth and his Gnostic posterity are ultimately based on a highly sophisticated exegesis of Gen. 4:25 (esp. the words ἕτερον σπέρμα). Comparable ideas are found in Hellenistic Jewish circles, as represented by Philo of Alexandria. Philo's treatise *On the Posterity and Exile of Cain* is particularly important for comparative purposes. In this treatise, commenting on Gen. 4:17–25, Philo remarks that all lovers of virtue are descendants of Seth (*Post.* 42), in contrast to the wicked race of Cain. To the term ἕτερον σπέρμα in Gen. 4:25 Philo observes that Seth is the "seed of human virtue" (*Post.* 173), sown from God (*Post.* 171). For Philo all virtuous men are the "race" of Seth. For the Gnostics, in a similar vein, all men of *gnosis* are symbolically the "race" of Seth. One might easily conclude that the Gnostic interpretation of Gen. 4:25 is influenced by, and probably derived from, a Jewish exegetical tradition similar to that encountered in Philo.

The Gnostic use of the terms "seed" and "race" includes other ideas, however, by which it is possible to arrive at a deeper understanding of the Gnostic self-definition. For the Gnostics see themselves, ultimately, as much more than the race of Seth; they regard themselves as nothing less than the "seed," "race," or "generation" of the highest God himself. This can readily be seen in the use of such expressions as "the seed of the

31. Cf. George W. MacRae, "Seth in Gnostic Texts and Traditions," *Society of Biblical Literature 1977 Seminar Papers* (Missoula: Scholars Press, 1977) 21.
32. For full particulars see chap. 4, above.

Father" (*Gos. Eg.* III 54,9–11) and "the unwavering race of the Perfect Man" (*Ap. John* II 2,24–25). As has already been noted,[33] "Man" is a designation for the highest God; with the use of the expression, "race of the perfect Man," the Gnostics identify themselves ontologically with the highest God and understand themselves as originating "from the Primeval Father" (*Hyp. Arch.* II 96,19–20). With such expressions we are confronted with the heart and core of the Gnostic religion, the idea of the consubstantiality of the self with God.[34]

Accordingly, we are not surprised to find that the Gnostics use as self-designations expressions normally used as attributes of God, such as "eternal" (*aiōnios*, e.g., *Steles Seth* VII 124,6.22), "imperishable" (*attako = aphthartos*, Norea IX 28,11), and "all perfect" (*panteleios, Zost.* VIII 20,2–3). Some of the divine self-designations are not particularly common; their use by the Gnostics seems to reflect a high degree of intellectual sophistication. One of the phrases already cited is a good example, "the unwavering race of the perfect Man" (*Ap. John* II 2,24–25). The Coptic expression translated variously as "unwavering," "immovable," or "unshakeable" *(ete maskim* or *atkim)* is very frequent in the Gnostic texts (*Ap. John* II passim; *Gos. Eg.* III 51,9 et passim; *Steles Seth* VII 118,12–13; *Zost.* VIII 6,27; 51,16) and probably translates, at least in some instances,[35] the Greek term *akinetos,* used of God by Aristotle (*Metaph.* 1073A; cf. 1012B) and by theologians influenced by his terminology (e.g., Athenagoras *Leg.* 22.5).

Another Gnostic self-designation of special interest is "the generation without a king over it" (ⲧⲅⲉⲛⲉⲁ ⲛ̄ⲛⲁⲧⲣ̄ ⲣ̄ⲣⲟ ⲉ2ⲣⲁⲓ ⲉⲭⲱⲥ, *Apoc. Adam* V 82,19–20; cf. "the undominated generation," ⲧⲅⲉⲛⲉⲁ ⲧⲉⲧⲙ̄ⲙⲛ̄ⲧⲉⲥ ⲣ̄ⲣⲟ, *Hyp. Arch.* II 97,4–5). This phrase translates the Greek term *abasileutos,* as is readily seen from its use in Hippolytus (ἡ ἀβασίλευτος γενεά, *Ref.* 5.8.2, a Naassene self-designation). The term is used of God in patristic literature (*Const. Ap.* 8.5.1). The Gnostics, with the use of this expression, declare themselves independent of any authority, human or divine

---

33. See discussion above, p. 129 and n. 26.

34. See the "Final Document" attempting to define Gnosticism, prepared at the Messina Colloquium on the Origins of Gnosticism, in Bianchi, *Origini dello gnosticismo,* xxvi–xxix. Cf. also the important article by Wolfgang Ullman, "Beziehungen zwischen gnostischen Gottesnamen und den Selbstbezeichnungen der Gnostiker in koptisch-gnostischen Quellen," in P. Nagel, ed., *Studia Coptica* (Berlin: Akademie-Verlag, 1974), pp. 191–200.

35. The other Greek term translated by the Coptic word, *atkim,* is *asaleutos,* also a term used in Greek philosophy. See now Michael A. Williams, *The Immovable Race: A Gnostic Designation and the Theme of Stability in Late Antiquity* (NHS 29; Leiden: E. J. Brill, 1985).

(especially the Creator of this world!), and thus also articulate their essential identity with the primal Father, "the Monad (who) is a monarchy with nothing above it" (*Ap. John* II 2,26–27).

Before concluding this discussion we must consider how the Gnostic self-designations we have discussed relate to each other, for only in so doing can we achieve a proper understanding of Gnosticism as a religious phenomenon. As we have seen, the Gnostics utilized various terms to express their essential identity with God; on the other hand, we also saw that they used terms to express their status as an elite religious group, such as "elect," "saints," "children of Seth," and so on. The latter category implies a process whereby their status is achieved and realized. At this point we have to do with yet another central feature of the Gnostic religion: the necessity for the divine seed in humans to be awakened in a salvific event, namely, through *gnosis*, "knowledge," more specifically, self-knowledge. The Gnostic, though he or she is essentially divine, must also become divine by the event of saving *gnosis*. In the Sethian Gnostic system Seth functions as a redeemer figure whose saving word of *gnosis* effects the salvation of the elect.[36] The Gnostics express their association with Seth the Savior with the use of such self-designations as "the seed of Seth." They become identified as such when they have awakened to *gnosis* and have thus been "born of the word" (*Apoc. Adam* V 85,27).

CONCLUSION

Gnosticism was a religious protest movement of late antiquity that, at least in its earliest history, based much of its mythology on Jewish scripture and tradition. It was a movement of intellectuals, and thus was able to incorporate ideas and traditions from the syncretistic milieu of the Hellenized Levant. The dominant impulse of the early stages of Gnostic history was its attitude toward Judaism. This attitude, as we have seen in our survey of the Sethian texts, is one of alienation and rejection, expressed in a very sophisticated, if perverse, way of reinterpreting biblical and Jewish traditions. Hence it seems most plausible to conclude that the earliest Gnostics were Jewish intellectuals eager to redefine their own religious self-understanding, convinced of the bankruptcy of traditional verities. It is quite possible that an important factor in the development of this Gnostic attitude was a profound sense of the

---

36. Cf. chap. 4, above.

failure of history. This appears to be reflected in the way in which the Gnostic sources depict the foibles and machinations of the Creator.[37] The essential feature of Gnosticism in its earliest history is its revolutionary attitude toward Judaism and Jewish traditions.

Early in the history of Gnosticism the expansion of Christianity resulted in the appropriation of Christian theologoumena into Gnosticism—as well as Gnostic theologoumena into Christianity—and Gnostic Christian groups were created. Some of the Sethian materials discussed in this chapter reflect influence from Christianity to a greater or lesser extent, especially in the appropriation of Jesus Christ as a redeemer figure. In the case of Sethian Gnosticism, in fact, we are confronted with serious problems in attempting to identify the particular communities from which our sources derive, and it has even been suggested that the quest for a Sethian Gnostic sect is as fruitless as the quest for the mythical unicorn.[38] In this view the Gnostic texts should be understood as individual efforts intended for individual meditation, and not for group use by members of a sect or community. Yet, despite the indications of a heightened individualism reflected in the texts (see esp. the expression, "perfect individuals," *Steles Seth* VII 124,8, etc.; *Zost.* VIII 60,23, etc.; *Allogenes* XI 45,7), there are, as we have already noted, indications of a *group* self-awareness in the various Gnostic self-designations. This suggests that there really were, over a period of time, religious communities of "Sethian" Gnostics, as the church fathers aver (esp. Ps.-Tertullian *Haer.* 8; Epiphanius *Haer.* 39). The texts also provide indications of the use of religious rituals among these Gnostics.[39] The very nature of the Gnostic religion, however, with its focus on self-realization and spiritual freedom, would mitigate against the establishment of an institutionalized "normative" group self-identity.[40] (The Manichaeans and the Mandaeans constitute important exceptions to this observation, a fact that also accounts for their relative "staying power."[41]) On the

37. Robert M. Grant's well-known theory that Gnosticism arose out of the debris of apocalyptic hopes shattered by the destruction of Jerusalem in 70 C.E. has often been criticized, and has subsequently been abandoned by Grant himself; see *Gnosticism and Early Christianity* (New York: Columbia University Press, 1959) 27–38. The socio-historical factors in the origins of Gnosticism are, nevertheless, worth pursuing, difficult as this task is. Cf. Rudolph, *Gnosis*, 275–94; and his "Forschungsbericht," *ThR* 36 (1971) 89–124.

38. See Wisse's article, "Stalking Those Elusive Sethians."

39. See esp. Schenke's important paper, "Gnostic Sethianism." On the place of ritual and sacraments in Gnosticism see Rudolph, *Gnosis*, 218–52.

40. Cf. Rudolph, *Gnosis*, 53–55.

41. For good summary discussions of Manichaeism and Mandaeism see Rudolph, *Gnosis*, 327–66. On the question of "institutionalization" in Gnosticism, or the absence

other hand, the Gnostic message was apparently attractive enough to be able to create cell groups of spiritual elitists within the growing Christian congregations all over the Mediterranean world, and perhaps also within Jewish synagogues both in Palestine and in the Diaspora (although this is harder to document).[42] The Gnostic religion thereby became an important negative factor in the institutionalization of the catholic church and in the development of normative Christian self-definition.[43]

---

thereof, the collaboration of scholars trained in sociological method would be of great value. The sociological study of Gnosticism is yet in its infancy. E. Michael Mendelson pointed out the usefulness of such study in his paper, "Some Notes on a Sociological Approach to Gnosticism" (in Bianchi, *Origini dello gnosticismo*, 668–75), as did Kurt Rudolph (in his "Forschungsbericht," *ThR* 36 [1971] 119–23). Since then a few sociological studies of Gnosticism have appeared: Hans G. Kippenberg, "Versuch einer soziologischen Verortung des antiken Gnostizismus," *Numen* 17 (1970) 211–31; Peter Munz, "The Problem of 'Die soziologische Verortung des antiken Gnostizismus,'" *Numen* 19 (1972) 41–51 [a critique of Kippenberg]; Petr Pokorný, "Der soziale Hintergrund der Gnosis," in Tröger, *Gnosis und Neues Testament*, 77–87; and Henry A. Green, "Suggested Sociological Themes in the Study of Gnosticism," *VC* 31 (1977) 169–80; cf. also Green, *The Economic and Social Origins of Gnosticism* (SBLDS 77; Atlanta: Scholars Press, 1985). Rudolph gives considerable attention to sociological questions in *Gnosis*, 204–72. In my view the most fruitful approach is one that is grounded in the texts. Gerd Theissen's sociological studies provide good models that might be appropriate also for Gnosticism; e.g., see his methodological study, "Die soziologische Auswertung religiöser Überlieferungen," *Kairos* 17 (1975) 284–99, esp. 296 n. 28 [on Gnosticism]. Cf. chap. 13 in this book, p. 208, n. 51.

42. Whereas the church fathers tell us even more than we want to know about "Christian" Gnostic groups, we are not well informed on the impact of Gnosticism on Jewish communities. Moritz Friedländer attempted to cull the rabbinic literature for such information in his *Der vorchristliche jüdische Gnosticismus* (see chap. 1, above). Of course, a developing "normative" Judaism would take steps to root out religious dissenters and "heretics," as we see, e.g., in the famous *birkat ha-minim* inserted into the Twelfth Benediction of the Amidah toward the end of the first century. On the *birkat ha-minim* see W. D. Davies, *The Setting of the Sermon on the Mount* (Cambridge: University Press, 1964) 275–79; but Davies does not give sufficient attention to the possibility that other "heretics" are under attack besides the Christians.

43. For discussion of some of the factors involved in the catholic Christian antipathy to Gnosticism see the papers by George MacRae, Jacques Ménard, Gérard Vallée, and Raoul Mortley, in E. P. Sanders, ed., *Jewish and Christian Self-Definition*, vol. 1: *The Shaping of Christianity in the Second and Third Centuries* (London: SCM/Philadelphia: Fortress, 1980).

9

Jewish Elements in
Corpus Hermeticum I
(Poimandres)

Tractate I of the *Corpus Hermeticum*[1] is a document of considerable importance for the history of Greco-Egyptian religious syncretism, and the history of Gnosticism in general. Entitled *Poimandres*, after the name of the god who reveals himself in the document, it is attributed in early tradition to the Egyptian god, Thrice Greatest Hermes (= Egyptian Thoth), revealer-god par excellence in Egyptian religion.[2] Probably the earliest document in the Hermetic corpus, it consists of a number of elements that apparently served as a sort of "canonical" basis for subsequent development of the Hermetic religion, as the references and allusions to the *Poimandres* in later Hermetic literature would tend to suggest.

The tractate consists of the following elements:

I. An introduction (chaps. 1–3), depicting the epiphany of the god "Poimandres" or "Mind" (the highest God) to the prophetic visionary, unnamed, whom tradition identifies as Hermes Trismegistus.

II. A revelation (4–26), consisting of
   A. A cosmogony (4–11);
   B. An anthropological section (12–23), including

---

1. See A. D. Nock and A.-J. Festugière, ed., *Corpus Hermeticum* (2d ed.; Paris: "Les Belles Lettres," 1960) 1.1–31. Translations of passages quoted in this chapter are my own. The most recent English translation of *Poimandres* is that of Layton, *Gnostic Scriptures*, 452–59.
2. The title "Ἑρμοῦ τρισμεγίστου Ποιμάνδρης" is probably secondary, but it is clear from *Corp. Herm.* XIII,15 that the *Poimandres* was attributed in early Hermetic tradition to Hermes Trismegistus. The name "Hermes" does not occur in the text of *Corp. Herm.* I itself.

1. An anthropogony (12–19), the most important element of
    which is the story of man's "fall," and
2. A section consisting of anthropological and ethical teach-
    ing (20–23); and
C. Eschatology (24–26), teaching the way of ascent to God.
III. An account of the prophet's apostolic mission to humanity, with
    an appeal to people to "repent" (27–29).
IV. A conclusion (30–32), the most important elements of which are
    hymns and prayers addressed to God.

It has long been noted, at least from the time of the Byzantine scholi-
ast Michael Psellus (tenth cent.),[3] that this document is replete with
Jewish elements, and even contains extensive scripture quotations and
allusions (esp. Genesis 1—2). In modern times, C. H. Dodd is the scholar
who has investigated these things most extensively.[4] He has argued that
the Cosmogony and the Anthropogony of the *Poimandres* is based in
large measure on the Genesis account of creation. Dodd has also noted
extensive influences from portions of the Greek Bible other than Genesis, and refers to influences from the kind of Hellenistic-Jewish literature
represented especially by Philo of Alexandria (though he does not claim
that *Corp. Herm.* I is dependent upon Philo).

Of course, it may well be the case that Dodd saw some allusions to
Genesis that really turn out to be illusory upon closer inspection of the
text. Ernst Haenchen has argued this rather forcefully.[5] The latter, in his
perspicacious analysis of the structure and theology of the *Poimandres*,
has also shown that the author of the tractate has utilized a number of
sources, some of which contradict one another. In any case, it is possible
that both the "Jewish" and the "Gnostic" elements in the Cosmogony
and Anthropogony are attributable to one or more "Jewish Gnostic"
sources.

More recently, H. Ludin Jansen, in a very interesting article,[6] has
argued that the Old Testament-Jewish emphasis in the *Poimandres* is so

3. See Psellus's scholium on *Corp. Herm.* I,18, excerpted in Walter Scott, ed.,
Hermetica, vol. 4: *Testimonia* (Oxford: Clarendon, 1936) 244–45.
4. *The Bible and the Greeks* (London: Hodder & Stoughton, 1935).
5. "Aufbau und Theologie des 'Poimandres,'" *ZTK* 55 (1956) 149–91. Cf. also R. McL.
Wilson, "The Gnostics and the Old Testament," in Geo Widengren, ed., *Proceedings of
the International Colloquium on Gnosticism, Stockholm August 20–25, 1973* (Stockholm:
Almqvist & Wiksell, 1977) 164–68, esp. 165f.
6. "Die Frage nach Tendenz und Verfasserschaft im Poimandres," in Widengren,
Proceedings, 157–63.

strong that it must have been written by a Jew who personally had lived through all of the mystical experiences described in the "autobiographical" sections of the text (esp. chaps. 1–3, 27–30). He thus implicitly denies any connection between the *Poimandres* and the Hermetic religion, though he does see it as a Gnostic document.[7] Its author must, therefore, have been a Jewish Gnostic. Unfortunately, Jansen's treatment, though rich in insight, is poor in documentation. Moreover, he takes no account of the problem of sources and redaction in the tractate.

In this study I shall first look at the structure of the document as a whole, that is, its final composition, and then concentrate on those sections that appear to belong to the final redaction and at the same time show features that are most characteristically Jewish. Then a tentative thesis will be proposed to account historically both for the "Jewishness" of the document, as well as its pagan—yes, Hermetic—thrust.

In looking at the form and structure of the *Poimandres*, one is struck by the similarity of this tractate to certain Jewish apocalypses, most notably 2 (Slavonic) *Enoch*, a document that probably emanates in its earliest form from first-century Egypt.[8] Indeed, the two documents show a remarkable degree of similarity not only in structure, but also in specific content. Here are some examples:

Poimandres	*2 Enoch*
Hermes,[9] almost asleep, receives a vision: chap. 1.	Enoch, first asleep, later awake, receives a vision: chap. 1.
A very large being appears and calls him by name: chap. 1.	Two very large men appear, and call him by name: chap. 1.
God reveals to Hermes the secrets of the cosmos and its origin: chaps. 4–11.	God reveals to Enoch the secrets of the cosmos and its origin: chap. 24.

7. Walter Scott, in his well-known edition of the *Hermetica*, has also pointed to Jewish influences in the *Poimandres*, and brings the tractate into close connection with the kind of Judaism represented by Philo of Alexandria. He also tends to think that the tractate was originally written independently of the Hermetic tradition. See *Hermetica* (Oxford: Claredon, 1925) 2.4–11. Karl-Wolfgang Tröger, however, refers to *Corp. Herm.* I as "ganz zweifellos hermetisch," a judgment with which I agree. See "Die hermetischen Gnosis," in Tröger, *Gnosis und Neues Testament*, 97–119, esp. 105.

8. I do not agree with J. T. Milik's late dating of *2 Enoch* in *The Books of Enoch: Aramaic Fragments of Qumran Cave 4* (Oxford: Clarendon, 1976) 107–16. See now F. I. Andersen's introduction and translation in *OTP* 1.91–213; cf. also Pearson, "Jewish Sources," 455f.

9. I refer to the unnamed visionary-prophet as "Hermes," in accordance with the Hermetic tradition; cf. nn. 2, 7.

God reveals to Hermes the creation of living things.	God reveals to Enoch the creation of living things. 28–30: 1–7.
The creation of man, sevenfold: chaps. 12–19 (seven *anthropoi*, chap. 16).	The creation of man, sevenfold (from seven substances): 30:8–9.
Eros is the cause of death: chap. 18.	Death comes to man through his wife: 30:17–18.
Two ways/possibilities for man, life and death, light, darkness: chaps. 19–23, cf. chap. 29 ("way of death").	Two ways for man, light and darkness: 30:15.
Blessings and curses: chaps. 22–23.	Blessing and curses: chap. 52.
Way of ascent revealed: chaps. 24–26.	Enoch ascends to heaven: chaps. 3–22.
The powers sing to the Father in the eighth sphere and in the ninth: chap. 26; cf. "Holy, Holy, Holy," chap. 31.	Angelic Powers sing to God in the seventh heaven, "Holy, Holy, Holy," chap. 21.
God is above the eighth sphere, either in the ninth or the tenth, receiving hymns of praise: chap. 26.	God dwells in the tenth heaven surrounded by hymns of praise: chap. 22.
Hermes is sent to preach to errant humankind: chaps. 27–29.	Enoch is sent to preach to errant humankind: chap. 22.
"I depart into life and light": chap. 32.	"I shall go up to heaven": 55:1–2.

Now although there is no solid evidence for the mingling of the Hermetic and Enochic traditions before the fourth century,[10] it is not out of the question that the author of the *Poimandres* was familiar with one or more apocalypses in the Enoch tradition of the sort represented by 2 *Enoch*, perhaps even 2 *Enoch* itself. In any case, it has all the earmarks of a Jewish apocalypse. (Specifically Egyptian "apocalypses" existed from ancient times, but differ radically from what we have in the *Poimandres*).[11]

10. Zosimus of Panopolis, who was immersed in the Hermetic tradition, utilizes Enoch material, both from 1 (Ethiopic) *Enoch* and (probably) from 2 *Enoch*. See, e.g., Scott, *Hermetica* 4.104–53. According to Muslim tradition Enoch (Idris) is equated with Hermes, and is credited with building the pyramids. Cf. Abu Salih, *The Churches and Monasteries of Egypt*, trans. B. Evetts (Oxford: Clarendon, 1895) 189.
11. See, e.g., C. C. McCown's important article, "Egyptian Apocalyptic Literature,"

The material from chapter 27 to the end of the *Poimandres* is especially important, for herein we see most clearly the basic thrust of the document as a whole. And precisely here the Jewish elements are pervasive. Here, too, we find the best evidence for reconstructing the document's historical *Sitz im Leben*.

Looking first at the apostolic preaching section, especially chapters 27 and 28, we see a number of elements reminiscent both of the scriptures (LXX) and of such Hellenistic Jewish literature as is preserved in the writings of Philo. For example, the use of the term δύναμις (power) as a designation for angelic beings (cf. also chaps. 7, 26) is common in Philo (*Plant.* 12–15; *Agr.* 167–71; *Spec. Leg.* 66–69; *Fug.* 68ff.), in the LXX (Ps. 110:21; 118:2–3); and related literature (e.g., *T. Jud.* 25:2). Indeed, even the name for God in the tractate, "Poimandres," may reflect the Jewish-biblical belief in God as "Shepherd of Men," especially of Israel (cf., e.g., Philo, *Agr.* 51: ὁ ποιμὴν καὶ βασιλεὺς θεός; Ps. 22:1: κύριος ποιμαίνει με).[12] He is called "Father of the All" as well (chaps. 27, 31), and this is a designation for God that occurs very often in Philo (*Det.* 148; *Op.* 71–73; *Leg. All.* 2,48–53; *Ebr.* 80–85; etc.). When "Hermes" addresses mankind as "earth-born men" (ἄνδρες γηγενεῖς), he is using a term that reflects Hellenistic-Jewish interpretations of Gen. 2:7 (e.g., Wis. 7:1; Philo, *Op.* 68–70; *Virt.* 195–99; etc.). The metaphor of "drunkenness," familiar from Gnostic texts,[13] is not absent from Jewish material, and is found in the prophets of the Bible as well as in extrabiblical Jewish literature (e.g. Isa. 28:1; Jer. 28:39; etc.).[14] In Philo, "drunkenness" and "sleep" are used together, as here, in a metaphorical sense (see esp. *Sobr.* 5). Moreover, when "Hermes" appeals to "earth-born men" to "repent" (μετανοεῖν), he is using an expression virtually restricted in antiquity to Jewish and Christian materials, as Eduard Norden noted long ago.[15] In general, the

---

HTR 18 (1925) 357–411. The most important Egyptian texts from the Hellenistic-Roman period are the *Demotic Chronicle*, the *Oracle of the Potter*, and the apocalypse preserved in the Hermetic *Asclepius*, *Corp. Herm.* IX, 24–26. NHC VI, tractate 8, is a Coptic version of the latter. See now also J. G. Griffiths, "Apocalyptic in the Hellenistic Era," in David Hellholm, ed., *Apocalypticism in the Mediterranean World and the Near East* (Tübingen: J. C. B. Mohr, 1983) 273–93.

12. ποιμὴν ἀνδρῶν is still the best etymology for the name "Poimandres," and is supported in the Hermetic tradition itself: Λόγον γὰρ τὸν σὸν ποιμαίνει ὁ Νοῦς, *Corp. Herm.* XIII, 19. Attempts to find an Egyptian etymology (*p3 mtr*, "the witness," or *p.eime n-Re*, "the knowledge of the Sun-god") are not convincing. Cf. Scott, *Hermetica* 2:16. See now NHC VI,3: *Auth. Teach.* 33,2, where God is called the "true Shepherd" of the soul; cf. also the name "Poimael" in NHC III,2: *Gos. Eg.* 66,1–2, probably based on the word ποιμήν ("shepherd") plus the suffix -ēl ("god").

13. See Jonas, *Gnostic Religion*, 68ff.

14. Cf. Dodd, *Bible and the Greeks*, 187–88.

15. *Agnostos Theos* (repr. Darmstadt: Wissenschaftliche Buchgesellschaft, 1956) 134–39.

whole of the message of our Hermetic preacher in these chapters has a prophetic ring about it, reminiscent of the accounts in the Bible of the preaching of the prophets.[16]

The results of Hermes's preaching are summarized in chapter 29: some of the hearers reject the message and thereby choose the "way of death"—this phrase reflects the Jewish "Two Ways" tradition[17]—whereas others wish to be taught more and thus to enter upon life. "Seeds of wisdom" are sown in the hearers—the terminology is akin to that employed by Philo[18]—and the product of this catechesis[19] is a worshiping community whose chief cultic activity is the offering up of "thanksgiving" (εὐχαριστία, chap. 29)[20] and "blessing" (εὐλογία, chap. 30)[21] to God.

It is precisely here, too, where we see the most striking examples of Jewish influence. For in the phraseology employed at the end of the *Poimandres*, from the end of chapter 29 through chapter 32, we are able to find fragments of Jewish liturgy, specifically prayers and formulas utilized in the daily worship life of pious Jewish communities at least from the turn of the era. The following are a few examples:

The words at the end of chapter 30, ἐκ ψυχῆς καὶ ἰσχύος ὅλης ("with [my] whole soul and strength"), clearly echo the last part of the *Shemaᶜ*. The LXX text of Deut. 6:5 reads, καὶ ἀγαπήσεις κύριον τὸν θεόν σου ἐξ ὅλης τῆς ψυχῆς σου καὶ ἐξ ὅλης τῆς δυνάμεώς σου ("and you shall love the Lord your God with your whole soul and your whole power"). The use of the word ἰσχύος in the *Poimandres* (for Hebrew וּבְכָל־מְאֹדֶךָ) instead of δυνάμεως as in the LXX is no problem, for in fact Origen noted that ἰσχύος is a textual variant in the manuscript tradition.[22] Indeed, the phrase ἐξ ὅλης τῆς ἰσχύος occurs in the New Testament, in the Markan form of the

16. So, rightly, Dodd, *Bible and the Greeks*, 179ff.

17. On the "Two Ways" tradition in Judaism and early Christianity see, e.g., Robert Kraft, *The Didache and Barnabas* (Robert M. Grant, ed., *The Apostolic Fathers*, vol. 3 [New York: Thomas Nelson & Sons, 1965]) esp. 4–16.

18. On Sophia ("Wisdom") as "sower" in Philo see *Fug.* 49–53; *Somn.* 1.199–202; on God or the Logos as "sower" of wisdom, see *Leg. All.* 1.43–51; 79–81; 3.180–83, 219–23; etc.

19. Haenchen refers to this section as "eine Art heidnischer Katechismus," in "Aufbau und Theologie," 185; Jansen calls it "ein Stück gnostischer Katechese," in "Die Frage nach Tendenz und Verfasserschaft," 158.

20. εὐχαριστία is a later variant of ἐξομολόγησις as a translation of Hebrew תּוֹדָה; see James M. Robinson, "Die Hodajot-Formel in Gebet und Hymnus des Frühchristentums," in *Apophoreta: Festschrift für Ernst Haenchen* (Berlin: Töpelmann, 1964) 198. Cf. also εὐχαριστεῖν (= ἐξομολογεῖσθαι = יָדָה) in chaps. 27, 29. On εὐχαριστία in Philo see Jean Laporte, *Eucharistia in Philo* (New York: E. Mellen, 1983).

21. εὐλογία = Hebrew בְּרָכָה; cf. Robinson, "Die Hodajot-Formel," 202. Cf. chap. 32: εὐλογητὸς εἶ = בָּרוּךְ אַתָּה, a common Jewish prayer-formula. See below.

22. See F. Field, ed., *Origenis Hexaplorum quae supersunt* (repr. Hildesheim: G. Olms, 1964) 1.283.

Shema͑ (Mark 12:30). This simply indicates that different Greek translations of the *Shema͑* existed in the worship life of Greek-speaking
synagogues of the Diaspora.[23]

The formulation δίδωμι . . . εὐλογίαν τῷ . . . πατρὶ θεῷ ("I render . . .
blessing to . . . God the Father"), here occurring with the words from the
Shema͑ quoted above, prepares for the blessing or hymn to follow, but
may also reflect the use of the biblical Psalms in corporate worship.
Compare, for example, Ps. 102(103):1: Εὐλόγει, ἡ ψυχή μου, τὸν κύριον
καί, πάντα τὰ ἐντός μου, τὸ ὄνομα τὸ ἅγιον αὐτοῦ ("Bless the Lord, my
soul, and, all that is within me, [bless] his holy name").

The hymn in chapter 31 reads as follows, concluding with a prayer
that the worshiper's "spiritual sacrifices" be accepted:

> Holy is God, the Father of the All.
> Holy is God, whose will is accomplished by his own powers.
> Holy is God, who wishes to be known, and is known to his own.
> Holy are you, who by (your) Word have established all that exists.
> Holy are you, of whom all of Nature became an image.
> Holy are you, whom Nature has not formed.
> Holy are you, who are stronger than every power.
> Holy are you, who are greater than every supremacy.
> Holy are you, who exceed (all) praises.
> Accept pure spiritual sacrifices from a soul and heart
> that is stretched out to you, (you who are)
> inexpressible, ineffable, invoked (only) by silence.

The prayer continues in chapter 32, and includes at the end the
doxological formula, "Blessed are you, O Father."

The ninefold ascription of "holiness" to God in this hymn, a hymn
later used even in Christian worship,[24] ultimately harks back to the
Kedusha, especially the part derived from Isa. 6:3. It will be noticed, too,
that the first three lines ascribe holiness to God in the third person, as in
the *Trishagion* of Isa. 6:3. Of course the Hermetic author has expanded
upon the text, adding his own characteristic formulations. But these
formulations themselves, together with their linguistic form,[25] are
nothing that could not have occurred in a Jewish community: "Father of
the All" (see above, with reference to Philo), "whose will is accomplished

23. The same passage from the *Shema͑* is used twice in a new Hermetic text, NHC
VI,6: *Disc. 8–9* 55,11–13 and 57,21–23. On this tractate see below.
24. Cf. Nock-Festugière, *Corpus Hermeticum* 1.xxxvii, referring to Pap. Berol. 9794, a
Christian text of the third century.
25. See Norden's remarks on the non-Hellenic character of the style of language
found here (article + participle), in *Agnostos Theos*, 203.

by his powers," that is, the angels (see above) who constantly sing the praises of God (as in Isaiah 6), "who wishes to be known, and is known to his own," language reminiscent of the Bible and of Hellenistic Judaism in general (e.g., Exod. 29:42–43 [LXX], Hos. 12:1 [LXX]).

Note, too, the connection between this hymn and the description of the heavenly praises of God in chapter 26, wherein the ascent to God is described, as well as the concluding word in chapter 32, "I depart into life and light." Here we find a phenomenon similar to that documented by Gershom Scholem in his studies of Jewish mysticism, namely, the use of the angelic hymns as vehicles of the mystic's ascent.[26] This coheres with a general observation that could be made for the religion of the *Poimandres*, that is, that personal piety and corporate piety are held in tension. We shall have to return to this point.

The ascription of holiness to God in the second person, "Holy are you," is, of course, also frequent in Jewish liturgy. See, for example, the third benediction in the weekday *Amidah*, which opens: קָדוֹשׁ אַתָּה ("Holy are you").[27] The simple address to God as "Father" in chapter 32, in the phrase, εὐλογητὸς εἶ πάτερ ("Blessed you are, Father"), has parallels ("our Father") in many Jewish prayers; and the benediction, "Blessed are you," is virtually ubiquitous in ancient (and modern) Jewish liturgy, as for example in the *Amidah*, the benediction said in connection with the *Shemaʿ*, and numerous other prayers.[28]

Now when these references to Jewish liturgy are brought up in connection with the *Poimandres*, I may lay myself open to the charge of anachronism. For where is the evidence for Jewish liturgy as early as the *Poimandres*? Did not the early rabbis forbid the writing down of *berakoth* until at least the sixth century?[29]

But we need not resort to the Hebrew liturgy for our parallels to the *Poimandres*, for we do have Greek examples of Jewish liturgy that reflect the worship practices of some Jewish communities at least as early as the *Poimandres*. I refer, of course, to the Hellenistic-Jewish prayers embedded in the *Apostolic Constitutions*, books 7 and 8, discussed by Wilhelm Bousset and others.[30] There is no need to discuss here the work that has

---

26. *Jewish Gnosticism, Merkabah Mysticism, and Talmudic Tradition* (New York: Jewish Theological Seminary, 1965) 20–23, esp. 23 n. 6, referring to *Corp. Herm.* I.26.

27. See D. W. Staerk, *Altjüdische Liturgische Gebete* (Berlin: Walter de Gruyter, 1930) 11; cf. also P. Birnbaum, *Daily Prayer Book* (New York: Hebrew Publishing, 1949) 85.

28. See, e.g., Staerk, *Altjüdische Gebete*, 4, 6, 7, etc.

29. *Šabbat* 115b, in the Gemara of the Babylonian Talmud.

30. Wilhelm Bousset, "Eine jüdische Gebetssammlung im siebenten Buch der apostolischen Konstitutionen," *Nachrichten von der Königlichen Gesellschaft der Wissenschaften*

been done on these fragments, but it is clear that they preserve important testimony to the use, in Hellenistic-Jewish communities, of both the
Amidah and the *Kedusha*. Here, then, are some selected parallels
between the *Poimandres* and these Jewish liturgical fragments:

Poimandres	*Apostolic Constitutions*
"Holy is God" (thrice): chap. 31	"Holy, holy, holy" (the *Kedusha*): 7.35.3 (*OTP* 2.680)
"Father of the All": 31	"Master of the All": 8.9.8 (*OTP* 2.689)
". . . his own powers": 31	"powers" (in the *Kedusha*): 7.35.3 (*OTP* 2.680)
"who wishes to be known and is known to his own": 31	"Lord God of knowledge" (LXX 1 Kgdms. 2:3): 7.35.9 (*OTP* 2.681) "the one who is known by all those who . . . seek you with rational (λογικαῖς) natures": 8.15.7 (*OTP* 2.695)
"who by (your) Word have estab-lished (συστησάμενος) all that exists (τὰ ὄντα): 31	"who framed (συστησάμενος) an abyss" 8.12.13 (*OTP* 2.691). "God of all beings (τῶν ὄντων)": 7:33.2 (*OTP* 2.677)
"whom Nature has not formed": 31	"invisible by nature": 7.35.9; 8.15.7 (*OTP* 2.681, 695)
"greater than every supremacy . . . who exceed (all) praises [lit. "greater than (κρείττων) the praises]": 31	"greater than (κρείττων) every cause and origin": 8.5.1 (*OTP* 2.687)
"Accept spiritual sacrifices (λογικὰς θυσίας)": 31	"Accept this our thanksgiving (εὐχα-ριστίαν)": 8.37 (Bousset 484)[31]
"from a soul and heart that is stretched out to you": 31	"with heart filled to the brim and with a willing spirit" (cf. 2 Macc. 1:3): 7.35.4 (*OTP* 2.681)

---

zu Göttingen, Philologisch-historische Klasse 1915 (Berlin, 1916) 435–89. Cf. Erwin R. Goodenough, *By Light Light* (repr. Amsterdam: Philo Press, 1969) 306–58; K. Kohler, "The Origin and Composition of the Eighteen Benedictions with a Translation of the Corresponding Essene Prayers in the Apostolic Constitutions," in *HUCA* 1 (1924), repr. in J. Petuchowski, *Contributions to the Scientific Study of Jewish Liturgy* (New York: Ktav, 1970) 52–90; H. Thuyen, *Der Stil der Jüdisch-Hellenistischen Homilie* (FRLANT 65; Göttingen: Vandenhoeck & Ruprecht, 1955) 28–31. See now also the introduction by D. A. Fiensy and the translation by D. R. Darnell in *OTP* 2.671–97. Translations of passages quoted here are essentially those of Darnell in *OTP* 2, but modified.
    31. This petition, not included in *OTP* 2, is attributed by Bousset ("Gebetssamlung," 484) to a Jewish evening prayer.

"Blessed are you, Father": 32   "Blessed are you, O Lord": 7.34.1
                                        (*OTP* 2.678)

While some of these parallels are more relevant than others, the conclusion can surely be drawn that the influence of Jewish liturgical usage on the *Poimandres* can hardly be doubted. This is made all the more evident as one looks at pagan Greek hymns and prayers, with which the material in *Poimandres* has nothing at all in common.[32]

But we must press on to inquire further into the cultic elements in the *Poimandres*, and consider the following question: What kind of community is reflected in this document? Or is such a question even capable of an answer? This, of course, is not the place to discuss the debates of scholars who have argued back and forth over the question of whether a Hermetic cultus ever existed.[33] In my view, we have ample evidence of such a thing in the *Poimandres* taken by itself, but this evidence is filled out by other documents in the *Corpus Hermeticum*, now recently enlarged by Coptic texts from Nag Hammadi.[34]

Looking at the *Poimandres* we can see the following important elements:

1. The (corporate? individual?) teaching of wisdom in a kind of catechesis, led by a "guide" (καθοδηγός) (29). The guide "enlightens" those in ignorance (32).

2. Possibly a baptismal ceremony, perhaps even including the drinking of baptismal water (29).[35]

---

32. Cf. the texts assembled by E. des Places, "La prière cultuelle dans la Grèce ancienne," in *RevScRel* 33 (1959) 343–59.

33. While Reitzenstein and others have posited a full-blown Hermetic religion, organized in religious *thiasoi*, Festugière and others have preferred to see the Hermetic texts as school products. For references and discussion see K. W. Tröger, "Die hermetische Gnosis," 118–19; and Jean-Pierre Mahé, *Hermès en Haute-Égypte* (BCNH, "Textes" 3; Québec: Université Laval, 1978) 1.54–59; and (BCNH, "Textes" 7, 1982) 2.3–38.

34. NHC VI,6: *The Discourse on the Eighth and Ninth;* VI,7: *The Prayer of Thanksgiving;* VI,8: *Asclepius* 21–29. While the two last-named texts were previously available in Greek (VI,7) and Latin (VI,7 and 8) versions, tractate 6 is an important new document in the Hermetic corpus, with close parallels to Corp. Herm. XIII, and numerous allusions to Corp. Herm. I. Complete editions with commentary are now available: J.-P. Mahé, *Hermès en Haute Égypte*, vol. 1, and Douglas Parrott, ed., *Nag Hammadi Codices V, 2–5 and VI with Papyrus Berolinensis 8502, 1 and 4* (NHS 11; Leiden: E. J. Brill, 1979). The edition of NHC VI,6 in the last-named volume was prepared by Peter Dirkse, James Brashler, and Douglas Parrott. On this text see also L. S. Keizer, *The Eighth Reveals the Ninth: A New Hermetic Initiation-Discourse (Tractate 6, Nag Hammadi Codex VI): Translated and Interpreted* (Seaside, Calif.: Academy of Arts and Humanities, 1974).

35. So also Haenchen, "Aufbau und Theologie," 185. For Hermetic baptism see also

3. The community thus formed engaging in sunset (and sunrise?) corporate devotions, characterized as εὐχαριστία (29), εὐλογία (30), and λογικαὶ θυσίαι (31).

4. Each member of the community returning to his own bed after devotions (29), that is, each member living alone in his own cell. The practice of asceticism is obvious.

5. Each member of the community also engaging in silent meditation: note the term σιωπή in chaps. 30 and 31.

What is reflected here, in fact, is a kind of "monastic" community, comparable to such first-century groups as the Therapeutae described by Philo (Vit. Cont.), or the "naked sophists" near Thebes encountered by Apollonius of Tyana (Philostratus Vit. Apol. 6,4–22). Indeed the parallels between the Poimandres and Philo's description of the Jewish Therapeutae are very striking. Unfortunately, we cannot take these up here.

It is, of course, important finally to acknowledge that we are not, after all, dealing with a Jewish text, but with a "Hermetic" one. For all the obvious Jewish elements in the Poimandres, it is not a Jewish document. I see no reason to doubt that it is, in fact, a Hermetic document, even though the name "Hermes Trismegistus" does not occur in the text itself.[36] And when all is said and done, the Hermetic "creed" differs radically from the Jewish. This "creed" is best summarized in those places in the text in which are found examples of a Hellenistic, gnosticizing reinterpretation of the ancient Delphic maxim, γνῶθι σαυτόν:[37] "Let the man who has mind (νοῦς) recognize himself as immortal" (chap. 18); "He who recognizes himself departs into him (God)" (chap. 21); "Let the man who has mind recognize himself" (chap. 21). The whole burden of the Poimandres, from beginning to end, is that knowledge of God is really knowledge of one's inner divine self. This is the essence of the Hermetic preacher's message of repentance (chaps. 27–28); this is the "wisdom" that is imparted—complete with revelatory cosmogony, anthropogony, ethical system, and eschatology—to the one who accepts the message of the Hermetic preacher. And, in the final analysis, those who choose Hermes Trismegistus as their καθοδηγός have left Moses behind.[38]

Corp. Herm. IV. For the drinking of baptismal water, see, e.g., the Gnostic system of Justin, described by Hippolytus (Ref. 5.27.2–3); the "Sethians," (Ref. 5.19–21); and the Mandaeans, on which see Eric Segelberg, Maṣbutā (Uppsala: Almqvist & Wiksell, 1958) 59ff.

36. Cf. nn. 2, 7.

37. Admirably treated by Hans-Dieter Betz, "The Delphic Maxim ΓΝΩΘΙ ΣΑΥΤΟΝ in Hermetic Interpretation," HTR 63 (1970) 465–84.

38. For Moses as a "guide" in Hellenistic Judaism see, e.g., Philo Migr. 23: θεσμοθέτῃ

How do we account for the curious mixture of Jewish piety, Gnosticism, and Hermetic paganism found here in the *Poimandres*? Is it possible to reconstruct the religious history of this text? To be sure, such a reconstruction would be, at best, tentative and incapable of proof. But I should like to suggest the following scenario:

An individual who has been closely associated, perhaps as a proselyte or "God-fearer," with a Jewish community somewhere in Egypt (Alexandria? Hermopolis?) forms a new group devoted to the Egyptian god Hermes-Thoth, the "thrice greatest," attracting like-minded followers to the new cult. In the formation of the group, familiar Jewish traditions and worship patterns are remodeled and recast, with the aid of further study of eclectic Greek philosophy and assorted other religious revelations readily available in Roman Egypt. The writing of an apocalypse credited to Hermes in such a context is no more problematical than the writing of an apocalypse credited to Enoch in a sectarian Jewish context.[39]

Such a process would most likely occur in a historical situation in which Judaism is on the wane, and other religions and philosophies, including native Egyptian ones, are on the rise. A specific point in time and space can be suggested for this development: the aftermath of the Jewish revolt in Egypt against the Emperor Trajan, 115–117 (or 118) C.E.[40] After this revolt Judaism ceased to represent an important religious force in Egypt, and other religions and philosophies filled the breach.

In the case of the *Poimandres*, as once the lore of the god Hermes-Thoth had served the cause of the religion of Moses (Artapanus is an obvious case in point!),[41] so now Mosaic religion is utilized to serve the cause of "Thrice Greatest Hermes." Of course, in the further development of the Hermetic tradition the Jewish elements gradually diminish. This diminution is quite noticeable in the later documents of the Hermetic corpus.

λόγῳ Μωυσῇ ποδηγετοῦντι. Philo seems to know an interpretation of the Delphic maxim such as is found here in the *Poimandres* (cf. Betz, "Delphic Maxim," 477–80), but ultimately rejects it. For Philo knowledge of God involves self-renunciation instead of self-realization (ἀπογιγνώσκειν ἑαυτόν, *Somn.* 1.60). On this point see Pearson, "Philo and Gnosticism," 307f., 339.

39. Indeed, we know as little of the religious and social history of such Jewish apocalypses as 2 *Enoch* as we do of the background of the *Poimandres*.

40. Cf., e.g., A. Kasher, "Some Comments on the Jewish Uprising in Egypt in the Time of Trajan," *JJS* 27 (1976) 147–58; and Pearson, "Christians and Jews," 213–14.

41. Artapanus, *Peri Ioudaiōn* (second century B.C.E.), fr. 3 (Eus. *Praep. Ev.* 9.27), wherein Moses is equated with Hermes, and credited with inventing the hieroglyphics, building Hermopolis, inventing philosophy, etc. See J. J. Collins's discussion and translation in *OTP* 2.889–903.

10

Gnosticism as Platonism

From ancient times it has been averred that the Gnostics derived their basic ideas from the Greek philosophers, especially Pythagoras and Plato. For example, Irenaeus (*Haer.* 2.14) argued that the Valentinian Gnostics borrowed their doctrines of the *pleroma* and *kenoma* from Democritus and Plato. Hippolytus (*Ref.* 1.11), more systematically, tried to show that the founders of the Gnostic heresies borrowed most of their ideas from Greek philosophy and religion. The Valentinian brand of *gnosis*, Hippolytus argues (*Ref.* 6.21–29), is derived from the philosophy of Pythagoras and Plato.[1] Tertullian (*Praesc.* 7) claimed that all of the heresies were based on Greek philosophy. Valentinus is stated specifically to be "of the school of Plato." Plotinus (*Enn.* 2.9.6), the reputed founder of Neoplatonism, claimed in a famous tract that his doctrinal opponents, whom he did not identify but who were obviously Gnostics,[2] based their doctrines on a misunderstanding of Plato. Porphyry's *Life of Plotinus* 16 provides us with more information on the Gnostic opponents of Plotinus, and refers to them as αἱρετικοὶ ἐκ τῆς παλαιᾶς ψιλοσοφίας ("sectarians from the ancient philosophy," i.e., Platonism).

---

1. As is well known, it was generally assumed in Hippolytus's time that Plato and Pythagoras taught the same basic doctrine, an opinion based to a large extent on Plato's own writings. See P. Merlan's remarks in *The Cambridge History of Later Greek and Medieval Philosophy* (Cambridge: Cambridge University Press, 1967) 86. Hippolytus argues this point himself (*Ref.* 6.21).
2. Porphyry attached the title πρὸς τοὺς γνωστικούς to *Ennead* 2.9. English translations, such as Armstrong's in the LCL edition, are misleading in that they tend to throw in here and there the designation "Gnostics" when, in fact, Plotinus's Greek text leaves the opponents unnamed. Plotinus's polemic is comparatively irenic, for his intellectual opponents were also his personal friends (*Enn.* 2.9.10). There is a probable allusion to the self-designation of the opponents in the phrase τοὺς ἤδη ἐγνωκότας ("those who already know" = τοὺς γνωστικούς) at 2.9.15.

In our own times scholars have referred to Gnosticism as a kind of Platonism. Willy Theiler calls the Gnosticism of the Imperial period, both Christian and pagan (*Chaldean Oracles, Hermetica*), "Proletarier-platonismus."[3] Simone Pétrement portrays Gnosticism as "un platon-isme romantique."[4] A. D. Nock prefers the designation "Platonism run wild."[5] John M. Dillon refers to the Gnostic and Hermetic writings and the *Chaldean Oracles* as "the 'underworld' of Platonism."[6]

It can hardly be doubted that the ingredients of the Gnostic religion in its origins and early history included a substantial dose of popular Platonism.[7] What I want to do in this chapter, however, is focus atten-tion on a comparatively late stage in the evolution of the Gnostic reli-gion, when it appears that a lively discussion is taking place in philo-sophical schools between Platonist philosophers and Gnostics, to the extent that one can speak of mutual influences. This stage in the history of Gnosticism has now been greatly illuminated by the publication of the so-called Nag Hammadi Library[8] of Coptic manuscripts. Of special interest for our topic are four interrelated texts from this collection: *The Three Steles of Seth* (NHC VII,5); *Zostrianos* (NHC VIII,1); *Marsanes* (NHC X,1); and *Allogenes* (NHC XI,3). In this essay I concentrate on the tractate *Marsanes*, not only because the other three have already re-

3. "Gott und Seele im kaiserzeitlichen Denken," in *Forschungen zum Neuplatonismus* (Berlin: Walter de Gruyter, 1966) esp. 113. This terminology is unfortunate, in my view, for it implies something misleading about the social class of the Gnostics. The ancient Gnostics can hardly be classified as "proletarians"!

4. *Le dualisme chez Platon, les Gnostiques et les Manichéens* (Paris: Presses Univer-sitaires de France, 1947) 129.

5. "Gnosticism," in Zeph Stewart, ed., *Essays on Religion and the Ancient World* (Cambridge: Harvard University Press, 1972) 2.949.

6. *The Middle Platonists* (London: Duckworth, 1977) 384–96.

7. Hans Joachim Krämer accords to Gnosticism, especially the Valentinian variety, an important role in the general history of Platonism from Plato to Plotinus. See *Der Ursprung der Geistmetaphysik* (Amsterdam: Schippers, 1964) 223–64. This view, of a historian of philosophy, should be compared with that of one of our most prominent historians of the Gnostic religion, Kurt Rudolph. Rudolph grants a certain degree of similarity between Gnostic and Platonic dualism, and the possible influence of the latter upon the former, but stresses the radical anticosmism of Gnosticism over against the "procosmic" nature of Platonic dualism. See Rudolph, *Gnosis*, esp. 60–62. In my view Rudolph understates the relationship between Gnosticism and contemporary Platonism. Nevertheless, I consider Rudolph's book to be the best full-scale treatment of the Gnostic religion available today.

8. All of the tractates in the Nag Hammadi corpus are now available in English translation; see *The Nag Hammadi Library*. It is assumed that the reader has ready access to this volume. Except where otherwise noted, all quotations from the Nag Hammadi texts are taken from *Nag Hammadi Library*. For bibliography on Gnosticism and the Nag Hammadi Codices see Scholer, *Nag Hammadi Bibliography*.

ceived more attention in published discussions,[9] but also because I have devoted considerably more attention to *Marsanes* in my own research.[10]

THE TRACTATE *MARSANES*

It should be stated at the outset that *Marsanes* is an exceedingly difficult document to deal with, for the single manuscript in which it is preserved is very fragmentary, and the Coptic text obviously corrupt. Yet I am convinced that *Marsanes* in its original form was a very important Gnostic document. Its putative author, "Marsanes" (possibly a pseudonym), was highly regarded as a Gnostic prophet, according to the testimony preserved in the untitled tractate of the Bruce Codex (chap. 7)[11] and Epiphanius's discussion of the (Sethian) Archontic Gnostics of Palestine (*Haer.* 40.7.6).[12] The tractate consists of a lengthy apocalypse containing an account of visionary experiences and revelations concerning the various levels of being and their natures. A prominent part of the document is also devoted to parenetical encouragement addressed to a group of Gnostics already presumed to have been schooled in the basic essentials of *gnosis*. Marsanes holds out the promise of heavenly ascent to those who are able to qualify, speaking also of his own ascent experiences. This tallies well with what Epiphanius reports of the prophet

9. See esp. Michel Tardieu, "Les trois stèles de Seth: un écrit gnostique retrouvé à Nag Hammadi," *RSPhTh* 57 (1973) 545–75; James M. Robinson, "The Three Steles of Seth and the Gnostics of Plotinus," in Geo Widengren, ed., *Proceedings of the International Colloquium on Gnosticism, Stockholm, August 20–25, 1973* (Stockholm: Almqvist & Wiksell, 1977) 132–42 (treating also *Zostrianos* and *Allogenes*); John H. Sieber, "An Introduction to the Tractate Zostrianos from Nag Hammadi," *NovT* 15 (1973) 233–40; Carsten Colpe, "Heidnische, jüdische und christliche Überlieferung in den Schriften aus Nag Hammadi II," *JAC* 16 (1973) 123–25 (on *Steles Seth*); "III," *JAC* 17 (1974) 113–15 (on *Allogenes*); "VI," *JAC* 20 (1977) 149–59, 161-70 (on *Zostrianos*); John D. Turner, "The Gnostic Threefold Path to Enlightenment," *NovT* 22 (1980) 324–51 (treating mainly *The Apocryphon of John, Trimorphic Protennoia, Zostrianos,* and *Allogenes*); and Maddalena Scopello, "Youël et Barbélo dans le Traité de l'*Allogène*," in Bernard Barc, ed., *Colloque International sur les Textes de Nag Hammadi (Québec, 22–25 août 1978)* (BCNH, "Études" 1; Québec: L'Université Laval/Louvain: Peeters, 1981) 374–82. Carsten Colpe has recently devoted some attention to *Marsanes*: "Überlieferung IX," *JAC* 23 (1980) 124–27; "X," *JAC* 25 (1982) 66, 89–91. Cf. also Alexander Böhlig, "Die griechische Schule und die Bibliothek von Nag Hammadi," in Alexander Böhlig and Frederik Wisse, eds., *Zum Hellenismus in den Schriften von Nag Hammadi* (Göttinger Orientforschungen 6; Reihe "Hellenistica" 3; Wiesbaden: Harrassowitz, 1975) 16–17.

10. See Pearson, *Codices IX and X*; cf. *Nag Hammadi Library*, 460–71. See also "Tractate Marsanes."

11. See Carl Schmidt, ed., and Violet MacDermot, trans., *The Books of Jeu and the Untitled Text in the Bruce Codex* (NHS 13; Leiden: E. J. Brill, 1978) 235.

12. For a discussion of these testimonies see my introduction to *Marsanes* in *Codices IX and X*, 230–33.

Marsanes (whom he calls "Marsianos"), who was reputedly "snatched up into the heavens and came down after three days" (*Haer.* 40.7.6).

The tractate *Marsanes* has been classified among those documents that reflect a basic Gnostic system variously called "Barbeloite" or "Barbelo-Gnostic" (these names are based on Irenaeus's report in *Haer.* 1.29)[13] or "Sethian."[14] The following Gnostic tractates are included in this category:

> *The Apocryphon of John* (NHC II,1; III,1; IV,1; BG 2)
> *The Hypostasis of the Archons* (NHC II,4)
> *The Gospel of the Egyptians* (NHC III,2; IV,2)
> *The Apocalypse of Adam* (NHC V,5)
> *The Three Steles of Seth* (NHC VII,5)
> *Zostrianos* (NHC VIII,1)
> *Melchizedek* (NHC IX,1)
> *The Thought of Norea* (NHC IX,2)
> *Marsanes* (NHC X,1)
> *Allogenes* (NHC XI,3)
> *Trimorphic Protennoia* (NHC XIII,1)
> Bruce Codex, Untitled Text[15]

The basic Sethian[16] Gnostic system includes the following elements: the figure of Seth, son of Adam, a heavenly savior figure who incarnates

13. See, e.g., Turner, "Threefold Path," 325 and passim. In that study Turner seems to distinguish between what he calls the "Barbeloite" system and Sethianism (327). See now his more recent treatment, "Sethian Gnosticism: A Literary History," in Charles W. Hedrick and Robert Hodgson, eds., *Nag Hammadi, Gnosticism, and Early Christianity* (Peabody, Mass.: Hendrickson, 1986) 55–86.

14. See esp. Schenke, "Das Sethianische System" and "Gnostic Sethianism."

15. So Schenke, "Gnostic Sethianism," 588. Colpe ("Überlieferung" II, 113) would include *The Paraphrase of Shem* (NHC VII,1) in this category. Louis Painchaud (*Le Deuxième Traité du Grand Seth* [BCNH, "Textes" 6; Québec: L'Université Laval, 1982] 6 and passim) has recently argued rather persuasively that *The Second Treatise of the Great Seth* (NHC VII,2) reflects a Sethian mythological background.

16. I prefer the designation "Sethian" to the other terms. We know that there were Gnostics who traced their spiritual ancestry to Seth. "Barbelo-Gnostic" is obviously a secondhand term invented by Irenaeus. In my view, Carl Schmidt was on the right track when he wrote at the turn of the century that "man statt Barbelo-Gnostiker auch den Namen 'Sethianer' einführen könnte, wenn man dabei die mannigfaltigen Schattierungen dieser grossen Gruppe im Auge behält" (*Plotins Stellung zum Gnosticismus und kirchlichen Christentum* [TU 20; Leipzig: Hinrichs, 1901] 63). Schmidt rightly included in this large group of Sethian Γνωστικοί the Gnostics described by Epiphanius in *Haer.* 39 and 40, the Gnostics known to Plotinus and Porphyry, and the Gnostics represented by *The Apocryphon of John* (BG) and Irenaeus *Haer.* 1.29, as well as the untitled text in the Bruce Codex. Of course, he did not know of the Nag Hammadi documents.

himself in various human prophets, and whose spiritual descendants constitute the Gnostic elect;[17] a primordial divine triad of Father, Mother ("Barbelo"), and Son; four "luminaries" ($\phi\omega\sigma\tau\hat{\eta}\rho\epsilon\varsigma$: Harmozel, Oraiael, Daveithe, and Eleleth), and other angelic beings subordinate to them; and an apocalyptic schematization of history. This system clearly underlies the tract *Marsanes*, though *Marsanes*'s system represents considerable proliferation of levels in the chain of being. Also, the name "Seth" does not occur in the extant portion of the text; but Marsanes, as a prophet-savior, can probably be taken as a manifestation of Seth the heavenly savior, like Allogenes in the tractate that bears his name, and Zostrianos in *Zostrianos*.[18]

It is clear that the Sethian Gnostic texts show important differences among them, though they can readily be divided into distinct groups. Some of them are Christian texts, or texts secondarily Christianized; some (in my view the earliest) show very prominent Jewish influences;[19] others display no Christian influence at all, and such originally Jewish features as remain in them are clearly to be reckoned to their prehistory, as part of the basic Sethian Gnostic tradition.[20] In this latter group belong *Marsanes* and the other three tractates mentioned earlier: *The Three Steles of Seth*, *Zostrianos*, and *Allogenes*, as well as the untitled text in the Bruce Codex. What holds these texts together, in addition to the basic Sethian system and their essentially pagan character, is their strong Platonizing tendency.

It is, of course, true that other varieties of Gnosticism display strong influences from Platonic philosophy, notably Valentinian Gnosticism (as observed by the Christian heresiologists mentioned at the beginning of this chapter). However, it is the (Sethian) Gnosticism of *The Three Steles of Seth*, *Allogenes*, *Zostrianos*, and *Marsanes*[21] that was known to, and resisted by, Plotinus and Porphyry in Rome in the third century of

---

17. See my discussion in chap. 4 of this book (pp. 76–79).

18. Ibid., p. 77, and my introduction to *Marsanes* in *Codices IX and X*, 242–43.

19. See chap. 8 in this book.

20. The history of Sethian Gnosticism can be outlined as follows (according to my reconstruction of the evidence): (1) origins of Sethian Gnosticism in a Jewish milieu; (2A) Christianization of Sethianism; (2B) Platonization of Sethianism in a pagan milieu. Stage 2B should be seen as basically independent of 2A, but probably later than 2A, so that some minor influence from Christian Sethianism cannot be ruled out. On the Jewish origins of Sethian Gnosticism see esp. Stroumsa, *Another Seed*. See now also Turner, "Sethian Gnosticism" (cit. n. 13).

21. *Zostrianos* and *Allogenes* are mentioned by name by Porphyry *Vit. Plot.* 16; the other two are possibly to be reckoned among the "others" ($\breve{\alpha}\lambda\lambda\omega\nu$ $\tau o\iota o\acute{u}\tau\omega\nu$) also mentioned. Porphyry mentions Nikotheos, too, who is closely associated with Marsanes in the Bruce Codex (see above, and n. 11).

our era (*Enn.* 2.9; *Vit. Plot.* 16). Indeed, we have in Porphyry and Plotinus some important information about the life-setting of third-century Gnostic-Platonist interaction in the very heart of the Roman Empire.[22] Of these four Gnostic texts, *Marsanes* may be taken as representing in some ways the strongest and most consistent influence from contemporary Platonic philosophy.

In what follows I shall take up for discussion the following aspects of *Marsanes*'s Platonism: (1) its ontology, (2) its doctrine of the soul and the soul's ascent, and (3) its surprising monism, based on Platonic doctrine.

MARSANES'S ONTOLOGY

The ontological/cosmological system of *Marsanes* can best be seen in the first part of the tractate, especially in a section of the text (2,12–4,24) presenting a graded structure of the universe under the symbolism of thirteen "seals," progressing from the lowest to the highest. A religious ascent experience is clearly in the background here. This passage is introduced as follows (2,12–16): "But as for the thirteenth seal, I (Marsanes) have established it, together with [the] summit of knowledge (γνῶσις) and the certainty of rest (ἀνάπαυσις)."[23] The text, unfortunately, is riddled with lacunae, but the extant material on the thirteen seals can be summarized as follows.

Seals 1–3 (2,16–26) are associated with the "worldly" (κοσμικός), "material" (ὑλικός), and "sense-perceptible" (αἰσθητός) levels of the cosmos. Seals 4 and 5 (2,26–3,17) probably deal with the soul and its "exile" or "transmigration" (παροίκησις) and "conversion" or "repentance" (μετάνοια); these terms are also found in *Zostrianos* and other sources.[24] With

22. Cristoph Elsas has devoted an important monograph to the Gnostic-Platonist discussions in Plotinus's school in Rome, based on an analysis of Plotinus's anti-Gnostic arguments (*Enn.* 3.8; 5.8; 5.5; 2.9): *Neuplatonische und gnostische Weltablehnung in der Schule Plotins* (Berlin/New York: Walter de Gruyter, 1975). Unfortunately, these four important tractates from Nag Hammadi were not available to him when he wrote his book. He links the Gnostic opponents of Plotinus with the Elchasaites and downplays the Sethian connection. F. Garcia Bazán (*Plotino y la Gnosis* [Buenos Aires: Fundación para la Educación, la Ciencia y la Cultura, 1981]) thinks that Plotinus's Gnostic opponents were Valentinians, but I find his arguments unconvincing. He, too, wrote without access to the new texts (see 11n).

23. Quotations from *Marsanes* are taken from the translation in *Codices IX and X*. A glance at the facsimile of Codex X (see *Facsimile Edition* [Leiden: E. J. Brill, 1977] plates 87–144) will enable the reader to perceive some of the difficulties posed by this document in its extant form.

24. See esp. *Zost.* 5,24–27, also in connection with an ascent experience as here in *Marsanes*. These technical terms also occur in the untitled Sethian tractate in the Bruce Codex (chap. 20) and were terms used by the Gnostics known to Plotinus (*Enn.* 2.9.6).

seal 6 (3,18–25) we progress to entities that are "self-begotten" (αὐτογεν-νητός) and "incorporeal" (ἀσώματον), but exist in a "partial" or "individu-ated" state (κατὰ μέρος). Seal 7 (3,17–4,2) deals with an "Intellect" (νοῦς) who "appeared [in the beginning]" and who may be equivalent to a figure called "Protophanes" in *Allogenes* 45,35. The "intelligible world" (κόσμος νοητός) is also mentioned in this connection. *Allogenes* also provides a clue to the identity of a power lost in a lacuna in the section dealing with seal 9 (4,7–10), namely, "Kalyptos" (45,31).[25] Seal 10 (4,10–12) deals with Barbelo, the "Mother" in the original Sethian divine triad.[26] Seals 11 and 12 (4,13–19) deal with the Invisible Three-Powered One and the non-being Spirit. The ultimate degree of transcendence is reached with seal 13 (4,19–24), the unknown God characterized by silence.

This tantalizing passage in *Marsanes* opens up the possibility of con-sidering a number of doctrines that stem ultimately from the Platonic tradition. I begin with the basic distinction, characteristic of Middle Platonism, between the "intelligible world" (κόσμος νοητός: 4,6–7; cf. 5,22; 41*,5–6) and the "sense-perceptible world" (κόσμος αἰσθητός: 5,18–19 and 24–25; 34*,20; 41*,2–3; cf. 2,22). The Middle Platonists used the term κόσμος νοητός to designate the immaterial world of Plato's intel-ligible "Ideas." Plato (*Tim.* 37CD) had used the term ζῷον νοητόν ("intel-ligible living being") for the immaterial "pattern" (παράδειγμα) of the material world. Middle Platonists used the term κόσμος νοητός instead, and included in this designation the totality of Plato's "Ideas." The earliest attestation of the distinction between the two "worlds," αἰσθητός and νοητός, is with Philo of Alexandria (e.g., *Op. mund.* 15–17, 24), but it is probably not original with him.[27] This terminology has become part of the basic ontological system of *Marsanes*. Here, as in Platonic philos-ophy in general, the "intelligible" realm is the realm of pure being.

μετάνοια occurs explicitly in *Marsanes* 3,15. παροίκησις is not found in the text, but ΝΕΤΟΥΗϨ (3,17) probably translates the related Greek verb παροικεῖν in the participial form, οἱ παροικοῦντες.

25. The system of *Marsanes* is most closely related to that of *Allogenes*. On *Allogenes* and its relation to contemporary Platonism see Turner, "Threefold Path," esp. 328–41.

26. Her name is restored in a lacuna in the text: [ΒΑΡΒΗΛⲰ Τ]ΠΑΡΘΕΝΟⲤ (4,11); but there is no doubt that "the virgin Barbelo" occurred in the original text. Her name occurs also at 8,28 and probably at 43*,21. It should be noted that asterisks are used in the pagination of *Marsanes*, from p. 13* on, to indicate that the page numeration is only postulated, not certain. There were probably more than the sixty-eight pages of text now identifiable from the extant fragments of Codex X. See my introduction to Codex X, in *Codices IX and X*, 211-27.

27. See, e.g., Dillon, *Middle Platonists*, 158–59; and M. Baltes, *Timaios Lokros über die Natur des Kosmos und der Seele kommentiert* (Leiden: E. J. Brill, 1972) 105.

As we have seen, however, *Marsanes* posits a transcendent level of divine reality regarded as above and beyond "being." The "Spirit which does not have being" (ⲡⲓⲡⲛ̄ⲁ̄ ⲉⲧⲉ ⲙⲛ̄ⲧⲉϥ ⲟⲩⲥⲓⲁ) is mentioned in the passage discussed above (4,17–18); presumably beyond him is the unknown Silent God associated with the thirteenth seal (4,20–23). Both of those figures occur again in the text; the latter is referred to as "that One who exists before all of them" (6,5–6). He is referred to in *The Three Steles of Seth* (124,18–21) as "the really Pre-existent One really existing, being the first Eternal" (ⲡⲏ ⲉⲧⲣ̄ ϣⲣ̄ⲡ ⲛ̄ϣⲟⲟⲡ ⲟⲛⲧⲱⲥ ⲉϥϣⲟⲟⲡ ⲟⲛⲧⲱⲥ· ⲉϥϣⲟⲣⲡ ⲡⲓϣⲟⲣⲡ ⲛ̄ϣⲁ ⲉⲛⲉϩ). The divine level of "pre-existence" (ὁ ὄντως προών) in *The Three Steles of Seth* is the level of divine *stasis* beyond movement (κίνησις), as taught, for example, by Numenius.[28] The notion of "non-being" transcendence is expressed with the use of a technical term, ⲁⲧⲟⲩⲥⲓⲁ = ἀνούσιος, in *Marsanes* 5,14 and in other Gnostic documents, both Sethian (*Allogenes, Zostrianos, The Three Steles of Seth*, the untitled text of the Bruce Codex)[29] and non-Sethian (Valentinian, Basilidian).[30] The term may, in fact, be a Gnostic coinage, but it is based on Plato's dictum (*Resp.* 6.509B) that "the Good is not being" (οὐκ οὐσίας ὄντος τοῦ ἀγαθοῦ) but is "beyond being" (ἐπέκεινα τῆς οὐσίας).[31] Plotinus refers to his First Principle, "the One," as "beyond being" and "non-being" (ἐπέκεινα οὐσίας μὴ οὐσία: *Enn.* 1.7.1; 5.6.6; 5.4.2; 6.7.40,42). It may be the case that Plotinus deliberately avoids the term ἀνούσιος just because he knows it to be a Gnostic coinage.[32] The concept itself is firmly rooted in the Platonic tradition.[33]

Looking now at the ontological system of *Marsanes* as a whole, as it is presented in the text discussed above, we can see reflected in it a basic four-level structure derived from Platonic tradition, into which have been incorporated specifically Gnostic entities created in the Sethian Gnostic tradition. The basic four-level metaphysic that underlies *Marsanes* (as well as *Allogenes* and the other related Gnostic texts)[34] is that

28. Frg. 15 (des Places). On these and related terms and concepts in *Steles Seth* see Tardieu, "Les trois stèles," esp. 560. Tardieu cogently includes *Steles Seth* among the "other" Gnostic texts discussed in Plotinus's school, according to Porphyry *Vit. Plot.* 16.

29. E.g., *Allogenes* 53,31–32; *Zost.* 79,7; *Steles Seth* 121,27; Cod. Bruc., *Untitled*, chap. 2.

30. Hippolytus *Ref.* 6.42 (Marcus); 7.21 (Basilides).

31. On this passage in Plato see John Whittaker, "ΕΠΕΚΕΙΝΑ ΝΟΥ ΚΑΙ ΟΥΣΙΑΣ," *VC* 23 (1969) 91–104.

32. Proclus specifically rejects the possibility that the Divine can be called ἀνούσιος. For him matter is ἀνούσιος; divine transcendence is expressed with the word ὑπερούσιος. See, e.g., *Inst. Theol.* 121, 197 in E. R. Dodds, ed., *Proclus: The Elements of Theology* (2d ed.; Oxford: Clarendon, 1963) 106, 172. Cf. n. 39, below.

33. For further discussion of this point, with additional texts, see Pearson, "Tractate Marsanes."

34. See Turner's excellent treatment in "Threefold Path," esp. 332–41.

which H. J. Krämer[35] traces back to the esoteric teaching of Plato via Speusippus:

1. The one (ἕν), beyond being
2. Intellect (νοῦς), the realm of pure being, including numbers and the Ideas
3. Soul (ψυχή)
4. Material bodies (σώματα)

This system underlies that of Plotinus (his three ἀρχαί plus the material level), as well as a number of other Platonic and Gnostic metaphysical systems. In *Marsanes* the highest level is that of Non-being (seals 12–13); the second main level is that of Barbelo (seals 8–10), presumably corresponding to Plotinus's Intellect; the third level is that of Soul (seals 4–6), and the lowest level is that of Matter (seals 1–3).[36] Into this metaphysical structure is fitted the original Sethian Gnostic divine triad: the unknown, transcendent Father; the Mother (Barbelo), his first emanation; and the Son (Autogenes).[37]

We note, however, that *Marsanes* is guilty of multiplying first principles, in the manner of those Gnostics against whom Plotinus argues (*Enn.* 2.9.2,6). For one thing, our text seems to distinguish between the Unknown Silent God and the Invisible Spirit in the level beyond being (seals 13–12). Subordinate to Barbelo in the level of Intellect (νοῦς) or perhaps understood as aspects of her (as in *Allogenes* 45,28–46,11; 58,12–22) are three entities identifiable as Kalyptos, Protophanes-Nous, and Autogenes (seals 10–7). With Autogenes we are on the borderline of the realm of Soul. Autogenes is a savior figure in *Marsanes*, who descends to the lower realms (5,27–6,5); yet he presumably retains his identity as an "intellect" (νοῦς: *Ap. John* II 7,4; BG 31,20), and may be identified as "the planning Intellect" (ὁ νοῦς διανοούμενος) of the Gnostics, referred to disapprovingly by Plotinus (*Enn.* 2.9.6).[38] The realm of the Soul in *Mar*-

35. *Ursprung*, esp. 193–223.
36. κοσμικός and ὑλικός (seals 1–3) seem to be used synonymously, something presumably impossible for Platonists for whom the concept of *kosmos* has no negative connotations. See, however, σῶμα τὸ κοσμικόν in frg. 68 of the *Chaldean Oracles* (des Places), which Lewy takes to be based on Plato *Tim.* 32C (τὸ τοῦ κόσμου σῶμα), and which he equates with πολυποίκιλος ὕλη ('variegated matter') in frg. 34 (des Places). See Hans Lewy, *Chaldean Oracles and Theurgy* (2d ed. M. Tardieu; Paris: Études Augustiniennes, 1978) 120 n. 204. For a new edition of the *Chaldean Oracles*, with extensive commentary, see Ruth Majercik, *Chaldean Oracles: Text, Translation, Commentary* (SGRR 5; Leiden: E. J. Brill, 1989).
37. See esp. *Ap. John* (NHC II) 2,25–27, 30.
38. Turner identifies Kalyptos, Protophanes, and Autogenes in *Allogenes* as νοῦς

sanes includes the individual "self-begotten" entities (seal 6), probably thought of as individual souls, with their "exiles" and their "repentings" (seals 5–4). The lowest level takes in the material realms (seals 3–1), including the "sense-perceptible power" (2,22) which, perhaps, may better be seen to belong to the lowest level of Soul. Thus the chain of being has received gradations and nuances in *Marsanes* of the sort that Plotinus felt compelled to reject, but which later Neoplatonists would have had less difficulty accepting.

Later Neoplatonist philosophy, indeed, tended to organize reality more and more into interlocking triads, with triads within triads; Proclus is a case in point.[39] One entity occurring in *Marsanes* that we have not yet discussed (associated with seal 11) may, in fact, represent a Gnostic contribution to Neoplatonic philosophy: "the Three-Powered One" (πλ τϣαμτε ν̄6λμ), a being who mediates between the unknown supreme God (Plotinus's "One") and the intelligible realm of Barbelo. The same figure occurs in *Allogenes* under the name "the Triple Power" (πιϣμν̄τ6ομ: 45,13 and passim). In *Marsanes* this divine being is said to "appear" and to "act" (ἐνεργεῖν) in filling the universe with divine power (6,20–23); he is the "activity" (ἐνέργεια) of the unknown Father (7,16–17). Whereas Plotinus was content to state that the One is his own ἐνέργεια (*Enn.* 6.8.12), *Marsanes* and *Allogenes* posit a separate mediating hypostasis for this purpose. He is, moreover, a triadic being, "triple-powerful." A comparable notion occurs in the *Chaldean Oracles* frg. 27 (des Places): παντὶ γὰρ ἐν κόσμῳ λάμπει τριάς, ἧς μονὰς ἄρχει ("for in every world there shines a triad, over which a monad rules"). Damascius (*De princ.* 43) interprets this oracle to mean that the one transcendent Father is prior to the Triad (ὁ εἷς πατὴρ ὁ πρὸ τῆς τριάδος).

The Greek word translated by the Coptic expressions πλ ϣαμτε ν̄6λμ and πιϣμν̄τ6ομ is τριδύναμος, found untranslated in the untitled text of the Bruce Codex (chap. 4 and passim) and other Gnostic sources. Indeed, the "three power" terminology is used in a number of various mythological contexts in Gnostic sources,[40] but it is especially important

---

νοητός, νοῦς θεωρητικός, and νοῦς διανοούμενος respectively. See "Threefold Path," 334. Cf. Plotinus's discussion in *Enn.* 2.9.6 concerning the distinctions made by the Gnostics among ὁ νοῦς ἐν ἡσυχίᾳ, ὁ νοῦς θεωρῶν, and ὁ νοῦς διανοούμενος.

39. See esp. his *Inst. Theol.* and E. R. Dodds's admirable commentary: *Proclus: The Elements of Theology.*

40. It is used of the supreme God in *Steles Seth* 121,31–32; of Barbelo in *Steles Seth* 121,32–33 and *Ap. John* II 5,8; BG 27,19–28,2; of Monogenes = Christ in Cod. Bruc. *Untitled*, chap. 4 and passim; of Christ in the "Peratic" system described by Hippolytus *Ref.* 5.12 (τριφυῆς . . . τρισώματος . . . τριδύναμος ἄνθρωπος); and of the "self-willed" Authades and other hostile powers in *Pistis Sophia*, chap. 29 and passim.

for our purposes to note that the term becomes a technical term in the vocabulary of Neoplatonism, used both of the human soul (e.g., Hierocles *Carm. Aur.* [Mullach 1, col. 462]) and of God (Marius Victorinus). Its use in the trinitarian theology of Marius Victorinus is especially important: "τριδύναμος est deus, id est tres potentias habens, esse, vivere, intellegere" ("God is triple-powerful, i.e., he has three powers: Existence, Life, and Intelligence": *Adv. Arium* 4.21). Victorinus relates "Existence" to the Father, "Life" to the Son, and "Intelligence" to the Holy Spirit.[41] This passage in Marius Victorinus has been shown by Pierre Hadot to be among those portions of Victorinus's writings based on Porphyry's lost commentary on Plato's *Parmenides*.[42] That Porphyry, in turn, got his triad of Existence, Life, and Intelligence from Sethian Gnostic sources is certainly possible. In *Allogenes*, which Porphyry knew (*Vit. Plot.* 16) and which is a likely source for Porphyry's triad, the "Triple Power" is defined exactly as in Marius Victorinus and Porphyry: "He is Life (ⲱⲚⲌ = ζωή) and Intelligence (ⲦⲘⲚ̄ⲦⲈⲓⲘⲈ = νόησις) and That Which Is (ⲡⲏ ⲈⲦⲈ ⲡⲀⲓ ⲡⲈ = τὸ ὄν) (49,26–28). The same triad of Being, Life, and Intelligence occurs in *Steles Seth* 125,28–32, and comparable triads occur in *Zostrianos* (ὕπαρξις, γνῶσις, ζωή: 15,2–12) and in *Marsanes* (γνῶσις, ὑπόστασις, ἐνέργεια: 9,16–18).[43] The term τριδύναμος itself may be a Gnostic coinage. If so, it found a natural environment in the speculations of the Neoplatonists, with their fondness for triadic ontological structures. In any case, we see in the use of the term τριδύναμος and the speculative triads mentioned above additional evidence of intellectual interaction between Gnostics and Platonist scholars in late antiquity.

THE SOUL IN MARSANES

In its treatment of the nature and destiny of the human soul *Marsanes* can be seen as essentially a Platonist work, and conversant with contemporary Platonist exegesis of, and speculation on, Plato's dialogues, especially the *Timaeus*. One interesting aspect of *Marsanes*'s doctrine of

41. Cf. Pierre Hadot's comments in P. Henry and P. Hadot, eds., *Marius Victorinus: Traités théologiques sur la Trinité* (SC 68; Paris: Cerf, 1960) 1.81–83. Hadot sees possible parallels to τριδύναμος in the terms τριγλώχις and τριοῦχος used in the *Chaldean Oracles* (frgs. 2, 26 [des Places]); see Pierre Hadot, *Porphyre et Victorinus* (Paris: Études Augustiniennes, n.d.) 1.294 n. 2. For the triad τὸ ὄν, ζωή, and νοῦς in Proclus see *Inst. Theol.* 103 (Dodds, *Proclus*, 92).

42. See *Porphyre et Victorinus*, esp. 1.293–94; 2.48.

43. For discussion of the Neoplatonic triad in relation to *The Three Steles of Seth*, *Zostrianos*, and *Allogenes* see Robinson, "Three Steles," 133–41; Tardieu, "Les Trois stèles," 559–64; and Turner, "Threefold Path," 334–36.

the soul is its treatment of the "spherical shape" ($\sigma\phi\alpha\iota\rho\iota\kappa\grave{o}\nu$ $\sigma\chi\hat{\eta}\mu\alpha$) of the soul, and the spherical parts of which it is made up. To be sure, the relevant passages are very garbled and difficult to construe (see esp. 25*,21–29*,1), dealing as they do not only with the soul but also with the letters of the alphabet in various combinations. Nevertheless, the basic notion of the sphericity of the soul is clear enough. In contemporary Platonist speculation on the Psychogonia in Plato *Tim.* 35A–36D, the human soul, as well as the world soul, is regarded as made up of seven parts conceived as circular or spherical (e.g., Plutarch *De an. procr.* 1028B; Diog. Laert. 3.71). The later Neoplatonists tie this doctrine of the sphericity of the soul to their concept of the soul's immaterial "vehicle" ($\ddot{o}\chi\eta\mu\alpha$: e.g., Proclus *In Tim.* 2.72.14; *Inst. Theol.* 210; Iamblichus *In Tim.* frg. 49 [Dillon]),[44] which is considered to be put on during the soul's descent from heaven.

Marsanes also seems to know Numenius's teaching on the descent of the soul into the world of generation, as presented in Macrobius's commentary on the "Dream of Scipio" found in Cicero's *Republic*.[45] In this doctrine the soul originates in heaven in the region of the fixed stars (Macrobius *In somn.* 1.11.10; cf. Num. frg. 35 [des Places]). From its original divine state as a "monad" (*In somn.* 1.12.5; cf. Num. frg. 42), it experiences "division" (*In somn.* 1.12.6,12), and becoming a "dyad" (*In somn.* 1.12.5) it descends through the intersection of the Zodiac and the Milky Way through the planetary spheres down to earth (*In somn.* 1.12.1–4,13–14). As usual, the text in *Marsanes* is fragmentary and garbled, but this basic doctrine can be seen nevertheless. At 25*,16–19, immediately after a fragmentary passage on the Zodiac, the soul's "division" ($\pi\omega\text{p}.\text{x} = \mu\epsilon\rho\iota\sigma\mu\acute{o}s$) "in these regions" (i.e., in the lower realms) is mentioned, followed by the passage cited above on the "spherical shapes" of the soul. In an earlier passage in *Marsanes* "soul garments" are mentioned ($\bar{\text{n}}$ɛ[ʙϲⲱ ⲙ]ⲯⲩⲭⲏ, 5,7–8), which may relate to the attributes put on by the soul in its descent (cf. Macrobius *In somn.* 1.12.13).

There are other examples of Platonic tradition utilized in *Marsanes*'s doctrine of the soul. *Marsanes* (41*,17–19), like *In somn.* 1.12.7–11 (cf.

44. On the vehicle of the soul in Neoplatonism see esp. Appendix II in Dodds, *Proclus*, 313–21. Cf. also Majercik, *Chaldean Oracles*, 31–40.

45. See Macrobius *In somn.* 1.10–12, based essentially on Numenius, according to E. R. Dodds, "Numenius and Ammonius," in *Les sources de Plotin* (Entretiens sur L'antiquité classique 5; Geneva: Hardt, 1960) 8; and H. de Ley, *Macrobius and Numenius: A Study of Macrobius, In Somn. I c. 12* (Brussels: Latomus, 1972). Porphyry is also sometimes credited as the source for Macrobius's description; see, e.g., R. van den Broek, "The Authentikos Logos: A New Document of Christian Platonism," *VC* 33 (1979) 263, n. 15.

Plotinus *Enn.* 2.9.6), teaches that embodiment dulls the intellect. In the same passage (41*,20–22) disembodied souls in heaven are mentioned, in a manner somewhat reminiscent of Plato's "Myth of Er" (*Resp.* 10.614A–621D) and later Platonist speculation thereon (e.g., Macrobius *In somn.* 1.11–12).

The destiny of the Gnostic soul is its ascent to the heavenly world and its reintegration into the divine. Precisely this ascent is held out throughout the text of *Marsanes* as the goal to be reached (see esp. 10,12–23); the prophet Marsanes's own ascent experience is treated as paradigmatic. In *Marsanes*, and in related Gnostic texts, the ultimate ascent of the soul is anticipated by means of an intellectual ascent experience described in ways reminiscent of traditional Platonic doctrines of ascent, especially those based on Plato's *Symposium* (210A–212A, Diotima's revelation to Socrates), with its goal of the vision of ultimate divine beauty and the achievement of immortality.[46] The passage on the thirteen seals in *Marsanes*, discussed above, may be an example of this *via eminentiae*, the way of ascending degrees, comparable to that presented in Plato's *Symposium*, wherein the Gnostic soul moves in contemplation from one stage to a higher one, reaching ultimately to a revelation of the ultimate stage, the unknown "Silent One" (2,12–4,25). The experience envisioned here is similar to that of Plotinus, as described by Porphyry (*Vit. Plot.* 23):

> So to this God-like man above all, who often raised himself in thought according to the ways Plato teaches in the *Symposium* to the First and Transcendent God, that God appeared who has neither shape nor any intelligible form, but is enthroned above Intellect and the Intelligible.[47]

Porphyry goes on to say that Plotinus was "united" (ἐνωθῆναι) with God four times, presumably in a transintellectual mystical experience, during the time Porphyry was with him. Plotinus himself describes the process of mystical union with the One (*Enn.* 6.9) and speaks of it as a "turning inward" of the soul (6.9.7), with concomitant "detachment from all things here below" (6.9.11). This kind of experience is reflected in *Marsanes*, too: "We have all withdrawn (ἀναχωρεῖν) to ourselves. We have become silent . . . we came to know him" (9,21–24).

Less lofty ideas pertaining to the ascent of the soul are also reflected in *Marsanes*. I refer now especially to that lengthy section of text dealing

---

46. On Gnostic ascent in *Allogenes, Three Steles of Seth,* and *Zostrianos,* and Platonic ascent traditions, see Turner, "Threefold Path," 341–46.
47. Armstrong's translation in the LCL edition, somewhat modified.

with the letters of the alphabet and their various combinations (esp. 26*,18–39,12), a passage closely tied to the sought-for ascent of the soul. This interesting passage reflects knowledge of technical grammatical discussion in the schools regarding the alphabet (Dionysius Thrax and his later commentators), but it is clear that the knowledge conveyed here has religious purposes akin, in fact, to those of the Valentinian Gnostic Marcus (Irenaeus *Haer.* 1.13–21). The letter combinations occurring here go beyond simple school exercises,[48] and have as their ultimate purpose "that you might collect them, and be separated from the angels" (32*,3–5). The various letters of the alphabet and their syllabic combinations are understood to have their counterparts in the angelic world (presumably located in the planetary and Zodiacal spheres), and the Gnostic adept must know their natures and their "nomenclature" (ὀνομασία: 27*,13; 30*,8; 31*,4) in order to ascend beyond these spheres occupied by the angels. Moreover, some of the various letter combinations have the character of *voces mysticae* or glossolalia and seem to have been intended to be chanted.

We are reminded that Plotinus scoffed at the Gnostics for their incantations addressed to the higher powers with the purpose of making them obey their commands (*Enn.* 2.9.14), but later Neoplatonists would have had less of a problem with this. Similar ideas and practices are reflected in the *Chaldean Oracles*, which loom so large in late Neoplatonism.[49] The theory, in any case, is already present in the *Theologoumena Arithmeticae* of the Pythagorean Nicomachus of Gerasa (fl. ca. 100 C.E.):

> For indeed the sounds of each sphere of the seven, each sphere naturally producing one certain kind of sound, are called "vowels." They are ineffable in and of themselves, but are recalled by the wise with respect to everything made up of them. Wherefore also here (i.e., on earth) this sound has power, which in arithmetic is a monad, in geometry a point, in grammar a letter (of the alphabet). And combined with the material letters, which are the consonants, as the soul to the body and the musical scale to the strings—the one producing living beings, the other pitch and melody—they accomplish active and mystic powers of divine beings. Wherefore when especially the theurgists are worshiping such (a divine being), they

48. The passage in 31*,23–29 is derived from a school exercise. See my notes to the text and translation in *Codices IX and X*.

49. Cf. Majercik's discussion in *Chaldean Oracles*, esp. 42–45. Majercik makes an explicit connection between the Chaldean use of "passwords" (συνθήματα) and *voces mysticae* as ascent techniques, and similar phenomena reflected in the Sethian Gnostic texts, including *Marsanes*.

invoke it symbolically with hissing sounds and clucking, with inarticulate and foreign sounds.[50]

PLATONIC MONISM IN *MARSANES*

Thus far we have concentrated on some major points of Platonic influence in the tractate *Marsanes*, and one could add to these a number of examples of Platonic vocabulary and technical terminology found in our Gnostic document.[51] We have also noted some specific connections between *Marsanes* (and the other documents related to it) and the Gnostic doctrines encountered by Plotinus and his disciples in his own school in Rome, including some very specific examples such as the Gnostic technical terms μετάνοια and παροίκησις. Nevertheless, there are some interesting omissions in *Marsanes* of specifically Gnostic doctrines and mythology also attacked by Plotinus, notably those most characteristic of the radical dualism of early Gnosticism, such as the myth of the Fall of Sophia[52] and the doctrine of the evil or foolish Creator (Enn. 2.9.4–5, 10–11). In fact, one can see reflected in *Marsanes* a definite tendency to move away from the radical dualism of early Gnosticism in the direction of a more monistic and procosmic understanding of reality. In my opinion this tendency is directly attributable to the influence of Platonic philosophy, and can be accounted for by positing a considerable degree of discussion between Gnostics and Platonists in schools such as that of Plotinus in Rome.

One notable example of what can be taken as a concession to Platonic monism is the following passage (*Marsanes* 5,17–26), where the Gnostic prophet says:

> I have deliberated and have attained to the boundary of the sense-perceptible world. ⟨I have come to know⟩ part by part the entire place of the incorporeal being, and ⟨I⟩ have come to know the intelligible world. ⟨I have come to know⟩, when I was deliberating, that in every respect the sense-perceptible world is [worthy] of being saved entirely.

50. Nicomachus *apud* C. Janus, *Musici Scriptores Graeci* (Leipzig: Teubner, 1895; repr. Hildesheim: Olms, 1962) 276–77, au. trans. On the use of the term "the theurgists" (οἱ θεουργοί) in this passage, see E. R. Dodds, "New Light on the Chaldean Oracles," in Lewy-Tardieu, *Chaldean Oracles*, 700 n. 31.

51. Some examples: *Marsanes*'s use of the term "incorporeal" (ἀσώματον) as an attribute of the intelligible (νοητόν) realm (3,8–9 and 20; 5,13 and 21; 36*,20), for which see, e.g., Numenius frg. 7 (des Places); *Marsanes*'s use of the term ἁπλοῦς ("simple") as a divine attribute (5,8–9), for which see Numenius frg. 11 (des Places); *Marsanes*'s references to "sameness" and "difference" as qualities built into the world (4,27–28), for which see esp. Plato *Tim.* 35A. For these and numerous other examples see my notes to the text and translation of *Marsanes* in *Codices IX and X*.

52. There is a possible allusion to the "salvation of Sophia" in *Marsanes* 4,2; the text is ambiguous.

Despite the corrupt state of the text, the import of this passage is clear. It is immediately followed by a statement on the descent of the "Self-begotten One," or "Autogenes," for the purpose of effecting salvation (5,2–6,16). That the "sense-perceptible world" is capable[53] of salvation is a rather surprising idea for a Gnostic text, but I think it can be accounted for with reference to a specific Platonic tradition, namely, that the purpose of the soul's descent into the material world is "for the perfection of the All" (εἰς τελείωσιν τοῦ παντός: Calvisius Taurus apud Stob. 1.378,25–28 [Wachsmuth]), based on Plato's Timaeus (41A–42A, esp. 41B).[54] Plato refers in this passage to the demiurgic activity of the lesser gods in fashioning the mortal beings. In Marsanes the salvific activity of Autogenes involves a descent to the lower world, and this activity is spelled out with even greater clarity in Allogenes 51,28–33, also probably under the influence of the Platonic theory under discussion: "He works successively and individually, continuing to rectify the failures from nature." Autogenes's activity in the lower realms is, in a sense, a demiurgic activity that effects the perfection, the "salvation," of the "sense-perceptible world."

Another example of Marsanes's monistic tendency—its tendency to place a higher value on the "world" (κόσμος) as a whole—is found in a passage where cosmic contemplation is given a positive value. The last line of p. 41* begins, "Blessed is" (the text is broken off at this point); the passage continues on p. 42* as follows: "whether he is gazing at the two (sun and moon) or is gazing at the seven planets or at the twelve signs of the Zodiac or the thirty-six Decans" (42*,1–7, with a break in the MS thereafter). It seems clear that "blessedness" is attributed to the one engaged in cosmic meditation, as a step toward enlightenment. Such an idea is based on a very popular tradition in Platonism, that meditation on the heavens leads to the vision of God. Humans, endowed by the Creator with an erect posture wherewith to gaze easily upward (Plato Tim. 90A–D), should fix their contemplative gaze on the heavens and thus achieve enlightenment. Numerous examples of this cosmic piety are found in later Platonic texts.[55] The attitude expressed here in Marsanes stands in marked contrast to the usual Gnostic attitude toward the

53. The text is restored at 5,25 as ϥⲙ̄[ⲡϣⲁ, "it (the sense-perceptible world) is worthy."

54. For discussion of this tradition see esp. Paul Kubel, Schuld und Schicksal bei Origines, Gnostikern, und Platonikern (Stuttgart: Calwer, 1973) 15–27.

55. See, e.g., Philo Plant. 16–27; Leg. all. 3.100–102; Vit. Mos. 2.69–70; Mut. Nom. 54–56; Somn. 2.226; Macrobius In somn. 1.14. On this tradition see the important monograph by Antonie Wlosok, Laktanz und die philosophische Gnosis: Untersuchungen zu Geschichte und Terminologie der gnostischen Erlöservorstellung (Abhandlungen der Heidelberger Akademie der Wissenschaften 2; Heidelberg: Winter, 1960).

heavenly bodies, especially the planets and the Zodiac.[56] Plotinus, in fact, criticizes the Gnostics for their attitude toward the heavenly bodies, and he recommends cosmic meditation (*Enn.* 2.9.16; 3.8.11). *Marsanes* clearly represents a Gnostic concession to the viewpoint expressed by Plotinus on this point, as on other important points already discussed.

In an important article, "Gnosis and Greek Philosophy," A. H. Armstrong[57] sums up the present state of scholarship on the question of the influence of Greek philosophy on Gnosticism. He says that the influence of Greek philosophy on Gnosticism is "not genuine, but extraneous, and, for the most part superficial."[58] In my view one can now go beyond that observation, by means of a closer look at such Gnostic tractates as *Marsanes* and the others we have discussed here, and argue that the influence of Greek philosophy, especially "Middle Platonism" in its more popular forms, is far more profound than heretofore thought. This is particularly so in the case of the later, more developed stages in the evolution of the Gnostic religion in late antiquity. It should also be stressed that the contact between Gnostics and Platonists was not by any means a one-way street. One must allow for the influence of Gnosticism upon late Platonism;[59] indeed, some examples of such influence have been given here, such as the term $\tau\rho\iota\delta\acute{v}\nu\alpha\mu\sigma\varsigma$, and the triad of Existence, Life, and Intelligence.

We can therefore conclude this essay with the observation that *Marsanes* and the other texts discussed here represent a significant intersection in the respective histories of Sethian Gnosticism and Platonic philosophy: in the development of the former "from mythology to mystical philosophy,"[60] and in the development of the latter in the opposite direction.[61]

---

56. E.g., *Ap. John* BG 39,6–12; *Exc. ex Theod.* 69–74; Cf. Kurt Rudolph, "Coptica-Mandaica: Zu einigen Übereinstimmungen zwischen koptisch-gnostischen und mandäischen Texten," in Martin Krause, ed., *Essays on the Nag Hammadi Texts in Honour of Pahor Labib* (NHS 6; Leiden: E. J. Brill, 1975) 204–5. Rudolph refers to *Marsanes*, but gives the wrong page reference and misunderstands the text. For an interesting discussion of the cosmic "rulers" in *The Apocryphon of John* as planetary and Zodiacal beings, see A. J. Welburn, "The Identity of the Archons in the 'Apocryphon Johannis,'" *VC* 32 (1978) 241–54.

57. In Barbara Aland, ed., *Gnosis: Festschrift für Hans Jonas* (Göttingen: Vandenhoeck & Ruprecht, 1978) 87–124.

58. Ibid., 109.

59. Armstrong allows for Gnostic influence on Numenius (ibid., 106–9).

60. Cf. Pearson, "Tractate Marsanes," 384; cf. also n. 20 above. The second volume of Hans Jonas's monumental work on Gnosis is subtitled "Von der Mythologie zur mystischen Philosophie" (*Gnosis und spätantiker Geist* [Göttingen: Vandenhoeck & Ruprecht, 1954]).

61. Cf. Carsten Colpe, "Überlieferung IX," *JAC* 23 (1980) 125.

11

Philo, Gnosis, and the
New Testament

The title of this chapter[1] might imply a wide-ranging treatment of a multitude of topics within three different and very large areas of study, or it might imply an attempt to find a connecting thread running through Philo, Gnosis, and the New Testament. One might also look upon one of them as the connecting link between the other two, for example, "Gnosis" as that which holds Philo and the New Testament together in some way. I take this latter option here, using the term "Gnosis" in a broad sense, and taking some current scholarship into account in the process. I begin this study in Corinth, and then move to Alexandria. There is also a movement in time, from the first century to the end of the second. Two of the Nag Hammadi tractates are taken briefly into account: *The Testimony of Truth* (NHC IX,3) and *The Teachings of Silvanus* (VII,4).

"GNOSIS" IN CORINTH?

In an article published some time ago, R. McL. Wilson poses the question, "How Gnostic were the Corinthians?"[2] Focusing on 1 Corinthians, he mentions in the course of his article the various motifs that have frequently been taken to reflect Gnostic influence among the Corinthians: a tendency to division, the terms "wisdom" and "gnosis," alleged libertine tendencies, denial or misunderstanding of the resurrection, spiritual enthusiasm, realized eschatology, misuse or misunderstanding of the sacraments, contrasts between *psychikoi* and *pneumati-*

---

1. This title was assigned to me by the editors of the Festschrift (to R. McL. Wilson) in which the essay first appeared. See Introduction, above.
2. 'How Gnostic Were the Corinthians?" *NTS* 19 (1972) 65–74.

koi, and the typology of Christ and Adam. Wilson grants that these items may add up to "what A. D. Nock[3] called 'a gnostic way of thinking,' such as we find later in the developed gnostic schools of thought" (70–71). He adds that the use of the term "Gnosis" is legitimate as a general description of the Corinthian situation (71). He even concedes that Paul himself "appears to be moving in a gnostic direction" in his view of the resurrection body (66–67). But he vigorously argues that it is illegitimate to read the developed Gnosticism of the second century back into first-century Corinth. "Gnosis in the broader sense is not yet Gnosticism" (71). What one finds in first-century Corinth, he concludes, is "only the first tentative beginnings of what was later to develop into fullscale Gnosticism" (74).

The careful distinction Wilson wants to make between the religion of the Corinthians, which he calls "Gnosis," and "Gnosticism" is surely cogent enough. I share his conviction that the religion of Paul's Corinthian congregation cannot reasonably be defined as "Gnostic" in the conventional sense of the term,[4] though I hasten to add that I make this judgment on exegetical grounds, leaving open the question whether "developed Gnosticism" actually existed in the first century.[5] But is

---

3. "Gnosticism," *HTR* 57 (1964) 278. Cf. chap. 10 in this book.

4. Cf. the well-known formulations found in the "Proposal for a terminological and conceptual agreement with regard to the theme of the Colloquium" drawn up at the Messina Colloquium on the Origins of Gnosticism, published in Bianchi, *Origini dello gnosticismo,* xxvi–xxix, English version. This document distinguishes *gnōsis,* as "knowledge of the divine mysteries reserved for an elite," from "the Gnosticism of the Second Century sects." The latter includes such elements as "the idea of a divine spark in man," a "devolution of the divine," and a saving *gnōsis* involving "the divine identity of the *knower* (the Gnostic), the *known* (the divine substance of one's transcendent self), and the *means by which one knows (gnōsis)."* Thus "not every *gnōsis* is Gnosticism." Wilson refers to these definitions of the Messina Colloquium with approval in several of his writings; see, e.g., *Gnosis and the New Testament* (Philadelphia: Fortress/Oxford: Blackwell, 1968) 17. Indeed, the distinction between "Gnosis" and "Gnosticism" is a basic presupposition of all of Wilson's publications on Gnosticism.

5. Although it is true that we do not have any *primary* textual evidence for Gnosticism earlier than the second century, it need not be concluded that Gnosticism could not have existed as early as the first century. In any case, it can no longer be held that Gnosticism developed as a "Christian heresy." On the whole question see now Rudolph, *Gnosis.* Simon Magus, e.g., has been taken by some (not all) scholars to represent a full-blown Gnosticism. See, e.g., Jonas, *Gnostic Religion,* 103–11; E. Haenchen, "Gab es eine vorchristliche Gnosis?" *ZTK* 49 (1952) 316–49; W. Foerster, "Die 'ersten Gnostiker' Simon und Menander," in Bianchi, *Origini dello Gnosticismo,* 190–96; and Rudolph, *Gnosis,* 294–98; Rudolph, "Simon—Magus oder Gnosticus? Zum Stand der Debatte," *ThR* 42 (1977) 279–359; G. Lüdemann, "The Acts of the Apostles and the Beginnings of Simonian Gnosis," *NTS* 33 (1987) 420–26. It should also be recalled that Wilson himself, in his important book, *The Gnostic Problem* (London: Mowbray, 1958), states the following: "Our earliest definite documentary evidence goes back to the middle of the first century, to the New Testament period. It may be that Gnosticism in the full sense is even older, but so far as can be seen at present it is more or less

"Gnosis" a better designation for the Corinthian situation than "Gnosticism"? Is this "Gnosis" simply a step in the direction of the "developed Gnosticism" of the second century? Wilson does make an important observation, with specific reference to "Wisdom Christology," to the effect that "something has happened to break the continuity of development and divert gnostic thinking into a different channel" (73), an important caveat against concluding that the religion of the Corinthians represents a point along a set "trajectory" leading inevitably to the "Gnosticism" of the second century. But then two items need further clarification: (1) In what specific first-century religious context should the Corinthian situation be placed? (2) What is that "something" that "divert(s) gnostic thinking into a different channel"?

Setting aside the second question for now, I want to take up the first, and reiterate here some points I made some years ago on the subject, namely, the historical contexts of the Corinthians' supposedly Gnostic traits.[6] In so doing I shall also call attention to some more recent contributions that shed additional light on this question.

The logical place to begin an appraisal of "Gnosis in Corinth" is the single passage in 1 Corinthians where *gnōsis* is discussed and even defined, 1 Corinthians 8. The burning issue in that chapter is whether or not it is permissible to eat meat that has been sacrificed to pagan gods ("idols," v. 4). The *gnōsis* on the basis of which certain Christians in Corinth felt free to eat such meat is specified as the knowledge that "there is no God but One," knowledge Paul and his Corinthian opponents have in common (v. 1). The *gnōsis* in question is the insight that enables Christians to make practical decisions in the community, based on the knowledge of God.[7] This kind of *gnōsis* pervades biblical and postbiblical Jewish thought, and has nothing whatever to do with Gnosticism.[8]

R. A. Horsley, in an article entitled "Gnosis in Corinth,"[9] has come to similar conclusions. But he makes some very interesting elaborations by putting the whole argument in 1 Cor. 8:1–6 squarely in the context of

contemporary with Christianity" (68). Cf. also his chap. on "The Earlier Gnostic Sects" (97–115).

6. Pearson, *Pneumatikos-Psychikos Terminology*. See also Pearson, "Hellenistic-Jewish Wisdom Speculation and Paul," in R. L. Wilken, ed., *Aspects of Wisdom in Judaism and Early Christianity* (Notre Dame: University of Notre Dame Press, 1975) 43–66.

7. See my discussion in *Pneumatikos-Psychikos Terminology*, 42–43.

8. Against Bultmann, TDNT 1.709, followed by U. Wilckens, *Weisheit und Torheit* (Tübingen: J. C. B. Mohr, 1959) 212, and W. Schmithals, *Die Gnosis in Korinth* (2d ed.; Göttingen: Vandenhoeck & Ruprecht, 1965) 134.

9. R. A. Horsley, "Gnosis in Corinth: 1 Corinthians 8:1–6," NTS 27 (1981) 32–51.

Hellenistic Jewish thought, especially as it is represented by Philo of Alexandria and the Wisdom of Solomon. It is in this context, too, that he places the *logos/sophia* Christology reflected in v. 6. I cannot take up his arguments in detail here; suffice it to say that his understanding of the background of Paul's argument in 1 Corinthians 8 is basically persuasive.

If one can speak of a "Gnosis" in Corinth in the sense that Wilson does, that is, as a "knowledge reserved for an elite,"[10] it must be added that such "gnosis" among the Corinthians was focused on the term *sophia* ("wisdom") rather than *gnōsis*. This is made abundantly clear especially in 1 Corinthians 1—4.[11] This passage (i.e., 1:10—4:20) constitutes a personal *apologia*, wherein Paul not only seeks to correct some fatal flaws in his Corinthian congregation's theology and conduct but also defends his apostolic authority against opponents who are challenging this authority. As part of their challenge they are claiming a special "wisdom" *(sophia)* and a special status as "spiritual" *(pneumatikoi)* and "perfect" (or "mature," *teleioi*) people, in contrast to others in the congregation who are still "babes" (or "immature," *nēpioi*). Paul cleverly takes his opponents' terminology, in which they express their elitist claims, and turns it back against them. Paul's opponents are using categories derived from Hellenistic Jewish wisdom, such as is represented especially by Philo of Alexandria and the Wisdom of Solomon. Paul himself argues out of a religious background more akin to Palestinian apocalypticism than to the speculative wisdom of his Corinthian opponents. I have discussed all of this in previous studies, and therefore do not wish to repeat the arguments here.[12] However, I do want to call attention once again to the work of R. A. Horsley, in which he comes to the same basic conclusions while providing additional arguments and evidence.[13]

To be sure, Horsley has taken issue with some of my contentions regarding the contrasting terms *pneumatikos* and *psychikos* as used in 1

10. See above, and n. 4.
11. That *gnōsis* in 1 Corinthians (chap. 8) is not the same as *sophia* is evident in 12:8, where the two are distinguished, as well as in 1:5, where Paul praises the Corinthians for their *gnosis* while proceeding to deny their claim to *sophia* in his main argument in chaps. 1—4. Cf. *Pneumatikos-Psychikos Terminology*, 42.
12. "Hellenistic-Jewish Wisdom Speculation"; cf. *Pneumatikos-Psychikos Terminology*, 27–42.
13. In addition to his article cited in n. 9 (esp. 43–51), see "Wisdom of Word and Words of Wisdom in Corinth," *CBQ* 39 (1977) 224–39; and "Pneumatikos vs. Psychikos: Distinctions of Spiritual Status among the Corinthians," *HTR* 69 (1976) 269–88, esp. 280–88.

Corinthians (2:13–15; 15:45–57); so I should like to take this up briefly here, particularly because this is the most important item brought up by those who want to point to an alleged "Gnostic" influence in 1 Corinthians.[14] My argument, in summary, is that the *pneumatikos-psychikos* terminology derives from Hellenistic Jewish exegesis of Gen. 2:7, wherein a differentiation is made between "spirit" *(pneuma)* and "soul" *(psychē)*. The starting point for this observation is 1 Cor. 15:44–47, where Gen. 2:7 is the point of the argument. Paul's eschatological targum on that passage is meant to counter his opponents' use of Gen. 2:7 to prove that man has an immortal element *(pneuma)* in him capable of surviving physical death. This is part of their argument against the resurrection of the body. Paul's point, based on his appropriation and reinterpretation of Palestinian resurrection traditions in which Gen. 2:7 is interpreted eschatologically, is that Christ is the "last Adam" and the "life-giving spirit" whose resurrection is the basis of future resurrection and eternal life for all believers. The best analogies to the Corinthians' interpretation of Gen. 2:7 are found in Philo and Wisdom.[15] Paul's opponents use the same Hellenistic Jewish exegetical traditions to bolster their classification of people in the community as "spiritual" *(pneumatikoi)*, those who live on the plane of the spirit *(pneuma)* by their devotion to wisdom, in contrast to those who live on the plane of their lower soul (the *psychikoi*) by not seeking after the higher wisdom.[16]

Horsley's critique of my argument consists of three points: (1) The specific *pneumatikos-psychikos* contrast does not occur in Philo or in other Hellenistic Jewish writings. (2) There is no fundamental contrast between "soul" and "spirit" in Philo or Wisdom. (3) There is no evidence in Philo or Wisdom for a preference of the term "spirit" instead of "mind" *(nous)* as a designation for the higher part of the soul.[17] The first point is obviously correct, nor did I ever claim to find that specific contrast in Philo or other Hellenistic Jewish writings. I did, and do, claim that the adjectival terms are based on a contrast between *pneuma* and *psychē*, analogous to the differentiation made in popular Greek philosophy of that era between the *psychē* of man and his rational *nous* ("mind").[18]

14. H. Jonas takes the *pneuma (pneumatikos)-psyché (psychikos)* contrast as a typical expression of Gnostic anthropology; see *Gnosis und spätantiker Geist*, vol. 1 (Göttingen: Vandenhoeck & Ruprecht, 1964) 210–14. Cf. R. Bultmann, *Theology of the New Testament*, vol. 1 (trans. K. Grobel; New York: Scribners, 1951) 174, 181, 204, with special reference to 1 Corinthians.

15. Cf. *Pneumatikos-Psychikos Terminology*, 15–26.

16. See above, and n. 12.

17. "Pneumatikos vs. Psychikos," 271.

18. Cf., e.g., *The Pneumatikos-Psychikos Terminology*, 9–11.

Point three of Horsley's critique is conceded. I should not have said that a "preference" for the term *pneuma* instead of *nous* is observable in Hellenistic Judaism.[19] But I still contend that the *locus classicus* in the LXX for a contrast between the soul and the spirit in man is Gen. 2:7, precisely the text whose interpretation is the bone of contention between Paul and his opponents in 1 Cor. 15:44–47. There is no question but that Philo uses the term *nous* for the higher faculty of the soul more frequently than he does *pneuma,* but even Horsley concedes that Philo uses *pneuma* for the higher soul sometimes; he counts "a dozen times" and cites as one of the texts *Special Laws* 1.171, which refers to "the rational spirit in us" (τοῦ ἐν ἡμῖν λογικοῦ πνεύματος; cf. *Spec. Leg.* 1.277).[20] As for point two, it is obvious that there is no consistent or "fundamental" contrast between "soul" and "spirit" in Philo or Wisdom—the terms are frequently seen as interchangeable as Horsley rightly points out[21]—but it can hardly be denied that the contrast occurs in Philo. Genesis 2:7 (LXX) certainly suggests such a contrast: God's inbreathing of the "breath of life" (πνοὴ ζωῆς) into man makes him a "living soul" (ψυχὴ ζῶσα). It is noteworthy that Philo sometimes substitutes the term *pneuma* for *pnoē* in his rendition of the passage (e.g., *Op. Mund.* 135; *Leg. All.* 3.161). And while it is true, as Horsley argues, that Philo often understands *pneuma* as the substance *(ousia)* of the soul,[22] consonant with a basic body-soul dualism, he can also differentiate between a lower (animal) soul and a higher soul *(Det. Pot. Ins.* 79–95; *Spec. Leg.* 4.123). In sum, while it is true that the contrast between a higher spirit and a lower soul is not a fundamental and exclusive one in Philo or Wisdom, such a contrast is fundamental to the contrast between the terms *pneumatikos* and *psychikos* as used by the Corinthian opponents of Paul.

Horsley does go on to show in an entirely convincing way that the contrast between the *pneumatikoi* and the *psychikoi* made by Paul's Corinthian opponents is ultimately based on Hellenistic Jewish categories, including exegesis of Gen. 2:7.[23] Horsley rightly sees Philo and Wisdom, in general, as providing the best analogies to the kind of religion espoused by the Corinthians, as reflected in Paul's argumentation.[24] This, then, brings up a basic historical question: How do we

19. Ibid., 11.
20. "Pneumatikos vs. Psychikos," 271 n. 8, and 273 n. 10.
21. Ibid., 271–73.
22. Ibid., 272.
23. Ibid., 274–88.
24. Cf. Pearson, *Pneumatikos-Psychikos Terminology,* passim.

account for the similarities between the Corinthians' "gnosis" (which I prefer to refer to as Christianized Hellenistic Jewish wisdom) and the religion of Philo? Paul's apologia in 1 Corinthians 1—4 provides a good basis for answering this question. It seems clear in his argumentation that he is especially concerned about the role of Apollos in the Corinthian congregation (esp. 3:5—4:5). He wants to express collegiality with Apollos, but at the same time he expresses his apostolic superiority to him in no uncertain terms. This suggests that the highly developed wisdom speculation in Corinth can be attributed to the teaching activity of Apollos. If we recall that Apollos was an Alexandrian Jew and a learned and eloquent teacher of scripture (Acts 18:24–26), we have a very plausible link between the religiosity of the Corinthians and that of Alexandrian Judaism as represented in Philo.[25] I am in any case convinced that virtually everything in 1 Corinthians thought to represent a "gnostic way of thinking"[26] can be explained on the basis of Hellenistic Jewish speculative wisdom such as that encountered in Philo.[27]

With this observation we move from Corinth to Alexandria.

HOW "GNOSTIC" IS PHILO?

If the "gnosis" of the Corinthians has basic affinities with the religiosity of Philo—which has been argued above—the extent to which Philo himself can be called a "Gnostic" becomes an issue. Here, again, we can profitably turn to what Wilson has written on the subject. I refer especially to his 1972 article, "Philo of Alexandria and Gnosticism."[28] In that article he reduces the various scholarly opinions on Philo's relation to Gnosticism to two: (1) Philo is part of the Gnostic movement.[29] (2) Philo is a precursor of the later Gnostic movement. Wilson prefers the second option, and in that connection makes the usual distinction between "Gnosis" and "Gnosticism." "Philo is not a gnostic in the strict sense of the term, although he does have affinities with Gnosticism" (215). Philo

25. See "Hellenistic-Jewish Wisdom Speculation," 46, 59. This point is also made with some force by Horsley, "Wisdom of Word" (cit. n. 13), 231–32, 237.
26. Cf. discussion above, p. 166.
27. This is Horsley's basic contention, too, in the three articles treated above.
28. "Philo of Alexandria and Gnosticism," *Kairos* 14 (1972) 213–19. Wilson treats Philo extensively in his book, *The Gnostic Problem* (cit. n. 5). I have discussed Wilson's treatment of Philo in that book, together with other important studies on Philo's relation to Gnosticism, in my article, "Philo and Gnosticism," 312–15.
29. The most important representative of this view is H. Jonas; see esp. *Gnosis und spätantiker Geist*, vol. 2 (Göttingen: Vandenhoeck & Ruprecht, 1954) 38–43, 70–121. See my discussion in "Philo and Gnosticism," 303–9.

marks "one of the preliminary stages" on the way to Gnosticism, but "he belongs mostly to Gnosis, not to Gnosticism. Indeed the case of Philo is one of the best examples of the value of this distinction" (ibid.).

Wilson specifies three "affinities with Gnosticsm" found in Philo: (1) emphasis in both on the complete transcendence of the supreme God, (2) interposition of a series of intermediaries between the supreme God and our world, (3) a general disparagement of the sense-perceptible world (216). The first point is further elaborated by pointing to Philo's unqualified denial of the possibility of knowing the divine essence and his tendency toward a *theologia negativa*, features he has in common with the Gnostics. Wilson adds that Philo does not use the term *agnōstos* ("unknowable") of God, "a point on which the gnostics were to carry the Platonic tradition further than either Plato or Philo ever did" (ibid.). But even the use of the term *agnōstos* of God is no necessary proof of Gnosticism. Josephus uses it of God (*Ap.* 2.167), and he can hardly be called a "Gnostic." Wilson's main point, however, is right: Philo's doctrine of the transcendence of God is based on a combination of Platonic philosophy with Old Testament theology (ibid.). The same, of course, could be said of the Gnostics' doctrine. So it is their radical dualism that separates the Gnostics from Philo, as Wilson rightly perceives (ibid., 219).

Wilson's second and third points bear upon the same basic issue, the radical dualism of the Gnostics versus the modified Platonism of Philo: Philo's intermediaries are not the wicked and rebellious archons of Gnostic myth (217–19), and Philo's disparagement of the sense-perceptible world, a basic feature of Middle Platonism,[30] is far removed from the Gnostic myth of a premundane Fall that places the world and its creator in the realm of evil (218).

All of this Wilson has stated with great perspicacity and eloquence. But then in what sense can one put Philo into the category of "Gnosis" at all, as Wilson does? If Philo has "not yet" taken the step toward Gnosticism (218),[31] under what circumstances *would* he have taken that step? Is

---

30. Philo, in fact, is our earliest evidence for the Middle-Platonic distinction between the *kosmos noētos* and the *kosmos aisthētos* (see, e.g., *Op. Mund.* 15–17, 24), but it is probably not original with him. See, e.g., J. Dillon, *The Middle Platonists* (Ithaca, N.Y.: Cornell University Press, 1977) 158–59, and M. Baltes; *Timaios Lokros über die Natur des Kosmos und der Seele kommentiert* (Leiden: E. J. Brill, 1972) 105. Cf. chap. 10, above, p. 154.

31. Cf. Wilson's statement in *The Gnostic Problem*, 67–68: "It must be admitted that there was a good deal of 'gnosticizing' thought in the early years of the Christian era, for example in Philo, but this is *not yet* definitely 'Gnostic' in the full sense" (emphasis added).

it that Gnosticism had "not yet" developed in the first century?[32] Or, rather, is it something in Philo's own religious makeup that prevented him from ever taking that step?[33] I think the latter is the case, and Wilson himself seems to share this view when he says of Philo: "He was a Jew, and it is difficult to imagine him having any sympathy for the gnostic repudiation of the God of the Old Testament" (219). Even if simply being a Jew did not necessarily preclude the possibility of his espousing Gnosticism—though such a step would surely involve apostasy from Judaism—we know what kind of Jew Philo was, one ultimately faithful to the religion of his people and totally committed to the one eternal God, Creator of, and Provider for, the world.[34]

There is, to be sure, a sense in which Philo's religiosity can be called a "gnosis," in the sense of "knowledge reserved for an elite." For throughout his writings, Philo distinguishes between an elite group in his community of persons who are capable of achieving "wisdom" (sophia), the "wise" or "perfect" (teleioi) versus the "immature" (nēpioi) who must be kept on a strict diet of milk (Migr. Abr. 28–29; Leg. All. 1.90–96; Agr. 8–9; etc.).[35] This is a feature Philo shares in common with the Corinthian opponents of Paul, discussed above.

Another definition of the kind of "gnosis" represented by Philo has been put forward by A. Wlosok. She postulates a "philosophical gnosis" involving a type of religious speculation based on Platonic themes and characteristic of first-century (and later) Alexandrian philosophy.[36] But all of this is considerably removed from the religious thought-world of the Gnostics. Though Philo's "gnosis" shares many themes with that of the Gnostics, there is a "new element" (as Wilson puts it) in Gnosticism: "the radical dualism which rejected this world and its creator, the divine tragedy, the tragic split in the Deity" (219). Wilson concludes his article with the observation that "this is something that still awaits explanation" (ibid.).

In order to get a clear grasp of what separates "Gnosticism" from "Gnosis" (as defined above) it is necessary to take a look at actual

32. Cf. n. 5 above, and n. 33.
33. I have elsewhere explored the possibility that Philo's own writings betray a knowledge and repudiation of an incipient Gnosticism in first-century Alexandria. See chap. 1 in this book.
34. See his moving credo at the end of his treatise on the creation of the world, Op. Mund. 170–72.
35. These and other texts are discussed in Pneumatikos-Psychikos Terminology, 27–30. Horsley has provided more evidence in his articles, cited above.
36. A. Wlosok, Laktanz und die philosophische Gnosis (Heidelberg: Carl Winter, 1960) 50–114. I have discussed her treatment of Philo in "Philo and Gnosticism," 309–12.

Gnostic texts. In the following section we shall stay in Alexandria, but move in time to the end of the second century, while taking a backward look at Philo and the New Testament.

PHILO, GNOSIS, AND THE NEW TESTAMENT IN SECOND-CENTURY ALEXANDRIA: TWO DOCUMENTS

The two documents to be taken up briefly here are meant to illustrate the distinction drawn by Wilson and others between "Gnosis" and "Gnosticism," as it may be applied to a situation late in the second century when everyone agrees that "Gnosticism" was flourishing. To be sure, many examples could be cited to illustrate this, but I have chosen for this purpose two texts from the Nag Hammadi corpus: NCH VII,4: *The Teachings of Silvanus*, and NHC IX,3: *The Testimony of Truth*. Both of these tractates presumably come from the same general milieu, Alexandria in Egypt; and they are roughly contemporaneous, datable to the end of the second century (*The Teachings of Silvanus* may be a little earlier). Both of them represent a milieu in which traditions from Hellenistic Jewish speculative wisdom and Middle Platonic philosophy are used to propagate a message in which Jesus Christ plays a central role; hence they are undeniably "Christian" texts. In both of them one can find numerous parallels to, if not actual use of, the writings of Philo. And both of them make use of the New Testament. But one (*The Testimony of Truth*) is clearly a Gnostic text; the other (*The Teachings of Silvanus*) can hardly be called "Gnostic" in any technical sense.

We consider first *The Testimony of Truth*,[37] a document that has aptly been called "one of the best examples of Christian Gnosticism."[38] It is a homiletic treatise in which its author contends vigorously on behalf of "the Truth" (as he understands it) against "the Law" and those who follow it. "The Law," for our author, is epitomized in the commandment given by the Creator "to take a husband (or) to take a wife, and to beget, to multiply like the sand of the sea" (30:2–5; cf. Gen. 1:28; 2:24; 22:17). The tractate advocates an extreme encratism based on a radical dualism between "Imperishability," "Light," and the "world" (30,12–21; cf. 40,27–

37. See Pearson, *Codices IX and X*; and *Nag Hammadi Library*, 448–59 (the most recent translation). For other bibliography see Scholer, *Nag Hammadi Bibliography*.

38. F. Wisse, "Die Sextus-Sprüche und das Problem der gnostischen Ethik," in A. Böhlig and F. Wisse, *Zum Hellenismus in den Schriften von Nag Hammadi* (Wiesbaden: Harrassowitz, 1975) 81.

28; 44,24–30; etc.), and between the "God of Truth" and the "God" who created the world and gave the Law (41,5; 45,3.24, etc.). Much of the tractate is devoted to the person and work of Christ, but it is nevertheless fair to say that it grounds salvation squarely on *gnōsis:* Christ will bring to eternal life in heaven those who have achieved *gnōsis* (36,2–7; 38,22–27). What sort of *gnōsis* this might be is not left in doubt:

> This, therefore, is the true testimony: When man comes to know himself and God who is over the truth, he will be saved, and he will crown himself with the crown unfading. (44,30–45,6)

Thus, in typically Gnostic fashion our tractate equates knowledge of God with knowledge of the self.[39]

All of this I have treated elsewhere;[40] what is of interest here is the tractate's reminiscence of, if not use of, Philo. The following examples illustrate this point. In the opening passage our author addresses "those who know to hear not with the ears of the body but with the ears of the mind" (29,6–9). The distinction between "the hearing of the mind" and the "hearing of the (bodily) ears" is made in Philo, too (*Decal.* 35). In similar fashion, *The Testimony of Truth* refers to the "eyes of (the) mind" (46,7) in its midrashic quotation of Gen. 3:5; Philo interprets the opening of the eyes referred to in Gen. 3:7 as "the vision of the soul" (*Quaest. in Gen.* 1.39). According to our tractate the "mind" *(nous)* of man is male (44,2–3); Philo routinely refers to the *nous* as male and sense perception *(aisthēsis)* as female (e.g., *Leg. All.* 2.38; 3.49–50; *Op. Mund.* 165).[41] Our tractate's denigration of the corruptible world of the flesh (40,27; 42,6) is almost matched in Philo (e.g., *Plant.* 53), as is its denigration of the body and its pleasures (e.g., 30,32–31,1; cf. *Gig.* 13–15; *Leg. All.* 3.77). To be "stripped" of the body is the goal of the Gnostic (37,2), and this is a goal not far removed from Philo, who in fact uses precisely these terms in describing the glorious end of Moses (*Virt.* 76). Our tractate speaks of the "dividing" power of the "word *(logos)* of the Son of Man" (40,23–41,4) in a manner reminiscent of Philo's discussion of the "cutting" and "dividing" power of the Logos (*Her.* 130–40).[42] Numerous other parallels could be cited between *The Testimony of Truth* and Philo, but let it suffice finally

39. Cf. the Messina definition referred to above (n. 4). For other examples of this emphasis on saving self-knowledge in *Testim. Truth* see 35,22–36,7; 36,23–28; 43,23–26.

40. See my introduction to the tractate in *Codices IX and X,* 101–20. See also chap. 12 in this book.

41. Cf. R. A. Baer, *Philo's Use of the Categories Male and Female* (ALGHJ 3; Leiden: E. J. Brill, 1970) esp. 38.

42. Cf. D. M. Hay, "Philo's Treatise on the Logos-Cutter," *SP* 2 (1973) 9–22.

to point out one final feature they have in common: the use of the allegorical method of interpreting scripture.[43]

All of this does not show that Philo is a Gnostic. It shows, rather, that this Gnostic text has utilized traditions, conceptions, and terminology at home in a milieu in which Hellenistic Jewish wisdom has been fused with Middle Platonic categories. The metaphysical dualism reflected in the Philonic texts cited above is typical of the Platonic philosophy of the day. *The Testimony of Truth* has utilized the same conceptions in the service of a radical Gnostic dualism profoundly different in spirit and intentionality from Philo's religiosity and Platonist philosophy.[44] The two parallels cited first are cases in point: in the first (*Decal.* 35) Philo is describing the scene of the giving of the Law on Mount Sinai (Exodus 20), and he says that the miraculous voice of God created in the souls of the Israelites a hearing superior to the hearing of the ears, that is, a hearing of the mind, wherewith properly to understand and obey the divine commandments. *The Testimony of Truth*, in contrast, has nothing but contempt for the Law. In the second (*Quaest. in Gen.* 1.39) Philo allegorically interprets the opening of the eyes of Adam and Eve (Gen. 3:7) as "the vision of the soul" which can perceive good and bad. *The Testimony of Truth*, on the other hand, describes the entire Paradise story in such a way that the Creator becomes the villain and the serpent the hero.[45] Here we have, in a nutshell, a prime example of the "revolutionary" character of Gnosticism,[46] that "new element," that, according to Wilson,[47] marks "Gnosticism" off from mere "Gnosis."

Similar observations can be made regarding the extensive use of the New Testament in *The Testimony of Truth*. All four Gospels are used, as well as Acts, the Pauline literature, Hebrews, James, 1 Peter, and Revelation. The Fourth Gospel and Paul have provided the greatest theological influence: the Son of Man Christology of John is very prominent in the document, and Paul's doctrine of the Law seems to have played a role in its depreciation of the Law and those "under the Law" (29,22–25; cf.

43. The passage just cited on the "dividing" power of the Logos is an example: the "saw" used to saw Isaiah the prophet in two "is the word of the Son of Man which separates us from the error of the angels." On scripture interpretation in *Testim. Truth* see Pearson, "Gnostic Interpretation," 311–19, and "Exegesis of Mikra," 641.

44. Cf. Plotinus's critique of Gnosticism in his well-known treatise "Against the Gnostics," *Enn.* 2.9.

45. On the Gnostic midrash embedded in *Testim. Truth* 45,23–49,7, see chap. 3 in this book, and *Codices IX and X*, 106, 111, 158–69.

46. On the "revolutionary" character of Gnosticism see, e.g., H. Jonas, "Delimitation of the Gnostic Phenomenon—Typological and Historical," in Bianchi, *Origini dello gnosticismo*, 90–104, esp. 101–2; and Rudolph, *Gnosis*, 54.

47. See discussion above.

Rom. 6:14; Gal. 4:4—5:21).[48] But the basic religious stance of *The Testimony of Truth* is ultimately as alien to the New Testament it appropriates as it is to Philo.

We now turn to the other document, *The Teachings of Silvanus*.[49] This document, the only non-Gnostic tractate in Nag Hammadi Codex VII, is an example of early Christian "wisdom," modeled upon the wisdom literature of Hellenistic Judaism and showing particular affinities with the Wisdom of Solomon. Loosely structured, it consists of admonitory sayings and proverbs, frequently introduced in typical wisdom style with the address, "my son," exhortations modeled on the Stoic-Cynic diatribe, and hymnic passages in praise of God and Christ. It has aptly been described as representing "a christianized form of Jewish wisdom which prepared the way for the thought of the great Alexandrian theologians of the third century."[50] Clement of Alexandria, indeed, shows manifest affinities with *The Teachings of Silvanus*,[51] but it is also of interest that a passage from the tractate (97,3–98,22) has been shown to have been used later in a sermon attributed to St. Anthony.[52] The author, of course, is unknown. The document is pseudonymously attributed to the companion of Paul and amanuensis of Peter mentioned in the New Testament (1 Thess. 1:1; 2 Thess. 1:1; 2 Cor. 1:19; 1 Pet. 5:12; referred to in Acts 15—18 as "Silas").

Numerous points of contact have been noticed between *The Teachings of Silvanus* and Philo, and some of these have been explored in an article by J. Zandee on *The Teachings of Silvanus* and Philo published in the Puech Festschrift.[53] Zandee is careful not to claim that Philo's writings were definitely known to the author of *The Teachings of Silvanus* (338), but he shows that they are remarkably similar both in method and specific content. Comparing specific passages in *The Teachings of Sil-*

48. On the use of the New Testament in *Testim. Truth* see *Codices IX and X,* 110, 112–113, as well as the indices and notes to the text.
49. For a critical edition of this tractate, with French translation and commentary, see Yvonne Janssens, *Les Leçons de Silvanos (NH VII,4)* (BCNH, "Textes" 13; Québec: Université Laval, 1983). Translations of passages quoted here are from *Nag Hammadi Library.*
50. W. R. Schoedel, "Jewish Wisdom and the Formation of the Christian Ascetic," in *Aspects of Wisdom* (cit. n. 6), 169–99, esp. 194.
51. See esp. J. Zandee, "*The Teachings of Silvanus*" and Clement of Alexandria. A New Document of Alexandrian Theology (Leiden: E. J. Brill, 1977).
52. W.-P. Funk, "Ein doppelt überliefertes Stück spätägyptischer Weisheit," *ZÄS* 103 (1976) 8–21.
53. "'Les Enseignements de Silvanos' et Philon d'Alexandrie," in *Melanges d'histoire des religions offerts à Henri-Charles Puech* (Paris: Presses Universitaires de France, 1974) 337–45.

vanus with texts in Philo, Zandee demonstrates that they have much in common in their conception of the transcendence of God, based on Platonic categories (338–39),[54] their doctrine of the personified "Wisdom" (340–41), their anthropology, also based on Platonism but showing Stoic features as well (341–42), their stress on morality and the struggle against the passions coupled with a decidedly negative attitude toward the body (343–44), and their use of the allegorical method of interpreting scripture (344–45). It can easily be concluded, on the basis of Zandee's study, that *The Teachings of Silvanus* exudes the same intellectual and religious atmosphere as Philo. The only basic difference between them in this regard is that *The Teachings of Silvanus* is a Christian document whereas Philo is Jewish. Thus, for *The Teachings of Silvanus* Christ is the ultimate teacher of wisdom (90,31–91,1; 96,32) instead of Moses:

> Know who Christ is, and acquire him as a friend, for this is the friend who is faithful. He is also God and Teacher. This one, being God, became man for your sake. (110,14–19)[55]

Indeed, the Logos and Sophia of Philo have become identified with Christ in *The Teachings of Silvanus*: "He is Wisdom; he is also the Word" (106,23–24). In this connection the author can paraphrase Paul's[56] words on the wisdom of God (1 Cor. 1:20–25): "For since he (Christ) is Wisdom, he makes the foolish man wise" (107,34; cf. 111,22–29). He can also paraphrase the praise of Sophia in Wisdom (7:25–26) in a hymn of praise to Christ:

> For he is a light from the power of God, and he is an emanation of the pure glory of the Almighty. He is the spotless mirror of the working of God, and he is the image of his goodness. For he is also the Light of the Eternal Light. (112,37–113,7)[57]

As has already been noted, *The Teachings of Silvanus* is not a Gnostic document; indeed, it shows some definitely anti-Gnostic features. It warns the reader not to be "defiled by strange kinds of knowledge (*gnōsis*)" (94,31–33). And Gnostics who refer to the Creator of the world

---

54. Cf. also Zandee's article specifically devoted to the Platonism of *Teach. Silv.*: "'Les enseignements de Silvain' et le platonisme," in J.-E. Ménard, ed., *Les Textes de Nag Hammadi* (NHS 7; Leiden: E. J. Brill, 1975) 158–79.

55. Philo (*Vit. Mos.* 1.158) is able to refer to Moses as a "god and king" on the grounds that he had entered into "the darkness where God was" (Exod. 20:21), and displayed in his life and career a "godlike pattern" (*theoidēs paradeigma*) for others to "imitate" (*mimeisthai*).

56. Paul is referred to by name at 108,30–31: "Paul, who has become like Christ." Cf. 1 Cor. 11:1.

57. On this hymn see Schoedel, "Jewish Wisdom" (cit. n. 50), 191–92.

as "ignorant"[58] are undoubtedly in view in the following warning: "Let no one ever say that God is ignorant. For it is not right to place the Creator of every creature in ignorance" (116,5–9). Nevertheless, some Gnosticizing features have been found in it by W. Schoedel and others, "notably in the tripartite anthropology which has to do with the 'three races' from which man originated (92:10ff.)."[59] A brief consideration of the passage in question (92,10–94,29) will therefore be in order before we bring this study to a close.

The key section of this passage reads as follows:

> But before everything (else), know your birth. Know yourself, that is, from what substance (οὐσία) you are, or from what race (γένος), or from what species (φυλή). Understand that you have come into being from three races: from the earth, from the formed (ⲉⲃⲟⲗ ⲅⲙ̄ ⲡⲉⲡⲗⲁⲥⲙⲁ), and from the created. The body has come into being from the earth with an earthly substance, but the formed, for the sake of the soul, has come into being from the thought of the Divine. The created, however, is the mind *(nous)*, which has come into being in conformity with the image of God (ⲕⲁⲧⲁ ⲑⲓⲕⲱⲛ ⲙ̄ⲡⲛⲟⲩⲧⲉ). The divine mind has substance *(ousia)* from the Divine, but the soul is that which he (God) has formed (ⲡⲉⲛⲧⲁϥⲣ̄ⲡⲗⲁⲥⲥⲉ) for their own hearts. (92,10–29)

This section is an exhortation to self-knowledge, considered as a prerequisite to living a "rational" *(noeron,* 94,14–17) life of "virtue" *(aretē,* 93,2).[60] It consists of an interpretation of the Delphic maxim, *gnōthi sauton* ("know thyself"),[61] amplified by a piece of Genesis exegesis focused on Gen. 2:7 and 1:27. It is a typical piece of Hellenistic Jewish wisdom, and reproduces concepts well known to Philo, if not in fact derived from him.[62] The exhortation to self-knowledge here is similar to Philo's injunction, "know thyself *(gnōthi sauton)* and the parts of which

58. This is a familiar topos in Gnosticism. A classic example occurs in *Ap. John* (NHC II,1) 11,15–22; see also *Testim. Truth* (NHC IX,3) 47,14–23, on which see chap. 3 in this book.

59. Schoedel, "Jewish Wisdom," 170. Cf. P. Perkins, *The Gnostic Dialogue. The Early Church and the Crisis of Gnosticism* (New York: Paulist Press, 1980) 182 n. 19, where influence from Valentinian Gnosticism is posited in this passage. On the threefold classification of mankind in Valentinian Gnosticism see Pearson, *Pneumatikos-Psychikos Terminology,* 76–81; and F.-M. Sagnard, *La gnose valentinienne et le témoignage de saint Irénée* (Paris: J. Vrin, 1954) esp. 387–415, 567–74.

60. Cf. H. Jonas's remarks on the absence of the concept of virtue *(aretē)* in Gnosticism, in *Gnostic Religion,* 266–69.

61. Cf. H. D. Betz, "The Delphic Maxim ΓΝΩΘΙ ΣΑΥΤΟΝ in Hermetic Interpretation," *HTR* 63 (1970) 465–84, esp. 477–82 on Philo. In my view, however, Philo's interpretation is not as close to the Hermetic one as Betz thinks. In the Hermetic (and Gnostic) interpretation, self-knowledge *is,* essentially, knowledge of God and salvation; this is far from the Philonic understanding. On the relevant passages in the *Poimandres* see chap. 9 in this book.

62. It is curious that these points have been overlooked by Zandee in his article on *Teach. Silv.* and Philo (cit. n. 53).

thou dost consist, what each is, and for what it was made, and how it is meant to work . . ." (*Fug.* 46). For Philo, as for *The Teachings of Silvanus*, the highest part in the human is "the Mind that is in thee" (ὁ ἐν σοὶ νοῦς, ibid.).[63] The three "substances" or "genera" are read out of Gen. 2:7 (LXX): "earth" (χοῦν ἀπὸ τῆς γῆς), the "formed" "soul" (ἔπλασεν . . . ψυχήν), and the "mind" *(nous)*, which has "substance from the divine" (cf. ἐνεφύσησεν . . . πνοὴν ζωῆς). Genesis 1:27 is also brought in, not only with the observation that it is the mind "which has come into being in conformity with the image of God," but also that it is the mind which is "created" (cf. Gen. 1:27: κατ᾽ εἰκόνα θεοῦ ἐποίησεν αὐτόν). Much of this exegesis is found in Philo, and in fact probably reflects influence from Philo. Some of the relevant Philonic texts have been mentioned already.[64] Philo says, for example, that the mind has for its "substance" *(ousia)* the spirit breathed into the human by God (*Rer. Div. Her.* 55–56). Philo also speaks of the mind *(nous)* as that which is created in the image of God (*Leg. All.* 1.90; *Plant.* 18–20; cf. *Rer. Div. Her.* 56–57). And Philo makes the distinction, observable here in our text, between that which is "formed" by God (*eplasen*, Gen. 2:7) and that which is created (*epoiēsen*, Gen. 1:27; see, e.g., *Leg. All.* 1.53).[65]

The main point of this passage is that the human has the innate capacity either to "live according to the mind" (93,34) or to live on a lower level of existence. If one cuts off the "male part" (i.e., the mind),[66] one becomes "psychic" (*psychikos*, 93,13–14), or, worse yet, "fleshly" (*sarkikos*), taking on "animal nature" (93,20–21). "God is the spiritual one (*pneumatikos*). Man has taken shape *(morphē)* from the substance of God" (93,25–27). In sum, "you will take on the likeness of the part toward which you will turn yourself" (94,3–5). Therefore "turn toward the rational nature and cast off from yourself the earth-begotten (ⲛ̄ⲭ̄ⲡⲟ ⲛ̄ⲕⲁ2 = γηγενής, cf. Philo, *Op. Mund.* 136; *Leg. All.* 1.31) nature" (94,16–19).

63. Colson's translation in the LCL ed. Cf. also *Migr. Abr.* 8–13, 137, 185f.; *Somn.* 1.52–60. The two last-cited passages speak of self-knowledge as a prerequisite to knowledge of God. But that self-knowledge is not the same as knowledge of God Philo makes abundantly clear in the passage immediately following in *Somn.*: "This is nature's law: he who has thoroughly comprehended himself, thoroughly despairs of himself (ἑαυτὸν λίαν ἀπέγνωκε), having as a step to this ascertained the nothingness in all respects of created being. And the man who has despaired of himself is beginning to know Him that IS" (*Somn.* 1.60, LCL ed.). On this and similar passages in Philo see Pearson, "Philo and Gnosticism," 307–9, 339.

64. In our discussion of 1 Corinthians, above, p. 170.

65. This point has been noticed by Zandee; see "*The Teachings of Silvanus*" and *Clement of Alexandria* (cit. n. 51), 46.

66. Cf. the texts from Philo cited above, p. 175.

This brings us, as it were, full circle back to the range of ideas at the heart of the controversy in Paul's Corinthian congregation. We see in this passage in *The Teachings of Silvanus* (and in others as well)[67] the same kind of speculative wisdom as was apparently taught in Corinth by Apollos of Alexandria, still vibrant for the second-century author of *The Teachings of Silvanus*. Whether this can be called "Gnosis" or "Gnosticizing" is a matter of semantics. If there was a "gnosis" in Corinth, or in Philo, there is the same kind of "gnosis" in *The Teachings of Silvanus*.

CONCLUSIONS

In this survey, touching upon aspects of first- and second-century Christianity, the speculative wisdom of Hellenistic Judaism, and second-century Gnosticism, we have had occasion to test the distinctions made by Wilson and others between "Gnosis" and "Gnosticism." These distinctions are valid to a point, in that "full-blown Gnosticism" was not found in the New Testament (i.e., in 1 Corinthians, our example) nor in Philo. A kind of "Gnosis" was arguably present, if one granted the broad definition proposed by Wilson and others, including the Messina Colloquium. But the "Gnosis" in question, in my view, might better be designated "speculative wisdom," in that "wisdom" is a far more central category in the literature in question—1 Corinthians, Philo and Wisdom, and *The Teachings of Silvanus*—than "knowledge" (*gnōsis*). The word "Gnosis" is too slippery a designation for the religiosity in question and lacks definitional utility, though there are cases where it might be more appropriate, such as the *gnōsis* espoused by Clement of Alexandria.

As for Gnosticism (which German scholars persist in calling "Gnosis"),[68] we are dealing with a scholarly construct that has definitional utility so long as the scholarly consensus is there. "The Gnostic religion" might be a better term, for in effect Gnosticism involves a radically new worldview and symbol system, and should be defined as a religion in its own right, with clearly recognizable historical parameters.[69]

Finally, we have encountered the tendency to use such terms as "not

---

67. For another example, see Pearson, "Hellenistic-Jewish Wisdom Speculation" (cit. n. 6), 47.
68. Cf., e.g., Rudolph, *Gnosis*, esp. his discussion of the Messina definitions, 56–57.
69. This is the view of Rudolph (ibid.) and many others. See, e.g., the very clear statement of the issues by K.-W. Tröger in his article, "The Attitude of the Gnostic Religion toward Judaism as Viewed in a Variety of Perspectives," in B. Barc, ed., *Colloque international sur les textes de Nag Hammadi* (BCNH, "Études" 1; Québec: Université Laval/Louvain: Peeters, 1981) 86–98. Cf. also the Introduction to this book.

yet" to distinguish between "Gnosis" or "Gnosticizing" ("pre-Gnostic," "proto-Gnostic") tendencies, and a "full-blown Gnosticism." The utility of this usage can also be called into question. In the case of *The Teachings of Silvanus,* for example, we have a document in which the religiosity of Hellenistic Judaism, as represented also by 1 Corinthians, Philo, and Wisdom, not only did "not yet" become a full-blown Gnosticism, but also never did so. One cannot project a "trajectory" from 1 Corinthians or Philo and necessarily expect to find "Gnostics" at the other end. Nor, for that matter, should we foreclose the possibility that there was a full-blown "Gnosticism" already in Philo's or Paul's time. To be sure, these issues remain open for further discussion.

12

Anti-Heretical Warnings in Codex IX from Nag Hammadi

"Heresiology" is one of the most characteristic expressions of catholic Christianity: the identification and refutation of unorthodox beliefs and practices. The origins of Christian heresiology are found in the New Testament itself, and it is well-developed by the time of the great heresiologist bishop, Irenaeus of Lyons.[1] Before the discovery of the Nag Hammadi library, it might have been thought that "heresiology" was solely the province of the "Great Church." To be sure, we do know from the fathers themselves that certain Gnostic sects spoke contemptuously of catholic Christians as "animal" ($\psi v \chi \iota \kappa o \iota$) men not in possession of gnosis.[2] And we have in *Pistis Sophia* and *The Second Book of Jeu* some polemics directed against immoral ritual practices apparently carried out by certain Gnostic groups, perhaps the same groups as are attacked by Epiphanius of Salamis (*Haer.* 25–26).[3] But now the Nag Hammadi corpus has expanded considerably our knowledge of Gnostic theological polemics in that several of the Gnostic tractates contain polemics directed not only against catholic Christianity but also against other Gnos-

---

1. See esp. F. Wisse, "The Epistle of Jude in the History of Heresiology," in M. Krause, ed., *Essays on the Nag Hammadi Texts in Honour of Alexander Böhlig* (NHS 3; Leiden: E. J. Brill, 1972) 133–43.
2. The Valentinians had a highly developed system of thought in which the "spiritual" ($\pi v \epsilon v \mu \alpha \tau \iota \kappa o \iota$), i.e., themselves, were distinguished from "psychic" (catholic) Christians, even to the differentiation of "spiritual" and "psychic" levels of salvation. On this see, e.g., E. Pagels, "A Valentinian Interpretation of Baptism and Eucharist—And Its Critique of 'Orthodox' Sacramental Theology and Practice," VC 65 (1972) 153–69, and esp. F.-M. Sagnard, *La gnose valentinienne et le témoignage de saint Irénée* (Paris: J. Vrin, 1947) 387ff. For the *pneumatikos-psychikos* terminology in the New Testament and in Gnosticism see Pearson, *Pneumatikos-Psychikos Terminology*.
3. *Pistis Sophia* 4, chap. 147 (C. Schmidt, ed., and V. MacDermot, trans., *Pistis Sophia* [NHS 9; Leiden: E. J. Brill, 1978] 381); *2 Jeu* 43 (C. Schmidt, ed., and V. MacDermot, trans., *The Books of Jeu and the Untitled Text in the Bruce Codex* [NHS 13; Leiden: E. J. Brill, 1978] 100). For Epiphanius's account see Layton, *Gnostic Scriptures*, 199–214.

tic groups. For example, *The Concept of Our Great Power* (NHC VI,4) may contain a polemic against the "Anomoeans" (40,7–9)[4] as well as against more orthodox Christians (45,15ff.). But even more interesting is the possibility that the "Antichrist" figure referred to in that document (44,13ff.) is to be identified as Simon Magus![5] *The Second Treatise of the Great Seth* (VII,2) contains obvious polemics against catholic Christians who worship the crucified Christ and who "persecute" the Gnostics (59,22–61,24). *The Apocalypse of Peter* (VII,3) presents as a revelation of the Savior a sketch of the history of early Christian doctrine that includes polemics against the catholic hierarchy (esp. 79,22ff.) and catholic doctrine (e.g., 74,5ff.), but also apparently against other Gnostic groups (74,15ff.).

Two such tractates from Codex IX are especially interesting, IX,1 and 3,[6] and in what follows a brief discussion of the theological polemics found in them will be presented.

THE TRACTATE *MELCHIZEDEK*

The first tractate in Codex IX, entitled *Melchizedek*,[7] comprises p. 1–p. 27, line 10 of the manuscript. Unfortunately, it is in very fragmentary condition, and the greater portion of it is lost.[8] However, the passage of greatest interest for the purposes of this essay is found on one of the best-preserved pages (p. 5), and is part of a prophetic revelation given presumably to Melchizedek. The previous context (pp. 1-4, very fragmentary and difficult to reconstruct) apparently concerns the ministry of "Jesus Christ, the Son of God," and his encounter with hostile powers who will initiate false charges against him,[9] his death and resurrection,

4. So F. Wisse, "The Nag Hammadi Library and the Heresiologists," *VC* 25 (1971) 208 n. 16. He suggests that this reference to a late fourth-century heresy helps us to date the document, and the Nag Hammadi library as a whole. But Krause interprets the word ΝΙⲀΝϨⲞⲘⲞⲒⲞⲚ as a neuter, which the (Greek) ending certainly suggests. See M. Krause and P. Labib, *Gnostische und Hermetische Schriften aus Codex II und Codex VI* (ADAIK Kopt. Reihe 2; Glückstadt: J. J. Augustin, 1971) 155.
5. Berliner Arbeitskreis, "Texte von Nag Hammadi," 52.
6. These tractates were as yet unpublished when this essay was first published; see now Pearson, *Codices IX and X*, and *Nag Hammadi Library*, 438–44; 448–59. See now also the important study by Klaus Koschorke, *Die Polemik der Gnostiker gegen das kirchliche Christentum* (NHS 12; Leiden: E. J. Brill, 1978).
7. The title, with decorations, is partially preserved on a fragment from the top of page 1: ⲘⲈⲖⲬⲓⲤ[ⲈⲆⲈⲔ].
8. About 47 percent of the total content is either extant or capable of restoration by scholarly conjecture.
9. "[They will] call him 'impious man, lawless (and) impure]," 3,7–9. Such a statement is reminiscent of anti-heretical attacks against alleged followers of "Cain" and

his postresurrection instructions to his disciples, and the coming of false teachers. Our passage follows:

> They will say of him that he is unbegotten though he has been begotten, (that) he does not eat even though he eats, (that) he does not drink even though he drinks, (that) he is uncircumcised though he has been circumcised, (that) he is unfleshly though he has come in flesh, (that) he did not come to suffering, ⟨though⟩ he came to suffering, (that) he did not rise from the dead ⟨though⟩ he arose from [the] dead.[10]

This text is admittedly not without its ambiguities at first glance, especially when one recalls a common tendency in Gnostic literature toward deliberate paradox, as the following passages illustrate:

> You hear that I suffered, yet I suffered not; and that I suffered not, yet I did suffer; and that I was pierced, yet I was not wounded; that I was hanged, yet I was not hanged; that blood flowed from me, yet it did not flow; and, in a word, that what they say of me, I did not endure, but what they do not say, those things I did suffer. (*Acts of John* 101)[11]

> Amen, I was seized; Amen again, I was not seized.
> Amen, I was judged; Amen again, I was not judged.
> Amen, I was crucified; Amen again, I was not crucified.
> Amen, I was pierced; Amen again, I was not pierced.
> Amen, I suffered; Amen again, I did not suffer.
> Amen, I am in my Father; Amen again, my Father is in me. (*Psalms of Heracleides*, p. 191).[12]

Of course, the style of these passages differs markedly from the one from Codex IX; the Manichaean text is religious poetry, and the one from the *Acts of John* is quasi-poetic "revelation language." In both, the Savior is the speaker addressing his disciples.

More to the point as a possible parallel to our text would be a "creedal" statement, such as the following from Ignatius of Antioch:

> There is one Physician, both fleshly and spiritual (σαρκικός τε καὶ πνευματικός), begotten and unbegotten (γεννητὸς καὶ ἀγέννητος), God come in

---

"Balaam" such as are found in the Epistle of Jude and elsewhere. Cf. F. Wisse, "Epistle of Jude" (cit. n. 1), who, however, goes too far in denying the existence of libertine groups in early Christianity. On Cain as a symbol of heresy, see my discussion in chap. 6, above. It has been suggested, presumably in all seriousness, that Jesus himself is the source for the licentious doctrines and practices of the groups attacked in the Epistle of Jude (Carpocratians?). See M. Smith, *Clement of Alexandria and a Secret Gospel of Mark* (Cambridge: Harvard University Press, 1973) esp. 201ff.

10. 5,2–11. Translations of passages from Codex IX quoted in this essay have been revised to conform to those published in *Nag Hammadi Library*.

11. *NTA* 2.234.

12. C. Allberry, ed. and trans., *A Manichaean Psalm-Book*, Part II (Stuttgart: Kohlhammer, 1938) 191.

the flesh (ἐν σαρκὶ γενόμενος θεός), in death true life (ἐν θανάτῳ ζωὴ ἀληθινή), both from Mary and from God (καὶ ἐκ Μαρίας καὶ ἐκ θεοῦ), first passible and then impassible (πρῶτον παθητὸς καὶ τότε ἀπαθής), Jesus Christ our Lord. (*Eph. 7.2*).[13]

In this passage the Antiochene bishop sets forth his christological creed over against the teachings and practices of heretics who "bear the Name" (i.e., of Christ) but behave (i.e., believe) like "rabid dogs" (*Eph.* 7.1). His creed is deliberately paradoxical and rather sophisticated, holding to *both* the spiritual and divine nature of Christ, along with his docetic opponents, and to the fleshly and human nature, which his opponents denied.

But upon closer examination we find that our text from Codex IX is unyieldingly nonparadoxical. The assertions of the opponents are, one by one, countered by the affirmation of the author's version of the truth (in the Coptic text rendered in circumstantial constructions, here translated with the word "though"). The opponents are arguing, among other things,[14] that Christ is "unbegotten" (Gr. ἀγέννητος),[15] "unfleshly" (Gr. ἄσαρκος), and impassible (cf. Gr. ἀπαθής), and that since he did not suffer he did not rise from the dead either. To all of these affirmations our Gnostic (!) author counters rigidly with the opposite, arguing almost naively against his docetic opponents with the result that he comes out with a more "primitive" Christology than that of the great anti-docetic bishop of catholic Christianity, Ignatius.

Most striking of all, however, in view of the overall Gnostic character of this tractate, is that the passage is formally similar to the eschatological warnings against "false prophets" and heretics that are found in the New Testament and other early Christian literature (e.g., *Didache* 16; Justin *Dial.* 35; *Epistula Apostolorum* 29; etc.). These false prophets and heretics will come "in his (i.e., Jesus') name" (5,1; cf. Matt. 7:22), that is, from within the Christian community itself (cf. Acts 20:30; Jude 4; 2 Pet. 2:1; 1 Tim. 4:1; 1 John 2:19; Rev. 2:2, 9, 14f., 20). Moreover, the kind of doctrine attributed to the false teachers in our document is strikingly similar to that attacked in 1–2 John, and the mode of attack is equally

13. Text: Funk-Bihlmeyer, *Die Apostolischen Väter* (Tübingen: J. C. B. Mohr, 1956) 84; au. trans.

14. That Jesus was not circumcised I find to be an interesting aspect of the docetic argument, and I know of no explicit parallels to this. Marcion, of course, would have stressed this point. Cf. Tertullian *Adv. Marc.* 3.8 (on Marcion's docetism), 1.19 and 4.6f. (on Marcion's deletion from his edition of Luke of the infancy narratives); *Carn. Chr.* 5 (where Jesus' circumcision is mentioned in an anti-Marcionite argument). Cf. Koschorke, *Polemik der Gnostiker* (cit. n. 6) 164–65.

15. Coptic ⲁⲧⲭⲡⲟϥ. It is assumed that this treatise was composed originally in Greek.

similar—that false teachers will arise who will deny that Jesus has "come in the flesh" (1 John 4:2; 2 John 7). Such a stance is most unusual in a Gnostic document, indeed unparalleled. It is usually assumed that Gnosticism tends naturally toward a "docetic" Christology;[16] and if in Gnostic sources one finds references to the physical suffering and death of Jesus such references are not without their ambiguity.[17]

Is our document Gnostic at all? Its Gnostic character can be seen in its references to well-known figures from the Gnostic hierarchy of the heavenly world such as Barbelo, Doxomedon, the four luminaries, Pigeradamas, and so on, from the reference to the elect as "the congregation of the children of Seth" (5,19f.), from the reference to such hostile spiritual powers as "archons," "angels," "word-rulers," "principalities," "authorities," "female gods and male gods" (2,8–10; 9,1), and from an apparent reference to the salutary effects of eating from the "tree [of knowledge]," enabling Adam and Eve to "trample [the Cherubim] and the Seraphim [with the flaming sword]" (10,3–6). The occurrence of Melchizedek as the central figure of our document,[18] however, may provide a hint that will enable us to explain the anti-docetic stance of this otherwise thoroughly Gnostic tractate.

Epiphanius of Salamis (*Haer.* 55) sets forth a somewhat confused account of a group whom he calls "Melchizedekians."[19] This group, according to Epiphanius, subordinates Christ to Melchizedek. Moreover, they are said to affirm that Christ originated from Mary, that is, was born as a man.[20] Of course, Epiphanius is notorious for his inaccuracies, but we find ready corroboration for a "low" Christology

16. "Die Gnosis kann von ihren Voraussetzungen aus weder eine wirkliche Inkarnation noch den leiblichen Tod Jesu denken"—K. M. Fischer, "Der johanneische Christus und der gnostische Erlöser," in Tröger, *Gnosis und Neues Testament,* 262. But cf. also L. Schottroff, *Der Glaubende und die feindliche Welt* (WMANT 37; Neukirchen: Neukirchener, 1970) 280ff. Cf. my review of Schottroff in *JBL* 91 (1972) 567–69.

17. Cf., e.g., *The Gospel of Truth* (NHC I,2) 18,24; 20,10ff. *The Second Treatise of the Great Seth* (NHC VII,2) 58,17ff.; but in the latter document the "docetic" position is dominant. Cf. J. A. Gibbons, "The Second Logos of the Great Seth. Considerations and Questions," *SBL 1973 Seminar Papers* (Cambridge, Mass.: Society of Biblical Literature, 1973) 242–61. See now also L. Painchaud, *Le Deuxième Traité du Grand Seth (NH VII,2)* (BCNH, "Textes" 6; Québec: Université Laval, 1982) esp. 17–19. And cf. the paradoxical assertions of the passages quoted above from the *Acts of John* and the Manichaean psalm.

18. See chap. 7 in this book.

19. Actually Epiphanius says that the "Melchizedekians" refer to themselves with this designation, and notes that they are also known as "Theodotianists" (*Haer.* 55.1.1).

20. Epiphanius argues vehemently: "For behold, these people have denied their master, the one who 'bought them with his own blood,' who did not, as they say, originate from Mary, but always was with the Father, God the Logos" (*Haer.* 55.9.1f., au. trans.).

amongst the "Melchizedekians" in Hippolytus and Pseudo-Tertullian. Both of these (though "Ps.-Tertullian," of course, may be Hippolytus himself) agree that the followers of Theodotus (whom Epiphanius calls "Melchizedekians")[21] affirmed the true humanity of Christ, stating that he was a "mere man," in contrast to the heavenly power Melchizedek, whose image Christ is.[22]

Thus, if our document is a product of,[23] or related in some way to, the "Melchizedekians," we have a ready-made explanation for its anti-docetic stance.

Two other passages in *Melchizedek* are worthy of note, for the purposes of this essay. Theological opponents may be referred to again at 7,1ff., where reference is made to the "unbelief," "ignorances," and "wicked deeds" of certain unnamed opponents. Unfortunately, the text is so fragmentary that nothing much can be made of this passage. Finally, at 25,5ff., the crucifixion and resurrection are mentioned, but again the fragmentary nature of the text leaves us without adequate context for detailed discussion, though we might here see, again, an anti-docetic thrust.

THE TESTIMONY OF TRUTH

Whereas the first tractate from Codex IX contains a theological polemic directed against docetic opponents (other Gnostics? Marcionites?), striking enough as that is, the third tractate presents a much more complicated picture. It contains polemics directed at several fronts of opponents, including most prominently "orthodox" Christians. Moreover, its Christology is at least mildly "docetic." The tractate comprises p. 29, line 6–end (p. 76 ?),[24] and, as no title is extant, it has been assigned the title *The Testimony of Truth*. Unfortunately it, too, is very fragmentary in

21. This Theodotus is referred to as a "banker" ($\tau\rho\alpha\pi\epsilon\zeta\iota\tau\eta s$) by trade and mentioned just after Theodotus of Byzantium (Hipp. *Ref.* 7.35; Ps.-Tert. *Haer.* 23). The Valentinian Theodotus whose works Clement of Alexandria excerpted is yet another individual.

22. Hippolytus *Ref.* 7.36; Ps.-Tertullian 24. The latter text states that the followers of Theodotus taught the virgin birth.

23. Epiphanius says that the Melchizedekians fabricated their own books (*Haer.* 55.1.5). Against a simple attribution of our document to the sect described by Epiphanius, however, is the occurrence in it of mythological personalia known from Sethian Gnosticism, a factor for which Epiphanius's account of the Melchizedekians does not prepare us. Moreover, the exact relationship between Jesus Christ and Melchizedek in our document is extremely difficult to pin down, but if anything "Melchizedek" seems not to function as a "heavenly power" to whom Christ is subordinate. On this see chap. 7, above, and Pearson, *Codices IX and X*, esp. 38–40.

24. For text and translation, with notes, see Pearson, *Codices IX and X*, 122–203.

crucial places, but the first several pages (29–48) are fairly well preserved.

Formally this document can be referred to as a "homiletic tract," and consists of two main parts: a well-constructed homily (29,6–45,6), plus miscellaneous additions attributable to the same author (45,6–end). It is addressed to "those who know to hear not with the ears of the body but with the ears of the mind" (29,6–9), who are distinguished from those who are not able to find the truth because of their adherence to "the Law" (29,9–15). The theological and ethical thrust of this document is radically encratic. The "Law" is tied to "lust" ($\epsilon\pi\iota\theta\upsilon\mu\iota\alpha$), "defilement," and "passion," and summarized, in our author's thinking, in the command "to take a husband (or) to take a wife, and to beget, to multiply like the sand of the sea" (30,2–5). Those who fulfill the Law "assist the world" and "[turn] away from the light" (30,12–14). Renunciation of the world is the mark of the Gnostic:

> No one knows the God of Truth except solely the man who will forsake all of the things of the world, having renounced ($\dot{\alpha}\pi o\tau\dot{\alpha}\sigma\sigma\epsilon\iota\nu$) the whole place, (and) having grasped the fringe of his garment. (41,4–10)

Salvation consists of one's leaving the world and returning to Imperishability whence he came (44,24–27):

> This, therefore, is the true testimony ($\mu\alpha\rho\tau\upsilon\rho\iota\alpha$): When man comes to know himself and God who is over the truth, he will be saved, and he will be crowned with the crown unfading. (44,30–45,6.)[25]

From this encratic point of view our author attacks the position of other Christians whose doctrines and practices deviate from his standards. Catholic Christians are certainly in view in the following passages:

> The foolish—thinking [in] their heart [that] if they confess, "We are Christians," in word only (but) not with power, while giving themselves over to ignorance, to a human death, not knowing where they are going nor who Christ is, thinking that they will live, when they are (really) in error—hasten towards the principalities and the authorities. They fall into their clutches because of the ignorance that is in them. (31,22–32,8)

> [These] are [empty] martyrs, since they bear witness only [to] themselves. And yet they are sick, and they are not able to raise themselves. But when

25. This passage looks like an ending, and functions as a peroration concluding the first part of the tractate, the homily. The tractate from that point on seems to be made up of a number of sources, though the overall thrust is the same as that of the first section, and functions as additional commentary on it.

they are "perfected" with a (martyr's) death, this is the thought that they have within them: "If we deliver ourselves over to death for the sake of the Name we will be saved." These matters are not settled in this way. (33,24–34,7)

Some say, "On the last day [we will] certainly arise [in the] resurrection." But they do not [know what] they are saying. (34,26–35,2)

In the first two passages it is evident that our author is attacking the readiness with which some Christians (catholic Christians) accept martyrdom, and the interpretation they place upon it. He does not explicitly state that Gnostics need not face martyrdom, though this is implied.[26] The last passage quoted attacks the resurrection doctrine of the catholic church, and the position of our document on that doctrine is made clear in another passage in which the "carnal resurrection" (σαρκικὴ ἀνάστασις)[27] is defined as "destruction" (36,30–37,1).

It has been observed in the case of some early Christian Gnostic teachers that there is a correlation between rejection of martyrdom, on the one hand, and espousal of a docetic Christology, on the other.[28] Can such a correlation be seen in The Testimony of Truth? In fact, the evidence is somewhat contradictory, probably owing to the use of disparate traditions.[29] Thus, as to Christ's origin, the "Son of Man"[30] is presented as coming directly from heaven to the world "by the Jordan River" (30,18–25), an idea that certainly implies a kind of docetism. On the other hand, Christ is said to have been "born of a virgin" (39,29–30). His birth also means that "he took flesh" (39,31), yet it is also said that "Christ passed through a virgin's womb," leaving Mary's virginity intact (45,14–18).[31] Unfortunately, nothing is said in this tractate concerning Christ's passion and death; so we do not know what interpretation our author

26. According to the Church Fathers the Gnostics tended to avoid a confession of Christ that might lead to martyrdom. See, e.g., Irenaeus Haer. 1.24.6 (Basilides) contradicted by Clem. Strom. 4.81ff.; Tertullian Adv. Val. 30 (the Valentinians); Irenaeus Haer. 4.33.9 and Clement Strom. 4.16f. (heretics in general). But a powerful exhortation to martyrdom is found in The Apocryphon of James (NHC I,1) 4,37–6,17.

27. The term σαρκικὴ ἀνάστασις also occurs in the Valentinian Treatise on the Resurrection (NHC I,4) 45,40–46,2.

28. See, e.g., Elaine Pagels, The Gnostic Gospels (New York: Random House, 1979) chap. 4: "The Passion of Christ and the Persecution of Christians" (70–101).

29. So Koschorke, Polemik der Gnostiker, 107f., 121f.

30. The "Son of Man" title is frequent in Testim. Truth, and the Johannine "Son of Man" pattern is dominant. For discussion see Pearson, Codices IX and X, 110.

31. This doctrine is reported to have been held by Valentinian Gnostics, according to Irenaeus (Haer. 1.7.2; 3.11.3), Tertullian (Adv. Val. 27.1), et al. On this see now M. Tardieu, "'Comme à travers un tuyau': Quelque remarques sur le mythe valentinien de la chair céleste du Christ," in B. Barc, ed., Colloque International sur les Textes de Nag Hammadi (Québec, 22-25 août 1978) (BCNH, "Études" 1; Québec: Université Laval/ Louvain: Peeters, 1981) 151–77.

would have placed upon it. The absence of such a discussion could mean that he rejected the reality of Christ's sufferings. In any case, one is left with the general impression that the Christology of *The Testimony of Truth* is predominantly docetic.

The catholic practice and interpretation of baptism is attacked in the following passage (unfortunately riddled with lacunae):

> There are some who, upon entering the faith, receive a baptism on the ground that they have [it] as a hope of salvation, which they call "the [seal,]" not [knowing] that the [fathers of] the world are manifest in that [place. But] he himself [knows that] he is sealed. For [the Son] of [Man] did not baptize any of his disciples. But [. . . if those who] are baptized were headed for life, the world would become empty. And the fathers of baptism were defiled. But the baptism of truth is something else; it is by renunciation (ἀποταγή) of [the] world that it is found. (69,7–24)

From this passage it is clear that our author rejects water baptism altogether, as a number of Gnostic groups are known to have done.[32] The reference to Jesus and the disciples is interesting,[33] and seems to indicate that Jesus and his disciples came to the Jordan to bear witness to the end of water-baptism. Something like that is stated in another passage early in the tractate:

> The Son of Man [came] forth from Imperishability, [being] alien to defilement. He came [to the] world by the Jordan river, and immediately the Jordan [turned] back.[34] And John bore witness to the [descent] of Jesus. For it is he who saw the [power] which came down upon the Jordan river;[35] for he knew that the dominion of carnal procreation had come to an end. (30,18–30)

---

32. In *The Paraphrase of Shem* (NHC VII,1) water is a symbol of chaotic darkness (cf. Gen. 1:2); water baptism is ascribed to a "demon" (30,23, called "Soldas" at 30,32f.) and referred to as "imperfect baptism" (30,25) and "impure baptism" (38,5–6; cf. also 31,17ff.). The Manichaeans, also, are known to have rejected water baptism. See, e.g., *Kephalaia*, chap. 6 (Böhlig ed., 33), and now also the Cologne Mani Codex, which shows that Mani grew up in an Elchasaite sect but repudiated some of this sect's teachings and practices, including water baptism; see A. Henrichs and L. Koenen, "Ein griechischer Mani-Codex," *ZPE* 5 (1970) 97–216. On the possibility of a Manichaean "baptism" with oil, see G. Widengren, *Mani and Manichaeism*, trans. C. Kessler (New York: Holt, Rinehart & Winston, 1965) 99ff.

33. Cf. John 3:22; 4:1–2.

34. This detail reflects influence from the OT narrative of the stopping of the Jordan River in Josh. 3:13ff., and esp. Ps. 114 (113 LXX):3: ὁ Ἰορδάνης ἐστράφη εἰς τὰ ὀπίσω. Psalm 114:3 is quoted in the Mandaean *Ginza* R. 5.2 (Lidzbarski, 178); and later, in the story of the baptism of Manda d Hayye by Yohana in *Ginza* R. 5.4 (Lidzbarski, 192), it is said that the waters of the Jordan turned backward at the glory of Manda d Hayye! Cf. also the Paris Magical Papyrus (*PGM* IV) 3053ff.: ὁρκίζω σε μέγαν θεὸν Σαβαωθ, δι᾽ ὃν ὁ Ἰορδάνης ποταμὸς ἀνεχώρησεν εἰς τὰ ὀπίσω.

35. In what follows the "Jordan" is allegorically interpreted as bodily senses and pleasures, and "John" as "the archon of the womb" (31,4f.).

In another section (38,27–39,12, unfortunately very fragmentary), there is an attack on those who are ruled by pleasure (ἡδονή), but it is not possible to determine what kinds of persons are referred to, whether catholic Christians (in which case the reference to ἡδονή is imprecise), or, less likely, libertine Gnostics.[36] In any case, the thrust of our document's polemics is directed obviously against catholic Christianity.

Yet, there is a very interesting section that looks very much like a catalogue of heresies and mentions well-known Gnostic figures. Unfortunately this section (beginning with p. 55, line 1)[37] is extremely fragmentary. "Valentinus" (56,2) and the "disciples of Valentinus" (56,5) are mentioned, as well as "Isidore" (57,6) and probably "Basilides" (57,8),[38] and possibly the "Simonians" (58,2f.).[39] Other names surely mentioned in this section are now lost. Interestingly enough such terms as "heretics" (59,4) and "schisms" (59,5) are used in this tantalizing section of the text, so riddled now with lacunae!

Why would a Gnostic teacher attack other Gnostics as "heretics" and "schismatics"? Or did the author of *The Testimony of Truth* simply lift this section on Gnostic heretical groups from a catholic ecclesiastical work, "with little concern for the fact that it was meant to expose and refute some of his spiritual ancestors?"[40] Such naiveté can hardly be attributed to our author. This Gnostic teacher attacks other Gnostics on grounds of substance, and, although the text is fragmentary, we can see in it that the issues revolve around matters of ritual and life-style. The Gnostics attacked here are said to practice water baptism ("the baptism [of death which they observe]—55,8–9), as do the catholic Christians. They are also reported to "take [wives] (and) beget children" (58,3–4), as the catholic Christian opponents also do. Thus, for the author of *The Testimony of Truth*, all Christians who do not conform to this "test of orthodoxy" in matters of practice—a resolute encratism and anti-sacramental-

36. Cf. Clement of Alexandria's arguments against libertine Gnostics in *Strom.* 3.42–44. But Julius Cassianus used the kind of argument found here in his attack against catholic practices (Clem. *Strom.* 3.91–93). I have argued elsewhere that Julius Cassianus could well have been the author of *Testim. Truth.* See Pearson, *Codices IX and X,* 104–5, 118–20. And see chap. 13 in this book.

37. Rather, it began somewhere on one of the missing pages before p. 55. Pages 51–54 are missing altogether, except for a single tiny fragment from each folio.

38. [ⲡⲃⲁⲥⲓⲗⲉⲓⲁ]ⲏⲥ.

39. ⲛ̄ⲥⲓ[ⲙⲱ]/ⲛⲓⲁⲛⲟⲥ. These are said to "take [wives] and beget children" (58,3f.), in contrast to another group that practices abstinence (ἐγκρατεύειν). All that remains of the name of the other group is ⲛ̄[. . . . .] /ⲁⲛⲟⲥ (58,4f.).

40. So Wisse, "Nag Hammadi Library" (cit. n. 4), 208, followed by Koschorke, *Polemik der Gnostiker,* 157. Koschorke, at least, sees the polemic against other Gnostics as based on substantial issues and grounded in the author's encratism (158–60).

ism—are fair game for polemical attack, whether they belong to the ecclesiastical camp or the "Gnostic" camp.

Our author is, of course, aware of theological polemics carried out by his ecclesiastical opponents. Probably such opponents are accused of using the apostle Paul's famous oath (Gal. 1:8) in their polemics: "[Even if] an [angel] comes from heaven, and preaches to you beyond that which we preached to you, may he be anathema!" (73,18–22). Our author mockingly retorts that such people are "immature" (73,25) and unable to keep their own law, "this law which works by means of these heresies" (73,27–29). Here we note that he can apply the term "heresy" to his ecclesiastical opponents as well as his Gnostic ones.[41]

We can see that *The Testimony of Truth*, from beginning to end, is filled with the polemical thrusts of a teacher who earnestly believed that his version of Christian faith (i.e., gnosis) and praxis was the only true one. Its author's hatred of "heresy" was certainly the match of an Irenaeus, or a Hippolytus, or a Tertullian. What is so fascinating in this case, however, is that this author is a kind of mirror image of the great heresiologists of the ecclesiastical establishment, for he represents the other side of their argument.[42]

CONCLUSION

These two tractates from Codex IX give us a very interesting and important glimpse of Gnostic theological polemics from the side of the Gnostics themselves. Of course, they differ the one from the other, and it is only a matter of coincidence that they are found in the same Codex. *Melchizedek* is anti-docetic and sacramental; *The Testimony of Truth* is docetic and anti-sacramental. Nevertheless, they represent well-defined points of view. While it may be true that much Gnostic literature was intended to function more like mystical poetry than statements of logical precision or coherent theological systems,[43] it is also clear that *some* Gnostics were very serious in their attempts to define and safeguard the truth. Though their versions of the truth were not the same as that of the catholic church fathers, we now see that their methods were not so different. As a result of the discovery of the Nag Hammadi library, we can now speak of "Gnostic heresiology."

41. See discussion above, p. 192.
42. For discussion of the historical setting of *Testim. Truth* in the context of Alexandrian Christianity, see chap. 13 in this book.
43. This point is made, and I think overdrawn, by F. Wisse, "The Nag Hammadi Library," 221f. One should also distinguish between the motivations of individual Gnostic authors and those of later compilers (or librarians) of Gnostic literature.

13

Gnosticism in
Early Egyptian Christianity

In a sense, this entire book has been about "Gnosticism in early Egyptian Christianity." While the previous chapters have dealt more specifically with other topics, especially the connection between Gnosticism and early Judaism, it can be seen that Egyptian Christianity was not far from the discussion. In chapter 1 we took up Moritz Friedländer's argument for the Alexandrian Jewish origins of Gnosticism; we could also see that many of the Gnostic sources he cited survive only in Christian dress. This is obviously the case with an original source not known to Friedländer, *The Apocryphon of John,* discussed in chapter 2. In chapter 3 we discussed Jewish haggadic material in a putative source now found in a Christian Gnostic text of Alexandrian provenience, *The Testimony of Truth.* The Gnostic traditions pertaining to the children of Adam and Eve, Seth, Norea, and Cain, discussed in chapters 4 to 6, likewise survive now in Christian Gnostic texts from Egypt; *The Hypostasis of the Archons* is an important example. All of the Gnostic sources featuring the figure of Melchizedek, discussed in chapter 7, are Christian texts of Egyptian origin. In our discussion of the development of Gnostic self-definition, in chapter 8, we concentrated on Sethian materials that reflect greater or lesser degrees of Christianization. Even the pagan Hermetic text, *Poimandres,* discussed in chapter 9, evidently did not escape the notice of Christians in Egypt, who did not shrink from using a portion of it in Christian worship.[1] The Tractate *Marsanes,* whose Platonism we discussed in chapter 10, could constitute an exception, in that

---

1. P. Berol. 9794: see p. 142 n. 24. I cannot accept the theory, recently put forward by Jörg Büchli, that the *Poimandres* is a "paganized" Christian text. See *Der Poimandres: Ein paganisiertes Evangelium* (WUNT 2:27; Tübingen: J. C. B. Mohr, 1987).

we detected no Christian influence in its content. Yet it was translated into Coptic by people who, whatever their Gnostic affiliation, were doubtless also Egyptian Christians. With our discussion of "gnosis" in Corinth and Alexandria, in chapter 11, we considered the Alexandrian origins of the apostle Paul's colleague (and rival) in Corinth, Apollos. Finally, in chapter 12, we moved to a later stage of Christian development in Egypt in our discussion of the tractates *Melchizedek* and *The Testimony of Truth* in Nag Hammadi Codex IX.

Thus it has already become evident that Gnosticism played an important role in the development of Christianity in Egypt. In this final chapter we shall address the very difficult problem of assessing just how important that role was. Indeed, we shall have to consider whether or not Egyptian Christianity, from its very beginnings in Alexandria, was essentially a Gnostic and thus, from a later perspective, heretical form of the Christian religion.

These questions are not at all easy to decide; for, as is widely acknowledged,[2] the origins of Egyptian Christianity are shrouded in obscurity, owing to a dearth of reliable evidence. As a result, scholarly opinion has varied greatly as to the sources and origins of Egyptian Christianity, and the nature and makeup of the Egyptian church in its earliest stages. It is nevertheless the case that Gnosticism and Gnostic influences play a large role in the discussion.

Nor can any responsible assessment of the existing evidence ignore the seminal and still very influential theory advanced by Walter Bauer in his provocative study, *Orthodoxy and Heresy in Earliest Christianity*.[3] That theory provides the basis for the question already posed: Was Egyptian Christianity originally a Gnostic and thus, from a later perspective, heretical form of the Christian religion?

---

2. Cf. the opening sentence in C. H. Roberts's important book, *Manuscript, Society, and Belief in Early Christian Egypt* (London: Oxford University Press, 1979): "The obscurity that veils the early history of the Church in Egypt and that does not lift until the beginning of the third century constitutes a conspicuous challenge to the historian of primitive Christianity" (1). See also Pearson, "Earliest Christianity"; and idem, "Christians and Jews."

3. Bauer, *Orthodoxy and Heresy*. The original German version was published in 1934: *Rechtgläubigkeit und Ketzerei im ältesten Christentum* (BHT 10; Tübingen: J. C. B. Mohr). His thesis has not been universally accepted by any means, and has been subjected recently to some critical scrutiny. See, e.g., Thomas A. Robinson, *The Bauer Thesis Examined: The Geography of Heresy in the Early Christian Church* (Lewiston/Queenston: Edwin Mellen, 1988), and literature cited there; Robinson concentrates mainly on Asia Minor. Cf. also James McCue, "Orthodoxy and Heresy: Walter Bauer and the Valentinians," *VC* 33 (1979) 118–30; McCue's article is more relevant to the Egyptian situation.

WALTER BAUER ON
EARLY EGYPTIAN CHRISTIANITY

The ancient and still common view regarding heresy is that it is already preceded by an orthodoxy, from which it is seen to deviate. In the Christian case, the orthodoxy in question is that pure doctrine purportedly handed down by Jesus to his apostles, and by the apostles to the church. While such a simplistic notion has long had its challengers— at least from the time of Ferdinand Christian Baur in the nineteenth century[4]—Walter Bauer first took up this question in a systematic way. The method he used was to examine the available evidence for the development of Christianity in various geographical areas. He concluded from his scrutiny of this evidence that heresies, as later defined in ecclesiastical circles, were often the original and only forms of Christianity in many areas. The orthodoxy that eventually came to prevail in such areas did so under the later influence of the Roman church and its ecclesiastical establishment.

While Bauer's theory has been criticized, especially with regard to certain individual geographical areas,[5] it is fair to say that it has gained most acceptance in the case of Egypt.[6] The very paucity of solid evidence for the early history of the Egyptian church provides Bauer with the foundation for his theory; for, he argues, there must surely have been evidence. Thus the question arises: "What reason could (churchmen) have had for being silent about the origins of Christianity in such an important center as Alexandria if there had been something favorable to report?"[7] The answer must be that the earliest form of Christianity in Egypt was not orthodox but heretical, specifically, Gnostic. The only

4. On Baur and his work as a church historian see esp. Peter C. Hodgson, ed. and trans., *Ferdinand Christian Baur on the Writing of Church History* (New York: Oxford University Press, 1968).

5. Cf. n. 3. Gary Burke has recently found interesting support for the traditional view of heresy, against Bauer, in the second-century pagan writer Celsus; see "Walter Bauer and Celsus," *The Second Century* 4 (1984) 1–7.

6. See, e.g., Hans Lietzmann, *A History of the Early Church* (trans. B. L. Woolf; Cleveland/New York: Meridian, 1961) 2.275; Robert M. Grant, *From Augustus to Constantine* (New York: Harper & Row, 1970) 198; Helmut Koester, *Introduction to the New Testament*, vol. 2: *History and Literature of Early Christianity* (Berlin-New York: Walter de Gruyter/Philadelphia: Fortress, 1982) 220. Koester's discussion of Christian origins in Egypt (219–39) is, however, more careful in that he speaks of the probability of "several competing Christian groups" in the earliest period (219). He also looks at a wider range of sources.

7. *Orthodoxy and Heresy*, 45. Bauer's discussion of Egypt is concentrated in chap. 2 (44–60), but he makes comments relevant to the Egyptian case elsewhere as well. In what follows I cite page numbers from his book in parentheses.

representatives of early Alexandrian Christianity of which we have any secure knowledge are all Gnostic arch-heretics: Basilides and his son Isidore, Carpocrates, and Valentinus, and their disciples (48).

What of Eusebius's account of the founding of the Alexandrian church by St. Mark?[8] And what of the bishops enumerated by Eusebius as Mark's successors? Bauer's answer is that the ten names of bishops listed between Mark and Demetrius[9] "are and remain for us a mere echo and a puff of smoke" (45). As for Mark himself and his connection with the founding of the Alexandrian church, it was the Roman church, argues Bauer, that lent to orthodox Alexandria the figure of Peter's interpreter for the purpose of creating a suitable founding legend and an apostolic grounding for episcopal rule and succession (60, 117). The earliest real glimpse that we get of "ecclesiastical" Christianity in Alexandria is with Demetrius, under whose episcopal rule (189–232 c.e.) an orthodox form of Christianity first developed (53–54), and to whom the fictitious succession list of Alexandrian bishops must ultimately be attributed (55).

In order for him to maintain his theory of the heretical (Gnostic) origins of Egyptian Christianity, Bauer must assess the earliest Christian literature attributable to Egypt in a manner consistent with the theory. Thus, the *Gospel of the Hebrews* and the *Gospel of the Egyptians* become products of "movements resting on syncretistic gnostic foundations" (50–53). The *Epistle of Barnabas* is seen to be given to "a thoroughly grotesque allegorization" and to be essentially "gnostic" in its content (47), with a Christology that "seems docetic" (48). With such characterizations, compared with the actual evidence (the texts themselves!), a large shadow of doubt begins to loom over the entire edifice of Bauer's reconstruction.

This is not the place to discuss the aforementioned early Alexandrian documents,[10] except to say that none of them is Gnostic in any meaningful sense of that term. They are, in any case, anonymous *(Gos. Heb.; Gos. Eg.)* or pseudonymous *(Barn.)*. So Bauer is essentially correct in his observation that the earliest Alexandrian Christians of which we have solid

8. *Hist. Eccl.* 2.16. On the Mark legend see Pearson, "Earliest Christianity," 137–45.
9. Annianus, Abilius, Cerdo, Primus, Justus, Eumenes, Mark, Celadion, Agrippinus, and Julian—Eusebius *Hist. Eccl.* 2.24; 3.14,21; 4.1,4,5,11,19; 5.9.
10. On *Gos. Heb.* and *Gos. Eg.* see *NTA* 1.158–78, and Koester, *Introduction* 2.223f., 229f., and literature cited. On *Barn.* see esp. R. A. Kraft, *Barnabas and Didache* (The Apostolic Fathers: A New Translation and Commentary 3; Toronto: Nelson, 1965), and cf. Pearson, "Christians and Jews," 211–14. See also *The Secret Gospel of Mark*, unknown to Bauer, on which see esp. Morton Smith, *Clement of Alexandria and a Secret Gospel of Mark* (Cambridge: Harvard University Press, 1973).

historical knowledge are the heresiarchs Valentinus, Basilides, and Carpocrates. But the significance of that fact is not so clear. In arriving at his
conclusions as to the heretical character of the earliest Christianity in
Egypt, Bauer must extrapolate backward in time from the reign of
Hadrian (117–138 C.E.), when these heretics were flourishing, and color
the result with the hues exhibited by the second-century Gnostics. We
know no more (and probably less) about Christian Gnosticism in first-
century Egypt than we do about non-Gnostic Christianity in first-century Egypt.

Are we left, then, with no recourse except groundless speculation? I
do not think so. I think we can make some progress in probing both the
prehistory of heresy, that is, pre-Valentinian Gnosticism, and the early
history of Egyptian Christianity in general, by studying the evidence
relating to the three heresiarchs themselves: Valentinus, Basilides, and
Carpocrates. Had Bauer done that, he might have come up with a
different assessment of Christian origins in Egypt, and a more nuanced
perspective on the position of Gnosticism in early Egyptian Christianity.

VALENTINUS

According to information preserved by Epiphanius of Salamis (*Haer.*
31.2.3), Valentinus was born in a village on the Egyptian seacoast and
educated in Alexandria. The year of his birth is not known, but we can
assume that he was born around the turn of the second century.[11]
Irenaeus (*Haer.* 3.4.3) reports that Valentinus moved to Rome in the time
of Hyginus (Bishop of Rome 138–141). Our interest is focused on the
period of his life spent in Alexandria, before he moved to Rome.

In Alexandria, Valentinus acquired his substantial learning in Greek
rhetoric and philosophy. He encountered Gnosticism there. He probably became a Christian there, too, and eventually a Christian teacher.
The relationship between Christianity and Gnosticism in Valentinus's
teaching, and the relationship between Valentinus's own elaboration of
gnosis and his source material, was apparently well known to Bishop
Irenaeus of Lyon. His summary assessment of Valentinus's teaching is:
"Valentinus adapted the fundamental principles of the so-called 'Gnostic' school of thought to his own kind of system."[12]

---

11. Bentley Layton's dates for Valentinus (ca. 100–ca. 175) seem reasonable. See his
valuable discussion in *Gnostic Scriptures*, 217–24.
12. *Haer.* 1.11.1, as translated by Layton (*Gnostic Scriptures*, 225); cf. also Tertullian
Adv. Val. 4. For a valuable discussion of the relationship between Valentinus and the
mythological system of *Ap. John*, see G. Quispel, "Valentinian Gnosis and the
Apocryphon of John," in Layton, *Rediscovery* 1.118–32.

What Irenaeus refers to here as "the so-called 'Gnostic' school of thought" is treated at length by him in Book 1, chapter 29 of his *Adversus Haereses*. There Irenaeus presents an account, obviously based on a written source, of the mythological system of a group of sectarians he refers to as "Gnostics" (*gnōstikoi*). The designation "Gnostic" is to be understood as a self-designation chosen by a specific group of people claiming to be in possession of a special, esoteric *gnōsis* ("knowledge").[13] As is well known by now, the system described by Irenaeus is essentially reproduced in a well-defined section of *The Apocryphon of John* (BG 2; NHC II,1; III,1; IV,1).[14] The kind of Gnosticism represented by this and other related texts is often referred to in modern scholarship as "Sethian" Gnosticism, on the basis of a prominence in the texts of the figure of Seth and the use of such terms as "seed of Seth" and "children of Seth" as a sectarian self-designation.[15] (Curiously, the term "Gnostic" does not occur in the Nag Hammadi texts.) Bentley Layton refers to the writings of this group as "classic gnostic scripture," and rightly sees in Valentinus both a Christian teacher bent on a "revision" of the Gnostic tradition and an innovative "mythmaker" in his own right.[16]

The essential relationship between the myth of *The Apocryphon of John* and the Valentinian myth as elaborated by Valentinus's pupil Ptolemy (Iren. *Haer.* 1.1.1–8.5) is evident when the two are compared. The problem here, though, is that Ptolemy's version was itself a revision of Valentinus's original system, which, in turn, was a revision of the Sethian Gnostic myth.[17] Unfortunately, we are imperfectly informed about Valentinus's own version, though Irenaeus presents a somewhat sketchy account (1.11.1), from which it can be inferred that Valentinus was indeed using a myth like that of *The Apocryphon of John*.

The extant fragments of Valentinus consist mainly of quotations from letters and homilies. Therefore, on the grounds of their literary genres, they cannot be expected to provide any systematic information on Valentinus's mythological system. Even so, allusions to the myth do occur. For example, fragment 1 (Layton C)[18] deals with the awe of the creator

13. For a valuable discussion of the term *gnōstikos*, see Morton Smith, "The History of the Term Gnostikos," in Layton, *Rediscovery* 2.796–807.

14. Cf. n. 12. See also the section on "Barbelognosis" in Foerster, *Gnosis* 1.100–20, containing a translation of Irenaeus *Haer.* 1.29.1–4 and the BG version (short recension) of *Ap. John*, with introduction. Cf. also Layton, *Gnostic Scriptures*, 163–69 (Irenaeus's account) and 23–51 (*Ap. John*, long recension [NHC II,1]).

15. Cf. Schenke, "Das sethianische System," and idem, "Gnostic Sethianism"; and chaps. 4, 8 in this book.

16. *Gnostic Scriptures*, 220f.

17. Ibid., 276–79. Layton's discussion is followed by a translation of Ptolemy's version of the myth (281–302).

18. The fragments of Valentinus are usually cited by the numbers assigned to them

angels in the presence of Adam; here we can easily see the use of the anthropogonic portion of a Gnostic myth like that of *The Apocryphon of John*. Allusions to the myth also occur in *The Gospel of Truth* (NHC I,3), a contemplative homily on the Christian message of salvation ("the gospel of truth") likely written by the great heresiarch himself.[19]

That Valentinus knew and used the basic myth of *The Apocryphon of John* is clear. But did he know and use the apocryphon itself? That seems to me to be highly unlikely. Indeed, it is doubtful that Irenaeus himself, in quoting part of the myth, was using what we know as *The Apocryphon of John* as his source.[20] That tractate, in the form(s) that we now know it, is probably later than Valentinus. It is clearly a composite document with a complicated literary history. Indeed, those elements in it that are clearly "Christian" seem to me to belong to the later stages of its redaction.[21]

So it is an open question whether the form of the Gnostic myth used by Valentinus in Alexandria already had some Christian elements in it, and, therefore, was at home among *Christian* Gnostics in Alexandria. The other possibility is that Valentinus took it over from a non-Christian group of Jewish Gnostics in Alexandria, and added Christian elements of his own.

Where did the myth originate? Alexandria? Or Syria? Syria is often regarded as the birthplace of Gnosticism, and some scholars, such as Helmut Koester, locate some of the most important Nag Hammadi texts there, including *The Apocryphon of John*.[22] It should be noted that the system of Saturninus (Satornil) summarized by Irenaeus (*Haer.* 1.24.1–2) presupposes the same myth as that of the apocryphon, or at least a simpler form of it. Saturninus, a Christian Gnostic, was active in Syrian Antioch. It is therefore possible that the myth used by Valentinus had been brought to Egypt from Syria by Gnostic Christians early in the second century, or perhaps even before the end of the first century. It is also possible that Saturninus in Antioch independently Christianized an earlier version of the myth that was available in both Antioch and Alexandria. In that case, the place of origin of the myth remains an open question.

---

in Völker, *Quellen* (57–60), followed by Foerster, *Gnosis* (1.239–43). Layton has recently devised a different system, arranging the fragments in a different order and identifying them with letters of the alphabet (*Gnostic Scriptures*, 229–49).

19. Layton, *Gnostic Scriptures*, 250–64.
20. Foerster, *Gnosis* 1.100-3; Pearson, "'Jewish Gnostic' Literature," 19–25.
21. Pearson, "'Jewish Gnostic' Literature," 19–25.
22. Koester, *Introduction* (cit. n. 6) 2.212f.

In discussing the Gnostic sources used by Valentinus, we must not overlook another important text from the Nag Hammadi corpus: *Eugnostos the Blessed* (II,3; V,3). This tractate, which shows no obvious Christian elements, is a learned philosophical-theological treatise devoted to an exposition of the true nature of God and the divine world. It was probably written in Alexandria by a Jewish Gnostic with considerable knowledge of Greek philosophy, especially Platonism. Its essential content is also preserved in a Christianized version, *The Sophia of Jesus Christ* (III,4; BG 3). In the latter tractate the material in *Eugnostos* has been "Christianized" by expanding the text into a postresurrection revelation discourse given by Christ to his disciples. *The Sophia of Jesus Christ* was probably edited in Alexandria by Christian Gnostics in the second century, probably after the time of Valentinus.[23]

The importance of *Eugnostos* for our purposes is that its speculations on Anthropos and Sophia seem to have been utilized by Valentinus in developing his doctrine of the divine Pleroma. This has recently been shown by Rouel van den Broek,[24] who accounts for the entities in Valentinus's primary Ogdoad (Iren. *Haer.* 1.11.1; cf. 1.1.1) with reference to the speculations in *Eugnostos*. Van den Broek also shows that the Gnostic speculations involved grew out of a Jewish milieu that was strongly influenced by Platonism. For example, the entities *Nous* ("Mind") and *Alētheia* ("Truth"), the second set of aeons in Valentinus's primary Ogdoad, ultimately derive from the sixth book of Plato's *Republic* (*Resp.* 490b), though Valentinus probably got them from a Jewish Gnostic myth such as is found in *Eugnostos*.[25]

In considering the background and intellectual milieu of Valentinus, we cannot overlook the strong possibility that Valentinus was personally acquainted with Basilides. Indeed, Layton has recently suggested that Basilides "may somehow have exerted a major influence upon the development of Valentinus' system."[26] We shall return to Basilides in the next section of this chapter.

Before we leave Valentinus, however, it is essential that we take into account the non-Gnostic background of his thought. We have already

23. Cf. Martin Krause's discussion and translation in Foerster, *Gnosis* 2.24–39.
24. Van den Broek, "Jewish and Platonic Speculations in Early Alexandrian Theology: Eugnostos, Philo, Valentinus, and Origen," in Pearson-Goehring, *Roots of Egyptian Christianity*, 190–203.
25. Ibid., 198f.
26. *Gnostic Scriptures*, 417. Layton also suggests that Valentinus had come into contact with Hermetic literature, such as the *Poimandres* (220, 413). On possible connections between *Poimandres* and the Valentinian myth see Jonas, *Gnostic Religion*, 171–73. On the *Poimandres* see also chap. 9 in this book.

alluded to his heavy indebtedness to Greek philosophy. We can go further and assert that Valentinus, like Philo Judaeus whose writings he probably knew,[27] belongs to the general history of Middle Platonism.[28] But more important for our purposes is Valentinus's use of non-Gnostic Christian sources. The best place to look for the evidence is in Valentinus's fragments, all of them presumably dating from his Alexandrian period. These fragments reflect the use by Valentinus of (at least) the canonical Gospel of Matthew (frg. 2 = Layton H) and the Pauline epistles (Romans in frgs. 5 and 6 = Layton D and G), and probably also the Gospel of John (frg. 3 = Layton E). Indeed, Valentinus refers in one of his homilies to the writings of "God's church" (frg. 6), which implies something like a collection of normative scripture. One need not add to this the numerous canonical scriptures alluded to in *The Gospel of Truth*[29]—which is probably a work of the master himself but perhaps not from his Alexandrian period—in order to see that many of the Christian writings that were destined to become canonical scriptures of the orthodox church were circulating in Alexandria in the early second century. Indeed, I would argue that precisely such writings gave Valentinian *gnosis* its special Christian character.

The implications of this for a proper assessment of the general character of early second-century Alexandrian Christianity are obvious, and will be taken up again later in this chapter. But first we must consider the other two heresiarchs, Basilides and Carpocrates.

BASILIDES

We know nothing of Basilides's background. We know only that he was active in Alexandria during the reigns of the emperors Hadrian (117–138) and Antoninus Pius (138–161; Clem. Alex. *Strom.* 7.17.106), but where he spent his early years is not at all clear. Eusebius, in his *Chronicle* (according to Jerome's Latin version) lists as one of the items

27. So Layton, *Gnostic Scriptures*, 217.

28. See John Dillon, *The Middle Platonists 80 B.C. to A.D. 220* (Ithaca: Cornell University Press, 1977) 384–89. G. C. Stead's study of Valentinus's thought lays heavy influence on his Platonism; see "In Search of Valentinus," in Layton, *Rediscovery*, 1.75–95.

29. On the use of canonical scripture in *Gos. Truth* see now Jacqueline A. Williams, *Biblical Interpretation in the Gnostic Gospel of Truth from Nag Hammadi* (SBLDS 79; Atlanta: Scholars Press, 1988). Williams has established as "probable" the use in *Gos. Truth* of the following NT books: Matthew, John, Romans, 1 Corinthians, 2 Corinthians, Ephesians, Colossians, Hebrews, 1 John, and Revelation; "possible" use adds Philippians to this list (see Table 2, pp. 181–83).

for the sixteenth year of Hadrian's reign (132): "Basilides the heresiarch was living in Alexandria. From him derive the Gnostics."[30] The implications of this terse comment seem to be that Basilides came to Alexandria from somewhere else. If that is the case, the most likely place for Basilides's point of departure is Antioch in Syria. Irenaeus (Haer. 1.24.1–2) puts Basilides in close association with Saturninus of Antioch, and claims that both of them were pupils of Menander, who had come to Antioch from Samaria (Justin Apol. 1.26.4).

We note that Eusebius traces the origin of the "Gnostic" sect to Basilides. This cannot be correct, if by "Gnostic" Eusebius means the sect so named by Irenaeus. It is, nevertheless, the case that Basilides's mythological system, like that of Saturninus, stands in close relationship to the basic myth identified by Irenaeus as that of the "Gnostics" (Haer. 1.29; cf. Ap. John).[31] Thus Basilides would appear to be one of the links in the nexus of the spread of the Gnostic religion between Antioch and Alexandria.

Basilides was reputedly a very prolific author; but, unfortunately, very little remains of his literary production. His Christian Gnostic teaching seems to have undergone considerable development in Alexandria, and was further modified by his son Isidore and other pupils. Indeed, in the case of the few fragments and testimonia that we have, it is not easy to distinguish between Basilides's own views and those of his followers. This problem is further compounded by the possible existence in the second century of another Basilides, a missionary to the Persians.[32] Bentley Layton has recently made a significant advance in scholarship on Basilides by isolating eight fragments that contain quotations from, or references to, Basilides's own works. Seven of these fragments are found preserved in the works of Clement of Alexandria; the other is preserved by Origen of Alexandria.[33]

It seems best, therefore, in our discussion of the work of Basilides and his use of sources, to confine our attention to the fragments that can

30. "Basilides haeresiarches in Alexandria commoratur. A quo gnostici," 201 in R. Helm, ed., Die Chronik des Hieronymus (in Eusebius Werke, 7.7, GCS 47, rev. ed.; Berlin: Akademie-Verlag, 1956). Cf. the Armenian version (ed. A. Schoene, Eusebi Chronicorum canonum quae supersunt [Dublin-Zurich: Weidmann, 1967] 2.168): "Basilides haeresiarcha his temporibus apparuit (Basilides the heresiarch appeared at this time)".
31. I accept the view of B. Layton (Gnostic Scriptures, 417–19) that Irenaeus's version of Basilides's system is the one closest to that of the heresiarch himself, rather than the version preserved by Hippolytus (Ref. 7.20.1–27.13).
32. "Fragment 1" (Völker, Foerster) has to do with this other Basilides; see Layton, Gnostic Scriptures, 418.
33. Layton, Gnostic Scriptures, 429–44 (frgs. A–H).

safely be attributed to him, and also cohere reasonably well with the account of Basilides's mythological system as reported by Irenaeus (*Haer.* 1.24.3–5), who, in turn, probably got it from Justin Martyr.[34]

Like that of Valentinus, Basilides's teaching was heavily imbued with Greek philosophy, but in his case, as has been shown by Layton,[35] the greatest influence was from the Stoic school. Also like Valentinus, Basilides was an exegete of scripture, and commented on some of the apostolic writings that would later become canonical in the catholic church.

The fragments of Basilides, all presumably from works produced after he came to Alexandria, show knowledge and use of the Pauline epistles (frg. F Layton) and the Gospel of Matthew (frg. G Layton = 2 Völker). The last-named fragment (G), the most extensive one preserved, is from Book 23 of Basilides's lost *Exegetica*,[36] and may constitute part of a commentary on 1 Peter 4.[37] If Irenaeus's discussion of Basilides's version of the crucifixion narrative is authentic, according to which Simon of Cyrene was crucified in Jesus' place (*Haer.* 1.24.4),[38] we have possible evidence of Basilides's use of the Gospel of Mark, for the wording of the narrative about Simon's bearing Jesus' cross is closer to that of Mark 15:20–21 than to its parallels in Matt. 27:32 and Luke 23:26.[39]

We thus find reflected in Basilides's writings, as we did in the case of Valentinus, the presence in Alexandria of scriptures destined to become canonical in the catholic church. We can also make the same assertion

34. Cf. n. 31. The section on Irenaeus's *Adversus Haereses* containing accounts of Simon, Menander, Satornil, and Basilides (1.23–24) is the material most likely based on Justin's lost *Syntagma* against heresies (referred to in *Apol.* 1.26). See esp. Adolf Hilgenfeld, *Die Ketzergeschichte des Urchristentums* (repr. Darmstadt: Wissenschaftliche Buchgesellschaft, 1963) 57, 200. For a good discussion of the problem of Irenaeus's sources see Frederik Wisse, "The Nag Hammadi Library and the Heresiologists," *VC* 25 (1971) 205–23, esp. 213–18.
35. *Gnostic Scriptures*, 418.
36. According to Clement of Alexandria, who quotes it (*Strom.* 4.81.1–83.1). Cf. Agrippa Castor's report (in Eusebius *Hist. Eccl.* 4.7.7) that Basilides composed "twenty-four books on the gospel," probably a reference to Basilides's *Exegetica* (commentaries).
37. So Layton, *Gnostic Scriptures*, 440.
38. Irenaeus may have misunderstood an account of the crucifixion such as that preserved in *Treat. Seth* (NHC VII,2) 55,30–56,19. At first sight this passage might suggest that it was Simon who was crucified, but that is not necessarily the case. The relevant part of the passage reads (in the *Nag Hammadi Library* translation): "It was another, their father, who drank the gall and the vinegar; it was not I. They struck me with the reed; it was another, Simon, who bore the cross on his shoulder. It was another upon whom they placed the crown of thorns. But I was rejoicing in the height . . ." (56,6–14). Cf. *Apoc. Pet.* (NHC VII,3) 82,17–83,15.
39. "Simonem quendam Cyrenaeum angariatum portasse crucem eius pro eo" (Völker) // ἀγγαρεύουσιν (παράγοντά) τινα Σίμωνα κυρηναῖον . . . ἵνα ἄρῃ τὸν σταυρὸν αὐτοῦ. Basilides is said to have produced, or edited, his own gospel (Origen *Hom. in Luc.* 1), but of this nothing remains.

about Basilides's Christian Gnosticism as we did about Valentinus's: His use of such non-Gnostic Christian writings gave Basilides's *gnōsis* its special Christian character.

CARPOCRATES

With Carpocrates we run into some special problems of definition. There is no question, of course, that Carpocrates was a heretic, according to the canons of later orthodoxy. But was he a Gnostic? Layton, for example, says that "the doctrine of the Carpocratians bears no noticeable resemblance to gnostic myth, and so there are no grounds to conclude that the Carpocratians were gnostics in the classic sense of the word, although they may have borrowed the name 'gnostic,' perhaps as a form of self-praise."[40] Morton Smith associates the core doctrines of the Carpocratians with early Palestinian Jewish Christianity, and downplays any connection with Gnosticism.[41]

In the case of Carpocrates, we are at a serious disadvantage, too, in that we have no writings of his at all. We do not even know that Carpocrates himself produced any, though the heresiologists do refer in general to writings of the Carpocratians. The evidence on the Carpocratians supplied by Irenaeus, which Smith describes as "the only account of Carpocratian theology which can pretend to reliability,"[42] is itself decidedly ambiguous, particularly as to any connection with Gnosticism. Reference to world-creating archons (*Haer.* 1.25.1) would seem to imply some connection with Gnostic myth, but may not be enough to classify the Carpocratians as Gnostics, even if Irenaeus does claim that the Carpocratians in Rome led by Marcellina "call themselves Gnostics" (*Haer.* 1.25.6). In any case, the emphasis on libertine practice sets Carpocrates apart from his Alexandrian contemporaries (or near-contemporaries),[43] Valentinus and Basilides. Nor is there any evidence at all of any contact between Carpocrates and either of the other two heresiarchs, though they were active in the same city.

The written sources used by Carpocrates are of primary importance for the present discussion, to the extent that we can ascertain them from the account presented by Irenaeus. These sources turn out to be, chiefly,

40. *Gnostic Scriptures,* 199.
41. *Clement of Alexandria* (cit. n. 10), 267–78.
42. Ibid., 270. In Appendix B of his book (295–350) Smith provides all of the references to Carpocrates found in patristic literature.
43. Carpocrates flourished before 125, according to Smith (ibid., 267).

New Testament books. The dominical saying about agreeing with one's adversary (Matt. 5:25–26; Luke 12:58–59) is used to bolster the doctrine that all sins must be completed in this life in order to escape reincarnation (*Haer.* 1.25.4). A saying in the Gospel of Mark (4:10–11) is used to bolster the Carpocratian claim to be in possession of Jesus' esoteric teaching (*Haer.* 1.25.5). And there is an allusion to the (deutero-) Pauline doctrine of salvation by faith (Eph. 2:8), cited as a basis for Carpocratian ethics (*Haer.* 1.25.5).

Unfortunately, the nature of our chief source, Irenaeus, prevents us from ascertaining more precisely what gospels were used by Carpocrates, in addition to an epistle or epistles in the Pauline corpus. The Gospel of Matthew, at least, seems to have been used, as well as a version of the Gospel of Mark. Clement's letter to Theodore, published by Morton Smith, raises the possibility that the version of Mark used by Carpocrates was really the longer version now known as *The Secret Gospel of Mark*.[44]

We can certainly conclude from the little evidence we have that Carpocrates had access in Alexandria to several of the writings that would later become part of the canonical New Testament of the church. There is little or no evidence that he used any written Gnostic sources. His doctrine of reincarnation reflects popular Platonism more than anything specifically Gnostic. Where he got his libertinism is uncertain, though again we may have to look eastward, to Syria. We recall in that connection that another expression of early Christian libertinism, the Nicolaitan sect (Rev. 2:6, 15), seems to have derived from Nicolaus of Antioch, one of the seven leaders of the Hellenist wing of the Jerusalem church in its earliest history (Acts 6:5).[45]

THE SHAPE OF
EARLY EGYPTIAN CHRISTIANITY

In our brief look at the three arch-heretics who, for Bauer, represent the core of Alexandrian Christianity in its earliest stages, we have cer-

---

44. Cf. n. 10. Clement's letter claims that Carpocrates obtained a copy of *The Secret Gospel of Mark* from an Alexandrian Christian presbyter and then produced a revised version of it (Smith, *Clement of Alexandria*, p. 446 [ET], 450 [text]).

45. The chief sources for the Nicolaitans are Irenaeus (*Haer.* 1.26.3), who affirms a connection with Nicolaus of Antioch, and Clement of Alexandria (*Strom.* 3.4.25–26), who tries to absolve Nicolaus himself of the charges tradition had brought against him and his sect. Epiphanius brings the libertine Gnostics he encountered in Egypt into association with Nicolaus and the Nicolaitans (*Haer.* 25–26). On these Gnostics see Layton, *Gnostic Scriptures*, 199–214.

tainly noted the presence of a pre-Valentinian, pre-Basilidian Gnosticism in Alexandria. But we have also noted the heavy reliance on the part of our heresiarchs on non-Gnostic writings of the (later) canonical New Testament. This itself is a strong indication that Alexandrian Christianity included in its mix groups of non-Gnostic Christians, people whom Bauer would have to put into the camp of the "orthodox," or (to use a better term) "proto-orthodox." Or were the people who brought the aforementioned apostolic writings to Alexandria all Gnostics? It is possible, but not likely. And what about the authors or compilers of the aforementioned apocryphal gospels and their respective communities, "Hebrews" and "Egyptians"? Perhaps such Christians were neither "orthodox" nor "proto-orthodox," but they were certainly not Gnostics. (Use of the term "orthodox" for this early period is, of course, an anachronism.) The *Epistle of Barnabas* also comes to mind here, a text whose "gnosis" consists of Christian "aggadah," that is, interpretation of the Old Testament (*Barn.* 1–17), and Christian "halakha" (18–21, the "Two Ways").[46] Yet another early second-century text could be mentioned here, the *Kerygma of Peter*, an apologetic work that is very likely a product of Alexandrian Christianity. Unfortunately it is lost, except for a few fragments in which no trace at all of Gnosticism can be seen.[47]

Thus there can be no doubt that in the time of Valentinus, Basilides, and Carpocrates there were non-Gnostic Christians in Alexandria as well as Gnostics. That can surely be maintained even if we want to discount entirely, as Bauer does,[48] Eusebius's reference to Agrippa Castor and his orthodox contemporaries. Referring to Basilides's "school of impious heresy" in Egypt (Alexandria), Eusebius assures the reader that Basilides did not go unchallenged:

> Now while most of the orthodox at that time were struggling for the truth, and fighting with great eloquence for the glory of the Apostles and of the Church, some also by their writings provided for their successors methods of defence against the heresies which have been mentioned. Of these a most powerful refutation of Basilides has reached us from Agrippa Castor, a most famous writer of that time, revealing the cleverness of the man's deception.[49]

Unfortunately, we know nothing more of Agrippa Castor. Nor do we have other names of "orthodox" Christians in Egypt from the time of the

46. Cf. references to Kraft and Pearson, n. 10.
47. *NTA* 2.94–102.
48. *Orthodoxy and Heresy*, 170–71.
49. *Hist. Eccl.* 4.7.5–7 (Lake's translation in the LCL edition). Eusebius goes on to provide some information on Basilides based on Agrippa Castor. Cf. n. 36, above.

arch-heretics and before, apart from the names of Mark and his alleged episcopal successors. We have already noted how Bauer assesses these.[50]

But having established that there were in Alexandria at least *some* non-Gnostic Christians, what was their relative numerical strength, over against the heretical groups? Were they a minority struggling to maintain their Christian life and faith in the face of the superior numbers of the Gnostics (as Bauer's theory would have it)? Or could they have been, in fact, a faceless majority?

Here is where the heretics themselves might come to our aid. Quite apart from the theoretical arguments that might be mounted by a sociologist of religion regarding the relationship between esoteric, elitist groups and their mainline cousins, and the statistical conclusions that could be drawn from such social theory,[51] we have the testimony of the heretics themselves. The Valentinians provide us with the best evidence, and this has to do with the very structure of their ecclesiology. Simply put, the "pneumatic" Gnostics were the elite few, over against the mass of ordinary "psychic" Christians, those who lacked the *gnosis* prerequisite for entering the eschatological pleromatic "bridechamber."[52] Scriptural proofs were even offered for this state of affairs. The pneumatic elite were referred to as the *eklektoi*, the "chosen," whereas the ordinary "psychic" Christians were the *klētoi*, the "called," recalling the words of the savior: "Many are 'called' but few are 'chosen'" (Matt. 22:14).[53] Indeed, one Valentinian text is very explicit on the relative strengths of non-Christians, non-Gnostic Christians, and Gnostics: "Therefore many are material (ὑλικοί), but not many are psychic (ψυχικοί), and few are spiritual (πνευματικοί)."[54]

---

50. Cf. discussion above, p. 197.

51. For a discussion of such little work as has been done on sociology and Gnosticism, see Henry A. Green, *The Economic and Social Origins of Gnosticism* (SBLDS 77; Atlanta: Scholars Press, 1985) 1–19. Green's own work reflects a Marxist approach. For an interesting theoretical discussion of how religious groups form and develop, see the seminal study by Rodney Stark and William Sims Bainbridge, *A Theory of Religion* (Toronto Studies in Religion 2; New York-Berne-Frankfurt-Paris: Peter Lang, 1987). Cf. chap. 8 in this book, p. 134 n. 41.

52. James F. McCue makes a major point of this in his study, "Orthodoxy and Heresy" (cit. n. 3).

53. This terminology is found in Clement of Alexandria's *Excerpta ex Theodoto* 58.1, part of a passage derived from an early Valentinian source also used by Irenaeus (*Exc. Theod.* 43.2–65 // *Haer.* 1.4.5–7.1). See, e.g., Otto Dibelius, "Studien zur Geschichte der Valentinianer, I: Die Excerpta ex Theodoto und Irenäus," *ZNW* 9 (1908) 230–47; Völker, *Quellen*, 104–18; and McCue, "Orthodoxy and Heresy," 125.

54. *Exc. Theod.* 56.2, as translated by Casey (*The Excerpta ex Theodoto of Clement of Alexandria* [SD 1; London: Christophers, 1934] 77). Cf. McCue, "Orthodoxy and Heresy," 127.

To be sure, the Gnostics were eager to convert to their groups individuals from the masses of ordinary Christians. We have already seen how they could utilize the non-Gnostic apostolic writings for their purposes, even devising commentaries that provided the "true" interpretation of these writings. (The Alexandrian Gnostics produced the first commentaries on the New Testament.) The later Basilidians and Valentinians even provided arguments based on apostolic succession: Basilides was said to have drawn his teachings from the apostle Peter through the mediation of one Glaukias; Valentinus drew his from the apostle Paul through one Theudas (Clem. Alex. *Strom.* 7.17.106). But, in the cases of Glaukias and Theudas, are we not entitled to borrow Bauer's phraseology (his reference to the Alexandrian episcopal succession list):[55] "a mere echo and a puff of smoke"?

However successful the Gnostic groups might have been in attracting converts to their groups, it must finally be concluded, with regard to Bauer's thesis, that (1) he was wrong on the question of the origins of Christianity in Egypt,[56] and (2) he was also probably wrong in his assessment of the relative numerical strengths of the non-Gnostic and Gnostic Christians there.

Yet he was not all wrong. It must be granted, for example, that Bauer was essentially right in his assessment of the importance of the role of Bishop Demetrius in the establishment of an ecclesiastical "orthodoxy" in Egypt. Properly called "the Second Founder of the church in Alexandria,"[57] Demetrius was clearly the first "monarchical" bishop in Alexandria. However, contrary to Bauer's view, it is doubtful that the impetus for Demetrius's career came entirely from Rome. The monarchical episcopacy was as late in developing in Rome (with Bishop Victor, 189–199)[58] as it was in Egypt (Demetrius 189–232). To be sure, ecclesiastical contact between Rome and Alexandria probably increased significantly from the time of Demetrius on; and the writings of Bishop Irenaeus of Lyon,[59] which probably came to Egypt via Rome, would surely have helped Demetrius and his theologians in the struggle to

55. Cf. discussion above, p. 197.
56. For my own views as to the Palestinian origin of the Alexandrian church and its predominantly Jewish character until the Jewish War of 115–117, see Pearson, "Earliest Christianity," and idem, "Christians and Jews"; cf. also chap. 11 in this book. See also the ground-breaking work of C. H. Roberts, *Manuscript, Society, and Belief* (cit. n. 2).
57. So W. Telfer, "Episcopal Succession in Egypt," *JEH* 3 (1952) 1–12, esp. 2.
58. See G. La Piana, "The Roman Church at the End of the Second Century," *HTR* 18 (1925) 201–77.
59. P. Oxy. (III) 405, a second-century fragment of Irenaeus's *Adversus Haereses*, dates to the time of Demetrius. See Roberts, *Manuscript, Society, and Belief*, 14.

define and enforce Christian orthodoxy for the Alexandrian church. Even so, some form of orthodoxy seems to have existed in Alexandria before Demetrius. This is indicated by Irenaeus himself, who, writing about 180, includes the church in Egypt among the churches scattered throughout the world that preserve the catholic faith with "one heart and one soul" (*Haer.* 1.10.2).

As for the intellectual life of the Alexandrian Christians, we can reasonably surmise, with Bauer, that the aforementioned heretics and their groups were dominant, at least until the time of the Christian Stoic Pantaenus, teacher and predecessor of Clement of Alexandria. Pantaenus, who flourished in the time of Emperor Commodus (180–192), was head of a theological school in Alexandria (the famous Catechetical School), which, according to Eusebius, had existed "from ancient custom" (*Hist. Eccl.* 5.10). C. H. Roberts has suggested that it was Pantaenus who purged that school of the influence of the Gnostics.[60] I would suggest, more guardedly, that Pantaenus took over the leadership of the school from a Gnostic teacher.[61] It can be surmised that Bishop Demetrius would subsequently have done all in his power to bring that school under the influence of the episcopal see.

In any case, during the time of Demetrius an all-out struggle began among competing groups of Christians, a struggle now more and more dominated by Christians loyal to the ecclesiastical establishment and its emerging standard of orthodoxy. In this setting we can situate two of the Nag Hammadi tractates discussed in previous chapters, *The Testimony of Truth* (NHC IX,3)[62] and *The Teachings of Silvanus* (NHC VII,4).[63]

In our discussion of *The Testimony of Truth* in chapter 12 we noted that its author was bent on safeguarding what, for him, was the true Christian teaching (gnosis) and life (encratism). His method was to attack his opponents and their "heretical" doctrines, and we noted that these opponents included not only adherents of the catholic ecclesiastical faith but also other Gnostics, including followers of Valentinus and Basilides. We could see that this author was part of a bitter struggle going on among rival Christian groups, both Gnostic and non-Gnostic, each vying for

60. Roberts, *Manuscript, Society, and Belief,* 54.
61. Who this might have been is anybody's guess; Basilides's son Isidore, for example, would have belonged to that generation. Gnostic students would not have been barred from attendance thereafter. We know that, many years later, Origen had some Gnostic students attending his lectures in the school. Among them was a certain Ambrose, a Valentinian, who was converted to ecclesiastical orthodoxy by Origen (Eusebius *Hist. Eccl.* 6.18).
62. See chap. 12, above, pp. 188–93.
63. See chap. 11, above, pp. 177–81.

some sort of spiritual and (no doubt) sociopolitical power. We can confidently situate *The Testimony of Truth* in the time of Bishop Demetrius of Alexandria. Under Demetrius, as we have seen, a Christian orthodoxy was in the process of being defined and imposed in the churches of Alexandria and elsewhere in Egypt. Under him, too, episcopal rule was being expanded in the Egyptian church by means of his consecration of new bishops.[64] The author of *The Testimony of Truth* represented an embattled group of Christians, and he did not shrink from taking up quill and ink against his adversaries.[65]

Can we know who this author was? I have argued elsewhere[66] that the information about its author that can be deduced from *The Testimony of Truth* fits very well what Clement of Alexandria reports about one Julius Cassianus. Clement (erroneously) refers to this man as "the originator of docetism." He had left the school of Valentinus and had written a book called *Concerning Continence and Celibacy* (*Strom.* 3.13.91–92). This information, together with the additional details provided by Clement, fits our author perfectly: a Gnostic teacher who espoused a docetic Christology and an encratic rejection of sex and marriage; and one who, though espousing and retaining certain Valentinian traditions, nevertheless repudiated the Valentinians because of disagreements with them in matters of ritual and life-style.

Whatever the truth might be concerning the identity of the author of *The Testimony of Truth*, he played a role in the theological battles waged in Bishop Demetrius's Alexandria, representing a cause that ultimately would fail.

The Teachings of Silvanus represents another side in the struggle. As we have already noted,[67] this is a document whose admonitory sayings, proverbs, and hymnic passages lie on a trajectory running from the Hellenistic Jewish wisdom of the Wisdom of Solomon and Philo Juda-

---

64. The tenth-century Melchite patriarch of Alexandria Eutychius, writing in Arabic (*Annales*, PG 111:982 [Latin trans.]), reports that when Demetrius became bishop there was no other bishop in Egypt. Demetrius appointed three bishops, and Heraclas, his successor, appointed twenty more. On this tradition see Eric W. Kemp, "Bishops and Presbyters at Alexandria," *JEH* 6 (1955) 125–42, esp. 138.

65. Cf. also *The Apocalypse of Peter* (NHC VII,3), which has "Peter" prophesying the future struggle of a Gnostic Christian minority: "And there shall be others of those who are outside our number who name themselves bishop and also deacons, as if they have received their authority from God. They bend themselves under the judgment of their leaders. These people are dry canals" (79,21–31, *Nag Hammadi Library* translation). On *Apoc. Pet.* see esp. K. Koschorke, *Die Polemik der Gnostiker gegen das kirchliche Christentum* (NHS 12; Leiden: E. J. Brill, 1978) 11–90.

66. For discussion see Pearson, *Codices IX and X*, 118–20.

67. See discussion in chap. 11, above, pp. 177–81.

eus, and a Christian form of the same represented by Apollos of Alexandria, to the Alexandrian theology of Clement of Alexandria. Though some of its themes could easily be espoused by Christian Gnostics, it ultimately comes down on the side of catholic Christianity in its rejection of those "strange kinds of knowledge" (94,32) whose proponents teach that God the Creator is "ignorant" (116,5–9).

These brief remarks concerning *The Teachings of Silvanus* lead us to Clement and his Christian *gnōsis*. Clement of Alexandria (ca. 150–215) is, so far as we know, the first adherent of catholic Christianity to lay claim to the designation *gnōstikos*, thus wresting the term from people deemed by him to be "heretics." To be sure, Clement's own theological orthodoxy has been called into question,[68] largely because of his willingness to see aspects of truth in the most unlikely sources, from pagan poets and philosophers to well-known Christian "heretics."[69] But, in the final analysis, Clement's loyalties are clear. This can be seen especially clearly in the seventh book of his *Stromateis*,[70] devoted to a discussion of the exemplary life of the true Christian "gnostic," together with a defense of the Christian faith against charges based on the proliferation of Christian sects. Clement, for all of his speculative inventiveness and ecumenical learning, can finally say,

> We ought in no way to transgress the rule of the Church. Above all the confession which deals with the essential articles of faith is observed by us, but disregarded by the heretics. Those, then, are to be believed who hold firmly to the truth. (*Strom.* 7.15.90)

We even see Clement espousing the view that the heretics are late innovators who have departed from "the oldest and truest Church" whose chief characteristic is unity:[71]

> The one Church, which they strive to break up into many sects, is bound up with the principle of Unity. We say, then, that the ancient and Catholic Church stands alone in essence and idea and principle and pre-eminence,

68. See esp. Salvatore R. C. Lilla, *Clement of Alexandria: A Study in Christian Platonism and Gnosticism* (Oxford: Oxford University Press, 1971). For a good survey of scholarship on Clement see Eric Osborn, "Clement of Alexandria: A Review of Research, 1958–1982," in *The Second Century* 3 (1983) 219–44.

69. Clement's attitude toward the teachings of Valentinus and Basilides is not altogether hostile. For an interesting comparison between Clement and Valentinus see James E. Davison, "Structural Similarities and Dissimilarities in the Thought of Clement of Alexandria and the Valentinians," *The Second Century* 3 (1983) 201–17.

70. A good English translation of Books 3 and 7 of the *Stromateis* is found in Henry Chadwick, ed., *Alexandrian Christianity* (LCC; Philadelphia: Westminster/London: SCM, 1954). The quotations from *Strom.* 7 that follow are taken from that volume.

71. We can detect here the influence of Irenaeus's *Adversus Haereses*.

gathering together, by the will of one God through the one Lord, into the unity of the one faith. (*Strom. 7.17.107*)

We do not know what sort of personal relations Clement had with Bishop Demetrius, but I dare say that the good bishop would have applauded such statements as these.

Of course, the Gnostic heretics did not capitulate so easily. Gnosticism persisted in Egypt for many centuries to come, and Gnostic writings proliferated throughout the country, as the Nag Hammadi corpus itself attests. It would take the full power of a Christianized imperium, working in conjunction with bishops and monastic abbots,[72] to stamp out the Gnostic heresies in Egypt. And we wonder if the project ever really succeeded![73]

But that's another book.

72. That Gnosticism was still rife in the Egyptian monasteries in the fifth century can be seen in an anti-Gnostic tract by Shenute of Atripe, on which see Tito Orlandi, "A Catechesis against Apocryphal Texts by Shenute and the Gnostic Texts of Nag Hammadi," *HTR* 75 (1982) 85–95. It is now widely acknowledged that the Nag Hammadi manuscripts were manufactured, inscribed, and ultimately buried by monks of the Pachomian system of monasteries. For recent discussions see James E. Goehring, "New Frontiers in Pachomian Studies," 236–57; and Armand Veilleux, "Monasticism and Gnosis in Egypt," 271–306, in Pearson-Goehring, *Roots of Egyptian Christianity*.

73. Readers of Lawrence Durrell's novel *Monsieur* (New York: Viking, 1975) are encouraged to believe that it never did.

Indices

I. GNOSTIC AND RELATED SOURCES

Origen
 Cels. 6.24–38, 18
 Cels. 6.27–29, 17
 Contra Celsum 6.24–38, 106
Ps.-Tertullian
 Haer. 2, 50
 Haer. 2.1, 13
Theodoret
 Haer. 1.14, 13, 97
"Peratae"
Hippolytus
 Ref. 5.12, 157
 Ref. 5.16, 46
 Ref. 5.16.8–9, 102
Saturninus
Irenaeus
 Haer. 1.24.1–2, 200
 Haer. 1.24, 37
"Sethians"
Epiphanius
 Haer. 39, 14, 53, 54, 103, 134, 151
 Haer. 39.1.2, 54
 Haer. 39.1.3, 54, 70, 74, 78
 Haer. 39.2.1, 62
 Haer. 39.2.4, 54, 62, 68
 Haer. 39.2.4–6, 70
 Haer. 39.3.1, 54
 Haer. 39.3.2–3, 54
 Haer. 39.3.5, 54, 74, 78
 Haer. 39.5.1, 54, 57, 66, 74, 75
 Haer. 39.5.2, 62, 85
 Haer. 39.5.2–3, 54
 Haer. 39.5.7, 66
 Haer. 40, 54, 103, 151
 Haer. 40.2.2, 65, 74, 75
 Haer. 40.5.3, 54, 62
 Haer. 40.7.1, 54, 65, 75
 Haer. 40.7.1-2, 75
 Haer. 40.7.2–3, 54
 Haer. 40.7.4, 65, 74
 Haer. 40.7.4–5, 54
 Haer. 40.7.5, 54
 Haer. 40.7.6, 150, 151
 Haer. 40.7.7, 57
Filastrius 3, 14
Hippolytus
 Haer. 5.19–21, 146

 Haer. 5.20, 55
 Haer. 5.22, 55
 Ref. 5.20, 70
 Ref. 5.20.2, 103
Irenaeus
 Ad. Haer. 1.29, 97, 199
 Haer. 1.29, 30, 55, 85, 126, 151, 203
 Haer. 1.29.1–4, 199
 Haer. 1.30, 53, 55, 61
 Haer. 1.30.1, 53, 85
 Haer. 1.30.5–7, 43
 Haer. 1.30.9, 53, 54, 61, 70, 85
Plotinus
 Enn. 2.9, 126
Porphyry
 Vit. Plot. 16, 126
Ps.-Tertullian
 Against All Heresies, 53
 Haer. 2.7, 14
 Haer. 8, 78, 134
Theodoret
 Haer. 1.14, 13, 53
"Severians"
Epiphanius
 Haer. 45.1, 43
 Haer. 45.1.4, 47
 Haer. 45.1.5ff., 47
Simon Magus, Simonians
 Pseudo-Clementine *Homilies* 2.22, 24
Valentinians
 Clement of Alexandria
  Exc. ex Theod. 43.2–65, 208
  Exc. ex Theod. 54.1, 55
  Exc. ex Theod. 58.1, 208
  Exc. ex Theod. 69–74, 164
 Eusebius
  Hist. Eccl. 6.18, 210
 Hippolytus
  Ref. 1.11, 148
  Ref. 6.21–29, 148
  Ref. 6.33, 48
  Ref. 6.42, 155
 Irenaeus
  Haer. 1.1.1–8.5, 199
  Haer. 1.2.5–6, 94

II. MODERN AUTHORS

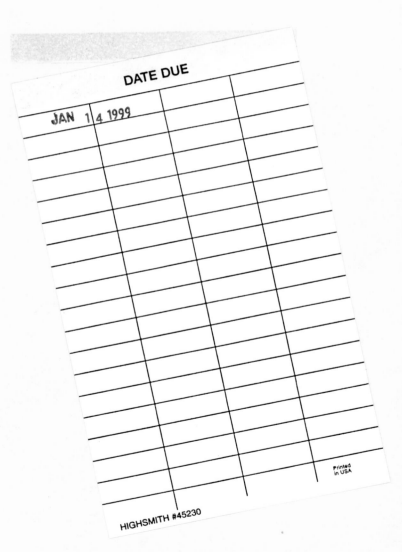